LUCY at the MOVIES

Cindy De La Hoz

RUNNING PRESS
PHILADELPHIA · LONDON

To Mom, Dad, and Tristan

9 8 7 6 5 4 3 2

Digit on the right indicates the number of this printing

Library of Congress Control Number: 2007924077

ISBN 978-0-7624-2706-2

Cover and interior design by Corinda Cook

Typography: Optima and Minion

This book may be ordered by mail from the publisher. Please include $2.50 for postage and handling.
But try your bookstore first!

Running Press Book Publishers
2300 Chestnut Street
Philadelphia, PA 19103-4371

Visit us on the web!
www.runningpress.com

CONTENTS

Introduction

When we think of Lucille Ball, it is most often in terms of our favorite Lucy Ricardo moment, for her work on *I Love Lucy* has been bringing joy to fans for over half a century. She is a legend embraced by each passing generation. These are words Lucille never would have imagined would be said of her that summer day in 1933 when she stepped off a train and into the Hollywood sunshine as a member of a troupe of starlets known as the Goldwyn Girls.

It is here that the tale of Lucille Ball's screen career begins. When *I Love Lucy* premiered on television in 1951, she had already been in Hollywood nearly twenty years, a veteran of some seventy films. Ever since I saw my first Lucille Ball movie, *The Big Street*, I have thought it is unfortunate that this substantial portion of her body of work is frequently overlooked completely. During these pre-television years, Lucille studied her trade from top to bottom, acquiring experience and knowledge that were essential to the immeasurable success she later achieved.

Early on, Lucille simply felt lucky to have found a place in Hollywood learning the profession that she loved—and earning a paycheck in the bargain! "I just wanted to be in there and learning," she said. Appearing first as a chorus girl, she later became the "Queen of the Bs" at RKO-Radio Pictures and then advanced to musical comedy star and supporting player at the preeminent film studio, MGM. By the '40s, she was already a popular performer and seen by critics as a first-rate comedienne. She was not in the super-star ranks with friends such as Ginger Rogers or Carole Lombard, but she did enjoy a very active career during the late '30s and '40s. Her movies are priceless records of the rise to fame of one of the world's most beloved stars, and they allow us to see her in an entirely new and fascinating light.

A naturally gifted entertainer, it did not take long for people to realize Lucille was a funny girl. Even on the set of her first film, *Roman Scandals*, comedian Eddie Cantor noticed her capacity for humor. Other starlets balked at the prospect of performing slapstick, but from the start Lucille was willing to put her glamour at risk in exchange for laughs. Because of this, we get to see the comedic actress we know and love from television in many of her films. At the same time, her dramatic performances prove that her talent extended beyond the realm of comedy.

Lucille Ball's entire film career is chronicled here—from her showgirl roles, to housewives, burlesque queens, shop girls, bad girls, socialites, movie stars, and yes, scatterbrained *Lucy* types, too.

Over the years she appeared alongside some of Hollywood's brightest stars, such as Katharine Hepburn, Henry Fonda, Gene Kelly, Bob Hope, and the Marx Brothers, and her earliest roles were in a few all time classics, including three of the Astaire-Rogers musicals. The photographs show Lucille at her most beautiful and glamorous as she romped through screwball comedies, strutted about in over-the-top Technicolor productions, and ran the gamut of emotions in film noir and

Lucille in 1937

melodramas. Her time on the big screen covered an extensive period in her career; though not her signature works, to miss her films is to pass up the perfect opportunity to see the versatile, always enjoyable talents of Lucille Ball as she made her way toward becoming America's favorite madcap.

Lucille Ball: A Biography

$\mathcal{L}$ucille's story began in the home of her maternal grandparents in Jamestown, New York, where the blue-eyed, brown-haired baby girl entered the world on Sunday, August 6, 1911. Her full name was Lucille Desirée Ball. The middle name came from her mother, Desirée Eveline Hunt, whom she and the rest of the family simply called DeDe. Her father was Henry Durrell Ball, a telephone lineman whose sense of humor Lucille's mother told her she inherited.

The little family first lived together in Montana. When Lucille was about two, her father's work took them to Wyandotte, Michigan, outside of Detroit, where he was employed at the Michigan Bell Company. In the winter of 1915, Henry Ball fell victim to typhoid fever, and on February 28, 1915, Lucille lost her father when she was three. She and her mother moved back to Jamestown shortly after, into the home of her grandparents, Fred and Flora Belle Hunt. Four months later, DeDe gave birth to her second child, a boy, whom she named Fred Henry, after her father and her late husband.

DeDe was remarried to a Swedish sheet metal worker named Edward Peterson in 1919. This marriage was short-lived, however, and it was Grandpa Hunt who stepped into the role of father for Lucille and Fred. They called him "Daddy." He was a skilled craftsman, a loving grandfather, and was always described by members of the family as a true "character" who dedicated himself to fighting for the underdog.

As the family struggled to keep afloat, DeDe and her second husband sought employment outside of Jamestown, so Lucille was sent to live with her stepfather's parents, the Petersons. Grandma Peterson taught Lucille the meaning of hard work and discipline, but also instilled in her a love of nature and gardening that would remain with Lucille throughout her life. This was an especially tough period in her childhood; yet when reflecting on what was actually a quite difficult upbringing, Lucille would speak of the positive aspects (the lessons learned from the stern Mrs. Peterson "never hurt me a bit.")

Lucille later wrote, "I wasn't unloved or an unwanted child, but I was moved around a lot, and then death and cruel circumstances brought many painful separations." When DeDe returned to Jamestown for good, Grandpa Hunt brought the family together again. They moved to a home in the nearby suburb of Celoron, where Lucille spent the happiest times of her childhood. For the rest of her life, she harbored idyllic memories of this three-bedroom, two-story dwelling with a hedge of lilac bushes in the backyard. The street where it is located is now called Lucy Lane.

At age four

DeDe entrusted a great deal of responsibility to Lucille. As the eldest, Lucille looked after her brother and her little cousin, Cleo (whom she called sister). While the adults of the family worked to put food on the table, the kids helped take care of the house, cleaning, doing some of the cooking, and taking care of the animals. Fred Ball recalled of their childhood, "We didn't play—we worked."

Of course, Grandpa Hunt did make time to take the kids to vaudeville shows, and during the summers, to a "fairyland" called Celoron Amusement Park. There they enjoyed the movies of Pearl

White and Tom Mix, rides, and other diversions. This is how Lucille first caught the acting bug. She fell in love with vaudeville and decided that was what she wanted to do—make people laugh! At home, she, Fred, and Cleo would reenact the shows they had just seen at Celoron Park, and at school she was encouraged to perform as well. Lucille and her friends would put on amateur plays in which she would take part in every aspect of production, from directing to costuming, and even sweeping the floors afterward. Performing became such a richly satisfying experience for her that she was soon auditioning for local plays.

The teenaged Lucille was inventive, athletic, and involved. She was also independent and headstrong. Acting became an outlet for her restlessness, but she still hungered to see new places. She ran away from home several times, often headed for New York, but she never got very far. DeDe sensed what might appease her daughter. Luckily for Lucille, her mother was not one to be constrained by the social standards of that time in Jamestown, which were still largely unaccepting of acting as a profession for a nice young woman. DeDe always encouraged Lucille's interest in the theater. Believing in her daughter's genuine ambition, she enrolled fifteen-year-old Lucille in the John Murray Anderson-Robert Milton school of dramatics in New York City.

In Manhattan, the skinny girl from Jamestown felt awkward and insecure and she showed it. Her stint at the acting school (whose star pupil a season

Lucille sits in front of her high school basketball team in 1925.

or two earlier was Bette Davis!) ended quickly. The heads of the school sent DeDe a letter stating that Lucille had no future as an actress; she should stop wasting her money.

Feeling lonely and homesick, Lucille returned to Celoron. There, in the summer of 1927, a tragedy struck that changed her family life forever. Grandpa Hunt was showing his grandson how to shoot a rifle. Another girl who joined them fired the gun just as a neighborhood boy dashed in front of their tin can target, and he was accidentally shot. The boy was paralyzed and his parents sued Fred Hunt. The family lost their home in Celoron and moved back to Jamestown. Lucille's cousin Cleo remembered the incident as "the tragedy that broke up the whole home life and sent everyone in different directions." Lucille felt an intense desire to take care of her family, but she knew she could not accomplish this in Jamestown, so that meant taking on the big city again.

Though still reticent and tongue-tied away from home, Lucille's ambition kept her pounding the pavement of New York looking for work in the theater. Several times she would be hired for the chorus only to rehearse for weeks (without pay, as was standard practice during rehearsal time) and wind up fired for one reason or another, including the show closing before it even debuted. At one point, Lucille landed a role as a showgirl in a road company production of *Rio Rita*, but was hired for little else. Struggling to make ends meet, she lived in cheap hotels, maintained a diet of coffee and doughnuts, and became adept at sneaking food into her purse at restaurants during dates.

Looking to "add a little glamour to my life," she became a blonde, told people she was from Butte, Montana (earning her the nickname "Two-Gun"), and even adopted a new name for a time—Diane Belmont. Lucille moved back and forth between New York and Jamestown several times during this period. "I'd run home for a while, then gather up my courage and go back." Lucille held on to her hope that it was only a matter of time before she would find success in the theater. But she still needed to make a living, so she did what she could. She became a model.

Lucille the model, 1932

New York modeling days

Lucille found work at Hattie Carnegie's, an upscale fashion house that catered to film stars and the social elite. It earned her thirty-five dollars a week. Though inexperienced, Lucille became a good high-fashion model and endeared herself to Carnegie. In addition to this, she took on other jobs, which made for a very hectic lifestyle. The lack of rest and proper nutrition soon took its toll. Though recovering from pneumonia, she continued working, and one day at Hattie Carnegie's, she suddenly collapsed. Racked with pain in her legs, she was told she had rheumatoid arthritis and was forced to go home—in a wheelchair.

Her recovery period lasted nearly two years, but Lucille was lucky. The medicine she was given was an experimental treatment that fortunately was successful for her. By mid-1930, she was sufficiently recovered to appear in a local production of *Within the Law*. Her performance as female gangster Aggie Lynch garnered excellent reviews in the town papers and gave her the confidence to return to New York. She moved into the Hotel Kimberly on Manhattan's West Side and resumed her modeling career at Hattie Carnegie's and other fashion houses. She also earned extra dollars posing for commercial agencies. One such job resulted in her becoming the latest figure on Chesterfield Cigarette ads.

One scorching Wednesday afternoon early in July 1933, Lucille was walking along Broadway in front of the Palace Theater when she was approached by talent agent Sylvia Hahlo. Hahlo recognized Lucille from the Chesterfield billboards and asked her if she would go out to Hollywood as

July 19, 1933—Lucille arrives in Los Angeles with six other poster girls chosen for Samuel Goldwyn's famed chorus line: Katherine Mauk, Rosalie Fromson, Mary Lange, Vivian Keefer (front), Barbara Pepper, and Theo Phane (in back with Lucille).

one of the Goldwyn Girls for Samuel Goldwyn's upcoming musical production, *Roman Scandals*. Lucille, then age twenty-one, jumped at the chance. Three days later, she boarded the Superchief bound for Hollywood, where she rented an apartment on Formosa Street, three blocks from the United Artists' studio where Goldwyn operated. After New York, she found the balmy atmosphere of California a welcome change.

Roman Scandals starred comedian Eddie Cantor. Sporting a thigh-length platinum blonde wig, in the picture Lucille played one of a group of

The Goldwyn Girl lineup of 1933—Lucille is fourth from left.

slave girls, but she was able to separate from the group by volunteering to have her face covered in a mudpack for one of the film's gags. Her initial contract with Goldwyn, dated July 11, 1933, guaranteed six weeks of employment, but production delays on *Roman Scandals* caused it to be extended, so she and the girls were loaned out to add charm to films at other studios.

Lucille joined the throng of young actresses aspiring to attain stardom. She had the advantage of arriving with a contract already in hand, but thought herself at a disadvantage because she believed she was not as beautiful as the other girls, so to stand out among the crowd, Lucille worked

longer and harder to improve her abilities and gain experience in the industry. Driven to succeed as an actress, she was further determined to make good in order to reunite her family—Fred, Cleo, DeDe, and Grandpa Hunt. She saw this as the perfect time and place. "I loved Hollywood. I saw in it a place I wanted to live, a place I wanted to bring my family. I had no thought of ever going back."

By the time *Roman Scandals* was finished, Lucille had played bits in other pictures for producer Darryl F. Zanuck's new company, Twentieth Century. In most of her early parts, she served no real purpose beyond dressing up a scene. While she was grateful for each new experience, Lucille had greater aspirations. When the opportunity arose for her to come under new management, she grabbed it. Although it meant taking a fifty-dollar-per-week pay cut, she signed a stock contract with Columbia Pictures in August 1934.

Fred Ball was the first of Lucille's family to join her in Hollywood. Her brother took a job at one of the town's famous nightspots, the Trocadero. The two saved money, rented a house at 1344 North Ogden Drive, and soon were able to send for the rest of the family. Then, on November 26, 1934, Lucille was notified that Columbia Pictures was cutting expenses by firing members of the stock company. Suddenly she was unemployed. Lucille told her family to move out to Hollywood anyway, that they would manage. It was a sound decision, because within a matter of hours, she found a new studio to call home.

RKO-Radio Pictures was casting for models to appear in *Roberta*, a lavish vehicle for Irene Dunne and Fred Astaire and Ginger Rogers, the pair who had caused a sensation a year earlier by stepping onto the dance floor in *Flying Down to Rio*. Lucille's model figure served her in New York and now brought her luck in Hollywood. The studio's newest costume designer, Bernard Newman, chose her for *Roberta*. Her meeting with him was the start of a long friendship between the two, and of Lucille's seven-year association with RKO.

DeDe and Grandpa Hunt came west shortly after. Later, her cousin Cleo joined them, making the household complete again. Lucille called holding together the family unit "the greatest thing that ever happened to me." As she would invariably do in the future, Lucille carried a similar feeling to the workplace. "I've always been a family person, and I adopted RKO as my studio family."

Lela Rogers, mother of Ginger, directed a workshop in the Little Theater on the RKO lot to help young contract players learn their craft. Over a period of two years, Lela was a mentor to Lucille, whom Lela in turn came to feel was her most

promising pupil. On the movie sets, Lucille observed the technical side of filmmaking, while appearing in plays produced at the Little Theater helped refine her dramatic skills and perform with more assurance. Some twenty years later, after she

Taking tips from Lela Rogers in 1936

and Desi bought the studio, Lucille established a similar workshop to pass on the guidance she received from Lela to a new generation of actors.

The country was still in the midst of the Depression, but RKO kept Lucille working steadily, and her career showed promise. She was an actress in training, becoming more at ease in front of the cameras by appearing in small roles. She took insignificant parts in films like *I Dream Too Much* and *Follow the Fleet* and made them memorable. Meanwhile, she earned a reputation for never complaining about anything she was asked to do, as well as for being a clown on the set. "Nothing was beneath me. I'd scream, I'd yell, I'd run through the set. I'd wear strange clothes. To me, it was just getting your foot in the door."

With her lively personality, Lucille was a popular girl. She went around with a group that

With Mack Grey
(right)

included Ginger Rogers, Phyllis Fraser (Ginger's actress cousin), and Anita Colby. Her social calendar included dates with actors like Ralph Forbes and Cesar Romero, whom she remembered as a great dancing partner, screenwriter Gene Markey, and Mack Grey, the assistant of screen tough guy George Raft. While she had fun casually dating many of the Hollywood handsomes, Lucille's most serious relationship of the late '30s was with Alexander Hall, a director seventeen years her senior. The romance began in late 1937 and lasted for more than two and a half years.

Lucille "graduated" from Lela's program in the spring of 1937. Her movie parts were steadily growing larger, but she began testing other mediums of the entertainment world as well. In December 1936, she took a part in the Barlett Cormack play *Hey Diddle Diddle*, featuring silent screen star Conway Tearle. It opened January 21, 1937, in Princeton, New Jersey. The company closed three weeks later, before reaching Broadway, and she went back to RKO. She tried radio as well, becoming a popular addition to the shows of Jack Haley and Phil Baker.

At the time of her return to RKO following *Hey Diddle Diddle*, the studio was mounting its adaptation of the hit Edna Ferber-George S. Kaufman play *Stage Door*, in which the two biggest female stars on the lot, Katharine Hepburn and

In *Hey Diddle Diddle*, a comedic play set in the film colony, Lucille played Julie Tucker, a sharp-witted starlet who shares a duplex apartment with fellow extra girls Martha Sleeper and Alice White. She received fine reviews.

Ginger Rogers, were to co-star. Lucille was chosen for a supporting role as one of a group of Broadway hopefuls who board together. The critics raved about the film, and Lucille made an impression (and won a raise in salary). She was assigned supporting roles in two A pictures, *Joy of Living* and *Having Wonderful Time*. Then she was given her first leading role opposite Joe Penner in the comedy *Go Chase Yourself*.

Lucille moved into the position of female lead in subsequent films for the duration of her RKO contract and the publicity machine whipped into action. Early on she was promoted as a clotheshorse. In 1936, she was named "Best-Dressed Girl in Town." Owing to her modeling experience, Lucille wore clothes well, so she could live up to the name. However, when it came to fashion,

her designers learned that she always insisted on comfort over the latest trends. She attributed much of her fashion sense to her favorite comedienne, Carole Lombard, and also to Joan Bennett.

A series of films was developed for Lucille about a glamorous movie star caught in a whirl of misadventures caused by her press agent, played by Jack Oakie. The series kicked off with *The Affairs of Annabel*, which was well received by both critics and audiences. Just two months later, its sequel, *Annabel Takes a Tour*, was released. Although it did not do as well as the first, it was a financial conflict between Oakie and the studio that brought a hasty end to the *Annabel* films.

Top-billed in a steady stream of small productions, Lucille became known as RKO's Queen of the Bs. "B" films were produced cheaply and

usually quickly. They were the training ground for many a future star, as they permitted rising actors to show what they could do in a role larger than they would have been given in "A" features. Lucille's low-budget films made money and were frequently above industry standards for B-picture production. During 1938 and 1939, she starred in no less than a dozen films. Some of her pictures may have been of questionable quality, but the critics consistently championed Lucille in their reviews and pleaded with the studio to give her better material. Orson Welles, then a newcomer to Hollywood, requested her for a farce he had in the works called *The Smiler with a Knife*, but the project fell through.

Lucille's second film assignment of 1940, *Dance, Girl, Dance*, offered one of the best parts of her film career. She played a hard-boiled burlesque queen who makes it to the top partly at the expense of a good-natured ballet dancer (played by Maureen O'Hara). During production, Lucille was told that her next film would be based on the Broadway musical *Too Many Girls*, to which RKO had just acquired the screen rights. Appearing alongside her would be Hollywood actors Ann Miller and Richard Carlson, as well as several actors from the stage cast, among them Desi Arnaz, a Cuban charmer who had set hearts aflutter with his conga rhythms in New York.

When Desi first caught sight of Lucille in the studio commissary, she was wearing a burlesque costume with tousled hair and a fake black eye for a scene in *Dance, Girl, Dance*. Desi could not believe that this woman was to play the ingénue of their film. Seeing her in regular makeup and dress later, he did not recognize her. Lucille remembered, "We met and it was, for me at least, true love from the start." She soon ended her relationship with Al Hall, and Desi ended his engagement to dancer Renée De Marco.

The twenty-three-year-old who had been the toast of New York before hitting Hollywood was born Desiderio Alberto Arnaz y de Acha III. His father was a doctor and mayor of Desi's hometown of Santiago de Cuba. The revolution of 1933 brought an end to the privileged upbringing he had enjoyed as the family lost everything. Desi and his father moved to Miami and later sent for his mother, Dolores. After working various odd jobs for pennies, Desi joined a band called the Siboney Septet, playing at the Roney Plaza Hotel. Eventually he organized his own band. Headed by Desi, they popularized *la conga* music and dance rhythms in Miami Beach. Success carried him to New York, where he headlined at the La Conga nightclub. There, Desi caught the attention of producer George Abbott and the famed composing team of Richard Rodgers and Lorenz Hart and suddenly

he found himself in a hit Broadway musical, *Too Many Girls*. RKO's purchase of the film rights brought Desi to Hollywood and Lucille in June 1940.

When production wrapped on their picture in August, the couple was separated. Desi went on the road, and in September, Lucille went to work on the Harold Lloyd comedy *A Girl, a Guy and a Gob*. For everything stacked against them—contrasting backgrounds, personalities, and religion, his playboy reputation, and her being five and a half years older than him—Lucille and Desi could not call off the romance, which continued via telephone and Western Union telegram over the next three months. After dating in Hollywood and New York, Lucille said he was "the first man I had ever met whom I immediately thought of as the prospective father of my children." Desi was no less spellbound, even when seated across from the exquisite Gene Tierney, whom he dated when they were both starring in different shows on Broadway. "I listened to Desi, over dinner, tell me how much he loved Lucille Ball," the actress later recalled.

On a publicity tour, Lucille made a stop in New York to see Desi, who had already made arrangements for them to marry. The day following her arrival, Saturday, November 30, 1940, Lucille and Desi eloped to Greenwich, Connecticut, where they were married by Judge John P. O'Brien at the Byram River Beagle Club. After a time in New York, the newlyweds returned to California and soon purchased a five-acre ranch, christened "Desilu," at 19700 Devonshire Boulevard in the Chatsworth section of the San Fernando Valley.

During the early part of their marriage, both were under contract to RKO. Lucille was still Queen of the Bs, but there were no visible plans for her career to advance beyond that point. Then writer-producer Damon Runyon arrived on the lot and requested her for the lead in *The Big Street*, a film based on "Little Pinks," one of his fables about the colorful characters of Broadway. The role of the self-centered Gloria Lyons would be the one Lucille most relished in movies, and her reviews were stellar.

Charles Koerner, head of the RKO theater chain and a friend of Lucille's, became the production chief of RKO in 1942. He confirmed her concern that in spite of her recent success, her prospects at the studio were dim. At this juncture, Lucille's career was resuscitated by an eminent producer from Metro-Goldwyn-Mayer, Arthur Freed. He had admired her work in *The Big Street* and wanted her for his next musical, *Du Barry Was a Lady*. Prompted by Freed, boss Louis B. Mayer made overtures to bring her into the MGM fold. They acquired half (and ultimately all) of her contract.

In the early '40s, RKO was perpetually in the midst of management upheavals. Their biggest attractions of the '30s—Katharine Hepburn, Fred Astaire, and Ginger Rogers—were no longer under exclusive contract. Though their fortunes improved with Koerner at the helm, the company was never on particularly solid ground for long. From this, Lucille entered MGM and into the most illustrious stable of stars at the finest filmmaking plant in Hollywood. Still, it depressed her to say goodbye to the crew she was fond of—her "studio family" at RKO.

The happy couple in New York, November 1940

Lucille's entire look was overhauled at MGM in preparation for the big-budget Technicolor film in which she was to star. At the time, she had strawberry blonde hair and was accustomed to wearing subdued colors. Hairstylist Sydney Guilaroff tried various hues before selecting a vivid shade of red that Lucille described as "a cross between carrots and strawberries." Meanwhile, costume designer Irene introduced her to clothing colors that would compliment this shade and accentuate her blue eyes. Lucille was ideal for Technicolor. *Du Barry Was a Lady*, co-starring Gene Kelly and fellow carrot-topped comic Red Skelton, went into production shortly after Lucille's thirty-first birthday, in August 1942. She followed it with *Best Foot Forward*, another musical, in which she starred as a movie queen named Lucille Ball.

Desi's film career was less fruitful as RKO had put him in a couple of lackluster films. In 1942, he also made the switch to MGM, where he won critical praise for his portrayal of an ill-fated soldier in *Bataan*. When America entered World War II, Desi immediately tried to enlist, but he was denied because his United States citizenship had not yet come through. However, by May 1943 he had become a citizen and was drafted. Lucille also did her part to support the war effort. She went to work on the morale-boosting musical *Meet the People*, sold war bonds across the country, and entertained the troops with the USO.

Soon after Desi went into the service, he suffered a knee injury, which prevented him from being sent overseas. He was instead stationed not far from the Arnazes' Chatsworth ranch, at Birmingham Hospital, where he arranged entertainment for the war-ravaged patients. In spite of his remaining close to home, Desi and Lucille barely saw each other. Lucille was lonesome and heartsick over the fact that they had been unable to have a child. The separation put a great strain on the marriage. Her despair was deepened by the death of her Grandpa Hunt in January 1944. She filed for divorce from Desi in September of that year. From the outset, the relationship was tempestuous, but their passionate love for each other brought them together in the face of numerous obstacles and would sustain them through difficult years to come. The very day that Lucille appeared in court for the interlocutory decree, she and Desi agreed to give their marriage another chance.

At MGM, Lucille's filming schedule, which had ebbed since *Meet the People*, picked up steam. In March 1945, production began on one of the highlights of her MGM career, an update of the studio's 1936 comedy *Libeled Lady*. Playing for all its worth the character originated by Jean Harlow, in *Easy to Wed* Lucille stole the show from her enormously popular co-stars, Van Johnson and Esther Williams. She starred in four films released during 1946 and made a cameo in a fifth, *Ziegfeld Follies*. The Associated Drama Guilds of America crowned her the year's "Queen of Comedy." During her spare time at MGM, Lucille was able to hone

Ziegfeld Follies, her scenes filmed in 1944

her skills with comic legend Buster Keaton and his frequent director, Ed Sedgwick. She later said they "were the first people to really teach me all about slapstick comedy and the importance of props. . . . I learned much from those two men, and I'll be forever grateful."

On November 16, 1945, Desi was released from the Army. He found it difficult to jumpstart his film career due to the scarcity of roles for Latin leading men with accents. In reality, making movies was not what he loved—making music was. He asked for his release from MGM and began reassembling his band. They played at Ciro's in Hollywood for a time, and then went on the road with considerable success.

At about the same time as Desi's discharge, Lucille completed the film *Two Smart People*, then left MGM soon after, later attributing the split to a conflict with the agent she had at the time. She felt he was mismanaging her career and found it necessary to leave the studio in order to remedy the situation. Difficulties in her personal and professional life brought on a bout of depression. Explaining her frame of mind during this period, Lucille later said, "I had been trying to embrace too much, taking on too many burdens—emotional and financial. As a result, I was exhausted, just completely depleted in every way." A new agent, Kurt Frings, and supportive coworkers on the set of her next film, *Lover Come Back*, helped snap her out of this state.

Now working as a freelance artist, Lucille opted to take a break from moviemaking. She enjoyed a happy time with Desi in New York during his engagement at the Copacabana in the summer of 1946 before reporting back to Hollywood to work on *Lured*, a thriller for Douglas Sirk. Wanting a change of pace, the next year she signed on to do *Dream Girl*, a play by Elmer Rice that would ultimately take her on a twenty-seven week cross-country tour between June 1947 and January 1948. In his review of the show, Edwin Schallert of the *Los Angeles Times* noted, "Miss Ball has efficiency as a comedienne. She can tinge a scene delicately with pathos. She has special facility in dealing with sharp-edged repartee."

During Lucille's run in the play, Desi was touring with his band. With Desi constantly on the road and Lucille based in Hollywood, their careers kept them apart. When her show reached Detroit, he flew in to see her for a surprise reunion. Meanwhile, the bus carrying his band to the next city was in a terrible accident. Desi had escaped serious injury or death by going to be with Lucille, and this incident strengthened their resolve to find a way to bring their lives together. She recalled, "We'd been married nine years and been together a year and two months—if that. You can't have children that way." They longed to make a family. To that end, they instituted a "stay-at-home" policy. Desi would arrange to maintain Los Angeles as his work base, playing in area nightclubs and performing on radio. He became the regular orchestra leader for Bob Hope's show and later would host his own

musical quiz program, *Your Tropical Trip*. In June 1949, the Arnazes renewed their marriage vows in a Catholic ceremony.

A few months after the *Dream Girl* tour, Lucille began a radio program based on the Isabelle Scott Rorick book *Mr. and Mrs. Cugat*. She hoped she and Desi could work on this together, but CBS-Radio felt they would not make a believable American couple. Tall, blonde, and accent-free Richard Denning was more their ideal. In July 1948, *My Favorite Husband* debuted as a weekly series. Lucille and Denning played "two people who live together and like it"—Liz, the scatterbrained wife, and George, her banker husband. The program became an audience favorite.

Having been off the screen for a year, Lucille returned in her first film with Bob Hope, *Sorrowful Jones*, for Paramount Pictures. Based on Damon Runyon's *Little Miss Marker*, it was originally made with Shirley Temple in 1934. The teaming of Hope and Ball was an inspired piece of casting that created a smash hit. *Easy Living* brought her back to the same studio where she had been Queen of the Bs a few years earlier, RKO. She followed that picture with *Miss Grant Takes Richmond*, costarring William Holden. It was the first of three films she signed to make for Columbia Pictures.

By early 1950, when she began the slapstick caper *The Fuller Brush Girl* for Columbia, CBS had

initiated plans to adapt *My Favorite Husband* to television. They wanted Lucille to continue in her role as the wife. This time she insisted she would do it only if Desi could play the husband. The CBS brass adamantly refused at first, saying the public would not accept the union of all-American Lucille and a Cuban "bongo-player," in spite of the fact that they had actually been married for ten years.

The Arnazes decided to prove the network wrong. Together with their friend Pepito, the Spanish clown, and the *My Favorite Husband* writers, they created a vaudeville act consisting of musical and comedy sketches and took it on the road in the spring and summer of 1950. Audiences across the country loved them.

That summer, the film version of *Born Yesterday* was being made. A year earlier, newspapers had hinted that producer Max Gordon had in mind Lucille taking over the stage role of Billie Dawn in Garson Kanin's play. In 1950, the property was to be filmed at the studio to which Lucille owed one more picture, Columbia, and she hoped the role might come her way. Boss Harry Cohn first wanted his top attraction, Rita Hayworth, to play the lead, while director George Cukor wanted no one but Judy Holliday, who had originated the part on Broadway. He lobbied ardently for her by fattening up a role in the Katharine Hepburn-Spencer Tracy courtroom comedy *Adam's Rib*. Her performance convinced Cohn to give Holliday the part that would eventually bring her an Oscar, while Lucille made *The Magic Carpet* in December. The routine adventure film allowed her to satisfy her contract and pick up her $85,000 paycheck quickly. Quickly was essential, for she had recently learned she was going to have a baby.

On the heels of the Arnazes' vaudeville success, CBS relented in early 1951 and agreed to let them do a television series together. The show would be produced by the company they had formed the previous year, Desilu Productions. With the team from *My Favorite Husband*—Jess Oppenheimer, Madelyn Pugh, and Bob Carroll, Jr.—they constructed a pilot that netted them a sponsor, Philip Morris Cigarettes.

New obstacles arose. Everyone wanted the show done before an audience because it brought out the best in Lucille. If shot in California, a low-quality kinescope would be sent to the bulk of TV viewers, who lived on the East Coast. The network wanted to broadcast live from New York, but the Arnazes did not want to relocate. Desi proposed that the program be shot in Hollywood on film, as if it were a movie, but before an audience, as if it were a stage play. This particular setup was untried. The Arnazes footed the extra cost by taking a pay cut in return for ownership of the shows (five years later, they sold them back to CBS for $5 million). Shooting on film allowed viewers across the country to receive the same quality picture. It also allowed *I Love Lucy* to be preserved and enjoyed in pristine reruns for generations to come.

With this business concluded, the creative team refined the characters of Lucy and Ricky Ricardo (originally called Lucy and Larry Lopez), then began the search for actors to portray their neighbors, the Mertzes. William Frawley, a character actor with more than a hundred movie credits to his name, was cast as the husband. Lucille insisted he "*was* Fred Mertz," that in creating the character, "the writers took Bill Frawley verbatim." After seeing stage actress Vivian Vance in the play *The Voice of the Turtle*, Desi and Jess Oppenheimer decided she was perfect for the part of Mrs. Mertz. Vance never got along with Frawley, but she and Lucille formed a sister-like relationship that lasted until Vance's death. They quarreled but always maintained a close bond.

In the midst of pre-production, Lucille had her first child, Lucie Desirée Arnaz, on July 17, 1951. The two major goals Lucille and Desi had dreamed of for more than ten years were finally coming to fruition at the same time: having children and being able to work side by side.

Some six weeks later, the first episode of the show was filmed; then, at 9 PM on Monday, October 15, 1951, *I Love Lucy* premiered. Due to technical problems with the first, the episode shown was actually the second filmed, "The Girls Want to Go to a Nightclub." *I Love Lucy* rapidly scaled the ratings charts. The public and critics were wild about the chemistry among the four stars. Lucille said in 1960, "I always felt our show was so successful because somehow, through the film and over the air, we communicated the fact that we were excited about each other. It wouldn't have been the same had we just been playing married."

In the spring of 1952, Lucille found out she was pregnant again. She and Desi presumed it meant the end of *I Love Lucy*. When they gave the news to producer Jess Oppenheimer, he thought it could be great for the show. The TV character of Lucy Ricardo would go through the pregnancy and

The expectant mother clowns with Desi in late 1952.

have a baby—another of many firsts the show ushered into the medium. After the idea was cleared with CBS and Philip Morris, they quickly commenced filming the second season in advance in order to give Lucille time off before and after her baby's birth. It had been planned that her baby

would be delivered by cesarean section. Desiderio Alberto Arnaz IV was born on the morning of Monday, January 19, 1953 and that evening Lucy Ricardo gave birth to "little Ricky" during one of the highest-rated half-hours in television history.

The following month, Lucille picked up an Emmy for Best Comedienne of 1952, and the show was named Best Situation Comedy. In March they resumed filming the second season. During their summer hiatus, Lucille and Desi went to work at MGM on *The Long, Long Trailer*. The movie had its premiere in February 1954 and smashed box-office records. Nearly three decades after she began trying to break in on Broadway, Lucille finally found her true place in show business—and international fame—through television. Unable to relax and enjoy it though, she became haunted by the thought that "All our good fortune was suddenly going to vanish."

It looked as if her fears would be realized when journalist Walter Winchell gave a report during his radio broadcast in September 1953 citing Lucille Ball a communist. In the days of the Hollywood blacklist, such an accusation, valid or not, spelled ruin for many creative people in the industry. The suspicion of Lucille's "red" affiliation stemmed from a voter registration card filed in 1936 in which she had registered as a communist voter. In 1952 she was questioned and cleared of suspicion

A family portrait,
1953

by the FBI, and a year later, she was called before the House Un-American Activities Committee. It seemed ridiculous, as Lucille never much involved herself in politics. She testified that both she and her brother Fred registered communist that year to placate their "Daddy," Grandpa Hunt. They did not vote, but only wished to please him. In her own words, "In those days that was not a big, terrible thing to do. It was almost as terrible to be a Republican in those days." She was cleared by the House Committee, but word that she had been questioned leaked to Winchell.

Newspapers followed suit and indicated that she was a communist on the strength of Winchell's report. This storm of adverse publicity coincided with the start of season three of *I Love Lucy*. The chairman of the House Committee held a press conference and cleared her name just hours before filming time of the season's premiere episode. Newspapers set the record straight the next day and, along with Winchell, apologized for earlier reports. The public loved Lucille all the more after the ordeal she had endured, and *I Love Lucy* remained at the top of the ratings.

The 1954–55 season featured top name guest stars, friends such as William Holden, Van Johnson, and Eve Arden (whose own series, *Our Miss Brooks*, was filmed next door to *Lucy*), even though in those days big stars generally shied away from television. It took long working hours for the Arnazes to maintain the level of success they had attained. The commute to and from the studio to their home in Chatsworth twenty miles away was tough on their schedules. This, coupled with a kidnapping scare against their children in early 1955, made Lucille and Desi decide to sell their cherished ranch (to actress Jane Withers) and purchase a home at 1000 North Roxbury Drive in Beverly Hills. The move came as they approached the end of the fourth *Lucy* season. No sooner was it completed than they began filming the movie *Forever, Darling*. Desi rightly concluded that at this point they could stop at the top, or keep going, which would require them to expand the business. The recent multimillion dollar sale of the *I Love Lucy* shows to CBS would keep them wealthy for the rest of their lives. Lucille's answer: "I don't want to quit."

Besides the show, which Lucille and Desi both loved to get on the set and perform, there was now also the organization to be considered. In addition to acting as co-star, Desi was also president of Desilu. Beyond *I Love Lucy*, their company was producing other successful shows, and Desi was engineering it all. With his reputation within Hollywood as a playboy, those in the industry

At the Emmys in February 1954 (awarded for the past year's work), *I Love Lucy* wins as Best Situation Comedy and Vivian Vance is named Best Supporting Actress.

underestimated the astute business and creative sense he possessed—all except Lucille. "He has a quick, brilliant mind; he can instantly find the flaw in any storyline;" she said. "And he has inherent good taste and intuitive knowledge of what will and will not play. He is a great producer, a great director."

The Arnazes' professional success had exceeded far beyond even their own expectations, but the responsibilities that accompanied the success also exacerbated their personal difficulties. All the while, Desi's working hours snowballed and the marriage began to disintegrate. Following the 1956–57 *Lucy* season, they alleviated part of their workload by halting the show's half-hour weekly format in favor of occasional hour-long specials. *The Lucille Ball-Desi Arnaz Show* (also called *The Lucy-Desi Comedy Hour*) aired on the Westinghouse *Desilu Playhouse* anthology series.

In need of additional operating space for their expanding TV empire, Desi finalized a deal to purchase RKO Studios from its latest owner, General Tire & Rubber, in November 1957. The acquisition took place during the filming of one of the five *Lucy-Desi* specials that aired in the 1957–58 season. For a price of $6,150,000, Desilu became larger than MGM.

In 1958, Desilu was more prosperous than ever, but Lucille and Desi were increasingly estranged. They worked hard to uphold the image of an ideal marriage, but it was impossible. Lucille would say they both had been at fault. "You can't go on and on for years being miserable about a situation and not have it change you." They agreed

In 1954

to divorce. Ironically, the show the Arnazes created to keep them together helped the marriage of many other couples instead. One fan wrote to Desi, "I was about to divorce my wife. After seeing *Lucy*, I realized that all women must be nuts, so I decided to stay."

Desi directed the final three *Lucy-Desi Comedy Hour*s. They completed the last of the series, "Lucy Meets the Mustache," guest starring Ernie Kovacs and Edie Adams, on March 2, 1960—Desi's forty-third birthday. Lucille filed for divorce the next morning. She and Desi remained on good terms up until Desi's death, and they shared custody of Lucie and Desi, Jr., who were ages eight and seven, respectively, at the time of the divorce.

Lucille decided that work was the best medicine for a broken heart. In June 1960, she began production on a first-rate film with Bob Hope, *The Facts of Life*. She then took on *Wildcat*, a musical play based on the N. Richard Nash book. In her only Broadway role, Lucille portrayed Wildcat Jackson, a character she described as nothing more than "a female 'Rainmaker'" (Nash's most famous character). The show opened in New York at the Alvin Theater on December 16, 1960. Though Lucille had the name to fill every seat, the play received poor notices. One critic said, "'Wildcat' hasn't much to offer in the way of lively song, dance, or merriment . . . Lucille Ball is pretty and vivacious, but the role doesn't offer her an opportunity to strut her comic stuff." The part was very physically demanding, however. Her health was completely run down, she suffered from exhaustion, and finally had to close the show the following June.

During her time in *Wildcat*, co-star Paula Stewart introduced Lucille to nightclub comedian Gary Morton. They began dating in New York and the relationship continued in Los Angeles after the play closed. "I was fed up with my life. Then, suddenly, there he was, like a breath of fresh air," Lucille later said. She and Morton were wed by her

friend and advisor, Dr. Norman Vincent Peale, on November 19, 1961. Desi was also remarried a year and a half later, on his forty-sixth birthday, to another redhead, Edith Mack Hirsch.

Lucille said *Wildcat* taught her that "the people came to the theater to see the Lucy they knew and I didn't give it to them." To rectify this, Lucille signed a deal with CBS in March 1962 to star in a television series based on *Life without George*, a book by Irene Kampen. Lucille, Vivian Vance at her side. Vivian had by then moved to Connecticut with her new husband, John Dodds (whom she married in January 1961), but Lucille coaxed her into doing *The Lucy Show*. Jimmy Garrett, Candy Moore, and Ralph Hart were cast as the children of Lucille and Vivian, who now played a widow and a divorcée, respectively. In their initial season, the show placed third in the ratings (tied with *Bonanza*). This did not measure up to *I Love Lucy*, but audiences did love having their favorite comedienne back in a weekly series.

Initially, Desi was executive producer of *The Lucy Show* and still president of Desilu Productions. It was an awkward situation with Gary Morton on the set as well. In November 1962, Lucille bought out Desi's stock in the company and thus relieved him of the burden of running a television empire. Desi Jr. said of his father, "Simple things like home and family and honesty

turn him on. Business doesn't, so when he got totally hung up on things that were fairly low on his scale of priorities, he ended up hating himself, and that's when he got into trouble." Lucille, who had been vice president of Desilu, moved into the top position. Studio mogul was not a role that she ever became comfortable in, but she did what had to be done, and did it effectively for the next few years. During her tenure as president, the company launched the landmark *Star Trek* television series as well as *Mission: Impossible.*

Making her second series, Lucille took on many more responsibilities than she had in her *I Love Lucy* days. In the past, Desi had been on hand to make adjustments to the production wherever needed. With him no longer there, she would find things were not always up to par and knew that she would have to take charge for the benefit of the show, which after all, she knew better than anyone else. Consequently, she became known as something of a taskmaster on the set. She was a woman and shouldered the responsibility for the program's success. Carol Burnett, who worked with her often, said, "Lucy . . . knew the lights, the scenery, the costumes, the music, the makeup. Everything. And she was always right!"

The second *Lucy Show* season brought Lucille's longtime friend Gale Gordon into the cast. Gordon, who had been Lucille's original pick for the role of Fred Mertz, had played her husband's banker boss in *My Favorite Husband* in the '40s, and now portrayed hardnosed Theodore J. Mooney, the banker in charge of her trust account. Vivian left after the third season. Happy in her second marriage, she preferred to spend more time at home in Connecticut and end the taxing weekly commutes between coasts.

The 1965–66 season introduced fans to Lucy in color. Ratings remained high. Though it became customary for Lucille to announce after each season that she would not return for another, family and friends insist she never wanted to quit. *The Lucy Show* continued for a total of six seasons, ending in 1968. Still considered the best in her field, Lucille won Emmys as Best Comedy Actress for the last two years of the series.

Here's Lucy featured teenaged Desi, Jr. and Lucie, as well as Gale Gordon.

Lucille made a brief return to movies in 1967 with a cameo in *A Guide for the Married Man*, starring Walter Matthau. During the summer of that year, she made *Yours, Mine and Ours* with Henry Fonda. It had first been slated for production in 1962, but it was put off time and again before shooting finally got under way five years later. The picture opened in April 1968 to both critical and public applause.

In February 1967, Desilu was sold to Gulf and Western Industries, Inc., owners of Paramount Studios. Soon after, Lucille Ball Productions was formed, and she decided to return to weekly television in a revamped format with a new title, *Here's Lucy*. Desi, Jr. and Lucie, who made appearances on *The Lucy Show*, became full-time cast members, playing her teenaged children. Gale Gordon was retained for the series, and Lucille's cousin, Cleo Smith, became the producer. The show aired Monday nights from September 1968 to 1974. Many of the biggest names in show business guest starred, most famously Elizabeth Taylor and Richard Burton. In one episode, Lucy even met Lucille Ball! The show ranked high on the Nielsen charts throughout most of its run in spite of formidable competition like *Rowan and Martin's Laugh-In*, which was broadcast at the same time during the first years.

Angela Lansbury had been tremendously

In spite of her recent skiing accident, Lucille could still make her high kicks reach above her head for the *Mame* numbers, but "dancing sideways was an agonizing thing."

successful in the musical *Mame* on Broadway in the late '60s, but Warner Bros. wanted an even bigger name for their film adaptation. December 1971 brought news that Lucille was to be the latest Auntie Mame. During a ski vacation the following month, Lucille suffered a serious leg injury. Then sixty years old, she rebounded sufficiently to return to work on season five of *Here's Lucy* before stepping in front of the cameras to do her high kicking in *Mame* in early 1973. The movie met with mixed, and frequently harsh, criticism upon its Easter 1974 release.

With her mother, DeDe, in 1943

After *Mame*, Lucille completed the last season of *Here's Lucy*. "It was a hell of a jolt to find myself unemployed with nothing to do after more than twenty-five years of steady work." The *Mame* disappointment, the conclusion of *Here's Lucy*, and the ski accident all put a tremendous strain on Lucille, both mentally and physically. She had never had a problem with the very physical comedy for which she was famous, but the accident put considerable limits on what she could do. This was crushing to a performer who once said, "I have to work or I'm nothing."

Throughout the '70s, she starred in several television specials produced by Lucille Ball Productions for the CBS network. One among them was "Lucy Gets Lucky" in 1975, with Dean Martin. It followed Lucy on her madcap adventures in Las Vegas. Her last special for CBS after a twenty-six year association was 1977's "Lucy Calls the President," which reunited her with past co-stars Vivian Vance and Gale Gordon, as well as former *I Love Lucy* director Marc Daniels.

That year was also marked by the death of Lucille's mother, DeDe. They had enjoyed an extremely close relationship, which friends described as sister-like. DeDe, who had encouraged Lucille since she first sparked an interest in acting, was in the audience of all her daughter's shows

With DeDe thirty years later, on the set of *Mame*.

from the very beginning. Lucille faced another major loss two years later, on August 17, 1979, with the death of Vivian Vance.

Besides being a career woman, Lucille was also a mother and concerned with her children's lives. Daughter Lucie took to the stage, starring on Broadway in the hit *They're Playing Our Song* in the early '80s, and in road shows such as *Cabaret* and *Annie Get Your Gun*. Lucie was married briefly to Phil Vandervort in the early '70s, then wed fellow actor Laurence Luckinbill in 1980. By 1985, she had provided Lucille and Desi with three grandchildren. Desi, Jr. later said he and his mother's relationship "went through some painful stages, but Mom's love was intense and tenacious." He came through headline-making relationships with Patty Duke and Liza Minnelli before marrying actress Linda Purl in 1979. The marriage was short-lived. In 1982, he sought help and overcame a battle with chemical dependency. Five years later he was married to dancer Amy Bargiel and, in time, they became parents to a daughter.

A few years after leaving his post at the helm of Desilu, Desi, Sr. launched his own company, which produced the moderately successful *Mothers-in-Law*, but he largely withdrew from the public eye. Much of his time was spent at his ranch and his home by the beach in Del Mar, near longtime friends such as Jimmy Durante and Dr. and Mrs. Marcus Rabwin. In 1976, he became a best-selling author by publishing his autobiography, *A Book*. Desi, Sr. struggled with alcoholism until he followed his son's example and sought recovery in 1985. The same year, he lost his wife, Edie, to cancer.

Lucille went back to CBS network television in 1985 in a role that was a far cry from Lucy. She played Florabelle, a cantankerous "bag-lady" living on the cold streets of New York in the made-for-television movie *Stone Pillow*. Filming had been set to take place on location in New York during the winter, but it had to be rescheduled until several months later, in the stifling heat. Beneath multiple layers of clothing worn for her part, Lucille's health

Presenters Bob Hope and Lucille at the 1989 Academy Awards presentation.

was ravaged. The movie placed in the top ten in the evening ratings. On the whole, critics praised Lucille's work, but many were aghast that she allowed herself to look the part of an unkempt homeless woman in her seventies.

The next year, Lucille returned to the weekly sitcom format as her last Lucy incarnation, in ABC's *Life with Lucy*. She and Gale Gordon co-starred as in-law grandparents. Previous *Lucy* show writers Madelyn Pugh Davis and Bob Carroll, Jr. were signed to write the show, which was produced by Lucille Ball Productions, in conjunction with Aaron Spelling's company. Network executives thought the series would be a surefire ratings champ; others thought it a bad idea, but Lucille aroused enthusiasm for getting back to work. The *Lucy* formula would not work this time. At age seventy-five, she could no longer get away with the same antics. Ratings plummeted after the first show. In November 1986, after eight episodes were broadcast (thirteen had been filmed), *Life with Lucy* was cancelled.

Weeks later, Lucille was dealt another devastating blow. Desi, who had been diagnosed with lung cancer earlier in the year, died on December 2 at the age of sixty-nine. Over the years, they had remained in close contact. She turned to him for professional advice right up to the end. As Lucie held the telephone to her ailing father's ear, Lucille spoke to him on his deathbed to say her last "I love you" and goodbye on November 30, 1986, the date that would have been their forty-sixth wedding anniversary.

Days after Desi's death, Lucille was the recipient of the Kennedy Center Honors, the nation's highest recognition of lifetime contributions to the performing arts. In her remaining years, she lived comfortably in her Beverly Hills home with husband Gary and occupied herself with her favorite games, particularly backgammon. Professionally, she made a few guest appearances on game shows and television specials, culminating in her appearance at the Academy Awards ceremony in 1989 with longtime friend and frequent co-star, Bob Hope. The two legends were met with a thunderous ovation. This was her final public appearance.

Lucille's health had been declining. In May 1988, she suffered a stroke. The following April, she was again rushed to Cedars-Sinai Medical Center, where she underwent surgery to treat an aortal aneurysm. She came through the operation and was expected to return home shortly. Days later, her abdominal aorta ruptured, she went into cardiac arrest, and died in the early morning hours of April 26, 1989. She was seventy-seven years old.

News of the death of Lucille Ball was met with a worldwide outpouring of grief. Her truly extraordinary work continues to be seen all over the globe. Thus she continues to achieve the desire she had since childhood—to make people laugh.

At the time of *Life with Lucy*

A Portrait Gallery

The photographs in this brief gallery were used to promote Lucille's latest films. In black and white, she was as stunning as any major glamor queen. In color, she earned the nickname "Technicolor Tessie" for her large blue eyes and vibrantly colored hair, which were brilliantly enhanced by the Technicolor of Hollywood's Golden Era.

The
Films
of
Lucille
Ball

*Films have been ordered according to production dates,

rather than by time of release.

The
Chorus Line
and
Small Roles

(1933 to 1937)

Lucille arrived in Hollywood in July of 1933 as a member of the Goldwyn Girls, chosen to appear in the film *Roman Scandals*. The initial six-week contract with Samuel Goldwyn stretched to over a year, a time in which she appeared in chorus lines and walk-on parts in numerous films.

Tired of being mere scenery, Lucille thought she might have better luck as a stock contract player at Columbia Pictures. There, her apprenticeship continued for all of three months, with more walk-ons and a line or two here and there. At the end of the three months, Columbia cut costs by dismissing the stock company and Lucille found herself out of a job.

Luckily though, she immediately answered a call for models at RKO Pictures and landed another contract. She began working with Lela Rogers, Ginger's mother, who ran a workshop in RKO's Little Theater. Lela was dedicated to nurturing the talents of promising new faces, and she saw in Lucille the potential for stardom. Lela used her influence to get Lucille and her other students small roles in films and produced plays in which they could develop their acting abilities.

Lucille was a popular girl around the lot, and as Ginger Rogers put it, "a laugh a minute." With this reputation as being the class clown, Lucille was often cast as gum-chewing blondes spouting one-liners. In spite of her beauty, she was perfectly willing to perform slapstick and never complained, which let producers and directors in on the fact that she was ideally suited to comedy.

During Lucille's first years in Hollywood, Jean Harlow was Hollywood's best-loved bombshell, causing every studio to churn out a slew of platinum blonde Harlow clones. Lucille was no exception, which makes it difficult to pick her out of the crowd of flaxen-haired starlets in some of her early films, but every attempt has been made to report on all of Miss Ball's big screen appearances, however brief.

Lucille the showgirl touches up her makeup on the set of *Kid Millions* in the summer of 1934.

Roman Scandals

A Samuel Goldwyn Production (1933)

Released by United Artists

Cast: Eddie Cantor (Eddie); Gloria Stuart (Princess Sylvia); Edward Arnold (Emperor Valerius); David Manners (Josephus); Ruth Etting (Olga); Veree Teasdale (Empress Agrippa); Alan Mowbray (Major-domo); John Rutherford (Manius); Willard Robertson (Warren C. Cooper); Lee Kohlmar (Storekeeper); Grace Poggi (Slave Girl); the Goldwyn Girls

Credits: Samuel Goldwyn (producer); Frank Tuttle (director); William Anthony McGuire, George Oppenheimer, Arthur Sheekman, and Nat Perrin (screenplay), from story by George S. Kaufman and Robert E. Sherwood; Gregg Toland and Ray June (photography); Alfred Newman (musical score); Busby Berkeley (dance director); Ralph Ceder (director of chariot sequence); John W. Boyle (photography of chariot sequence); Richard Day (art director); Vinton Vernon (sound); Stuart Heisler (editor)

Songs: "Build a Little Home," "No More Love," "Keep Young and Beautiful," "Put a Tax on Love" (Harry Warren and Al Dubin)

Release date: December 23, 1933 (Rivoli Theater)

Run time: 85 minutes

In the roundup of slaves for the elaborate "No More Love" production number, Lucille was given prime placement, above the "AL" in "Valerius" in this photo.

Synopsis

When Eddie (Eddie Cantor), a humble delivery boy, takes a stand against the crooked chamber of commerce president of West Rome, Warren Cooper (Willard Robertson), the courageous young man is cast out of town. Eddie begins thinking such injustice could never take place in ancient Rome, and in that moment, he is magically transported back in time. He soon winds up sold to the highest bidder at the slave market! However, he makes friends with his owner, Josephus (David Manners), who bought Eddie only to set him free.

At the palace, the tyrannical emperor of Rome, Valerius (Edward Arnold), has taken a new prisoner, Princess Sylvia (Gloria Stuart). After a botched rescue mission, Eddie is appointed the emperor's official food taster—a dangerous duty considering that the Empress Agrippa (Veree Teasdale) is trying to poison her husband. She now seeks help from Eddie.

Meanwhile, Josephus, who is in love with Princess Sylvia, is banished from Rome for attempting to take her away from the palace. Before leaving, he plans for her and Eddie to go away with him. Disguised as an Ethiopian beauty specialist to gain access to the girls' area, Eddie relays the message to the princess and gives the slave girls (including Lucille) tips on how to "Keep Young and Beautiful"—before stumbling onto evidence of the emperor's treacherous deeds.

Empress Agrippa forces Eddie to try to kill the Emperor. When the plot goes amiss, Eddie is sentenced to death. As guards chase him through the city on chariots, Princess Sylvia is delivered to Josephus. They escape, but Eddie is captured. Just then, he is transported back to his own time. There he finds incriminating documents that will put Warren Cooper out of power, and the people of West Rome celebrate with their hero.

As a wistful Roman slave girl

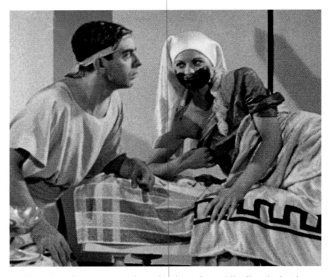

Wearing only a flesh-toned bodysuit under heaps of hair.

Roman Scandals started it all for Lucille in Hollywood. When a fearful mother pulled her daughter out of the group that had been selected for the film's chorus, one space was left open for the Chesterfield Cigarettes poster girl of the moment, Lucille Ball. Samuel Goldwyn's first Eddie Cantor musical, *Whoopee* (1930), had been an adaptation of a

Goldwyn Girls give lessons on how to "Keep Young and Beautiful."

Lucille (standing, right) and the girls are positioned for a shot.

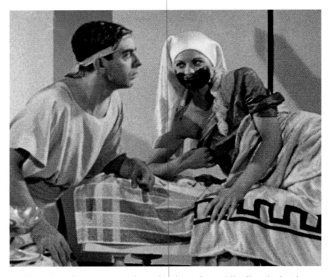

Lucille and Eddie Cantor startle each other when Eddie disturbs her beauty regimen and she lets out a familiar Lucy scream.

Ziegfeld show. In answer to the Ziegfeld Girls, the producer introduced his own lineup of gorgeous gals—the Goldwyn Girls. Other stars to emerge from these ranks were Betty Grable (who was among the first crop), Paulette Goddard, and Virginia Bruce.

The Goldwyn-produced Eddie Cantor films were annual extravaganzas featuring the eye-rolling entertainer in screwball situations while uniting the juveniles and toppling villains, musical numbers staged by Busby Berkeley (often performed by Cantor in blackface), and of course, the girls—all in exotic locales. *Roman Scandals*, fourth in the cycle, followed this formula and made a bundle of profits.

Besides introducing the Goldwyn Girls, *Whoopee* had also introduced master choreographer Busby Berkeley to the Hollywood musical. During the production of this picture, Berkeley was moonlighting at Warner Bros. on *Footlight Parade*. Consequently, the *Roman Scandals* numbers were not up to his usual high standard. After the film, Goldwyn lost Berkeley to Warners, where his career blossomed with musical classics like *42nd Street* and the *Gold Diggers* series.

In new surroundings, Lucille's ambition and desire to be noticed made her shed the shyness that had overcome her in New York. She became known for her constant clowning on the Goldwyn lot,

which earned her Eddie Cantor's favor. She also became known as the showgirl more than willing to do anything less than glamorous that the other girls were uncomfortable with, such as having her face covered in a mudpack for one scene.

On the set, leading lady Gloria Stuart met and fell in love with one of the writers, Arthur Sheekman, whom she married the next year. Stuart, who thought young Lucille incredibly beautiful and funny, introduced her to Sheekman. Lucille cajoled the writer and his partner, Nat Perrin, into adding a couple of extra lines for her to speak including her first words on screen— "He said the city put us here and we should live here." She actually had a dual role in her first movie. In the ancient Rome sequences, she was a slave girl and joined the chorus of "Keep Young and Beautiful," and in contemporary West Rome, she was one of the townspeople featured prominently in the "Build a Little Home" number.

Lucille (left) and a friend on one of the modern outdoor sets, used for the "Build a Little Home" sequence.

The Bowery

A Twentieth Century Picture (1933)

Released by United Artists

Cast: Wallace Beery (Chuck Connors); George Raft (Steve Brodie); Jackie Cooper (Swipes McGurk); Fay Wray (Lucy Calhoun); Pert Kelton (Trixie Odbray); Herman Bing (Max Herman); Oscar Apfel (Ivan Rummel); Ferdinand Munier (Honest Mike); George Walsh (John L. Sullivan); Lillian Harmer (Carrie A. Nation); Harold Huber (Slick); Fletcher Norton (Googy); Lucille Ball (Extra)

Credits: Presented by Joseph M. Schenck; Darryl F. Zanuck (producer); William Goetz and Raymond Griffith (associate producers); Raoul Walsh (director); Howard Estabrook and James Gleason (screenplay), from novel by Michael L. Simmons and Bessie Roth Solomon; Barney McGill (photography); Alfred Newman (musical director); Richard Day (art director); Allen McNeil (editor)

Release date: October 4, 1933 (Rivoli Theater)

Run time: 92 minutes

Wallace Beery and Jackie Cooper starred together in four films, of which this was the second.

Synopsis

Saloon-owner Chuck Connors (Wallace Beery) reigns in prominence in the Bowery of the Gay Nineties, while Steve Brodie (George Raft) rates second, making them fierce rivals. Chuck's brash manner and contemptible view of women has rubbed off on an orphan he has taken in, Swipes (Jackie Cooper). The gentle Lucy Calhoun (Fay Wray) changes Chuck. He gives the crestfallen girl a job in his home, much to the annoyance of Swipes, who soon runs away to live with Steve.

Steve has ambitions to own a popular tavern like Chuck's. To gain notoriety, he proclaims he is going to take a dive off of the Brooklyn Bridge. He then bets his nemesis that if he makes the jump, he (Steve) will take over Chuck's place. Steve goes through with the stunt. Chuck loses his bar, his reputation, Swipes, and finally Lucy, who has fallen in love with Steve.

On the brink of the Spanish-American war, Chuck enlists. That night, Swipes returns to him, renewing Chuck's conviction to get back on his feet. Then, Steve's enemies tell Chuck that a dummy went off the bridge, not Steve. Swipes knows that Steve indeed made the jump himself, but Chuck is convinced he was cheated out of his bar.

Inevitably, Chuck and Steve come to blows. Chuck prevails, thereby regaining his big-shot status. Swipes admires both men. He makes Chuck and Steve see that the Bowery is big enough for both of them. Lucy sees off the new pals, who decide to use their brawn to fight in the war.

Notes and Comments

Twentieth Century Pictures was launched by former Warner Bros. production chief Darryl F. Zanuck in April 1933 with Joseph Schenk, the president of United Artists. Samuel Goldwyn helped the fellow UA producing unit get started by loaning out his showgirls, since Goldwyn himself made few films per year and only one Cantor musical. Lucille was put to work as an extra (possibly in a scene at the beach) in *The Bowery*, the new company's first production, filmed in the summer of 1933.

The story featured several characters based on actual turn-of-the-century Bowery figures. Chuck Connors, the "Mayor of Chinatown," was known for his thrilling tours of that district, and the real Steve Brodie was legendary for his claim to have jumped off the Brooklyn Bridge in 1886. Temperance advocate Carry Nation and fighter John L. Sullivan were also portrayed. The picture collected $1,494,294 in domestic rentals upon its release. It's full of boisterous, colorful characters, picturesque ornamentation and costumes, and bawdy Gay Nineties Bowery jargon. Decades later, many of the remarks and situations would be justly considered offensive toward women and various ethnic groups, the comic slant notwithstanding.

With MGM helping to finance Twentieth Century, Zanuck was granted access to their stable of stars. He was loaned Wallace Beery and Jackie Cooper, the pair who made *The Champ* MGM's biggest hit of 1931. A post-*King Kong* Fay Wray was cast as leading lady.

Paramount provided George Raft, the actor and dancer best known for gangster portrayals (*Scarface*, 1932). He befriended Lucille. The day that her family joined her in Hollywood in late 1934, Raft loaned Lucille his car so that she could make an impression when she picked them up at the bus terminal in style. Lucille also double-dated with Raft often after she began dating his assistant, Mack Grey. Grey was one of her longest lasting boyfriends of the mid-'30s.

Snapshot taken outside of Lucille's first apartment in Hollywood.

Reviews

"Punctuated [with] ribald mirth, brawls, fights, noises and vulgarity . . . Whatever one may say against the coarse interludes in this production, there is no gain-saying that the sight on the span between Manhattan and Brooklyn is really funny. . . . Mr. Beery acts in his usual robust but nevertheless effective fashion. Mr. Raft is on his mettle as Brodie and Jackie Cooper does well with his part."

—*New York Times*

"As long as the atmosphere of the film is being provided, even though it is laid on with a trowel, 'The Bowery' is lively and rather effective entertainment, but when it goes in for plot manipulations it is less happy."

—*New York Herald-Tribune*

" . . . as rewritten the two practically legendary characters make good entertainment. . . . Color contributed by the Bowery atmosphere and the manners, fashions and people of the day are a natural source of material for the script, which rests easily on the background when the action momentarily lags."

—*Variety*

Blood Money

A Twentieth Century Picture (1933)

Released by United Artists

Cast: George Bancroft (Bill Bailey); Judith Anderson (Ruby Darling); Frances Dee (Elaine Talbart); Chick Chandler (Drury Darling); Blossom Seeley (Singer); Etienne Girardot (Bail Bond Clerk); George Regas (Charley); Theresa Harris (Jessica); Kathlyn Williams (Mannish Woman); Lucille Ball (Drury's Date at Racetrack)

Credits: Presented by Joseph M. Schenck; Darryl F. Zanuck (producer); William Goetz and Raymond Griffith (associate producers); Rowland Brown (director); Rowland Brown and Hal Long (screenplay); James Van Trees (photography); Alfred Newman (musical director); Albert D'Agostino (art Director); Hal Long (continuity); Lloyd Nosler (editor)

Songs: "Melancholy Baby" (Ernie Burnett, George A. Norton, and Maybelle E. Watson); "San Francisco Bay"

Release date: November 15, 1933 (Rivoli Theater)

Run time: 65 minutes

Synopsis

Bill Bailey (George Bancroft), a prosperous bail bondsman, falls for a new client charged with theft, Elaine Talbart (Frances Dee). The society beauty has a fascination for crime. Bill's only appeal to her is his association with outlaws. She discards him as soon as bank robber Drury Darling (Chick Chandler) enters the scene.

Drury is a friend and frequent client of Bill's. Following the bank caper, Bill posts bail to keep Drury out of prison pending trial in return for a share of the stolen bonds. When things become dangerous for him, Bill advises Drury to skip town. Before leaving, he sends Elaine to deliver Bill's share of the bonds, but she cheats him out of the spoils by giving him worthless registered bonds. Convinced Drury was behind the swindle, Bill informs the police of his whereabouts. The underworld, led by Drury's sister, Ruby (Judith Anderson)—whose love Bill had rejected in favor of Elaine—turns on Bill. Claiming jealousy was the reason her brother was turned in, Ruby has her gangland cronies embark on a campaign to ruin Bill. He strikes back by collaborating with the police, further antagonizing the racketeers, who arrange a plot against Bill's life.

Elaine visits Drury in jail and proudly tells him that she cheated Bill. Drury promptly gets word of this to Ruby, who then rushes to warn Bill that he is in danger. She reaches him just in time to save his life and make him realize that they make a perfect pair.

After her arrival in 1933, as she played bit parts in films like *Blood Money*, the starlet very quickly felt at home in Hollywood.

Notes and Comments

Darryl Zanuck was at the forefront of making the underworld ubiquitous on movie screens when he produced *Little Caesar* in 1931. The crime wave spread into the next year with films such as *I am a Fugitive from a Chain Gang* and *Scarface*. In late 1933, Zanuck banked on the public's continued fascination with the subject when he invested in the production of *Blood Money*. It ultimately showed a loss of $62,301.

This was the last in a trio of crime dramas written and directed by Rowland Brown (*Angels with Dirty Faces*), and the screenplay was based on a story of his titled "Bail Bond." With its corrupt characters and gangland setting, *Blood Money* is an intriguing product of Hollywood's pre-code era, those years in the early '30s before effective enforcement of the Production Code brought strict censorship to the movies. Less than a year after its initial release, it would be banned by the Catholic Church's Legion of Decency.

George Bancroft, once one of the silent screen's leading tough guys, headed the cast. Australian actress Judith Anderson was a star on Broadway before making her motion picture debut in *Blood Money*. She won stellar reviews but

Reviews

"More about the underworld, but some novel twists to the story. . . . sequence by sequence, the feature has production smartness embroidered along the seams."

—*Variety*

"This whimsical little tale of thievery, thuggery and attempted slaughter was mistaken for entertainment by Darryl Zanuck, who obviously thought that the part of Bill Bailey, the racketeering bail expert, would give George Bancroft an opportunity to shine once more on the screen."

—*New York Times*

"A tawdry tale, peopled by a thoroughly obnoxious set of characters, this glorification of bail-bondsmen, burglars, bandits and street-walkers creates a definitely unpleasant reaction . . . With the exception of one or two good lines, the dialogue is dull and halting, the continuity lacks cohesion and only in a single sequence is suspense created and sustained. . . . The players are good in bad parts."

—*New York American*

returned to the stage until 1940. That year she gave her best-known film performance as the sinister Mrs. Danvers of Alfred Hitchcock's *Rebecca*. At various times, Loretta Young and Tallulah Bankhead were up for the lead female role in *Blood Money*. Instead, screen ingenue Frances Dee was borrowed from RKO and cast against type, shocking her fans by playing a trouble-seeking young woman with a mean masochistic streak. At this very time, she could also be seen in theaters in *Little Women*. Lucille appears as one of two girls paid to keep gangster Chick Chandler company at the racetrack, only to be spurned when Frances Dee turns his head.

Blood Money, which began filming on August 14, 1933, was the second offering from Zanuck's Twentieth Century Pictures. Lucille was put to work on its first four features. In its brief lifespan, the company turned out some ambitious productions—such as *The House of Rothschild*, *Les Misérables*, and *Call of the Wild*—and picked up several Oscar nominations for their films, most with William Goetz (Louis B. Mayer's son-in-law) and Raymond Griffith (a comedy star of the silent era) as associate producers under Zanuck. Twentieth Century-Fox was born after the production unit's merger with the Fox Film Corporation in May 1935.

Broadway Thru a Keyhole

A Twentieth Century Picture (1933)

Released by United Artists

Cast: Constance Cummings (Joan Whelen); Paul Kelly (Frank Rocci); Russ Columbo (Clark Brian); Blossom Seeley (Sybil Smith); Gregory Ratoff (Max Mefooski); Texas Guinan (Tex Kaley); Hugh O'Connell (Chuck Haskins); Hobart Cavanaugh (Peanuts Dinwiddie); C. Henry Gordon (Tim Crowley); William Burress (Thomas Barnum); Helen Jerome Eddy (Esther Whelen); Lucille Ball (Girl at Beach); Abe Lyman and His band; Frances Williams; Eddie Foy, Jr.; Barto and Mann

Credits: Presented by Joseph M. Schenck; Darryl F. Zanuck (producer); William Goetz and Raymond Griffith (associate producers); Lowell Sherman (director); Gene Towne and Graham Baker (screenplay), from story by Walter Winchell; Barney McGill and Peverell Marley (photography); Alfred Newman (musical director); Jack Haskell (dance director); Richard Day and Joseph Wright (art directors); Maurice Wright (editor)

Songs: "Doin' the Uptown Lowdown," "When You Were the Girl on the Scooter and I was the Boy on the Bike," "Past, Present and Future," "I Love You Pizzicato" (Mack Gordon and Harry Revel)

Release date: November 1, 1933 (Rivoli Theater)

Run time: 90 minutes

Synopsis

The well-known racketeer Frank Rocci (Paul Kelly) uncovers his soft side when a childhood pal appeals to him for help in finding chorus work for her sister, Joan Whelen (Constance Cummings). Rocci's influence gets her hired at the Club Kaley, and he quickly becomes infatuated with the beautiful and curiously ingenuous girl. To make her dreams of stardom come true, Rocci buys the club and springs Joan from the chorus into center stage. The grateful Joan is willing to marry him, but Rocci knows he must first ensure their future safety by retiring from the underworld.

Eventually, New York becomes too dangerous. Rocci sends Joan out of town while he attempts to settle matters with his gangland rival Tim Crowley (C. Henry Gordon). At Miami Beach, Joan meets and falls in love with crooner Clark Brian (Russ Columbo). Word of the

Nightclub star Joan tours the new domicile of her gangster benefactor Frank Rocci.

Reviews

"Not a big picture, but it's good entertainment . . . The dialog does not display distinct strength, but in general production value the picture has enough to raise it to the plane where it will satisfy. . . . Surprise of the picture is Russ Columbo. He screens unusually well and suggests a type who, with development and screen tutelage, may go places."

—*Variety*

"The film has popular values, unquestionably, and affords photographic effects that are notable in one of the musical numbers, and offers commendable acting by Kelly and Constance Cummings, while the romantic theme is appealing, but the picture is not unusual in essential idea."

—*Los Angeles Times*

"The nightclub show in 'Broadway Thru a Keyhole' is genuinely entertaining. The various numbers are endowed with originality . . . Although many of the incidents are highly improbable, the narrative has a certain strength, chiefly through Mr. Kelly's adroit impersonation of Rocci."

—*New York Times*

romance reaches Rocci up North. He orders her to return, and Joan obediently complies. Feeling indebted to Rocci, she resolves to forget Clark.

Unable to stay away from Joan, Clark goes to New York amid speculations as to what will happen when he comes face to face with Rocci. Clark convinces him that he deeply loves Joan, and Rocci agrees to let her go. Joan and Clark are married, but she is snatched from his arms following the ceremony. The entire town thinks Rocci is behind it, and this results in his being shot by the police. Soon however, it comes out that the kidnapping was orchestrated by Crowley. Joan is delivered back to Clark, and Rocci is shown to be one gangster with a fair share of good points.

Notes and Comments

Made under the working title of *Broadway Love*, the backstage gangster/showgirl story of *Broadway Thru a Keyhole* was penned by Walter Winchell. It caused a stir because of its parallels to incidents in the life of Ruby Keeler, and led to blows exchanged between Winchell and Keeler's husband, Al Jolson, at a boxing match a month before this film went into production.

Actor-turned-director Lowell Sherman (who had just directed Katharine Hepburn in *Morning Glory*) guided a cast studded with New York stage performers including Paul Kelly, Hugh O'Connell, Blossom Seeley, Frances Williams, and the Prohibition-era hostess known as the "Queen of the Night Clubs," Texas Guinan (who died only days after the film's release). The star, Constance Cummings, also had great success on the stage, in Britain and the United States.

Russ Columbo, an orchestra leader and radio singer with matinee idol looks, was romantically linked to Carole Lombard. *Broadway Thru a Keyhole* gave him his first major film role. He received positive notices, but did not have a chance to develop in movies. His life was cut short a year later in a mysterious accident. Details of the story vary, but during the course of a visit

Constance Cummings, Gregory Ratoff, and Blossom Seeley

to the home of a photographer friend, an antique gun was accidentally fired and the bullet reportedly ricocheted from the floor, to a table, to Columbo's head.

Playing a beach-bunny in a scene filmed by the shore in Santa Monica, Queen of Comedy Lucille Ball cracked her first on screen joke in *Broadway Thru a Keyhole*. After her companion is slighted by Constance Cummings she quips, "Well you certainly were the life of the party, Louie, while it lasted." Lucille was constantly shuffling from one set to the next during this time, simply changing costumes and doing whatever was assigned to her. She later said she did not know of her *Broadway Thru a Keyhole* appearance until she saw the movie many years later. At least her director made an impression on her. In a 1939 magazine feature, Lucille said that Sherman was another notable to offer her encouragement at the outset of her career.

Nana

A Goldwyn Production (1934)

Released by United Artists

Cast: Anna Sten (Nana); Lionel Atwill (Colonel Andre Muffat); Richard Bennett (Gaston Greiner); Mae Clark (Satin); Phillips Holmes (Lieutenant George Muffat); Muriel Kirkland (Mimi); Reginald Owen (Bordenave); Helen Freeman (Sabine Muffat); Lawrence Grant (Grand Duke Alexis); Jessie Ralph (Zoe); Ferdinand Gottschalk (Finot); Lucille Ball (Extra)

Credits: Samuel Goldwyn (producer); Dorothy Arzner (director); Willard Mack and Harry Wagstaff Gribble (screenplay), suggested by Émile Zola novel; Gregg Toland (photography); Alfred Newman (musical score); Richard Day (art director); Willard Mack (dialogue director); Travis Banton, Adrian, and John W. Harkrider (costumes); Frank Maher (sound); Frank Lawrence (editor)

Song: "That's Love" (Richard Rogers and Lorenz Hart)

Release date: February 1, 1934 (Radio City Music Hall)

Run time: 88 minutes

Synopsis

Nana (Anna Sten), an impoverished French girl, is determined to emerge from the gutter to high society. One night at a local dive, show business impresario Gaston Greiner (Richard Bennett) discovers her and gives the ambitious young woman her chance to become a star in her own show. When Nana takes the stage on opening night, her magnetic performance seduces every man in attendance.

To the annoyance of her svengali, Nana encourages the attention of rich and powerful men. But her heart belongs to no one until she finds young soldier George Muffat (Phillips Holmes). The two fall madly in love. After George's brother Andre (Lionel Atwill) discovers that they intend to marry, he uses his influence in the military to have George sent to Algeria. Then he tries to bribe Nana to let his brother's heart go. When she refuses to accept the money, Andre has Greiner destroy her position in the theater. Stripped of her fame, fortune, and George's company, Nana endures with the hope that she and her beloved will one day reunite.

Thanks to "friends" who intercept George's letters, Nana has no word from him in months. When Andre resurfaces, offering to make her a star

Anna Sten and Richard Bennett (renowned stage star and father of Constance, Joan, and Barbara).

Andre attempts to buy off the love-struck Nana. Lionel Atwill's role was to have been played by Warren Williams.

again, she accepts his helping hand and they begin a love affair, though she still pines for his brother.

Shortly after, France goes to war, bringing George back to Paris. He arrives at Nana's home to reclaim his love. As Nana prepares to go away with him, George finds out that the woman he loves and his brother have betrayed him. Convinced she has ruined their lives, Nana takes her own life as a final, desperate effort to unite the feuding brothers.

Notes and Comments

Lucille merely served to beautify the background as a showgirl of Goldwyn's next picture after *Roman Scandals*, but this was a very special production to Goldwyn. The producer yearned to develop a female attraction to compete with the likes of those at the major studios—Garbo, Shearer, Harlow, Dietrich, West, the emerging Hepburn and Davis. He saw a picture of Ukrainian-born actress Anna Sten in a newspaper, then, after viewing the German film *Der Mörder Dimitri Karamasoff* (*The Brothers Karamazov*, 1931), decided she had the makings of a great American cinema star—even though she spoke no English.

Sten, who was already well known in Europe, arrived stateside in April 1932. She was hidden away for well over a year of preparation, with English lessons,

Reviews

" . . . if many of the patrons were not moved by the dramatic quality of the narrative, they felt that their visit to the theater was amply repaid by the commendable performances of Miss Sten, Richard Bennett, Reginald Owen and Lawrence Grant. . . . [Miss Sten] is more beautiful and gives even a more finished performance than she did in any of her foreign films."

—*New York Times*

" . . . for all its script shortcomings, 'Nana' is a money production. Certainly this heretofore unknown star seems possessed of sufficiently undeniable allure to go places. Miss Sten has beauty, glamour, charm, histrionic ability (although there are a couple of moments which seemed a bit beyond her), and vivid sex appeal. That's the difference between just a good leading woman and a potent gate-getting star."

—*Variety*

" . . . a mild, over-written and leisurely romantic drama, pretty, but also pretty thin. Indeed, it suggested mainly that once again a really great actress had been scratched by Hollywood and that the result was less acting than a series of beautifully photographed poses."

—*New York World-Telegram*

makeup tests, singing, dancing, and physical training. Goldwyn originally planned to make an American version of *The Brothers Karamazov*, co-starring Sten and Ronald Colman, but after abandoning this idea, he turned to Émile Zola's novel about a nineteenth-century French courtesan called Nana.

On August 18, 1933, Sten and *Nana* were finally ready to go before the cameras, with George Fitzmaurice directing. They began with the opening shot in the film, an exterior scene set in a misty graveyard where Nana bids farewell to her departed mother. After several weeks of filming, Goldwyn was dissatisfied with the daily rushes and he decided to scrap the footage and begin anew with Dorothy Arzner (who had recently directed Katharine Hepburn in *Christopher Strong*) replacing Fitzmaurice. New cast members were brought in as well. Three top designers were required to come up with Sten's wardrobe: Adrian, Travis Banton, and John Harkrider. Rodgers and Hart contributed her song, and she was glorified in the photography of master cinematographer and innovator Gregg Toland.

Nana opened nearly two years after Sten's arrival in the US. Contemporary reviews show that the critics were indeed enthusiastic about her, if not the film itself. But the public was the deciding factor. Comparisons to Garbo and Dietrich were inevitable, but Sten did not fascinate and fire the imaginations of movie fans as they did. *Nana* died at the box office. The film adaptation strayed so far from Zola's novel that the author's heirs called it a "complete deformation" of the original work and set out to have it withdrawn from the French market. For European release, the title was changed to *Lady of the Boulevards*.

Undaunted, Goldwyn produced two more Anna Sten films. *We Live Again* in 1934, co-starring Fredric March, was followed the next year by *The Wedding Night* with Gary Cooper, which became famously known as "Goldwyn's Last Sten." Neither generated the reception he hoped for. Sten did appear in a handful of films over the next two decades, but never came close to the status envisioned for her by Goldwyn.

Moulin Rouge

A Twentieth Century Picture (1934)

Released by United Artists

Cast: Constance Bennett (Helen Hall/Madame Raquel); Franchot Tone (Douglas Hall); Tullio Carminati (Victor "Vicky" Le Maire); Helen Westley (Mrs. Morris); Andrew Tombes (McBride); Hobart Cavanaugh (Drunk); Georges Renavent (Frenchman); Fuzzy Knight (Eddie); Ivan Lebedeff (Ramon); Lucille Ball (Showgirl); the Boswell Sisters; Russ Columbo

Credits: Presented by Joseph M. Schenk; Darryl F. Zanuck (producer); William Goetz and Raymond Griffith (associate producers); Sidney Lanfield (director); Nunnally Johnson and Henry Lehrman (screenplay), from story by Nunnally Johnson; Charles Rosher (photography); Alfred Newman (musical director); Russell Markert (dance director); Richard Day and Joseph Wright (art directors); Gwen Wakeling (costumes); Lloyd Nosler (editor)

Songs: "Coffee in the Morning," "Song of Surrender," "Boulevard of Broken Dreams" (Al Dubin and Harry Warren)

Release date: February 7, 1934 (Rivoli Theater)

Run time: 70 minutes

Lucille is the slouching blonde at far left.

Sheet music picturing Constance Bennett as "The Girl from the Moulin Rouge."

Synopsis

Former vaudevillian Helen Hall (Constance Bennett) gave up her career when she married playwright Doug (Franchot Tone), who adamantly opposes her still-burning theatrical ambitions. He refuses even to grant Helen an audition for his new show. Instead, Doug and producer Vicky Le Maire (Tullio Carminati) import from Paris the star of the Moulin Rouge, Madame Raquel (also played by Bennett), who, unbeknownst to them, was the other half of Helen's sister act. Fed up, Helen walks out on Doug.

Reviews

"It's a nice combination of a brisk story, smartly edited, good acting under competent direction and general good photography. . . . Production numbers are gorgeous and generally exquisitely photographed."

—Variety

"[Constance Bennett's] vehicle this time is a backstage story which has been well furnished with a pleasing levity in the course of its bright lines. Also it can boast of its tuneful music and of giving less heed than usual to the spectacle angle. . . . In her dual role Miss Bennett is thoroughly enjoyable. . . . Franchot Tone lends able support as Douglas, and Tullio Carminati is most engaging as Le Maire."

—New York Times

"Fast and funny in the manner of a French farce and with its frail plot structure handsomely ornamented with song and dance and lavish investiture, this new Constance Bennett picture provides good fun . . . The songs, dances, witty sayings, the amusing situations, the cleverness of the cast, the beauty of the settings are what count. And all these attributes are profusely present in 'Moulin Rouge.' . . . Miss Bennett does beautifully in her dual role, giving it all the fire and sparkle that situation calls for."

—New York American

She tells Raquel of her troubles. Their striking resemblance allowed them to play sisters on vaudeville, and now allows Helen to fool Doug. By adopting a French accent and a blonde wig, Helen becomes Raquel. The real Raquel leaves town and Helen sets out to prove she has talent.

After one rehearsal, Doug dubs her "a great artist." Mission accomplished, Helen is anxious to end the ruse. But plans change when Doug becomes enamored of "Raquel." She tests his fidelity and he fails miserably. To find

Lucille stands on the bottom step, ready to adorn the revue scenes.

out if she has truly lost him, Helen invites Doug to go away with her. To her despair, he accepts.

Distraught, Helen sends for Raquel on the show's opening night, but she is unable to arrive in time. Helen goes on in her place, finally realizing her stage dreams. After this triumph, she ends the masquerade.

Doug admits he is overflowing with pride and Helen receives the message he had sent to Raquel earlier in the evening that established his intention to call off the rendezvous because he loves his wife.

Notes and Comments

Moulin Rouge commenced filming two weeks after *Broadway Thru a Keyhole*, in September 1933. Fair-haired fashion plate Constance Bennett donned a black wig for one half of her dual role. The movie provided a change of pace from her popular melodramas, so registered on the screen was the charming comedienne of future films such as *Topper* (1937).

The full lineup of chorus girls as they appear in the "Boulevard of Broken Dreams" musical sequence.

Franchot Tone starred opposite her in a role intended for Robert Montgomery, whom Zanuck tried to borrow from MGM. Montgomery was called back to his home studio, and Metro offered Tone as a substitute. Theatre Guild actress Helen Westley made her movie debut playing Bennett's aide-de-camp. Twentieth Century's second musical also featured Russ Columbo and the popular singing trio of the Boswell Sisters, along with Al Dubin and Harry Warren's tuneful "Coffee in the Morning" and "Boulevard of Broken Dreams," which were composed for this film.

Moulin Rouge director Sidney Lanfield went on to direct many of Bob Hope's pictures, including his first with Lucille, *Sorrowful Jones*. Nunnally Johnson's story for the film was inspired by the 1925 silent *Her Sister from Paris*. That picture, which starred Constance Talmadge and Ronald Colman, was in turn derived from a play by Ludwig Fulda. The same premise turned up again in Lucille's 1940 film *You Can't Fool Your Wife* and in Greta Garbo's swan song, *Two-Faced Woman* (in which Bennett was also featured). Moreover, they all bear a strong resemblance to the Ferenc Molnár play *The Guardsman*.

Shown with a halo of blonde curls in a few fleeting close-ups, Lucille was a chorus girl in the revue sequences. The routines were staged by Russell Markert, with whom she struck up a friendship. The dance director was founder of the Radio City Music Hall Rockettes and was their choreographer for decades.

Detail of Lucille from the above photo

Hold That Girl

A Fox Film (1934)

Cast: James Dunn (Barney Sullivan); Claire Trevor (Tony Bellamy); Alan Edwards (Tom Mallory); Gertrude Michael (Dorothy Lamont); John Davidson (Ackroyd); Robert McWade (McCloy); Effie Ellsler (Grandmother); Jay Ward (Warren); Lucille Ball (Girl)

Credits: Sol M. Wurtzel (producer); Hamilton MacFadden (director); Dudley Nichols and Lamar Trotti (story and screenplay); George Schneiderman (photography); Samuel Kaylin (musical director); Duncan Cramer (art director); Royer (gowns); Al Protzman (sound)

Release date: March 23, 1934 (Roxy Theater)

Run time: 68 minutes

Synopsis

Since their meeting, a running feud between Barney Sullivan (James Dunn), an easy-going detective, and Tony Bellamy (Claire Trevor), an enterprising newspaper gal, makes for an amusing series of run-ins, but keeps them from showing that they are actually crazy about each other.

Tony is anxious to get the goods on a band of jewel thieves, but her close investigation of the criminals quickly puts her in certain danger. She witnesses a murder. The crooks make sinister plans to keep her from reporting what she has seen and take her to the hideout of gang leader Tom Mallory (Alan Edwards). Mallory has a soft spot for her, so he allows her to escape, sees her to safety, and then gets bumped off for the noble gesture. Barney soon arrives on his own rescue mission and wins the girl while the bad guys are brought to justice.

Notes and Comments

In November 1933, Lucille had another extra assignment in this Fox program comedy that re-teamed James Dunn and Claire Trevor, a popular pair that had clicked the previous year in *Jimmy and Sally*. They made a cheery combination in a trio of light comedies. *Hold That Girl* was followed by *Baby Take a Bow* (1935), in which they played the doting parents of another of Dunn's frequent female co-stars, Shirley Temple. After her debut in 1933, Trevor was one of Fox's busiest actresses during the decade, mostly in Bs, but she later made more memorable films, including *Stagecoach* and *Key Largo*. Dunn's feature debut was opposite Sally Eilers in *Bad Girl* (1931), a hit that led to six more pairings,

Claire Trevor and James Dunn

making Eilers his regular leading lady. The affable Irishman of *Hold That Girl* was very much the type Dunn was known for in the '30s.

Before its release, the film's title was changed from *Every Girl for Herself* and *Women and the Law*. Dudley Nichols and Lamar Trotti collaborated on the story. Both Oscar winners (Nichols for *The Informer*, Trotti for *Wilson*), they joined forces on several films of the mid-'30s, but their greatest successes were apart from each other. Not among their more distinguished works, *Hold That Girl* was a mild but amusing addition to the reporter and law enforcement feud films of this period, taking inspiration from Ben Hecht's play *The Front Page*, which reached the screen in 1931 (later remade into the classic *His Girl Friday*).

Lucille was playing bit parts regularly at Twentieth Century Pictures at this time, and she did two at Fox. The two companies merged a year later. Though Fox was the bigger corporation, Zanuck took charge. It would be eleven years before Lucille returned to Twentieth Century-Fox, for *The Dark Corner*.

Bottoms Up

A Fox Film (1934)

Cast: Spencer Tracy (Smoothie King); Pat Paterson (Wanda Gale); John Boles (Hal Reede); Sid Silvers (Spud Mosco); Herbert Mundin (Limey Brock); Harry Green (Louis Wolf); Thelma Todd (Judith Marlowe); Robert Emmett O'Connor (Detective Rooney); Dell Henderson (Lane Worthing); Suzanne Kaaren (Secretary); Douglas Wood (Baldwin); Lucille Ball (Showgirl)

Credits: B. G. DeSylva (producer); David Butler (director); B. G. DeSylva, David Butler, and Sid Silvers (story and screenplay); Arthur Miller (photography); Constantine Bakaleinikoff (musical director); Harold Hecht (dance director); Gordon Wiles (art director); Joseph Aiken (sound); Russell Patterson (editor)

Songs: "Turn on the Moon," "I'm Throwing My Love Away," "Little Did I Dream," "Waitin' at the Gate for Katy" (Richard A. Whiting and Gus Kahn; Harold Adamson and Burton Lane)

Release date: April 13, 1934 (Radio City Music Hall)

Run time: 85 minutes

Synopsis

Shrewd, fast-talking Smoothie King (Spencer Tracy) arrives in Hollywood assured of becoming a movie mogul in no time. He discovers pretty, unemployed actress Wanda Gale (Pat Paterson) in a coffee shop and decides to take her with him to the top. To give her distinction, he has her pose as the daughter of an English nobleman. Smoothie's pal Limey (Herbert Mundin) is to be her father, "Lord Brocklehurst."

Wanda's reservations about Smoothie's scheme fade as they make contact with the film colony at a party where she meets her dream man, matinee idol Hal Reede (John Boles). Discontented with his career, Hal douses his sorrows in a few too many drinks and Wanda takes him home. Limey informs producer Louis Wolf (Harry Green) of this. Fearing widespread news of the incident would compromise Reede's reputation, Wolf gives "Miss Brocklehurst" and her friends their hearts' desires—contracts with the studio. Wanda becomes Hal's leading lady both onscreen and off.

Before long, Wanda is exposed as phony, but it is too late for Wolf to do anything, as she is in the midst of making a big-budget musical. A sidelined movie queen (Thelma Todd) tells her that Hal pretended to be in love with her only to find out who she was. Heartbroken, Wanda cries on Smoothie's shoulder. Smoothie is in love with her. He investigates and finds out that Hal loves her regardless of who she is. Smoothie delivers the news to Wanda, then bows out graciously.

Notes and Comments

British actress Pat Paterson made her American screen debut in Fox's *Bottoms Up*. She married shortly after her arrival at Fox, however, and

Lucille (back row, left) and other chorus girls costumed for the "Waitin' at the Gate for Katy" number.

made only a handful of films before retiring as Mrs. Charles Boyer. Her co-star, Spencer Tracy, had a longer tenure at the studio. Under contract since 1930, he played a succession of tough guys in crime dramas and comedies at Fox. *Bottoms Up* was his first musical. It was at MGM a year later that Tracy's career took off. Lucille would have a chance to act with the five-time Oscar winner a decade later, in *Without Love*. Featured in a relatively small role was comedienne Thelma Todd. During the '20s and early '30s in Hal Roach shorts and feature films, she was a foil for a host of the day's top comics, most famously for the Marx Brothers in *Monkey Business* and *Horse Feathers*.

Producer B. G. DeSylva also co-wrote the script of *Bottoms Up*, with supporting actor Sid Silvers and director David Butler. DeSylva was a writer-producer in Hollywood and Broadway and composer of songs like "California, Here I Come." Writer-director (and former actor) David Butler later made *That's Right—You're Wrong* with Lucille. He and DeSylva teamed up on a string of Fox musicals and comedies, including three starring Shirley Temple.

Reviews

" . . . a musical film so thoroughly tuneful and amusing, so thoroughly free from the usual spectacular song and dance numbers lavished on such productions, that it is one of the special cinema delights of recent weeks. . . . the acting of the entire cast, notably that of Spencer Tracy, is excellent."

—*New York World-Telegram*

"Bottoms Up is tiptop. It's good cinematic fare from every angle, particularly the elements of comedy and plot, of which aspects most filmusicals are singularly devoid. Seemingly recognizing the film fans' basic penchant for an arresting story, or at least a plot that plausibly makes the musical trimmings jell, the screen artificers of 'Bottoms Up' have given this phase more than passing attention. . . . Pat Paterson [is] a pert and cute personality . . . "

—*Variety*

" . . . an agreeable surprise, for although the narrative is light and frivolous it nevertheless is one that captures the attention. . . . The scheme results in many hilarious incidents, and largely through the author and the director's will the efforts of King and his cohorts are highly successful."

—*New York Times*

Advertisement for *Bottoms Up* featuring Spencer Tracy, Pat Paterson, and John Boles.

"23 skidoo!" *Bottoms Up* publicity still of Lucille and two showgirl friends. Barbara Pepper is at left.

Bottoms Up was a well-received Hollywood satire with music and modest production numbers that were secondary to the plot. This was appreciated in musicals that followed the surge of mediocre revues that came in the early sound era. The dance sequences were created by Harold Hecht, who later became a producer (*Marty*, *Separate Tables*).

Lucille is seen looking beautiful and elegantly gowned in the party sequence, then in turn-of-the-century garb for the production number "Waitin' at the Gate for Katy." Lynn Bari, future star of Fox's low-budget product and popular supporting actress, had a small role in *Bottoms Up* as well.

Murder at the Vanities

A Paramount Picture (1934)

Cast: Carl Brisson (Eric Lander); Victor McLaglen (Detective Bill Murdock); Jack Oakie (Jack Ellery); Kitty Carlisle (Ann Ware); Dorothy Stickney (Norma Watson); Gertrude Michael (Rita Ross); Jessie Ralph (Mrs. Helene Smith); Charles B. Middleton (Homer Boothby); Gail Patrick (Sadie Evans); Donald Meek (Dr. Saunders); Toby Wing (Nancy); Otto Hoffman (Walsh); Charles McAvoy (Ben); Beryl Wallace (Beryl); Barbara Fritchie (Vivien); Lona Andre (Lona); Colin Tapley (Stage Manager); Mitchell Leisen (Orchestra Leader); Lucille Ball (Extra); Duke Ellington and His Orchestra

Credits: E. Lloyd Sheldon (producer); Mitchell Leisen (director); Carey Wilson, Joseph Gollomb, and Sam Hellman (screenplay), from play by Earl Carroll and Rufus King; Leo Tover (photography); Larry Ceballos and LeRoy Prinz (dance directors)

Songs: "Cocktails for Two," "Where Do They Come From (and Where Do They Go)?," "Live and Love Tonight," "Marihuana," "Ebony Rhapsody," "Second Hungarian Rhapsody" (Arthur Johnston and Sam Coslow)

Release date: May 19, 1934 (Rivoli Theater)

Run time: 89 minutes

Synopsis

On the opening night of Earl Carroll's *Vanities*, the show's stars, Eric Lander (Carl Brisson) and Ann Ware (Kitty Carlisle), announce their engagement. This infuriates their co-star, Rita Ross (Gertrude Michael), who wanted Eric for herself.

When Ann scarcely escapes two would-be fatal accidents, Detective Murdock (Victor McLaglen) is called in to investigate. Ann is unharmed, but a female private eye hired by Eric turns up dead. Evidence points to Eric's mother, Mrs. Smith (Jessie Ralph), as the killer. The spurned Rita strikes out against Eric by further incriminating his mother. She has

Kitty Carlisle and Carl Brisson

When viewing the film it is not possible to identify Lucille among the hundreds of Vanities girls, but this production still reveals her in the "Where Do They Come From (and Where Do They Go)?" musical number. See page 75.

Reviews

"Pulchritude, indeed, is the keynote of the production . . . The plot [leaves] loose ends, but the motivation is well enough established, and if the finger of guilt points somewhat obviously, it doesn't matter. For what counts most is the spectacle. The rest is just the dummy for its handsome draperies."

— *New York American*

"It can boast of its lavish staging, certain tuneful melodies, and its host of attractive girls. But the mystery is never particularly disturbing. . . . the spectacular items are far more interesting than the story."

— *New York Times*

"Of the genus backstage musical, long familiar in the films, it has more life and bloom than the great majority of such potpourris . . . with melodrama, drama, and near tragedy all melanged with songs and dances, most colorfully staged . . . For the wisecracks there is Jack Oakie . . . Carl Brisson [is] a chap of prepossessing personality . . . Kitty Carlisle promises to improve with acquaintance."

— *Los Angeles Times*

learned a dark secret from Mrs. Smith's past: She once committed a crime that has tormented her for years, but that went unpunished by the courts. Rita threatens to inform the police, but before she can do so, she becomes the second murder victim of the night. Eric and Mrs. Smith are the prime suspects.

Throughout the tragedy and mayhem going on backstage, the *Vanities* has gone on as scheduled. Once the performance is over, Eric is to be arrested on suspicion. Just then, Rita's maid, Norma (Dorothy Stickney), reveals the truth behind all that has happened.

Norma first witnessed Rita attempt to kill Ann. When Eric's private eye intervened, Rita killed her. Later, while Rita was performing on stage, Norma, tired of being beaten and belittled by the volatile star, shot Rita. With the mystery solved, Mrs. Smith's secret is safe and Eric and Ann can proceed with their plans to elope.

Notes and Comments

Earl Carroll's *Murder at the Vanities* played for six months on Broadway between 1933 and '34. The famed showman co-wrote the play with Rufus King, an author of thrillers, who provided the twist and turns of the murder mystery. Their story inspired Paramount Pictures to translate to the screen for the first (and only) time an edition of Carroll's legendary *Vanities* revue.

Early cast considerations were Cary Grant, Dorothy Dell, and radio singer Lanny Ross. Instead, top roles went to Danish actor (and former middleweight boxing champ of Europe) Carl Brisson and Broadway's Kitty Carlisle, making her motion picture debut. Carlisle made only a few films, the best being the Marx Brothers classic *A Night at the Opera*. Other important roles were filled by Dorothy Stickney, primarily a stage actress, and the more familiar Hollywood names of Victor McLaglen and Jack Oakie. A pre-stardom Ann Sheridan was cast as well, in a minor part.

The director, Mitchell Leisen, was also a costume designer and art director who focused on visuals in his films, and this comes through clearly in *Murder at the Vanities*. In the tradition of Earl Carroll, the production was opulent and teemed with girls in pretentiously mounted musical numbers. "Cocktails for Two" was the standout of the Johnston-Coslow score, which also featured an odd tune about "sweet Marihuana," sung by Gertrude Michael against a background of cacti.* Decades later, the number is alarming. At the time, the plant was not yet illegal and many, including

star Kitty Carlisle, did not know what it was. In early 1934, Joseph Breen, director of the Studio Relations Committee, which enforced the production code, approved the film, only to have the Department of State raise objections to the song a year later. Cuts were ordered before the film could be reissued in 1935, but not every print met with

Detail of Lucille from photo on page 74

the censors' scissors. The complete version has been released on home video.

As the mystery unfolds during the *Vanities* opening night, scenes flash back and forth between the lavish stage show and backstage intrigue. Except as noted below the photo on page 74, Lucille was lost amid the throng of body-baring chorines, billed as "The Most Beautiful Girls in the World," who were used in creating the spectacles.

*For obvious reasons the song was later given a new title, "Sweet Lotus Blossom."

The Affairs of Cellini

A Twentieth Century Picture (1934)

Released by United Artists

Cast: Constance Bennett (Duchess of Florence); Fredric March (Benvenuto Cellini); Frank Morgan (Alessandro de' Medici, Duke of Florence); Fay Wray (Angela); Vince Barnett (Ascanio); Jessie Ralph (Beatrice); Louis Calhern (Ottaviano); Jay Eaton (Polverino); Paul Harvey (Emissary); John Rutherford (Captain of the Guards); Irene Ware (Girl); Lucille Ball (Lady-in-Waiting)

Credits: Presented by Joseph M. Schenck; Darryl F. Zanuck (producer); William Goetz and Raymond Griffith (associate producers); Gregory La Cava (director); Bess Meredyth (screenplay), from play by Edwin Justus Mayer; Charles Rosher (photography); Alfred Newman (musical score); Adolph Bolm (ballet master); Richard Day (art director); Gwen Wakeling (costumes); Thomas T. Moulton (sound); Fred Fox (assistant director); Barbara McLean (editor)

Release date: September 5, 1934 (Rivoli Theater)

Run time: 80 minutes

Synopsis

The famed roguish craftsman Benvenuto Cellini (Fredric March) is to be hanged by order of the Duke of Florence (Frank Morgan) for insulting a member of the aristocracy. But when the Duke himself arrives with soldiers to arrest him, Cellini steers the half-witted monarch's attention to his lovely model, Angela (Fay Wray). The execution is at once forgotten and the Duke takes Angela off to the palace to be his mistress.

Among Florentine women, Cellini is as well known for his romantic prowess as he is for his art, and the word has spread to the Duchess (Constance Bennett). She beckons him to the palace. Cellini keeps the date, but then finds Angela and steals her away. Both the Duke and Duchess are incensed.

Once again, Cellini's execution is ordered. This time he reconciles with the Duchess and becomes her lover. She then saves his life by convincing the Duke that killing him would inflame the people. In return for the pardon, the Duke commands Cellini to return Angela to him. So as not to give rise to rumors when she is returned to the palace, the girl is to pose as Cellini's guest at a banquet to be held that evening.

The Duchess's fury over Angela's presence at the gathering is intensified when the Duke lies to her by saying that Cellini is engaged to the girl. To punish her paramour, the Duchess has poison put in his glass. He takes a drink, then collapses. Her anger vanishes and she pronounces her love for Cellini. Soon it is revealed that he did not actually drink of the cup containing poison. The Duke's intrigue with Angela is also exposed. With no further secrets between her and the Duke, the Duchess departs with Cellini for her winter palace.

The Duchess pays a visit to Cellini's workshop. It was rare to find Constance Bennett, the modern beauty and renowned style star, in a costume picture.

Notes and Comments

The Firebrand, a play by Edwin Justus Mayer inspired by the exploits of sixteenth-century Florentine artisan Benvenuto Cellini, served as the basis for Darryl Zanuck's film. The producer commissioned Bess Meredyth, a veteran scenarist who wrote romance scripts for Greta Garbo and Norma Shearer, to compose the adaptation. Filmed under the same name as the play during February and March of 1934, prior to release the title was switched to *The Affairs of Cellini*.

Gregory La Cava (Lucille's *Stage Door* director three years later) elicited entertaining performances from his notable cast, lead by Constance Bennett and Fredric March, who was riding the crest of his great success as *Dr. Jekyll and Mr. Hyde*. The hardworking Fay Wray supported them. She appeared in nearly a dozen 1934 releases, almost as many as Lucille, only in Wray's case it was starring roles and second leads she was rushed in and out of. Beloved character actor Frank Morgan had played the Duke of Florence in the stage edition of

As one of the Duchess's handmaidens, Lucille, with dark tresses, can often be spotted over Bennett's shoulder.

Reviews

"'The Affairs of Cellini' is a polite bedroom farce with the quick tempo of good comedy, the swashbuckling melodrama of an old Fairbanks film and the gorgeous trappings of a lavish historical drama. . . . It is all played up to the hilt by a cast that seemed to enjoy the proceedings hugely."

—*New York Sun*

"Magnificently acted by Frank Morgan, Fredric March and Constance Bennett, directed with delicacy by Gregory La Cava, The Affairs of Cellini is an uproarious and gracefully ribald costume play, rarely informative, but almost always funny. . . . would be a notable comedy if its only merit were Frank Morgan's performance as the Duke."

—*Time*

"Practically, it is a Lubitsch type of comedy transferred to another era. Lightness and gayety [sic] are emphasized throughout, and gorgeousness surrounds the somewhat trifling plot. But all of it spells smart and different entertainment."

—*Los Angeles Times*

Suspicion reigns supreme in the Palazzo de' Medici. Lucille observes over Bennett's shoulder, at left.

the film a decade earlier. He came to recreate his performance on the screen after Zanuck was unable to obtain the services of Charles Laughton. Morgan earned an Oscar nomination as Best Actor in the role. The film itself garnered additional nominations for cinematography, art direction, and sound recording. *The Affairs of Cellini* was made for $549,000 and garnered $860,000 in US film rentals.

Draped in robes and topped in a brunette wig, Lucille played one of the four ladies-in-waiting who attend Duchess Constance Bennett about the palace. Lucille had first met Constance in New York when Constance and her sister Joan were frequent patrons of Hattie Carnegie's salon. Because of Lucille's resemblance to them, with the same hair color, style, and lean figure, it was often Lucille who modeled for the Bennett sisters. Joan in particular made an impression. Lucille patterned her own hair and fashions on the actress then and after the famous blonde became a brunette in 1938.

Two months after *Cellini* and before beginning her next film assignment, Lucille took a trip back home to Jamestown to visit with relatives and old friends. There she found that being a Goldwyn Girl had made her the pride of the town.

Bulldog Drummond Strikes Back

A Twentieth Century Picture (1934)

Released by United Artists

Cast: Ronald Colman (Hugh "Bulldog" Drummond); Loretta Young (Lola Field); Warner Oland (Prince Achmed); Charles Butterworth (Algy); Una Merkel (Gwen); C. Aubrey Smith (Colonel Nielson); Arthur Hohl (Dr. Owen Sothern); George Regas (Singh); Ethel Griffies (Lola's Aunt); Mischa Auer (Hassan); Douglas Gerrard (Parker); Halliwell Hobbes (First Bobby); E. E. Clive (Second Bobby); Kathleen Burke (Lady Jane); Wilson Benge (Watkins); Lucille Ball (Bridesmaid)

Credits: Presented by Joseph M. Schenck; Darryl F. Zanuck (producer); William Goetz and Raymond Griffith (associate producers); Roy Del Ruth (director); Nunnally Johnson and Henry Lehrman (screenplay), from novel by H. C. McNeile; Peverell Marley (photography); Alfred Newman (musical score); Richard Day (art director); Gwen Wakeling (costumes); Allen McNeil (editor)

Release date: August 15, 1934 (Rivoli Theater)

Run time: 83 minutes

Synopsis

When his partner Algy (Charles Butterworth) takes a wife, Captain Hugh "Bulldog" Drummond (Ronald Colman) decides to give up his adventures in favor of peace and tranquility. Strolling through the foggy London streets, he loses his way, wanders into the home of Prince Achmed (Warner Oland)—and discovers a corpse. He summons a police officer, but when they return, the prince and his staff feign bewilderment. No dead body is found, but Hugh knows something is amiss.

The stars, Ronald Colman and Loretta Young

Reviews

"A jolly pot-pourri, which is not intended to be taken seriously for a moment, the picture is full of quite effortless nonsense and is highly entertaining throughout. Directed with a brilliantly sure, silky touch by Roy Del Ruth, and acted by a cast selected with unerring shrewdness, it moves along blissfully in a light-hearted, galumphing mood from beginning to end. . . . The cast is perfect from top to bottom."

— *New York World-Telegram*

"Fast moving, laugh-studded, smartly produced melodrama as incredible as it is engrossing. . . . Not for a moment does it lag and although it really does not make logic it has that eerie plausibility that a well-written mystery novel achieves when perused in the wee hours."

— *Variety*

"Ronald Colman, the stellar player in 'Bulldog Drummond Strikes Back,' gives another of his ingratiating and flawless performances as the redoubtable Captain Hugh Drummond. Owing to his keen sense of humor, Mr. Colman succeeds in making the extravagant adventures of the master sleuth almost possible."

— *New York Times*

Captain Drummond is in a tight spot—but never for long. Clockwise in this scene are George Regas, Warner Oland, Mischa Auer, and Ronald Colman.

Failing to interest Scotland Yard's Colonel Nielson (C. Aubrey Smith) in the mystery, Hugh drags Algy from his bride (Una Merkel) to help crack the case. Damsel in distress Lola Field (Loretta Young) turns up at Hugh's door. Her uncle, the captain of Prince Achmed's ship, has disappeared. She tells Hugh that the prince had a cargo of precious furs aboard. En route to London, her uncle received a distressing radiogram concerning the cargo. After reaching port, he went to relay the message to the prince and never returned. Lola has the radiogram, but it is encoded. Worse yet, soon her aunt disappears as well.

Hugh is immediately on the job. Each time he uncovers evidence of the prince's misdeeds, he awakens Nielson, but before they return, the proof disappears. The exasperated colonel is ready to have Hugh arrested. Lola too is kidnapped and Hugh returns to the prince's home. After numerous comic turns and close calls, he rescues Lola and her aunt (it is too late for her uncle—the murdered man Hugh had seen earlier in the night).

Piecing clues together, Hugh hits upon the mystery of the radiogram. The furs are infected and must be destroyed before they are unloaded. Hugh heads to the port and sets fire to the ship. Algy decodes the radiogram for the authorities. To save his fortune, the prince was willing to unleash a plague upon London. Hugh imposes upon Algy's wedding night once more—to ask the newlyweds to witness his marriage to Lola.

Notes and Comments

Films about author H. C. "Sapper" McNeile's suave sleuth, Bulldog Drummond, began in the silent era and continued intermittently, both in America and the UK, over several decades. Ronald Colman was already a star in silent pictures, but the introduction of his "velvet voice" in early talkies like 1929's *Bulldog Drummond* advanced his celebrity and earned him his first Oscar nomination. In 1934, he reprised the role in Twentieth Century's *Bulldog Drummond Strikes Back*. The character was subsequently portrayed by various actors, including Ray Milland, Walter Pidgeon, Ralph Richardson, and most frequently, John Howard, who starred in the Paramount series of the late '30s.

The groom's best friend poses with the bride at the start of a highly eventful night—for all except the bride!

Influenced by contemporary best-selling novelists Ellery Queen and Dashiell Hammett, producer Darryl Zanuck viewed the trend in mystery films of the day as "toward a lighter type of horror story, with as much emphasis placed on characterization and dialogue as on plot." *Bulldog Drummond Strikes Back* mingled drama, adventure, and suspense with liberal doses of comedy—an increasingly prevalent melange following the exceptional *Thin Man* series opener that was released earlier in the year.

The picture brought Colman back to the screen after a split with Samuel Goldwyn, to whom he had been under contract since the mid-'20s. It further enhanced his career and sent him on to greater roles. Loretta Young was his winsome leading lady. Charles Butterworth was amusing as his pal Algy, as was Una Merkel, as Algy's exasperated bride of a few hours. Warner Oland took a break from doing his own sleuthing as Chinese detective Charlie Chan at Fox to play the film's villain. Lucille, meanwhile, adorned the wedding reception scene, gabbing amongst the bridesmaids.

Kid Millions

A Goldwyn Production (1934)

Released by United Artists

Cast: Eddie Cantor (Eddie Wilson, Jr.); Ann Sothern (Joan Larrabee); Ethel Merman (Dot); George Murphy (Gerald Lane); Berton Churchill (Colonel Larrabee); Warren Hymer (Louie the Lug); Paul Harvey (Sheik Mulhulla); Jesse Block (Ben Ali); Eve Sully (Fanya); Otto Hoffman (Khoot); Stanley Fields (Oscar); Edgar Kennedy (Herman); Jack Kennedy (Pop Wilson); John Kelly (Adolph); Doris Davenport (Toots); Stymie Beard (Stymie); Tommy Bond (Tommy); Guy Usher (Slade); the Nicholas Brothers; the Goldwyn Girls of 1934

Credits: Samuel Goldwyn (producer); Roy Del Ruth (director); Arthur Sheekman, Nat Perrin, and Nunnally Johnson (story and screenplay); Ray June (photography); Ray Ringer (special effects); Alfred Newman (musical director); Seymour Felix (dance director); Richard Day (art director); Omar Kiam (costumes); Vinton Vernon (sound); Stuart Heisler (editor)

Songs: "An Earful of Music," "When My Ship Comes In," "Okay Toots" (Walter Donaldson and Gus Khan); "Your Head on My Shoulder," "I Want To Be a Minstrel Man" (Burton Lane and Harold Adamson); "Mandy" (Irving Berlin); piano number (Jacques Fray and Mario Braggiotti)

Release date: November 10, 1934 (Rivoli Theater)

Run time: 90 minutes

Synopsis

The death of Edward Grant Wilson sets off a frenzy of imposters laying claim to the vast fortune he uncovered in an archeological dig. The rightful heir is Eddie Wilson, Jr. (Eddie Cantor), who must travel to Egypt to collect. On board the *S.S. Luxor*, the unsuspecting Eddie encounters his competitors . . .

First is Dot (Ethel Merman), whose boyfriend, Louie (Warren Hymer), has talked her into alleging to have been Wilson's common-law wife. She presents herself to Eddie as his long-lost mother, while Louie plots to bump him off. Colonel Larrabee (Berton Churchill), also after the treasure, says it was his Egyptian Society that financed Wilson's expedition. He is traveling with his niece, Joan (Ann Sothern), whose sweetheart, Gerald Lane (George Murphy), was Wilson's assistant and knows that the one and only true heir is Eddie.

Upon arrival in Egypt, Eddie meets Fanya (Eve Sully), daughter of the sheik (Paul Harvey). The princess, infatuated, takes him to the palace to meet her father. Little does he know, the sheik has vowed to kill the son of Professor Wilson for the desecration of his ancestral burial ground. Un-

Surrounded by the wives of the sheik, Eddie pines for the girl he left behind.

Lucille cuddles up to star Eddie Cantor in costume for "Okay Toots."

aware of Eddie's relation to Wilson, the sheik welcomes him into his home, but when the troupe of claim jumpers converge on the palace, Eddie's identity is revealed. The sheik declares he must die and throws the others into the dungeon.

As they are about to brew a pot of Eddie Wilson soup, Fanya tells her father she wishes to marry the young man. Eddie makes his escape by stepping into a burial casket and speaking to the sheik from inside. Pretending to be an ancient spirit, he demands that the prisoners be set free. Eddie makes it back to New York by plane, one in which larcenous Louie had stashed stolen treasures from the palace. With the money from the goods, Eddie opens a free ice cream factory for children, employing his friends from the Egyptian adventure, as well as the beautiful Goldwyn Girls.

Notes and Comments

Kid Millions, fifth in Samuel Goldwyn's Eddie Cantor series, had the usual mix of music, mirth, and madness, along with a color "Ice Cream Fantasy" finale that became Goldwyn's chief concern during production. The newly developed

"'Kid Millions' finds Mr. Cantor at his funniest . . . Mr. Goldwyn's production has been wise not only in the handsome mounting but in the selection of the supporting players. Ethel Merman, Warren Hymer, Ann Sothern and Eve Sully may be singled out as lending particularly valuable aid."

—*New York Evening Post*

" . . . a superior screen comedy into which the generous Mr. Goldwyn has poured almost everything that seemed helpful to the cause of pleasure. . . . Not all of 'Kid Millions' is as good as its best, but it is invariably diverting, a continuously reliable bazaar of gayety [sic] and music."

—*New York Times*

"Another Goldwyn-Cantor musical comedy extravaganza and again strong entertainment . . . Comparisons with earlier productions will be made, but are pointless [since] 'Kid Millions' is up to standard. And that's good enough. . . . Plot is musical comedy strictly carried along by Cantor's breeze and the Goldwynesque showmanship. Picture should have no trouble. It's packed with dames and giggles."

—*Variety*

three-strip Technicolor process could register all the colors of the rainbow—as well as vanilla, strawberry, and chocolate. In addition to the chorus numbers, Lucille made it into this novelty sequence as one of the beauties running the ice cream factory.

Kid Millions was filmed in the summer months of 1934. Alongside Cantor in the large supporting cast of the picture was Broadway legend Ethel Merman, the vaudeville team of Block and Sully, and the young Nicholas Brothers—best known for their specialty acts in musicals of the '40s—in their second film. With top-drawer production values and Irving Berlin's old-time "Mandy," the musical did well at the box office, but only one Goldwyn-Cantor show followed—*Strike Me Pink*, released in 1936.

George Murphy, who had just come west from the Broadway company of *Roberta*, made his cinematic debut as the juvenile to Ann Sothern's ingénue. On the set, Murphy observed the efforts of a certain blonde chorine to be "noticed." She would customarily turn up missing after breaks during filming and assistant director Ben Silvey would call out, "Miss Ball—on the set please." When Murphy advised her to be careful, she said they may fire her, "But one thing you can be sure of—they'll know who I am."

Indeed, Lucille was anxious to get out and sign with a new studio because as long as she remained a Goldwyn Girl, she could hope for little more than showgirl parts. Shortly after her work was through on *Kid Millions*, she moved to Columbia Pictures. Even though the $75 per week she would be making was a $50 pay cut, she thought there she would at least have a chance to break out of the chorus line.

Cantor, Hollywood's highest-paid actor this year, talks with his favorite chorus girl. She said the supportive comic told her, "Lucille, you have a gift for comedy and a sense of timing that's priceless. Why don't you break away from this [lineup] and try to act?"

Dance director Seymour Felix basks in the company of the Goldwyn Girls. Lucille is furthest right.

The Fugitive Lady

A Columbia Picture (1934)

Cast: Neil Hamilton (Donald Brooks); Florence Rice (Ann Duncan); Donald Cook (Jack Howard); Clara Blandick (Aunt Margaret); Nella Walker (Mrs. Brooks); William Demarest (Steve Rogers); Matt McHugh (Bert Higgins); Wade Boteler (Rudy Davis); Ernest Wood (Joe Nelson); Rita La Roy (Sylvia Brooks); Rita Gould (Mrs. Clifford); Harvey Clark (Mr. Creswell); Lucille Ball (Beauty Operator)

Credits: Sid Rogell (associate producer); Al Rogell (director); Herbert Asbury and Fred Niblo, Jr. (story and screenplay); Al Siegler (photography); George Cooper (sound); Moreley Lightfoot (assistant director); John Rawlins (editor)

Release date: December 6, 1934 (Strand Theater)

Run time: 66 minutes

Synopsis

A trusting beauty operator, Ann Duncan (Florence Rice), falls for Jack Howard (Donald Cook), a suave thief, and becomes his bride. She finds herself on the lam instead of a honeymoon when Jack steals some jewels and makes a getaway, leaving her to take to take the rap. A train wreck en route to prison prevents Ann from serving her term. In the tumult of the wreck, her identity becomes confused with that of Sylvia Brooks (Rita La Roy), a femme fatale who was on her way to cause trouble for the family of the wealthy husband she hooked, Donald Brooks (Neil Hamilton).

Ann continues on the woman's path to the Brooks country estate, where she is taken in by the charitable family and hidden from the authorities after they hear her story. Ann and Donald quickly begin to fall in love. Later, unexpected visitors arrive on the scene: Ann's thieving husband, to rob the Brookses and to claim his bride, Sylvia Brooks's brother, to claim his sister, and the police, to claim their fugitive lady. After a few chaotic moments, the confusion is cleared up and Ann is proven innocent of the charges against her. Jack is headed for jail and Ann is headed for a happy marriage with Donald.

Notes and Comments

Florence Rice, who had just come from starring in the hit play *She Loves Me Not* on Broadway, made her screen debut as the title character of *The Fugitive Lady*. The daughter of renowned sportswriter Grantland Rice, she appeared in Bs at Columbia before hitting her stride at MGM, where she played supporting roles as well as leads in the late '30s, frequently paired with Robert Young. Her *Fugitive Lady* co-star was Neil Hamilton,

Reviews

"Miss Rice turns in a competent performance and gives promise of developing into a useful lead. Neil Hamilton is a personable hero and Donald Cook shows briefly as the gentleman thief. William Demarest and Clara Blandick handle most of the comedy and they turn in good scores . . . If the story were up to the acting and directorial average this would have been strong material. As is, fair and unimportant."

—Variety

"Florence Rice possesses an aristocratic profile and natural poise. Neil Hamilton does not disappoint as the hero, and Donald Cook forsakes his former leading man tactics to give a clever crook characterization. Rita La Roy is well cast as the first Mrs. Brooks."

—Los Angeles Times

1934—Retaining the mien of New York days that made her the ideal model for the famous Bennett sisters.

a leading man in the '20s who played the snobbish Lonny Borden in *What Price Hollywood?* and was later Commissioner Gordon of *Batman* fame.

The Fugitive Lady was filmed between September 19 and October 2, 1934 under the supervision of producer Sid Rogell, a future RKO studio chief. His brother, Al Rogell, directed from a script by Herbert Asbury and Fred Niblo, Jr. The screenwriters and director, who worked as a team on low-budget dramas in 1934, came up with a fairly entertaining programmer that opened to tepid reviews.

Lucille is seen in the opening sequence as a beauty operator in a cosmetics salon. It was another small part, but she was also doing a great deal of publicity work and co-starring in a few shorts during this period, including *Three Little Pigskins* with the Three Stooges, a first encounter with knockabout comedy performed by its most intense partisans.

Men of the Night

A Columbia Picture (1934)

Cast: Bruce Cabot ("Stake-Out" Kelly); Judith Allen (Mary Higgins); Ward Bond (Detective John Connors); Charles Sabin (Packey Davis); John Kelly (Chuck); Arthur Rankin (Pat Smith); Matthew Betz (Schmidt); Walter McGrail (Louie); Maidel Turner (Mrs. Webbley); Charles C. Wilson (Benson); Frank Darien (Mr. Webbley); Al Hill, Louis Natheaux (Hold-up Men); Eddie Foster (Pedro); Gladys Gale (Mrs. Everett); Robert Graves (Mr. Everett); Ernie Adams (Sandy); Lucille Ball (Peggy)

Credits: Lambert Hillyer (director, story, and screenplay); Henry Freulich (photography); Lodge Cunningham (sound); C. C. Coleman (assistant director); Al Clark (editor)

Release date: November 27, 1934 (Loew's Ziegfeld Theater)

Run time: 58 minutes

Synopsis

Detective "Stake-Out" Kelly (Bruce Cabot) sets out to round up a gang of Hollywood jewel thieves headed by Packey Davis (Charles Sabin). In the midst of his duties, Kelly becomes enamored of Mary Higgins (Judith Allen), a drive-in waitress with ambitions to become a movie star, but their potential romance comes to a halt when he begins to suspect she is entangled with Davis. The police department arranges a plan for one of the gang members to be formally identified. When the plot is foiled, Kelly believes Mary tipped off Davis, but she is actually working undercover with the police. Just as Mary's proximity to Davis puts her in deadly peril, Kelly and his men are able to save her and put Davis and his crew behind bars. Kelly finds out Mary was working on the side of the law all along. He sends her home to Iowa—and quickly follows.

Notes and Comments

Lambert Hillyer took a break from horse operas to tell this cops and robbers yarn, which was essentially a western set in Hollywood. The prolific writer-director began in the teens with westerns starring William S. Hart and continued operating primarily in that genre for decades, making serials with Buck Jones, "Wild" Bill Elliot, Tex Ritter, and Johnny Mack Brown. *Men of the Night*, whose working title was *Stake Out*, was part of Judith Allen's brief career as a B movie star in the early '30s. She was cast opposite Bruce Cabot (*King Kong*'s heroic Jack Driscoll), who later supported Lucille and Bob Hope in *Sorrowful Jones* and *Fancy Pants*. Ward Bond, as Cabot's partner, provided light moments to the action-filled crime drama. The actor played hundreds of bit parts and

Review

some second leads in films, but is known for starring in the television series *Wagon Train.*

In Lucille's first release from her new studio, she took the small part of Peggy. In the year she arrived at Columbia Pictures there were many bright moments in the company's history as it emerged from "poverty row" status with the brilliant comedy *It Happened One Night.* That film alone brought home all the top Oscars, while *One Night of Love* won two others. Carole Lombard in *Twentieth Century* was another triumph. With these 1934 releases, Columbia set off two trends that took hold in movies immediately: screwball comedies featuring frivolous heiresses and the mass importation of opera stars to Hollywood, both of which would touch Lucille's career in the next couple of years.

During her brief time as a Columbia Pictures contract player, 1934.

Jealousy

A Columbia Picture (1934)

Cast: Nancy Carroll (Josephine Douglas); George Murphy (Larry O'Roark); Donald Cook (Mark Lambert); Raymond Walburn (Phil); Arthur Hohl (Mike); Inez Courtney (Penny); Robert Allen (Jim); Clara Blandick (Mrs. Douglas); Arthur Hoyt (Smith); Josephine Whittell (Laura); Arthur Vinton (Tony); Ray Mayer (Hook); Ray Cooke (Line); Huey White (Sinker); Lucille Ball (Extra)

Credits: Roy William Neill (director); Joseph Moncure March and Kubec Glasmon (screenplay), from play by Argyll Campbell; John Stumar (photography); Viola Lawrence (editor)

Release date: November 22, 1934 (Strand Theater)

Run time: 66 minutes

George Murphy and Nancy Carroll

Synopsis

Prizefighter Larry O'Roark (George Murphy) is on the road to the championship and engaged to a lovely girl, Jo (Nancy Carroll). Only his jealous nature hinders their happiness. The night of an important bout, Jo must work late with her boss, Mark Lambert (Donald Cook), causing a heated argument between her and Larry. Mark allows her the night off, but then accompanies her to the fight. Larry sees them from the ring, gets caught off guard, and his opponent knocks him out cold.

The loss puts Larry's career in shambles, but he and Jo marry. Larry trains for his comeback, but in the meantime, Jo helps with the finances by returning to work, not telling Larry that her employer is still Mark. Finally Larry gets a break—a major fight. The night he brings home the

Reviews

news, Jo is working late at Mark's apartment. Larry finds out and charges in, filled with rage. The confrontation turns fatal when Larry gets hold of a gun. Mark is killed. In a state of shock, Larry walks out, leaving Jo to manage the ordeal on her own.

In trying to protect Larry, Jo ends up charged with murder. Elsewhere, Larry's sanity is restored. From a newspaper, he learns that Jo is on trial for her life. He rushes to court, confesses to the murder, and is sentenced to death. As he takes the final steps to his doom, Larry regains consciousness in the ring where it all began when he was knocked out. It had been a dream—an all-too-real one that serves to mend Larry and Jo's relationship. Larry overcomes his jealousy and befriends Mark.

Notes and Comments

Nancy Carroll was the effervescent baby-faced star of both musical comedies and dramas for a time in the early sound era, but at this point, her career was fading. After the former Paramount Pictures actress signed with Columbia, she was paired in three films with newcomer George Murphy in quick succession, with *Jealousy* being the first.

Writers Joseph Moncure March (*Hell's Angels*) and Kubec Glasmon (*The Public Enemy*) adapted their script from the Argyll Campbell play *Spring 3100*, which had a brief run in New York in 1928. They came up with a dismal tale that met with a poor reception.

Lucille was not the only member of the *Kid Millions* cast to move to Columbia directly after the film's completion. George Murphy, here in his second picture, spent a year at Columbia in which he did not fare very well, but Lucille was making out worse. She had switched studios in search of better parts. In *Jealousy* she was again used merely as scene filler. She would unite with members of the cast again in her own movies a few years later: Inez Courtney in *Beauty for the Asking* and Murphy in *A Girl, a Guy and a Gob*.

Broadway Bill

A Columbia Picture (1934)

Cast: Warner Baxter (Dan Brooks); Myrna Loy (Alice Higgins); Walter Connolly (J. L. Higgins); Helen Vinson (Margaret Higgins); Douglas Dumbrille (Eddie Morgan); Raymond Walburn (Colonel Pettigrew); Lynne Overman (Happy McGuire); Clarence Muse (Whitey); Margaret Hamilton (Edna); Frankie Darro (Ted Williams); George Cooper (Joe); George Meeker (Henry Early); Jason Robards, Sr. (Arthur Winslow); Ed Tucker (Jimmy Baker); Edmund Breese (Presiding Judge); Irving Bacon (Hotdog Stand Owner); Charles C. Wilson (Collins); Harry Todd (Pop Jones); Charles Lane, Ward Bond (Morgan's Henchmen); Helen Flint (Mrs. Early); Helene Millard (Mrs. Winslow); Bob Tansill (Whitehall's Jockey); Clara Blandick (Mrs. Peterson); Inez Courtney (Mae); Claude Gillingwater (J. P. Chase); Paul Harvey (James Whitehall); James Blakely (Interne); Alan Hale (Orchestra Leader); Lucille Ball (Telephone Operator)

Credits: Frank Capra (producer and director); Robert Riskin (screenplay), from story by Mark Hellinger; Joseph Walker (photography); Gene Havlick (editor)

Release date: November 30, 1934 (Radio City Music Hall)

Run time: 104 minutes

Raymond Walburn, Myrna Loy, and Warner Baxter

Synopsis

Dan Brooks (Warner Baxter) hates being a puppet of his wealthy father-in-law, J. L. Higgins (Walter Connolly). His passion is horses, not running one of the Higgins enterprises. Fed up, he and his beloved horse, Broadway Bill, leave Higginsville to enter the world of racing. His wife Margaret (Helen Vinson), not interested in leaving behind her luxury, permits Dan to go without a fight. But her little sister Alice (Myrna Loy) follows after him.

Dan's first move is to enter Broadway Bill in the Imperial Raceway Derby, but he must pay a hefty entry fee. He puts the horse in a small race to raise money, but has to stop racing him when Broadway Bill takes ill and needs to conserve his energy for the Derby. Alice comes through with the entry fee, but Dan's neglect of his other debts lands him in jail

Back at the track, gambler Eddie Morgan (Douglas Dumbrille) has rigged the big race in favor of his own horse, Sun-Up. A gag wager placed

Reviews

"A sly and impertinent screen comedy, painlessly whimsical and completely engaging, 'Broadway Bill' unfolds the fresh and inventive talent of Frank Capra in a mood of high good humor. . . . The players who work for Mr. Capra have a habit of performing at the top of their talent. . . . Myrna Loy reaffirms our faith in her, both as a light comedienne and as a person."

—*New York Times*

"For a starter Capra has a fine pair of leads in Warner Baxter and Myrna Loy, and then he has a yarn in which the tempo appears to have been especially suited to his directorial talents. The rest was up to Capra, and the rest is very much okay."

—*Variety*

" . . . one of the best bets of the current season in the way of gay, polite, literate and otherwise highly agreeable screen romances. It must be seen for its two charming romantic lovers, its amusing gallery of secondary characters, its ingenious and touching climax and its really fine—yes, super-fine—direction."

—*New York World-Telegram*

on Broadway Bill by a millionaire sets off a betting frenzy on the long shot. This makes Morgan stand to win even more if Sun-Up wins. When he hears Dan has to scratch Bill, Morgan springs Dan from prison and sees to it that his horse is in the race so that the odds on Sun-Up will not drop again.

Finally, the big moment arrives. If Broadway Bill wins, Dan will never have to go back to Higginsville. He is not let down—Broadway Bill triumphs—but it was too much for the not-fully-recovered champ. He dies on the track. Dan is despondent, but he has won respect and even affects the heart of J. L. Higgins. Once he gets back on his feet with a new stable of horses, Dan returns to Higginsville—but only long enough to take Alice away with him.

Notes and Comments

In 1934, Frank Capra's *It Happened One Night* put Columbia Pictures on the map, and the film would win him the first of his three Best Director Oscars at the Academy Awards ceremony held the following year. The star filmmaker next

Warner Baxter, Myrna Loy, Clarence Muse, and a rooster named Skeeter. This was Loy's first and only time working under the direction of Frank Capra. He had asked her to make *It Happened One Night* with him, but she passed up the plum role based on an early version of the script.

wanted to make *Broadway Bill*, based on a story by Mark Hellinger and adapted by Robert Riskin, the ace scribe who penned many Capra classics.

For the female lead, Capra borrowed Myrna Loy from MGM. She had just become one of Hollywood's hottest (and busiest) actresses with the recent successes *Manhattan Melodrama* and *The Thin Man*. For the star, the producer-director wanted an actor who showed a true affinity for horses. Warner Baxter assured him that he fit the bill, but as production got under way, it became apparent that Baxter was afraid of horses! *Broadway Bill* still turned out wonderfully Capra, filled with all the heartwarming spirit and touches of pathos for which he was noted.

The story remained a favorite of Capra's and he decided to remake *Broadway Bill* years later at Paramount as *Riding High* (1950), starring a more ideal Dan Brooks—Bing Crosby—opposite Coleen Gray. Racing scenes filmed at San Francisco's Tanforan racetrack from this version were edited into the remake, and many members of the original cast were employed, including Clarence Muse, Margaret Hamilton, Frankie Darro, Douglas Dumbrille, and Raymond Walburn. (Capra also remade his 1933 hit, *Lady for a Day*, as *Pocketful of Miracles* in 1961.)

Lucille played a telephone operator who helps spread the tip about a sure bet—"I just heard that

Obviously not dressed for her role as a phone operator in this publicity photo from the period *Broadway Bill* was in production—Lucille's modeling experience, coupled with her easy-going personality, made her a favorite of Columbia's still photographers.

J. P. Chase bet two Cs on Broadway Bill." She formed at least two long-standing friendships on the set. Charles Lane and Irving Bacon, who played small parts in this picture, later turned up in various roles in her television series. Among their memorable guest spots on *I Love Lucy* are Lane as a clock-watching passport office clerk in "Staten Island Ferry," and Irving Bacon as Ethel's father, Will Potter, in "Ethel's Home Town."

Carnival

A Columbia Picture (1935)

Cast: Lee Tracy (Chick Thompson); Sally Eilers (Daisy); Jimmy Durante (Fingers); Florence Rice (Miss Holbrook); Thomas Jackson (Mac); Dickie Walters (Poochy); Fred Kelsey (Detective); Oscar Apfel (Mrs. Lawson); Lucille Ball (Nurse)

Credits: Samuel J. Briskin (producer); Walter Lang (director); Robert Riskin (story and screenplay); Al Siegler (photography); Edward Bernds (sound); Edward Bernoudy (assistant director); Gene Milford and Richard Cahoon (editors)

Release date: February 15, 1935 (Rialto Theater)

Run time: 77 minutes

Synopsis

Marionette show conductor Chick Thompson (Lee Tracy) loses his wife during childbirth. His father-in-law labels Chick an unfit parent because of his connection with the carnival and demands sole custody of newborn Poochy (Dickie Walters). To keep the welfare services from taking his son, Chick steals away with him from the hospital. He leaves the carnival, spending the next two years dodging authorities and becoming a doting father.

Some time later, Chick regroups with his former assistants in the puppet show, Daisy (Sally Eilers) and "reformed" pickpocket, Fingers (Jimmy Durante). They join the carnival as a team under the name of "Doc Crawford's Australian Marionettes." With social workers still after Poochy, Chick seeks to secure custody of the boy by finding him a suitable mother. Daisy loves both Chick and Poochy, but she remains frustrated because Chick never gets around to realizing this fact.

Chick and Fingers get into trouble when Fingers stuffs the ballot box at a baby contest in order to ensure that Chick wins the prize money, which they hope will convince the children's care society that he is capable of providing for his son. While the two evade the authorities, a fire overtakes the carnival. Daisy saves Poochy, making Chick finally see that in her he has found a loving wife as well as an ideal mother for his boy. The police catch up with Chick and Fingers to escort them to a six-month stay in prison. Thanks to the wily Fingers' ability to literally slip the key to freedom away from their jailer, they will not remain locked up for long!

Jimmy Durante, Dickie Walters, Lee Tracy, and Sally Eilers

Notes and Comments

Carnival, made at Mack Sennett Studios from October 23 to December 1934, finally gave Lucille a taste of the career advancement she sought at Columbia Pictures; it was the first film to give her onscreen billing.

The star, Lee Tracy, was trying to rebuild his career after a drunken spectacle he created the previous year by urinating from a balcony over a passing parade while on location in Mexico for *Viva Villa!*. The resultant disgrace had ended his MGM contract. Prior to that, the talented stage and screen actor turned in notable performances in exceptional comedies such as *Blessed Event* and *Bombshell*. Sally Eilers provided the romantic interest in *Carnival*. With *Bad Girl* in 1931, she had established herself as an enjoyable lead in minor Fox comedies and dramas. Aiding them in supporting roles were Jimmy Durante, slightly more restrained than usual, Florence Rice, with very little to do, and two-year-old Dickie Walters, who performed well his task of making Poochy an adorable tot.

This sentimental, whimsical, and romantic tale set against a carnival backdrop was told by Robert Riskin, foremost Columbia writer responsible for some of the most beloved screenplays of all time, and smoothly directed by Walter Lang. Lang went on to guide many splashy Technicolor musicals, including *State Fair* (1945) and *The King and I* at Twentieth Century-Fox, where he was Betty Grable's preferred director.

Reviews

"Robert Riskin, one of the most gifted of the studio writers, has invented a number of merry situations to demonstrate the difficulties of being an unmarried father. Up to the time when 'Carnival' collapses weakly into straightforward melodrama, a calamity which Mr. Riskin thoughtfully defers until the last twenty minutes, the new film proves to be an enjoyable sentimental comedy."

—*New York Times*

"The picture isn't a super-colossal, but it is a lively, shrewdly concocted, roundly wrought little piece, well written by Bob Riskin, well directed by Walter Lang and played to the hilt by the glib Master Tracy. There's a [sic] deal of first rate aiding and abetting, too."

—*New York American*

"Not much to this plot, but the action carries along well without more than the necessary peg on which to hang the incidents, with Lee Tracy doing a sincere, if slightly overstressed performance, and Jimmy Durante in for the life-saving. Manages to hold interest and to maintain fair suspense. . . . On the strength of the performances, more than the story, this should hold its own . . . "

—*Variety*

Behind the Evidence

A Columbia Picture (1935)

Cast: Norman Foster (Tony Sheridan); Donald Cook (Ward Cameron); Sheila Mannors (Ruth Allen); Geneva Mitchell (Rita Sinclair); Samuel S. Hinds (J. T. Allen); Frank Darien (Herbert); Pat O'Malley (Lieutenant James); Gordon De Main (Captain Graham); Edward Keane (Hackett); Lucille Ball (Secretary)

Credits: Lambert Hillyer (director); Harold Shumate (story and screenplay); Henry Freulich (photography); Arthur Black (assistant director); George Cooper (sound); Richard Cahoon (editor)

Release date: January 25, 1935 (Palace Theater)

Run time: 70 minutes

Synopsis

Tony Sheridan (Norman Foster), the well-known globetrotting millionaire, has recently lost his fortune and takes a job as a society reporter for the *Daily Herald*. He is sent to cover the engagement party of an old flame, Ruth Allen (Sheila Mannors), who is now betrothed to a shady broker by the name of Ward Cameron (Donald Cook). There, in addition to learning that Ruth is still in love with him, Tony finds evidence regarding a hold-up gang the police are after. Cameron is revealed as their leader. Tony protects Ruth by hiding this fact for the time being.

Tony embarks on an investigation of Cameron's gang while turning his column into front-page material. As his case against them stacks up and Tony becomes a hero, he becomes a walking target for the vengeful criminals. The police step in to guard Tony, but even so he winds up kidnapped by Cameron's henchman. The police arrive in the nick of time, Cameron is killed in the ensuing action, and Tony gets his girl back.

Notes and Comments

Lucille played a secretary in this recently discovered addition to her list of film credits. *Behind the Evidence* was a run-of-the-mill news reporter film from the Irving Briskin programmer unit of the Columbia lot. Its working title was *Against the Evidence.*

Norman Foster, who in the film finds work as a society columnist to be a succession of dangerous adventures, acted in dozens of movies of the early '30s. He had a more durable career as a director, however. Shortly after completing *Behind the Evidence*, he began directing and writing *Mr. Moto* and *Charlie Chan* mysteries at Fox and went on into the '40s,

'50s, and '60s in films and television. Sheila Mannors, played bit parts for years. The lead female character of Ruth Allen was one of her first co-starring roles. She later changed her name to Sheila Bromley and remained in motion pictures for several more years, but rarely rose above supporting roles in B productions at a variety of studios. Co-star Donald Cook went on to success as one of Broadway's foremost leading men.

A sultry pose from her Columbia days

Reviews

"'Behind the Evidence' makes no attempt at novelty. Culled from the headlines, it tells a brisk and lightly entertaining story of bandits in flight. The acting is up to the general tone of the production, nonchalant, quick-paced and untroubled by subtleties."

—*New York Sun*

" . . . a friendly and harmless little specimen of the wood-pulp school of film melodrama . . . 'Behind the Evidence' is performed with appropriate zest by Norman Foster as the reporter, Donald Cook as the gang leader, and Sheila Mannors, a fair to middling newcomer, as the society girl in whom they are both interested."

—*New York Times*

"Employing a static and unimaginative camera to relate all the nickel-weekly cliches about murders, hold-ups and newspaper reporters who solve crimes that baffle the police, 'Behind the Evidence' is, in spite of its excess of invention, a thin and wispy piece of murder entertainment . . . "

—*New York World-Telegram*

The Whole Town's Talking

A Columbia Picture (1935)

Cast: Edward G. Robinson (Arthur Ferguson Jones/Killer Mannion); Jean Arthur (Miss Clark); Arthur Hohl (Detective Sergeant Boyle); James Donlan (Detective Sergeant Howe); Arthur Byron (District Attorney Spencer); Wallace Ford (Healy); Donald Meek (Hoyt); Etienne Girardot (Seaver); Edward Brophy (Slugs Martin); Paul Harvey (J. G. Carpenter); J. Farrell MacDonald (Warden); John Wray (Henchman); Effie Ellsler (Aunt Agatha); Virginia Pine (Seaver's Secretary); Lucille Ball (Extra)

Credits: John Ford (producer and director); Jo Swerling and Robert Riskin (screenplay), from story by W. R. Burnett; Joseph August (photography); Viola Lawrence (editor)

Release date: February 28, 1935 (Radio City Music Hall)

Run time: 93 minutes

Synopsis

Arthur Jones (Edward G. Robinson), mild-mannered office clerk, has the misfortune of having the same face as Public Enemy No. 1, "Killer Mannion." One afternoon, this uncanny resemblance nearly gets him thrown into prison. The district attorney releases Jones with a "passport"—a note explaining his situation in case the police should apprehend him again. The story is the talk of the town, and inevitably reaches Mannion himself.

The killer forces his way into Jones's home and makes him relinquish the passport each night so that he can roam the streets freely. Meanwhile, a newspaper hires Jones to write a series of articles about Mannion, which Mannion himself begins ghostwriting. Filled with thrilling details, they win Jones the admiration of his peers and, more importantly, of his dream girl, Miss Clark (Jean Arthur).

The police soon tire of having two Mannions running around town, so they put "Jones" in prison for safekeeping and announce that the real Mannion will be shot on sight. Unbeknownst to them, the man they imprison is the real Mannion, who soon escapes. Mannion decides it is time to eliminate Jones so that the police will think it is the criminal that has been eradicated. He sends Jones to a bank, then tips off the police where "Mannion" is headed. The police prepare to shoot as soon as he enters.

At the bank doors, Jones notices that he has left money behind and returns to retrieve it at Mannion's hideout. There he finds out about the trap that was set for him. The timid clerk gathers all his courage and fools Mannion's own mob into killing their leader. Jones is hailed a hero and sets sail on a richly deserved vacation with his lovely bride, Miss Clark.

Arthur Byron, Wallace Ford, and Arthur Hohl huddle around stars Edward G. Robinson and Jean Arthur.

Notes and Comments

Edward G. Robinson cemented his reputation as the screen's fiercest gangster as *Little Caesar* (1930), a character created by W. R. Burnett. In 1934, the actor's career was in a slump, and Warners loaned him out for the first time for *The Whole Town's Talking*, based on another Burnett story, "Jail Breaker." In his dual role, Robinson displayed his soft side as the timid office clerk and evoked Little Caesar by instilling terror as the ruthless hood, giving his career the boost it needed.

The co-starring role of the clever Miss Clark, meanwhile, advanced Jean Arthur's stature and exposed her natural gift for comedy. After toiling in westerns and other undistinguished fare since the mid-'20s, she turned her focus to the stage. Then, signing with Columbia Pictures in 1933, she got a terrific break by being chosen for this movie, her fourth assignment under the new term contract. Arthur's confident, sassy character would come to full bloom over the next few years in Frank Capra films like *Mr. Smith Goes to Washington*, making her the director's favorite actress and one of the cinema's top comediennes.

"Swell entertainment. . . . Basic idea has been kneaded over many times, yet a few ingenious touches, a slick cast, electric tempo, and the finished loaf will probably deceive everybody outside the trade, a high compliment for the scenarists and John Ford, who directed."

—*Variety*

"Pungently written, wittily produced and topped off with a splendid dual performance by Edward G. Robinson, it may be handsomely recommended as the best of the new year's comedies. . . . Under John Ford's persuasive direction, the entire cast is on its mettle."

—*New York Times*

"'The Whole Town's Talking' is melodrama told from a comedy angle, with no lessening of the suspense and no softening of the outcasts' heart. Expert timing on the part of director and star, an excellent script, and an original story, keep the thrills and laughs fairly even."

—*New York Sun*

With more extra work in *The Whole Town's Talking*, Lucille was kept busy in the studio's portrait gallery.

John Ford guided the filming of *The Whole Town's Talking* from October 24, 1934 through mid-December. It was made under the working titles of *Jail Breaker* and *Passport to Fame*. Often overlooked among the director's many illustrious credits, the film is a tremendously well-acted and skillfully directed comedy-drama with much to enjoy. This picture is listed among Lucille's credits in many sources, but it is difficult, if not impossible, to place her among the mob of extras employed for its numerous crowded scenes.

It is believed that she can be spotted in the bank sequence where, as police rush in, a lanky platinum blonde that appears to be her stands in the background at a teller's booth. In his memoirs, Robinson wrote of Lucille and her presence in the movie: "I have tried very hard to remember, but I do not recall the role. I think I recall everything else she ever played. I know her very little, but if it's any joy for her to know, she makes me laugh, and I don't laugh easily."

I'll Love You Always

A Columbia Picture (1935)

Cast: Nancy Carroll (Nora Clegg); George Murphy (Carl Brent); Raymond Walburn (Charlie); Arthur Hohl (Jergens); Jean Dixon (Mae Waters); Robert Allen (Joe); Harry Beresford (Henry Irving Clegg); Paul Harvey (Sandstone); Lucille Ball (Lucille)

Credits: Everett Riskin (producer); Leo Bulgakov (director); Vera Caspary and Sidney Buchman (screenplay), from story by Lawrence Hazard; Joseph August (photography); George Cooper (sound); Richard Cahoon (editor)

Release date: March 29, 1935 (Roxy Theater)

Run time: 75 minutes

George Murphy, Nancy Carroll, and Jean Dixon

Synopsis

Actress Nora Clegg (Nancy Carroll) gives up a promising stage career for domestic bliss as the wife of the overconfident Carl Brent (George Murphy). Carl sets out to amaze the engineering world, but the Depression makes a job that he is qualified to fill impossible to come by, and he is too proud to take anything less. Before long, Carl takes out his frustrations on Nora, and the marriage suffers. He finds out that Nora has taken a job in a taxi-dance hall to help make ends meet. They quarrel bitterly, separate, and Nora accepts a stage role out of town.

Carl is driven to theft merely to impress Nora with an Atlantic City spree. Their reunion is shortlived. Carl must repay his debt by going to prison. But owing to a softhearted officer (Arthur Hohl), the truth is kept from Nora. She is made to believe that Carl has left for Russia on an important engineering job.

Reviews

Likewise, Nora is concealing something from him—she is expecting their child. Once Carl is freed from jail, Mr. Sandstone (Paul Harvey), the head of an engineering firm (and the same man from whom he had stolen money), forgives Carl and offers him employment. A changed Carl meets his newborn baby, and the Brents resume their married life with a much more promising outlook.

Notes and Comments

Nancy Carroll and George Murphy's follow-up to *Jealousy*, *I'll Love You Always* was another rather dreary story. Their next and final film together was *After the Dance*, still another romantic melodrama, but with music added. They made a cute pair, but their lackluster co-starring vehicles seemed ill-suited to their personalities and talent. Carroll, the bigger name at the time, exited motion pictures soon after. Murphy, on the other hand, was just starting out. He later recalled that his three-time co-star "wasn't too easy to work with." Jean Dixon played Carroll's acerbic best friend, and Lucille, in another bit, played Lucille.

The script was conceived by two leading writers, Vera Caspary, author of the novel *Laura* (upon which the 1944 film was based), and Sidney Buchman (*Talk of the Town*, *Holiday*). While most movies of this period attempted to make audiences forget the country's problems, their story mirrored the struggles faced by young Depression-era newlyweds. Russian-born Broadway producer and performer Leo Bulgakov made his entry into the cinema would as director of *I'll Love You Always*.

Shortly after her brief task in this picture was performed, Lucille, along with a large group of stock company players, was released from her contract with Columbia. She had been employed there for only three months. That could have been the end of the line for an actress of less ambition and fortitude, but for Lucille it was only a matter of hours before she went on the payroll at another major studio.

Roberta

An RKO-Radio Picture (1935)

Cast: Irene Dunne (Stephanie); Fred Astaire (Huck Haines); Ginger Rogers (Liz Gatz, "Countess Scharwenka"); Randolph Scott (John Kent); Helen Westley (Minnie, "Roberta"); Claire Dodd (Sophie); Victor Varconi (Prince Ladislaw); Luis Alberni (Voyda); Ferdinand Munier (Lord Delves); Torben Meyer (Albert); Adrian Rosley (Professor); Bodil Rosing (Fernande); Lucille Ball (Model)

Credits: Pandro S. Berman (producer); William A. Seiter (director); Jane Murfin, Sam Mintz, Allan Scott, and Glenn Tryon (screenplay), from play by Jerome Kern and Otto Harbach, based on novel *Gowns by Roberta* by Alice Duer Miller; Edward Cronjager (photography); Max Steiner (musical director); Fred Astaire (dance director), Hermes Pan (assistant); Zion Myers (production associate); Van Nest Polglase (art director), Carroll Clark (associate); Thomas Little (set decoration); Bernard Newman (gowns); John Tribby (recording); P. J. Faulkner, Jr. (music recording); George Marsh (sound); William Hamilton (editor)

Songs: "Let's Begin," "Yesterdays," "Smoke Gets in Your Eyes" (Jerome Kern and Otto Harbach); "I'll Be Hard to Handle" (Kern and Bernard Dougall); "I Won't Dance" (Kern and Oscar Hammerstein II, revised lyrics by Dorothy Fields and Jimmy McHugh); "Lovely to Look At" (Kern, Fields, and McHugh)

Release date: March 8, 1935 (Radio City Music Hall)

Run time: 106 minutes

Synopsis

In Paris, Huck Haines (Fred Astaire) and his Wabash Indianians search for a job. With no place to turn, they arrive at the salon of Minnie (Helen Westley), the aunt of Huck's pal, John Kent (Randolph Scott). Minnie is better known as Roberta, owner of Paris's premier fashion house. There, John and Minnie's assistant, Stephanie (Irene Dunne), spark to each other, and Huck runs into his childhood sweetheart, Liz Gatz (Ginger Rogers). Liz now poses as the Countess Scharwenka. The title helped her become the continent's leading entertainer. Huck is sworn to secrecy about her prosaic past, and in return, Liz gets the band hired at the Café Russe.

Minnie passes away unexpectedly and John inherits Roberta's. Admitting he knows nothing of fashion, he takes Stephanie on as a partner. As their working relationship develops into something more, his ex-girlfriend Sophie (Claire Dodd) arrives in Paris. Her superior manner

Counterfeit Countess Ginger Rogers tells Fred Astaire the unthinkable, "I Won't Dance."

Reviews

" . . . Mr. Astaire and 'Roberta' have dashed right along and established a model for lavishness, grace and humor in the musical film. If there is any flaw in the photoplay, it is the unfortunate circumstance that Mr. Astaire and his excellent partner, Miss Rogers, cannot be dancing during every minute of it."
—*New York Times*

"'Roberta' is musical picture-making at its best—fast, smart, good looking and tuneful. . . . Astaire has found an ideal partner. Miss Rogers dances well enough to be able to hold her own in the stepping numbers, which is something when dancing with Astaire. Besides which she looks better and works better in each succeeding picture. . . . Irene Dunne looks like a million and sings like just as much."
—*Variety*

" . . . Roberta stands in a good way of being the best musical comedy to come out of Hollywood. [It] is so thoroughly lively, so exciting to the eye and ear, and so imbued with an unstrained-for gaiety that it glides smoothly and pleasantly through the vaguely motivated tale."
—*Liberty*

soon makes John overcome his infatuation. He eats his heart out upon seeing Stephanie on the arm of Prince Ladislaw (Victor Varconi), an exiled Russian nobleman. Befuddled by drink and believing Stephanie is interested in Ladislaw because he is a prince, John insults her and she calls an end to their partnership.

After John also walks out on Roberta's, Huck is placed at the helm. Fear that he will ruin the business draws Stephanie back. She, Huck, and Liz arrange an elaborate musical fashion show to display her new line, with entertainment provided by Huck and Liz. Their success on the dance floor leads to a marriage proposal.

After the show, John returns with a heavy heart to say goodbye to Stephanie, whom he thinks he has lost to Ladislaw. She reveals that the prince is actually her cousin, she is an exiled princess, and John is the man she loves.

Notes and Comments

To the tune of the Oscar nominated "Lovely to Look At," Lucille made her RKO debut descending a flight of stairs modeling a flamingo pink ostrich feather cape

It was the elaborate fashion show sequence that brought Lucille to RKO-Radio Pictures, the company she would one day own. Photo inscribed by Lucille, likely to her future mentor, Ed Sedgwick, "Ed— Remember this in 'Roberta'—'Sme—"

over a form-fitting gown embellished with the same plumage. The very evening she was dropped by Columbia, Lucille answered a call for models to be featured in *Roberta*. Costume designer Bernard Newman hired her, and after the film's completion, she signed a six-month contract with RKO that eventually extended to seven years.

Roberta was an adaptation of a hit Broadway musical that played in 1933–34, featuring Bob Hope, George Murphy, and Lyda Roberti in its cast. Hope and Murphy's characters were combined and played by Fred Astaire, and Roberti was succeeded by Ginger Rogers. The Astaire-Rogers partnership had been established when they introduced the Carioca in *Flying Down to Rio* (1933). Their brief but impressive scenes led from *Rio* to *The Gay Divorcee* to *Roberta*. The story focused mainly on Irene Dunne and Randolph Scott, but as in *Rio*, Astaire and Rogers stole the show with their comedy scenes and spectacular musical numbers. The year *Roberta* was released, 1935, their names (together) appeared fourth on the list of top ten box-office draws.

Although she had been a musical performer on the stage before coming to Hollywood, Irene Dunne was acclaimed for her dramatic portrayals from the outset of her career in films and did not often put to use her lilting vocals for the screen. In *Roberta*, her grandest musical to date, she

sang four melodies, including "Smoke Gets in Your Eyes." Randolph Scott, in a departure from westerns, was cast opposite Dunne. Bernard

The heart-pounding "I'll Be Hard to Handle" number

Newman, whom RKO imported from Bergdorf-Goodman's in New York, was a star behind the scenes. Showcasing $250,000 worth of extreme costumes, the entire film was a parade of his designs.

Filming began on *Roberta* on November 26, 1934, and continued through most of January 1935. RKO earned profits of $770,000 from the production. *Roberta* was later remade by MGM as *Lovely to Look At* (1952), starring Kathryn Grayson and Howard Keel, with Marge and Gower Champion as the young dancers.

Old Man Rhythm

An RKO-Radio Picture (1935)

Cast: Charles "Buddy" Rogers (Johnny Roberts); George Barbier (John Roberts, Sr.); Barbara Kent (Edith Warren); Grace Bradley (Marian Beecher); Betty Grable (Sylvia); Eric Blore (Phillips); Erik Rhodes (Frank Rochet); John Arledge (Pinky Parker); Johnny Mercer (Colonel); Donald Meek (Paul Parker); Evelyn Poe (Honey); Dave Chasen (Andy); Joy Hodges (Lois); Douglas Fowley (Oyster); Margaret Nearing (Margaret); Ronald Graham (Ronald); Sonny Lamont (Blimp); William Carey (Bill); Lucille Ball, Marian Darling, Jane Hamilton, Maxine Jennings, Kay Sutton, Jack Thomas, Erich von Stroheim, Jr., Carlyle Blackwell, Jr., Bryant Washburn, Jr., Claude Gillingwater, Jr. (College Students)

Credits: Pandro S. Berman (producer); Zion Meyers (associate producer); Edward Ludwig (director); Sig Herzig, Ernest Pagano, and H. W. Hanemann (screenplay), from story by Lewis Gensler, Sig Herzig, and Don Hartman; Nick Musuraca (photography); Roy Webb (musical director); P. J. Faulkner, Jr. (music recording); Hermes Pan (choreographer); Sam White (staging of songs); Van Nest Polglase (art director), Perry Ferguson (associate); John Tribby (recording); George Crone (editor)

Songs: "There's Nothing Like a College Education," "Boys Will Be Boys," "When You Are in My Arms," "Come the Revolution Baby," "I Never Saw a Better Night," "Old Man Rhythm" (Lewis Gensler and Johnny Mercer)

Release date: August 2, 1935 (RKO Colonial Theatre)

Run time: 75 minutes

Synopsis

Johnny Roberts (Buddy Rogers) has the love of the amiable Edie Warren (Barbara Kent) but is infatuated with Fairfield College's campus vamp, Marian Beecher (Grace Bradley). Alarmed by the effect Marian has on Johnny's academic performance, John Roberts, Sr. (George Barbier), abandons his doll manufacturing company and enrolls in college to see to it that his son stops fooling around and gets together with Edie.

This portrait of Lucille, made a short time after *Old Man Rhythm*, captures the image of a hopeful Hollywood starlet, and in the look shows the inspiration of stars like Harlow and Lombard.

Roberts immerses himself in the high-spirited Fairfield atmosphere, and does his best to quell Johnny's romance with Marian. Tipped off that the girl is a fortune hunter, Roberts determines he need only give the impression that the family business is failing to send her packing. There is more truth in this than he realizes. While Roberts relives his youth at Fairfield, the doll company has begun to go under.

By prom night, Johnny still sees Edie as a sister, and plans to elope with Marian. That evening, Roberts's partner, Rochet (Erik Rhodes), arrives to tell Roberts that if he does not return to work at once, he will lose the company. When Marian hears this, she walks out on Johnny. Seeing her true colors, Johnny realizes what his father had known all along—that Edie is the girl for him. Roberts can now return to business.

Notes and Comments

Charles "Buddy" Rogers, "America's Boyfriend" in the late 1920s and early '30s, returned after a year's absence from the screen in *Old Man Rhythm*.* The low-key campus musical placed him alongside Barbara Kent, Grace Bradley, character actors George Barbier, Eric Blore, and Erik Rhodes, as well as several singers and dancers. Edward Ludwig, a veteran of comedy shorts, directed the cast, and Hermes Pan put them through their musical routines. Pan collaborated with Fred Astaire in the creation of the breathtaking dances of the ten Astaire-Rogers musicals.

Along with contract players Marian Darling, Jane Hamilton, Maxine Jennings, and Kay Sutton, Lucille helped fill out the student body in *Old Man Rhythm*. The large cast gave her the chance to form friendships with members of the RKO family. She is visible in several group scenes—roasting marshmallows and swaying to the music. Fellow platinum-topped beauty Betty Grable, who appeared in many college films of the '30s, was prominently featured. She displayed talent and verve as a tap-dancing co-ed, yet by this time,

*"America's Boyfriend" married "America's Sweetheart," Mary Pickford, in 1937.

Reviews

"The sight of a grey-haired gentleman in a college cap and other educational accoutrements is productive of a fair amount of amusement, while occasional helpings of song and dance are additional assets. . . . a bright specimen that should entertain most popular patrons for an hour or so."
—unknown 1935 press clipping

"Aside from some well staged tunes and a few juicy comedy moments, 'Old Man Rhythm' stacks up as inconsequential fare. Old Siwash gets another fantastic going-over, with the frail story counteracted by the smooth pacing and breeziness of the direction. . . . Cast is topheavy with lookers, while the dancing interludes leave little wanting."
—*Variety*

" . . . an unpretentious musical film . . . photoplay's appeal—if any—will be to those who like musical comedy routine in the collegiate manner."
—*New York Daily News*

she had been in movies for six years and another five would pass before she reached major stardom in 1940's *Down Argentine Way*.

Old Man Rhythm cost $243,000 to make. Its working title was *Papa's in the Cradle*, a modest production with a silly but entertaining plot and a pleasing score (that is heard in the background of many RKO films of this period). The lyricist, Johnny Mercer, also appeared on camera in a small role as one of the singing students. Some of his future hits were "Jeepers Creepers," "You Must Have Been a Beautiful Baby," "Hooray for Hollywood," "Moon River," and "That Old Black Magic."

Lucille has some fun with her friend and *Old Man Rhythm* supporting player Betty Grable. Grable made her screen debut at the age of twelve, in 1929, and by the mid-'40s would be the highest paid woman in America. The two actresses would enjoy themselves around a racetrack of another kind when Grable guest starred in a 1958 installment of *The Lucy-Desi Comedy Hour*, "Lucy Wins a Racehorse."

Top Hat

An RKO-Radio Picture (1935)

Cast: Fred Astaire (Jerry Travers); Ginger Rogers (Dale Tremont); Edward Everett Horton (Horace Hardwick); Erik Rhodes (Alberto Beddini); Eric Blore (Bates); Helen Broderick (Madge Hardwick); Gino Corrado (Venice Hotel Manager); Edgar Norton (London Hotel Manager); Leonard Mudie (Flower Salesman); Lucille Ball (Flower Shop Clerk); Frank Mills (Lido Waiter)

Credits: Pandro S. Berman (producer); Mark Sandrich (director); Dwight Taylor and Allan Scott (screenplay), from story by Dwight Taylor; David Abel (photography); Vernon L. Walker (special effects); Max Steiner (musical director); Hermes Pan (dance director); Van Nest Polglase (art director), Carroll Clark (associate); Thomas Little (set decoration); Bernard Newman (gowns); Hugh McDowell, Jr. (recording); P. J. Faulkner, Jr. (music recording); George Marsh (sound); William Hamilton (editor)

Songs: "No Strings," "Isn't This a Lovely Day (To Be Caught in the Rain)?," "Top Hat, White Tie and Tails," "Cheek to Cheek," "The Piccolino" (Irving Berlin)

Release date: September 6, 1935 (Radio City Music Hall)

Run time: 101 minutes

Synopsis

While in London for the opening of his new show, dancer Jerry Travers (Fred Astaire) meets the lovely Dale Tremont (Ginger Rogers). After a less than favorable first impression, he sends her a roomful of flowers and they share an enchanted afternoon in the park. The budding romance looks bright until a misunderstanding causes Dale to think Jerry is Horace Hardwick (Edward Everett Horton), the husband of her friend Madge (Helen Broderick).

Madge had plans for Dale and Jerry to join her in Venice—and hopefully fall in love. Once there, Dale tells Madge of "Horace's" flirtations. Madge believes her but does nothing for the time being. Instead, she gets to work pairing Dale off with the man Dale thinks is Madge's husband! Jerry meanwhile, continues pursuing Dale. She hates having to report more occurrences of Horace's unfaithfulness to Madge. This eventually earns the real Horace a black eye, causing still more confusion when he thinks Madge has found out about one of his past indiscretions.

Reviews

"It is a plain fact that 'Top Hat' is the best of the Fred Astaire-Ginger Rogers vehicles, which is to say, it is the top in screen musicals. . . . For, though 'Top Hat' may not boast of a spectacularly original plot, there is at least an ebullience which keeps the story divertingly alive, and the dialogue has more genuinely funny gags than all the rest of the screen musicals put together. . . . There is individual brilliance in the work of Edward Everett Horton, Helen Broderick, Erik Rhodes and Eric Blore . . . "
— *New York Post*

"Mr. Astaire is the tops in 'Top Hat.' He has never done anything better than the dance which he does to the music of the title song. . . . The picture has been expertly directed by Mark Sandrich and elaborately mounted by RKO. It is lively and tuneful entertainment . . . "
— *New York Daily News*

"The theatres will hold their own world series with this one. It can't miss and the reasons are three—Fred Astaire, Irving Berlin's songs and sufficient comedy between numbers to hold the film together."
— *Variety*

Could that sincere face make Jerry believe Dale's tall tale of a rendezvous in Paris?

All the while Jerry is bewildered by Dale's aversion to him. Though she is falling in love, the thought of Madge causes her to take flight the moment Jerry comes into view. In an effort to discourage him once and for all, she marries her other suitor, fashion designer Alberto Beddini (Erik Rhodes). Soon after, Jerry finally discovers that Dale has been mistaking him for Horace. He explains the situation to her and with the help of Horace's valet, Bates (Eric Blore), they are afforded time alone to make amends. They spend the evening dining and dancing to the strains of "The Piccolino."

Now they only have to arrange for Beddini to grant Dale a divorce. This measure is found unnecessary after a confession from Bates—Horace had told him to keep an eye on Dale, whom he considered a "dangerous woman." Having disguised himself as a priest, Bates had performed the service for Dale and Beddini. They are not married after all, which leaves the door open for her to marry Jerry.

Notes and Comments

The fourth musical in the Astaire-Rogers cycle, which began filming in April 1935, is, along with *Swing Time*, regarded by most fans and critics as the peak of the team's ten pairings. Fred Astaire disapproved of the original screenplay and sent a letter to producer Pandro Berman stating in part, "I cannot see that there is any real story or plot to this script." Changes were made, and the finished product had many similarities to 1934's *The Gay Divorcee* (based on a play by *Top Hat* writer Dwight Taylor), but the production had many other virtues to offer in the way of individuality and superior entertainment that made it RKO's box-office champion of the decade.

"Isn't This a Lovely Day (To Be Caught in the Rain)?"

One of the Oscar-nominated art deco sets is seen in the "Cheek to Cheek" number, featuring Rogers in the famous molting dress that danced beautifully with her and Astaire.

Lucille was given a bit part as a clerk in the hotel flower shop. The role started very differently than what is seen in the final print. As originally staged, she spoke the first lines in a Cockney accent and the man with her in the scene responded. She later said that when it came time to shoot the scene

The stars with Irving Berlin, who later called the score he composed for this film his "personal favorite." "Cheek to Cheek" garnered an Oscar nomination, but Harry Warren's "Lullaby of Broadway" took home the honor.

she was extremely tense and kept flubbing her lines. Eventually Lela Rogers saved the day (and kept her from being replaced) by advising director Mark Sandrich to have the salesman speak the first lines (spreading gossip about Miss Tremont), as Lucille replies by nodding and inquiring, "What can he say?" and "Really?" She remained forever grateful to Lela, and to Sandrich, for agreeing to the suggestion. Sandrich directed five of the Astaire-Rogers films. His son, Jay, later worked with Lucille as well, as second assistant director on *I Love Lucy*.

Lending a hand in the success of *Top Hat* was a quartet of expert character actors. One among

them was a stage actress relatively new to movies, Helen Broderick, who, like the character she portrayed, was apparently also an amateur matchmaker. At her prompting, Lucille and Helen's son, actor Broderick Crawford, dated for a brief period. The enthusiastic press corps announced they were engaged in June 1936.

Top Hat boasted a musical score comprising five hit Irving Berlin songs that accompanied dance sequences created by Astaire and Hermes Pan, among them the breezy "Isn't This a Lovely Day (To Be Caught in the Rain)?" and the timeless "Cheek to Cheek." For the dance that accompanied the latter, Ginger wore a blue satin evening gown covered in ostrich feathers that floated upwards and fell to the ground every time she moved. Astaire dubbed her "Feathers," and it caused a minor controversy on the set when they tried to make her wear a different dress. As Ginger had dreamed up the feather creation herself, she stood her ground, and so helped to make "Cheek to Cheek" one of the most memorable sequences in movie history.

Top Hat grossed nearly $3.2 million and earned four Oscar nominations: Best Song ("Cheek to Cheek"), Best Dance Direction ("The Piccolino" and "Top Hat"), Best Art Direction for the twist on Venice brought to life by the art department, and Best Picture.

The Three Musketeers

An RKO-Radio Picture (1935)

Cast: Walter Abel (d'Artagnan); Paul Lukas (Athos); Margot Grahame (Milady de Winter); Heather Angel (Constance); Ian Keith (de Rochefort); Moroni Olsen (Porthos); Onslow Stevens (Aramis); Rosamond Pinchot (Queen Anne); John Qualen (Planchet); Ralph Forbes (Duke of Buckingham); Nigel de Brulier (Richelieu); Murray Kinnell (Bernajou); Lumsden Hare (de Treville); Miles Mander (King Louis XIII); Wade Boteler (Peylerand); Stanley Blystone (Villard); Ralph Faulkner (Jussac); Lucille Ball (Member of the Court)

Credits: Cliff Reid (associate producer); Rowland V. Lee (director); Dudley Nichols and Rowland V. Lee (screenplay), from novel by Alexandre Dumas; Peverell Marley (photography); Vernon L. Walker (special effects); Max Steiner (music); Robert Sisk (production associate); Otto Brower (director of chase scenes); Fred Cavens (fencing arrangements); Louis Vandenecker (technical advisor); Van Nest Polglase (art director), Carroll Clark (associate); Thomas Little (set decoration); Walter Plunkett (costumes); John L. Cass (recording); P. J. Faulkner, Jr. (music recording); George Hively (editor)

Release date: October 31, 1935 (Radio City Music Hall)

Run time: 96 minutes

Synopsis

Trouble is brewing within the French royal palace. The treacherous Count de Rochefort (Ian Keith), agent of Cardinal Richelieu (Nigel de Brulier), plots to seize power by taking advantage of growing tension between France and England provoked by the Duke of Buckingham's (Ralph Forbes) love for France's Queen Anne (Rosamond Pinchot). De Rochefort sets out to convince Richelieu that the queen is a traitor.

Unaware of this palace intrigue, d'Artagnan (Walter Abel) leaves Gascony for Paris to become a member of the royal guard—a musketeer. In Paris, he is welcomed into the alliance of the three bravest of musketeers, Athos (Paul Lukas), Porthos (Moroni Olsen), and Aramis (Onslow Stevens). On his first night, his new lodgings become the scene

Heather Angel is at center. Lucille is the blonde over her left shoulder in this scene from the end of the film, in which Count de Rochefort is revealed as a traitor.

Reviews

of a fateful meeting between Queen Anne and Buckingham. The queen gives the duke her most precious diamond brooch as a symbol that there must be peace between France and England. D'Artagnan vows to keep this Her Majesty's secret—and wins the love of Constance (Heather Angel), the queen's lady-in-waiting.

De Rochefort learns of the secret meeting from his spy network. He uses it against the queen by having her husband, King Louis XIII (Miles Mander) order her to wear her diamond brooch at the king's anniversary celebration in eight days. To save Queen Anne, d'Artagnan and his three comrades depart to recover her jewels before then.

The count puts into action his most potent accomplice, Milady de Winter (Margot Grahame). She has seized the queen's diamonds and fools d'Artagnan into believing that she is an ally of Buckingham. D'Artagnan becomes her prisoner, but soon the musketeers come to his rescue. Lady de Winter is made to relinquish the diamonds. The diamonds are then returned to Queen Anne and de Rochefort is exposed as a traitor, thanks to d'Artagnan and the three musketeers. For their valor, they are appointed King Louis's Guard of Honor.

Notes and Comments

Of the many American film adaptations of Alexandre Dumas' *The Three Musketeers*, RKO's 1935 version is among the least well-known. Various d'Artagnans over the years include Douglas Fairbanks, Don Ameche, Louis Hayward, Gene Kelly, Cornel Wilde, and Michael York. Stage actor Walter Abel made a valiant attempt to fill the immortal swordsman's boots, but RKO's casting choice was uninspired, though he was not the first choice. Early on Francis Lederer had been slated for the role.

The film was shot primarily from mid-June to August 1935. Director Rowland V. Lee, who had just made *Cardinal Richelieu* for Twentieth Century,

On the arm of Ralph Forbes a year before the making of *The Three Musketeers*, and not long before his marriage to Heather Angel.

had a cast consisting of relatively unknown actors. For Abel, it was the first of very few lead roles he was ever given. The Musketeers were Paul Lukas (later named Best Actor for *Watch on the Rhine*), Moroni Olsen, in his screen debut as Porthos, and Onslow Stevens. Nigel de Brulier played Cardinal Richelieu for the third time in his career. He portrayed him once more in the 1939 edition starring Don Ameche. Among the female players were Rosamond Pinchot, in her only motion picture, and British actress Margot Grahame.

In resplendent seventeenth-century regalia, Lucille was a member of the court flanking Queen Anne in the final sequence. Ralph Forbes, a British actor who played the Duke of Buckingham, had been a beau of hers in 1934, during her Goldywn days. Shortly after their romance ended, he married Heather Angel (he was married to actress Ruth Chatterton before that), who played Constance in *The Three Musketeers*. The British actress was a leading lady at Fox and Universal in the mid-'30s, and later played Phyllis in several installments of Paramount's *Bulldog Drummond* series.

The Three Musketeers had location filming in the heat of the San Fernando Valley in summertime. Lucille was known as a girl who never complained. She did not mind getting dirty or taking falls, but one thing she could never bear was sweltering heat coupled with a heavy costume. After fainting in layers of petticoats during this production, Lucille finally spoke up to her bosses and nearly quit RKO. The audacity of this young contract actress may have earned her respect, as Lucille was indeed elevated to credited parts a short time after.

I Dream Too Much

An RKO-Radio Picture (1935)

Cast: Lily Pons (Annette Monard); Henry Fonda (Jonathan Street); Eric Blore (Roger Briggs); Osgood Perkins (Paul Darcy); Lucien Littlefield (Mr. Dilley); Lucille Ball (Gwendolyn Dilley); Mischa Auer (Pianist); Paul Porcasi (Uncle Tito); Scott Beckett (Boy on Merry-Go-Round); Esther Dale (Mrs. Dilley)

Credits: Pandro Berman (producer); John Cromwell (director); Edmund North and James Gow (screenplay), from story by Elsie Finn and David G. Wittels; David Abel (photography); Vernon L. Walker (special effects); Max Steiner (musical director); Andre Kostelanetz (orchestra conductor); Hermes Pan (dance director); Van Nest Polglase (art director), Charles Kirk (associate); Bernard Newman (gowns); Hugh McDowell, Jr., P. J. Faulkner, Jr., and J. G. Stewart (sound); William Morgan (editor)

Songs: "Bell Song" from opera *Lakmé* (Delibes); "Caro Nome" from opera *Rigoletto* (Verdi); "Jockey on the Carousel," "I'm the Echo," "I Got Love," "I Dream Too Much" (Jerome Kern and Dorothy Fields)

Release date: November 28, 1935 (Radio City Music Hall)

Run time: 97 minutes

Synopsis

Gifted operatic soprano Annette Monard (Lily Pons), tired of training day in and day out, sneaks away from the watchful eye of her taskmaster uncle in search of excitement. She finds it with aspiring composer Jonathan Street (Henry Fonda). They share laughs and a few drinks, and the next morning, find they are married! Jonathan allows Annette to stay with him and they come to adore each other.

As he composes an opera, she takes care of the home. But everything changes when Jonathan discovers her remarkable voice. He decides their combined talents would create a sensation. Annette submits only to please

A most unusual first encounter between Jonathan and Annette leads to home and marriage.

him, but has no desire for stardom herself. She takes Jonathan's opera to producer Paul Darcy (Osgood Perkins), but when she sings, Darcy is interested only in her voice, not in Jonathan's music.

Within a short time, Annette becomes a star in spite of herself. She arranges to have Jonathan's opera produced, but when he finds out what she has done, his pride is hurt and he leaves her. Successful but miserable, Annette soon walks out on Darcy—and runs into Jonathan, now a taxi driver. They reunite until Darcy arrives and ridicules Jonathan's lifestyle. Again Jonathan lets his ego come before love. He sends her back to her career.

Annette hatches an idea to help her husband. She adapts his opera into a musical comedy, which Darcy agrees to produce. *I Dream Too Much* opens to rave reviews, and this time, Jonathan's music receives the accolades. When the couple has a baby, Annette achieves her own dream—that of domesticity.

Notes and Comments

The unexpected success of Grace Moore in Columbia's Oscar-winning *One Night of Love* (1934) made Hollywood studios look to the Metropolitan Opera House for potential stars. Fox enlisted Lawrence Tibbett; Jesse Lasky: Nino Martini; Warners: Everett Marshall; Paramount: Gladys Swarthout. At MGM, even the Marx Brothers joined the fray this year with a raucous *Night at the Opera*. French coloratura soprano Lily Pons, age thirty-seven but with very youthful dark good looks, a diminutive frame, and an extraordinary voice that reached the high F, seemed a natural recruit to RKO executive Pandro Berman.

From August through September 1935, Pons was put to work on what went into production as *Love Song*, but came out as *I Dream Too Much*, with a script by *One Night of Love* scenarists Edmund North and James Gow. Her director, John Cromwell, had made the critically acclaimed *Of Human Bondage* with Bette Davis the previous year. Leading man Henry Fonda was a rising star following his debut in *The Farmer Takes a Wife* (1935). *I Dream Too Much* was his third film.

Reviews

"[Lily Pons] fortifies her brilliant singing with an engaging quality of bird-like charm and a sense of what her countrymen happily call joie de vivre. . . . 'I Dream too Much' suffers from inaction and a limited sense of humor. But it is amiably managed, admirably played, and provides a reasonably painless setting for the gifted soprano."
—*New York Times*

"Treated with lightness and brightly handled sentiment, Lily Pons's screen debut affords an evening of lilting pleasure. . . . Aided by brilliant support from the always capable Osgood Perkins and given the freshly talented Henry Fonda for a leading man, 'I Dream Too Much,' even with its occasional lapses and thinness, is an item of genuine and tuneful gaiety."
—*Liberty*

"'I Dream Too Much' is a gay and sparkling musical, slowed up occasionally by the directorial pace. The script is full of pleasant fantasy, the cast a handsome and engaging one, the score and Lily Pons's voice equally delightful to music lovers."
—*New York Sun*

Anxious for a taste of Parisian depravity, Lucille's onscreen family, the Dilleys, are taken to a cabaret by their tour guide, played by Henry Fonda.

Supporting them were Eric Blore, a trained seal, and Osgood Perkins (father of the movies' favorite *Psycho*, Anthony Perkins). Five-year-old Scotty Beckett, of the *Little Rascals*, was featured in the exhilarating "Jockey on the Carousel" number, and Lucille spoke with flair a couple of tart lines as an American tourist who prefers to see the nightlife to traditional Parisian landmarks.

The score selected to present Pons's voice to the mass public included operatic arias as well as Jerome Kern melodies. The well-known Russian orchestra leader André Kostelanetz worked on the film. He and Pons married three years later. *I Dream Too Much* received an Oscar nomination for sound recording, but did not win the prize. It disappointed at the box office too. The critical reception was generally favorable, however, and the stage was set for a follow-up to Lily Pons's movie debut.

Chatterbox

An RKO-Radio Picture (1936)

Cast: Anne Shirley (Jenny Yates); Phillips Holmes (Philip Greene, Jr.); Edward Ellis (Grandfather Uriah Lowell); Erik Rhodes (Archie Fisher); Margaret Hamilton (Emily "Tippy" Tipton); Granville Bates (Philip Greene, Sr.); Allen Vincent (Harrison); Lucille Ball (Lillian Temple); George Offerman, Jr. (Michael Arbuckle); Maxine Jennings (Miss Jennings); Richard Abbott (Blythe)

Credits: Robert Sisk (associate producer); George Nicholls, Jr. (director); Sam Mintz (screenplay), from play by David Carb; Alberto Colombo (musical director); Robert de Grasse (photography); John E. Burch (production associate); Van Nest Polglase (art director), Perry Ferguson (associate); George D. Ellis (recording); Arthur Schmidt (editor)

Release date: February 14, 1936 (RKO Albee Theater)

Run time: 68 minutes

Synopsis

Jenny Yates (Anne Shirley), a guileless girl from rural Vermont, is thrilled by the arrival of a theatrical company in her town. She haunts the local theater and moons over a painter with the troupe, Philip Greene (Phillips Holmes). Her grandfather, Uriah Lowell (Edward Ellis), forbids her to attend the show, adding that he will lock his door to her if she does. Jenny disobeys. Grandfather cannot bring himself to lock her out, but the hired hand can—and does.

With nowhere to go, Jenny hides in the rumble seat of Philip's car, following the company to New York, determined to become an actress.

Erik Rhodes, playing a director, pleads with a certain mercenary leading lady to save his show on opening night.

Reviews

Philip's producer friend, Archie Fisher (Erik Rhodes), casts her in a play, replacing his uncooperative star, Lillian Temple (Lucille Ball). Not realizing that it is a satire, Jenny takes her role to heart and plays it seriously—precisely what Fisher wants. Philip knows the audience's reaction will break her heart, but Jenny's over-enthusiasm makes the difficult task of telling her impossible.

Jenny's grandfather arrives in search of Jenny. He tracks down Philip, and they attend her opening night. Jenny is humiliated as her performance elicits roars of laughter. She believes Philip deliberately hurt her by not telling her what would happen. In truth, he is in love with Jenny. Fisher puts Temple back in the lead, and Jenny heads back to Vermont with her grandfather. This time it is Philip who stows away in Jenny's car. With restored optimism, she forgives him.

Notes and Comments

Chatterbox was an unpretentious vehicle for RKO's resident country girl, Anne Shirley. Age seventeen at the time of filming (October-November 1935), she had been in movies for thirteen years. After her triumph in 1934's *Anne of Green Gables*, Dawn Eveleen Paris, who had taken the stage name of Dawn O'Day, adopted the name of the story's heroine, "Anne Shirley." While never a top star, she was Oscar-nominated for her supporting role in *Stella Dallas* (1937) and, like Lucille, extremely active in RKO's B unit. She retired after *Murder, My Sweet* (1944), at age twenty-six, having been in movies most of her life.

As Jenny Yates, a girl akin to Katharine Hepburn's Eva Lovelace of *Morning Glory* and *Alice Adams*, Shirley's charming performance rated best in *Chatter-box*. Like the *Gables* character, Jenny was a dreamer with a limitless supply of gab. *Anne of Green Gables* screenwriter Sam Mintz and director George Nicholls, Jr. worked with Shirley again on this film, which was an adaption of the David Carb play *Long Ago Ladies*. A former editor, Nicholls made his directorial debut with *Finishing School* (1934), starring Frances Dee and Ginger Rogers. It was the first of several pictures he made with Shirley, who was also featured in the cast.

Portrait made of Lucille as
stage actress Lillian Temple

Philips Holmes, a leading man in early talkies and son of stage and screen stars Taylor Holmes and Edna

Phillips, co-starred in *Chatterbox*. Lillian Temple, an actress more interested in money than her art, was

Lucille's most substantial role to date—the first to offer dialogue in multiple scenes and wardrobe changes.

Other players were Erik Rhodes as a stage director, minus the famous Italian accent he affected as Tonnetti/

Beddini in Astaire-Rogers musicals, *The Wizard of Oz*'s Wicked Witch, Margaret Hamilton, Edward Ellis, the

original *Thin Man* of the mystery film series, and Granville Bates. Ellis and Bates played one of the film's

funniest scenes, in which they engage in an inebriated battle of boasts over the achievements of their ancestors.

Chatterbox was budgeted at $188,809 ($550 of which was allotted for three costumes for Lucille) and

completed production on November 29, 1935.

Muss 'Em Up

An RKO-Radio Picture (1936)

Cast: Preston Foster (Tippecanoe "Tip" O'Neil); Margaret Callahan (Amy Hutchins); Alan Mowbray (Paul Harding); Ralph Morgan (Jim Glenray); Guinn "Big Boy" Williams ("Red" Cable); Maxie Rosenbloom (Snake); Molly Lamont (Nancy Harding); John Carroll (Gene Leland); Florine McKinney (Corinne); Robert Middlemass (Inspector Brock); Noel Madison (Spivalli); Maxine Jennings (Cleo); Harold Huber (Maratti); Clarence Muse (William); Paul Porcasi (Luigi Turseniani); Ward Bond, John Adair (Gangsters); Lucille Ball (Extra)

Credits: Pandro S. Berman (producer); Charles Vidor (director); Erwin Gelsey (screenplay), from novel by James Edward Grant; J. Roy Hunt and Joseph August (photography); Roy Webb (musical director); Van Nest Polglase (art director), Perry Ferguson (associate); Denzil A. Cutler (recording); Jack Hively (editor)

Release date: February 1, 1936 (Rialto Theater)

Run time: 70 minutes

Synopsis

Detective Tip O'Neil (Preston Foster) is summoned to protect Paul Harding (Alan Mowbray), recipient of a series of threatening messages believed to come from one of the suspicious characters who frequent his home. Among them are Harding's daughter, Nancy (Molly Lamont), his ward, Corinne (Florine McKinney), Corinne's fiancé, Gene (John Carroll), and Tip's favorite, Harding's pretty, gun-toting secretary, Amy (Margaret Callahan).

The mystery intensifies when Corinne is kidnapped. Nancy empties her trust fund to raise a $200,000 ransom, but Corinne is not released. Tip's investigation leads him to the chauffeur, William (Clarence Muse). William is about to tell all he knows when he is shot. Later, Amy is attacked for a briefcase but she holds onto it—and its seemingly worthless contents. Corinne's captors now demand and collect $50,000, provided by Gene. This time, the girl is returned.

After Corinne's abductors are apprehended, the puzzle comes together. The men say they never asked for or received the first $200,000,

Lucille is pictured with Margaret Callahan (left) and Molly Lamont.

which was supposedly delivered by Harding. They were hired by someone merely to hold Corinne, who went along with them willingly. Harding himself was behind the sham. William was killed because he knew.

Harding and Corinne had a scheme to take Nancy's money and run away together. Their mistake came when Corinne held out for an extra $50,000. The briefcase Amy was assaulted for contained proof of their guilt. Tip has found them out. Harding and Corinne are seized as they try to escape the grounds of Harding's estate.

Notes and Comments

In some credit listings of *Muss 'Em Up*, Lucille is attributed the part of a "departing train passenger." In screenings of the film she could not be found, but the photo on page 122 places her with cast members Margaret Callahan and Molly Lamont around the time of filming. It is possible that she strolled before the *Muss 'Em Up* cameras as an extra between scenes of *Chatterbox*. The films were shot concurrently, primarily in November 1935.

Based on *The Green Shadow*, a novel by James Edward Grant (*Boom Town*, *The Alamo*), the film's final title was inspired by New York police commissioner Lewis J. Valentine, who issued the directive to his department as a means of capturing the bad guys. Preston Foster's character was more hardboiled and rougher around the edges than most of the suave detectives that filled movie screens of the mid-'30s, but he was an equally potent crime-solver.

Foster was surrounded by a large cast of suspects: Ralph Morgan (brother of Frank); the prolific Alan Mowbray; Guinn "Big Boy" Williams, tough guy in forty years worth of films; and British starlets Margaret Callahan and Molly Lamont. The former light heavyweight champion Maxie "Slapsie" Rosenbloom also appeared in brief scenes. They all were under the direction of Charles Vidor, whose fondly remembered *Cover Girl* and *Gilda*, both with Rita Hayworth, would come in the following decade.

Reviews

"'Muss 'Em Up,' [proves] increasingly surprising—and surprisingly good mystery film entertainment . . . Charles Vidor has directed it all at a rapid pace, and the picture moves deftly and amusingly to its well-concealed dénouement. Preston Foster is capital as Tip . . . "
—*New York Times*

"Frankly a program mystery picture, it is peopled with enough likeable and convincing actors to make it amusing. The direction is brisk; the conversation lively; the situations surprising. It is the cast, however, that makes 'Muss 'Em Up.'"
—*New York Daily Mirror*

"a fascinating melodrama of the early Dashiell Hammett and Raoul Whitfield school . . . tense and thrilling murder drama which mixes comedy and sudden death in a black, but altogether engrossing manner."
—*New York World-Telegram*

Follow the Fleet

An RKO-Radio Picture (1936)

Cast: Fred Astaire (Bake Baker); Ginger Rogers (Sherry Martin); Randolph Scott (Bilge Smith); Harriet Hilliard (Connie Martin); Astrid Allwyn (Iris Manning); Harry Beresford (Captain Hickey); Russell Hicks (Nolan); Brooks Benedict (Sullivan); Ray Mayer (Dopey); Lucille Ball (Kitty Collins); Addison Randall (Lieutenant Williams); Betty Grable, Joy Hodges, Jeanne Gray (Trio Singers); Maxine Jennings (Hostess); Jane Hamilton (Waitress); Edward Burns, Tony Martin, Franks Mills, Frank Jenks (Sailors)

Credits: Pandro S. Berman (producer); Mark Sandrich (director); Dwight Taylor and Allan Scott (screenplay), from play by Hubert Osborne, as produced by David Belasco; David Abel (photography); Vernon L. Walker (special effects); Max Steiner (musical director); Hermes Pan (dance director); Van Nest Polglase (art director), Carroll Clark (associate); Darrell Silvera (set decoration); Bernard Newman (gowns); Harvey S. Haislip (technical advisor); Hugh McDowell, Jr. (recording); P. J. Faulkner, Jr. (music recording); George Marsh (sound cutter); Henry M. Berman (editor)

Songs: "We Saw the Sea," "Let Yourself Go," "Get Thee Behind Me Satan," "I'd Rather Lead a Band," "Here am I, But Where Are You," "I'm Putting All My Eggs in One Basket," "Let's Face the Music and Dance" (Irving Berlin)

Release date: February 20, 1936 (Radio City Music Hall)

Run time: 110 minutes

In a show within the show, Lady Luck does not smile upon gambler Fred Astaire in spite of the presence of lovely Lucille and his other fair-weather friends, who depart as his wallet empties.

Synopsis

When the Navy drops anchor in San Francisco, sailors Bake Baker (Fred Astaire) and Bilge Smith (Randolph Scott) drop into the Paradise dance hall in search of fun. There, Bake finds his old dancing partner, Sherry Martin (Ginger Rogers), and they rekindle the old magic. Upon seeing Bilge, Sherry's homely sister, Connie (Harriet Hilliard), goes in for a makeover performed by Sherry's friend, Kitty (Lucille Ball). Her new look turns his head, but Bilge quickly decides she is too serious and instead hooks up with a frivolous blonde named Iris (Astrid Allwyn). Not realizing he lost interest, Connie goes out the next day and salvages her father's old ship—for Bilge.

Meanwhile, Sherry lands an audition with an important producer. Unaware of this, Bake goes to see the same producer to arrange a tryout for Sherry, just when she is in his office. When Bake hears that the girl currently auditioning is making a great impression, he sabotages her chances. After Sherry finds out what he did, she gets even, then forgives Bake without delay; they have a much bigger problem to face.

Connie has found out about Bilge and Iris and wants to leave town, but she cannot yet. A kind old friend talked his company into salvaging her ship without paying in advance. He will have trouble if the job is not paid. Connie must find a way to raise money. Bake has an idea—put on a benefit show!

The night of the performance, Bake is denied shore leave so he jumps ship. Bilge is sent to arrest him. Bake tells him that the show is to help Connie, who spent her last dime on a ship for him. Bilge allows them to proceed and finally realizes what a great girl he almost lost. Bake and Sherry are a hit in the show. The team of Baker and Martin is back together, off the dance floor as well as on.

Follow the Fleet took Astaire and Rogers out of upper-class foreign settings and into a San Francisco taxi-dance hall. Frank Jenks, Tony Martin, and Frank Mills are among the sailors watching the stars' nimble stepping during a dance contest.

"With Ginger Rogers again opposite, and the Irving Berlin music to dance to and sing, Astaire once more legs himself and his picture into the big time entertainment class. . . . Dwight Taylor and Al Scott's dialog is good and can be counted on for laughs, with the Astaire-Rogers dancing sure to do the rest."

—*Variety*

"Screen musical comedy has seldom been more entertaining . . . [Astaire's] comedy here is remarkably adroit, and of course, his dancing is brilliant and breathtaking. As Sherry, Miss Rogers has never appeared to better advantage. . . . Her comedy work and her dancing are superb, and she comes nearer to matching Mr. Astaire in both these departments than ever before."

—*New York World-Telegram*

" . . . even though it is not the best of their series it still is good enough to take the head of this year's class in song and dance entertainment. . . . it should be assurance enough to hear that [Astaire and Rogers] tap as gayly [sic], waltz as beautifully and disagree as merrily as ever."

—*New York Times*

Fred Astaire singles out Lucille from among the starlets.

Notes and Comments

The 1922 Hubert Osborne play *Shore Leave* served as the basis for *Follow the Fleet*. The production brought some changed elements into the Astaire-Rogers series while echoing their earlier films, most strongly *Roberta*, with a story centered on two young couples.

Roberta's Randolph Scott was again borrowed from Paramount to play the flighty sailor of the second romantic pair. Unable to secure Irene Dunne, RKO recruited the popular singer from Ozzie Nelson's band, Harriet Hilliard, to make her feature film debut. The blonde vocalist became a brunette to contrast with Ginger. Hilliard sang two songs from the Irving Berlin score, including "Get Thee Behind Me, Satan," a Rogers number that had been cut from *Top Hat*.

Lucille had the part of a showgirl, Kitty Collins, her delivery of a few quips she was given to speak making it memorable. Other *Fleet* cast

The hauntingly beautiful "Let's Face the Music and Dance" number. Ginger's heavily beaded bell sleeves proved problematic for dancing. Astaire struggled to keep from being struck in the face by them during twirls she made with arms raised.

members with bright futures were crooner Tony Martin, seen among the sailors, and Betty Grable, generously billed sixth though seen all too briefly as one of Ginger's backup singers. Dance extras for the picture were plucked right from Hollywood dance halls by choreographer Hermes Pan. The two best, a twenty-year-old secretary and an eighteen-year-old dishwasher, got to compete against the stars in the finals of the "Let Yourself Go" dance contest sequence. The production cost RKO $747,000 to produce. With Astaire and Rogers ranked third in the year's popularity ratings, naturally *Follow the Fleet* was an unqualified hit.

Hubert Osborne's play had previously been filmed as *Shore Leave* (1925). The work was also

Three future stars: Lucille, Harriet Hilliard, and Betty Grable. Like Lucille, Harriet, with her husband, Ozzie Nelson, would have great success on television years later.

converted into *Hit the Deck*, a musical play by Vincent Youmans. That in turn became a 1930 Jack Oakie film of the same name and the 1955 MGM remake with Jane Powell and Tony Martin.

With Fred Astaire and Ginger Rogers (center)

The Farmer in the Dell

An RKO-Radio Picture (1936)

Cast: Fred Stone (Ernest Boyer, "Pa"); Jean Parker (Adelien Boyer); Esther Dale (Loudelia Boyer, "Ma"); Moroni Olsen (Chester Hart); Frank Albertson (Davy Davenport); Maxine Jennings (Maud Durant); Ray Mayer (Spike); Lucille Ball (Gloria Wilson); Rafael Corio (Nicholas Ranovitch); Frank Jenks (Crosby); Spencer Charters (Milkman)

Credits: Robert Sisk (associate producer); Ben Holmes (director); Sam Mintz and John Grey (screenplay), from novel by Phil Strong; Nick Musuraca (photography); Alberto Colombo (musical director); John E. Burch (production associate); Van Nest Polglase (art director), Al Herman (associate); John L. Cass (recording); George Hively (editor)

Release date: March 6, 1936 (Palace Theater)

Run time: 67 minutes

Synopsis

Iowa farmer Ernie Boyer (Fred Stone) and his family move to Hollywood. Ma (Esther Dale) has one aim in mind—to get daughter Adie (Jean Parker) into the movies. Adie's own foremost wish is to marry young Davy Davenport (Frank Albertson), but Ernie takes her to a studio to please Ma. On the soundstage, Adie goes unnoticed, but director Chester Hart (Moroni Olsen) takes a liking to Ernie and casts him in the picture he is making.

So as not to disappoint Ma, Ernie tells her that it was Adie they hired. Trouble starts between Adie and Davy, and Ernie soon tires of lying. He tells Ma the truth and decides to quit movies, hoping it will return his home life to normal. The studio bosses see great potential in Ernie and offer him a salary he cannot refuse. Thinking of how it could help the family, Ernie accepts. He then has to leave immediately for location filming.

Meanwhile, greed overtakes Ma. She rents a lavish house in which to entertain the Hollywood set, as Adie throws Davy over for a movie extra who poses as Russian nobility. Ernie returns from filming angry and hurt by what he sees. He sends for Davy to go back to Iowa without the women. Lou and Adie finally come down to earth when Ernie shows them that Adie's aristocrat is only a fortune hunter. Adie goes back to Davy. Ma apologizes, promising not to try to run their lives anymore.

Notes and Comments

Fred Stone was a Broadway musical comedy favorite since the first years of the twentieth century and the star of a handful of films in the

With Frank Jenks, Fred Stone, and Moroni Olsen

"With a story which has been screened before, though not by that name nor under Phil Strong's sponsorship, there is no particular appeal to the outline, and a careful production and nice acting does not save it. . . . The chief merit of the production is the genuineness with which the story has been told."

—*Variety*

"Fred Stone makes it endurable with his warm and believable characterization . . . Granting that it has a few amusing scenes, our thumb still points down."

—*New York Times*

"For about one-half of its unreeling, 'The Farmer in the Dell,' [is] an animated satire cruelly razzing the insanities of Hollywood as well as some of those who want to crash its loony portals. . . . After a grand beginning the film dwindles into [an] ambling, uninteresting story. . . "

—*New York World-Telegram*

early '20s. Coming to RKO in 1935, he returned to the screen after an eleven-year absence with a heartwarming performance as Katharine Hepburn's father in *Alice Adams*. His natural, homespun manner was seen as reminiscent of Will Rogers, who died that year at the height of his fame. *The Farmer in the Dell*, from a novel by *State Fair* author Phil Strong, was the studio's first starring vehicle for Stone.

Associate producer Robert Sisk handed the modest picture to Ben Holmes, a writer and director of short subjects. As his bucolic family, Stone was given Jean Parker (*Lady for a Day*, *Little Women*) for a daughter, a wife in Esther Dale, and a prospective son-in-law in Frank Albertson. Again Tony Martin is visible in a bit part.

The Farmer in the Dell was shot just after the holidays, in January 1936, with some location filming in the San Fernando Valley, where the company had to contend with an intimidating swarm of bees. Fortunately for her, Lucille's scene took place indoors. She was a script girl, Gloria Wilson. It was the last character she played as a platinum blonde, which was virtually the standard for starlets in the Harlow-conscious mid-30s. With her career slowly but surely advancing, she began looking for a more singular look.

Bunker Bean

An RKO-Radio Picture (1936)

Cast: Owen Davis, Jr. (Bunker Bean); Louise Latimer (Mary Kent); Robert McWade (J. C. Kent); Jessie Ralph (Grandmother); Lucille Ball (Rosie Kelly); Berton Churchill (Professor Balthazer); Edward Nugent (Mr. Glab); Hedda Hopper (Mrs. Kent); Ferdinand Gottschalk (Dr. Meyerhauser); Leonard Carey (Butler); Russell Hicks (A. C. Jones); Sibyl Harris (Countess); Pierre Watkin (Mr. Barnes); Patricia Wilder (Secretary); Maxine Jennings (Receptionist)

Credits: William Sistrom (associate producer); William Hamilton and Edward Killy (directors); Edmund North, James Gow, and Dorothy Yost (screenplay), from play by Lee Wilson Dodd, based on novel by Harry Leon Wilson; David Abel (photography); Roy Webb (musical director); Van Nest Polglase (art director), Al Herman (associate); Clem Portman (recording); Jack Hively (editor)

Release date: June 26, 1936 (Palace Theater)

Run time: 67 minutes

Synopsis

Everyone takes advantage of Bunker Bean (Owen Davis, Jr.), an office clerk at the Kent Aircraft Corporation—particularly his boss, J. C. Kent (Robert McWade). Bunker has an idea that learning who he was in past incarnations would embolden him. Told by a fortuneteller that he was once Napoleon, Bunker begins behaving like an all-powerful emperor and hopes this will win over the boss's daughter, Mary (Louise Latimer). Her reaction is decidedly negative.

Bunker returns to the crystal gazer. This time he used to be "Ram Tah," an Egyptian pharaoh. He purchases the pharaoh's mummy to inspire him to assume the ancient ruler's traits of bravery and nobility.

Bunker inherits the patent to a gyro-stabilizer, a device for airplanes. Kent needs it badly and offers to purchase it for $100, but Bunker suspects it must be worth much more. A. C. Jones (Russell Hicks), president of a rival

Miss Kelly, the secretary, is astonished by the newfound forwardness of her once-timid coworker.

aircraft company, counters with $15,000. Rather than enter a bidding war, Kent and Jones join forces and make Bunker a paltry offer. His gumption to fight the businessmen is crushed when he discovers that the mummy of Ram Tah is a fake.

Mary, who by now has fallen in love with Bunker, makes him realize that his recent accomplishments were his own doing, not the power of a phony mummy. Bunker opens a company to compete with Kent. Mary looks on with pride as Bunker's newfound business savvy forces her father to make him a fair offer for the prized patent, and they go into business together.

Notes and Comments

Along with *Ruggles of Red Gap* and *Merton of the Movies*, *His Majesty, Bunker Bean* was one of Hollywood's favorite Harry Leon Wilson stories. It had been adapted for the screen first in 1918 by Paramount, starring Mary Pickford's brother, Jack Pickford, and then in 1925 by Warner Bros., with Matt Moore.

Owen Davis, Jr., primarily a stage actor and the son of a Pulitzer Prize-winning playwright, had his first lead film role in 1936's *Bunker Bean*. Opposite him was Louise Latimer, with whom he was paired four times that year. William Hamilton and Edward Killy, an editor and assistant director, respectively, on RKO's A-list productions, co-directed the comedy.

Lucille played Rosie Kelly, a gum-churning office secretary with biting wit. Joan Davis, another future TV comedienne with a knack for physical comedy, played a receptionist, and the soon-to-be-renowned gossip columnist, Hedda Hopper, appeared as a society matron.

Though still playing small roles, Lucille was forging an identity and developing her own style. For *Bunker Bean* she darkened her tresses to a chestnut shade and experimented with bangs. In the same month of the film's release, Hollywood costume designers named her, rather than an established star, the year's "Best-Dressed Girl in Town." Thus the studio found a perfect way to promote their rising starlet—as a clotheshorse.

Reviews

"It will make good with those who see it, for lack of names does not mean absence of acting and story value. . . . The script has been well constructed for speed, action and laughs, all of which are enhanced by a smooth and finished direction . . . It is a workmanlike job all around."

—*Variety*

"It is a sprightly and diverting little film though its superficialities may disappoint the admirers of the original Mr. Bean, whose complexities and inspirations were more sly than those represented in the screen version. . . . Davis, Jr. [plays] the role with skill and relish."

—*New York Daily Mirror*

"It's a fresh and amusing little program picture—'B.B.'—better than average in production, dialogue and acting. . . . it benefits by modern treatment [of an old story] and especially by Owen's interpretation of the title role."

—*New York Evening Post*

This portrait of Lucille in costume as Rosie Kelly was used to promote *Bunker Bean*, made in April 1936.

Winterset

An RKO-Radio Picture (1936)

Cast: Burgess Meredith (Mio Romagna); Margo (Miriamne); Eduardo Ciannelli (Trock Estrella); John Carradine (Bartolomeo Romagna); Edward Ellis (Judge Gaunt); Paul Guilfoyle (Garth Esdras); Maurice Moscovitch (Esdras, Sr.); Stanley Ridges (Shadow); Willard Robertson (Policeman in Square); Mischa Auer (Radical); Myron McCormick (Carr); Helen Jerome Eddy (Mrs. Romagna); Barbara Pepper (Girl); Alec Craig (Hobo); Fernanda Eliscu (Piny); George Humbert (Lucia); Murray Alper (Louie); Paul Fix (Joe); Lucille Ball (Girl in Square)

Credits: Pandro S. Berman (producer); Alfred Santell (director); Anthony Veiller (screenplay), from play by Maxwell Anderson, as produced by Guthrie McClintic; Peverell Marley (photography); Nathaniel Shilkret (musical director); Maurice De Packh (musical arrangements); Vernon L. Walker (special effects); Van Nest Polglase (art director), Perry Ferguson (associate); Darrell Silvera (set decoration); John L. Cass (recording); William Hamilton (editor)

Release date: December 3, 1936 (Radio City Music Hall)

Run time: 77 minutes

Synopsis

After a paymaster's murder, the innocent Bartolomio Romagna (John Carradine) is framed and sentenced to death. Sixteen years later, his case is re-examined in a law school classroom. Students declare the ruling was unjust and uncover evidence that a Garth Esdras (Paul Guilfoyle) witnessed the killing. The highly publicized story reaches Trock Estrella (Eduardo Ciannelli), the man behind the crime. Trock threatens Garth to keep him quiet, but Esdras breaks down and confesses his involvement in the crime to his father and sister.

Romagna's son, Mio (Burgess Meredith), has sought for years to clear his father's name. He comes across a very sad-looking girl, Miriamne

Young stars Burgess Meredith and Margo perform over the airwaves during filming in August 1936. Margo made her Broadway debut in *Winterset*. After the film version, she continued to work on stage and occasionally in films. Meredith is remembered by several roles: The Penguin in TV's *Batman*, Mickey the trainer of *Rocky*, and lively ninety-five-year-old Grandpa Gustafson of *Grumpy Old Men*.

Reviews

"Once in a very great while a beautiful picture is made, a picture with a story that carries weight, with performances that dig deep into the living flesh of tragedy, with artistic honesty. And it's so different from the usual movie that lots of guys and gals wonder what the hell it's about. Such a picture is Maxwell Anderson's 'Winterset,' . . . "

—*New York Post*

" . . . a mature, purposeful drama, frankly outspoken in its argument, courageous in its conclusions and zealously played by a superbly chosen cast."

—*New York Times*

"By cutting and editing rather than change of dialogue or characterization, the film emerges more vivid and forceful than the play . . . [Those who] found the play a grand gangster melodrama, which took itself much too seriously, will rejoice that the film has stripped 'Winterset' of its pretentiousness. There is still the theme. There is still the blank verse, now cut down so that speeches do not hold up the action."

—*New York Sun*

(Margo), unaware that she is Garth's sister. There is an instant connection between them. Mio tells her about his father. Without saying what she knows, Miriamne tells him he must go away immediately to save himself, leaving Mio hungry for more information.

Mio finds the Esdras home. Garth and the now mentally disturbed Judge Gaunt (Edward Ellis), who sentenced Romagna to death, talk Mio into considering that his father was guilty. Trock arrives, revealing enough to reaffirm Mio's faith in his father's innocence. Holding the criminal at gunpoint, Mio obtains a full confession, but soon the tables are turned, and Trock is in control. Trock leaves the house and has an assassin stand by to kill Mio. Tired of living with guilt, Garth walks to the street and is shot but Mio, with Miriamne, remain trapped in an alley just out of the killer's range. Suddenly Mio sees a sign to save them—he begins playing a barrel organ on the street, attracting a cop who had previously shown his hatred of the instrument. The couple is taken away from the danger zone by police escort. Trock is then shot down by his own hired assassin, and the truth lives with Mio.

Notes and Comments

Maxwell Anderson's *Winterset*, telling of a miscarriage of justice echoing the real-life case of Sacco and Vanzetti, opened on Broadway in September 1935. The New York Drama Critics Circle deemed the play the season's best, and RKO's film adaptation was considered even better. From the stage company, Burgess Meredith, Margo, and Eduardo Ciannelli were enlisted to recreate their roles in the picture. For Meredith, it would be his movie debut.

An eager George Stevens was first appointed to *Winterset*, but he was called away to direct a Katharine Hepburn costume comedy, *Quality Street*, while *Winterset* was handed to Alfred Santell. In the film's early stages, Lionel Barrymore, Anne Shirley, and later Sylvia Sidney, were to be cast. By the time filming got under way in late July 1936, Barrymore had to be

Winterset

substituted by Edward Ellis, while Mexican actress and dancer Margo was selected to reprise her role in place of Shirley or Sidney, leaving no familiar "names" in the cast.

A keen eye is needed to spot Lucille in long skirt, sweater, and hat watching the townspeople dance to the music of a barrel organ. This was her final appearance without dialogue or credit. Also in this scene was Barbara Pepper, a New York model who arrived in Hollywood with Lucille as a Goldwyn Girl in 1933, and who is recognizable to *I Love Lucy* fans. The two remained friends, and Pepper can be spotted in many episodes of the show.

Producer Pandro Berman took a risk in bringing *Winterset* to the screen. The play's appeal to mass audiences was anything but certain. Anthony Veiller's adaptation, which retained the essence of Anderson's work, replaced the original tragic conclusion with a happy ending as a relief to the prevailing melodrama. Happy ending or not, *Winterset* was not a box office film. It was, however, widely praised for its artistic merits and nominated for two Oscars (Best Art Direction and Best Score).

Menacing Eduardo Ciannelli (right) enters the sanctuary of Burgess Meredith, Margo, Maurice Moscovitch, Edward Ellis, and Alec Craig.

That Girl from Paris

An RKO-Radio Picture (1936)

Cast: Lily Pons (Nikki Martin); Jack Oakie (Whammo); Gene Raymond (Windy McLean); Herman Bing (Hammacher); Lucille Ball (Claire Williams); Mischa Auer (Butch); Frank Jenks (Laughing Boy); Patricia Wilder (Hat Check Girl); Vinton Haworth (Reporter); Willard Robertson (Immigration Officer); Gregory Gaye (Paul de Vry); Ferdinand Gottschalk (Uncle); Rafaela Ottiano (Marie); Harry Jans (Purser); Landers Stevens (Ship's Captain); Edward Price (Photographer); Alec Craig (Justice of the Peace)

Credits: Pandro S. Berman (producer); Leigh Jason (director); Joseph A. Fields, P. J. Wolfson, Dorothy Yost, and Howard Kussell (screenplay), from story by Jane Murfin suggested by J. Carey Wonderly story; J. Roy Hunt (photography); Nathaniel Shilkret (musical director); Andre Kostelanetz (orchestra conductor); Van Nest Polglase (art director), Carroll Clark (associate); Darrell Silvera (set decoration); Edward Stevenson (gowns); Hugh McDowell, Jr., (recording); William Morgan (editor)

Songs: "Una Voce Poco Fa" from opera *Barber of Seville* (Rossini); "Tarantella" (Panofka); "Blue Danube Waltz" (Johann Strauss, orchestration by Arthur Schwartz); "Call to Arms," "Love and Learn," "Seal it with a Kiss," "Moon Face," "My Nephew from Nice" (Schwartz and Edward Heyman)

Release date: December 31, 1936 (Radio City Music Hall)

Run time: 104 minutes

Synopsis

Singer Nikki Martin (Lily Pons) shocks all Paris by running out on her wedding to Paul de Vry (Gregory Gaye)—an impresario whose primary interest is her career rather than Nikki herself. The runaway bride flees to the countryside and latches onto an American musician she meets on the road, Windy McLean (Gene Raymond), who is sailing back home that afternoon with his band. Nikki stows away on the ship without his knowledge.

Once they dock in America, Nikki tracks down Windy to the apartment he shares with band mates Whammo (Jack Oakie), Butch (Mischa Auer), and Laughing Boy (Frank Jenks). Immigration officials soon arrive, blaming the four men for Nikki's illegal entrance into the country. Facing imprisonment if she is found with them, the troupe takes a job out of town in an effort to keep her concealed.

As she is in love with Windy, Nikki clashes with his girlfriend, Claire (Lucille Ball). The band is a sensation with Nikki singing (photos of the "French Doll" are strictly prohibited). When Windy begins to warm to the endearing troublemaker, Claire notifies the police of the star's identity.

Center, with (from right) Herman Bing, Frank Jenks, Jack Oakie, Gene Raymond, and Mischa Auer.

Lucille, as Claire, fumes while Nikki and Windy display their fondness for each other.

After narrowly escaping the authorities, the boys decide that one of them should marry Nikki and make her a legal resident. Windy confesses his feelings for her and soon proposes.

Before the wedding, it slips that the four men initially high-carded to choose which man would be her husband. Likely recalling her ex-fiancé, Nikki believes that any one of them was willing to marry her simply to keep her with the band. Insulted, she runs away, deciding that if her career is to be most important in life she may as well go back to de Vry. She resolves her legal status, but the boys end up in prison—until Nikki bails them out. Just as she is to be married, the band members convince her that Windy has been truly in love with her all along. Again she runs out on her wedding, this time to marry the man she loves.

Notes and Comments

The second showcase for French opera star Lily Pons was a remake of RKO's first official production, *Street Girl* (1929), starring Betty Compson and based on a J. Carey Wonderly story called "The Viennese Charmer." The tale was retold once more in 1942 as *Four Jacks and a Jill*, starring Anne Shirley, with Desi Arnaz in a supporting role.

Because *I Dream Too Much* had lost money, in *That Girl from Paris*, the Metropolitan diva was placed in a lighter story, linked to a swing band, and surrounded by comics, including Jack Oakie, who had been in the 1929 version. The score was designed to converge modern music and classical in a brisk and inventive manner. This aim was climaxed by Arthur Schwarz's exciting arrangement of Strauss's "The Blue Danube." The revised formula for Pons clicked with audiences, making the picture one of the studio's top moneymakers of the year.

Lucille was given a far greater opportunity in *That Girl from Paris* than she had in the first Pons film. She played the second feminine lead, Pons's rival for Gene Raymond. Her big scene was a highlight: In an attempt to sabotage her rival's act, Pons's character rubs soap on the bottom of

A page from one of Lucille's many scrapbooks. The center photo shows her as Claire. Before her comic ballroom dance, Claire exhibits her fancy footwork in an audition.

her dancing shoes. Wearing a billowy Edward Stevenson gown and the slippery footwear, Lucille proceeds onto the dance floor and executes a series of exquisite pratfalls. In reality, however, she did not anticipate how slick the floor would actually be made for this sequence, resulting in many painful tumbles for the game actress.

Lucille worked hard for three years to win her first really important role. The summer of 1936, which preceded this film's production, had been an eventful one for Lucille. She played only one bit part in a film, opting instead, under the tutelage of Lela Rogers, for more chances to *act*. She took bigger parts in a couple of shorts and played the lead in the RKO Little Theater production *Breakfast with Vanora*. That summer, she also received a fair share of notoriety from being romantically linked with Broderick Crawford, and from her new label as Hollywood's most stylish girl about town.

One more Pons vehicle followed this one before the singer's time in the movies came to an end. The deceptively titled *Hitting a New High* (1937) cast her as Oogahunga, the Bird-Girl. The opera craze that had been initiated with Columbia's *One Night of Love* was now running its course, and Pons herself wanted out to return to grand opera. She continued quite successfully in her true profession for many years.

Don't Tell the Wife

An RKO-Radio Picture (1937)

Cast: Guy Kibbee (Malcolm J. Winthrop); Una Merkel (Nancy Dorset); Lynne Overman (Steve Dorset); Thurston Hall (Major Manning); Guinn Williams (Cupid); Frank M. Thomas (Sergeant Mallory); William Demarest (Larry Tucker); Lucille Ball (Ann Howell); Harry Tyler (Mike Callahan); George Irving (Warden); Bradley Page (Hagar); Cy Jenks (Sam Taylor); Harry Jans (Martin); Bill Jackie (Rooney); Alan Curtis (Customer's Man); Donald Kerr (Smith); Charlie West (Joe Hoskins); Aggie Herring (Charwoman); Barney Furey (Sign Painter); Hattie McDaniel (Nancy's Maid)

Credits: Robert Sisk (associate producer); Christy Cabanne (director); Nat Perrin (screenplay), from play by George Holland; Harry Wilde (photography); Vernon L. Walker (special effects); Van Nest Polglase (art director), Feild Gray (associate); John E. Tribby (recording); Jack Hively (editor)

Release date: February 18, 1937 (Palace Theater)

Run time: 62 minutes

Synopsis

Once operator of an investment racket, Steve Dorset (Lynne Overman) has retired to a farm with his wife, Nancy (Una Merkel). One of his former cohorts comes out of prison with a new slant on the old business. He has obtained the "Golden Dream" mine—there is no gold in it, but they can sell stock and at least do have a mine this time. Nancy protests, but Steve is coaxed into the crooked organization again.

To make Nancy believe the venture is legal and so agree to assist them financially, Steve furnishes a gullible front man, Malcolm J. Winthrop (Guy Kibbee). They set him up with a pretty secretary (Lucille Ball) and name the firm after him. A team of fast-talking salesmen is hired to push Golden Dream stock, with one stipulation—never put anything in writing. The well-meaning Winthrop sends word of the stock to his pals. One of these letters reaches Police Sergeant Mallory (Frank M. Thomas), who begins examining Steve and the gang more closely.

At left, with Lynne Overman, Frank M. Thomas, and Guinn "Big Boy" Williams.

Steve tries to make his business enterprise appear legitimate to wife Nancy by presenting her to the credulous Malcolm J. Winthrop.

Before long, the truth is exposed. Winthrop learns that the business is crooked. Nancy is set to walk out on Steve. Hoping to keep the couple together, Winthrop comes up with an alternative to turning Steve over to the police. He resolves to legitimize the House of Winthrop. He investigates and discovers that there is indeed gold in Golden Dream, then spreads the news that the mine is a sound investment. Through his maneuvers, Winthrop saves the money of many innocents and makes Steve and his cronies the "suckers" for once. Nancy gets back her own monetary contribution, while Steve promises to mend his ways.

Notes and Comments

Lucille wrapped up her film assignments for 1936 with *Don't Tell the Wife*, which was adapted from George Holland's play *Once Over Lightly* by veteran comedy writer Nat Perrin. The film's prolific director, Christy Cabanne, had been in movies since the early teens as an actor, writer, and director. He made several features with the rotund character actor Guy Kibbee, beginning with *Don't Tell the Wife* and continuing in the '40s with RKO's *Scattergood Baines* series.

Kibbee's co-star, Una Merkel (on loan from MGM), was a prime supporting actress of the '30s, probably best known for her barroom brawl with Marlene Dietrich in *Destry Rides Again*. She played the wife of the title with her customary wit, and Lynne Overman was her shyster husband. Lucille was cast as the fashionable "secretary" and lone female member of a gang of con artists. She wore a suit—likely from her personal wardrobe—that would turn up on her again in *Stage Door*.

Don't Tell the Wife was filmed in November and December 1936. Following production, RKO gave Lucille leave to head east with *Hey Diddle Diddle*, a play by Bartlett Cormack in which she had earned a part after producer-director Anne Nichols saw her in *That Girl From Paris*. The star, Conway Tearle, took ill and the show closed during out-of-town try-outs before reaching Broadway. Lucille lost nothing. Her reviews were stellar. *Variety* noted, "Lucille Ball, making her first stage appearance, fattens a fat part and almost walks off with the play." She returned to Hollywood in mid-February 1937 to continue her budding career at RKO. She was about to make a splash in the studio's most distinguished production of the year.

Conway Tearle, standing, left in above photo, is seen in his role of a beleaguered movie director. Beside him are clockwise Alice White, Don Beddoe, Lucille, and an actor believed to be Alfred White. Beddoe portrayed Tearle's assistant and Lucille's beau. The reviews for the play (below) were mild, but *Variety* thought Lucille was the highlight. "She outlines a consistent character and continuously gives it logical substance."

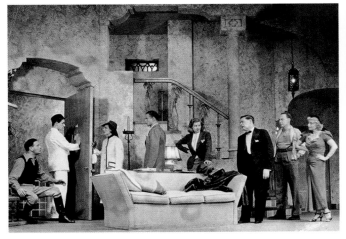

RKO's Queen of the Bs

(1938 to 1942)

Lucille finally had a chance to shine in a prestigious film in 1937's *Stage Door*. Her supporting role as the wisecracking Judy Canfield was a standout among a team of memorable ladies that made the bosses at RKO take notice of the talented comedienne they had under contract. Though not a star of the first order, she emerged as the queen of the studio's B-picture unit.

No longer just another platinum blonde, her look became more distinctive and she was cast in film after film (twenty-one in the course of four years), playing every kind of character. She was constantly praised as being the greatest asset of these low-budget films, and they were consistently popular with audiences. Her Bs were considered "B pluses" as far as production values, and she was known for the fashionable wardrobe she wore in them. Lucille later said she "loved every minute of it" because of the opportunities and constant new filmmaking experiences they provided.

The Affairs of Annabel (1938), in which the *New York Times* said Lucille was "rapidly becoming one of our brightest comediennes."

Stage Door

An RKO-Radio Picture (1937)

Cast: Katharine Hepburn (Terry Randall); Ginger Rogers (Jean Maitland); Adolphe Menjou (Anthony Powell); Gail Patrick (Linda Shaw); Constance Collier (Catherine Luther); Andrea Leeds (Kaye Hamilton); Samuel S. Hinds (Henry Sims); Lucille Ball (Judy Canfield); Franklin Pangborn (Harcourt); William Corson (Bill); Pierre Watkin (Richard Carmichael); Grady Sutton (Butch); Frank Reicher (Stage Director); Jack Carson (Mr. Milbanks); Phyllis Kennedy (Hattie); Eve Arden (Eve); Ann Miller (Annie); Margaret Early (Mary Lou); Jean Rouverol (Dizzy); Elizabeth Dunne (Mrs. Orcutt); Norma Drury (Olga Brent); Jane Rhodes (Ann Braddock); Peggy O'Donnell (Susan); Harriett Brandon (Madeline); Katharine Alexander, Ralph Forbes, Mary Forbes, Huntley Gordon (Cast of Stage Play)

Credits: Pandro S. Berman (producer); Gregory La Cava (director); Morrie Ryskind and Anthony Veiller (screenplay), from play by Edna Ferber and George S. Kaufman; Robert de Grasse (photography); Roy Webb (musical director); Van Nest Polglase (art director), Carroll Clark (associate); Darrell Silvera (set decoration); Muriel King (gowns); Trabert & Hoeffer–Mauboussin (jewelry); John L. Cass (recording); William Hamilton (editor)

Song: "Put Your Heart into Your Feet and Dance" (Hal Borne and Mort Greene)

Release date: October 8, 1937 (Radio City Music Hall)

Run time: 91 minutes

Synopsis

Heiress Terry Randall (Katharine Hepburn), out to take Broadway by storm, moves into the Footlights Club, a theatrical boarding house inhabited by a group of wisecrackers who face the heartache of the theater by maintaining their sense of humor. The prim and proper Terry is hopelessly misplaced. She and her caustic roommate, Jean Maitland (Ginger Rogers), are at each other's throats immediately. One girl befriends Terry, however—Kaye Hamilton (Andrea Leeds), who only a year ago had been a star. This year, she cannot even get an audition.

Jean also has a running feud with housemate Linda Shaw (Gail Patrick), the latest girlfriend of producer Anthony Powell (Adolphe Menjou). To spite Linda, Jean responds when Powell makes advances to her, then she loses her head and falls for him. With help from Terry, however, she soon recovers her senses.

With Ann Miller, Eve Arden, and Ginger Rogers. Arden is standing left of Lucille. *I Love Lucy* and Arden's own popular television series, *Our Miss Brooks*, were shot on adjoining stages at Desilu studios some fifteen years later.

Jean prepares for a double date with a couple of Judy's lumbermen from back home in Seattle.

A birthday celebration for the club's most promising actress, Kaye.

In addition to leading his complicated love life, Powell is also producing the play *Enchanted April*. His backer for the show agrees to finance the production only if Terry is given the lead. Unbeknownst to Powell, his "angel" is her father, who is trying to snap Terry out of her stage ambitions by making her the star of what he hopes will be a flop. Her emotionless performance in rehearsals seems to indicate her father will get his wish.

Meanwhile, Jean and the girls despise Terry for taking the part Kaye had her heart set on. Heartbroken but not bitter, Kaye soothes Terry's jitters on opening night. After seeing her off, the sights and sounds of her own opening swirl through Kaye's mind and she commits suicide by leaping from a window. Jean informs Terry of the tragedy just before curtain time. She goes on with the show and gives a poignant, emotionally charged performance, which she dedicates to Kaye in the curtain speech.

Months later, the Footlights Club is back to normal, and Terry is one of the girls. It is an average day, full of wisecracks and the familiar sounds of Jean and Linda fighting. One of the girls, Judy (Lucille Ball), has gotten married and they give her a send-off to a more traditional lifestyle. After her departure, a new girl arrives with a quality seen in both Kaye and Terry, one that makes her seem just a bit different from the rest.

Notes and Comments

RKO paid $125,000 for the rights to film the George S. Kaufman-Edna Ferber play *Stage Door*, which had starred Margaret Sullavan on Broadway. In their adaptation, scriptwriters Morrie Ryskind and Anthony Veiller removed the decidedly anti-Hollywood essence of the original work and came out with something quite distinct that was deemed superior to the play.

Shooting began on June 7, 1937 (the day Hollywood and the rest of the country was stunned by the death of twenty-six-year-old Jean Harlow). Director Gregory La Cava was an immense talent, with credits like *My Man Godfrey* (1936) to his name. Seeking to present the hopes, frustrations, and troubles of aspiring actresses in a realistic manner, he had secretaries on hand at all times to observe the interactions between cast members, record conversations, and then report back to him. Though the actresses were handed new pages of script daily, La Cava encouraged them to improvise. However unorthodox his methods may have seemed, they lent authenticity and spark to the dialogue.

Katharine Hepburn had gone to Broadway in 1933 in *The Lake*. The show was a famous fiasco, but she was able to poke fun at the experience in *Stage Door*. *The Lake* served as a template for the play within the film, *Enchanted April*, and provided the immortal line that every Hepburn imitator recites, "The calla lilies are in bloom again." With her box-office standing on shaky ground after a string of costume pictures that failed, Hepburn realized during production that it was not intended for her to carry *Stage Door* on her own. Not until the last part of the film does she begin to dominate.

Producer Pandro Berman saw pairing Hepburn with Ginger Rogers as an ideal arrangement. Ginger rivaled (and at this point was surpassing) Hepburn as the studio's top leading lady. She and Fred Astaire were still top box-office draws, but Ginger yearned to prove herself in dramatic parts. *Stage Door* gave her that opportunity and her talent shined in one of her greatest performances. Lucille was elated to be working along-

Relaxed, Lucille reflects the natural atmosphere La Cava encouraged on the set of *Stage Door*.

side these two actresses. "Being at RKO so long gave me years of observing these two big stars. They were very opposite. And both very worth observing."

Though the stars were at their best, the ensemble cast was an essential element of *Stage Door*'s excellence. The best of RKO's crop of starlets, including Eve Arden and fourteen-year-old Ann Miller, left their mark as tenants of the Footlights Club. Andrea Leeds (borrowed from Goldwyn) was named the "real discovery of the picture" by the *New York Times*. As it turned out, Leeds bowed out of movies in 1940, while several of the others continued for decades.

Lucille would later say that she would not have been cast in *Stage Door* if not for the urging of Lela Rogers, because she was certain La Cava did not want her. Lucille could undoubtedly identify with the character of Judy Canfield, having struggled to break into the New York theatrical scene herself only a few years earlier. She demonstrated her impeccable timing in the part and won critical praise. This put Lucille's career on a new level, elevating her to supporting player in A pictures and leading lady in Bs. It also led to a revised contract with RKO at an increased salary.

Though its $81,000 profit margin fell short of expectations, *Stage Door* was a critical triumph, nominated for Academy Awards in four categories: Best Picture, Best Director, Best Screenplay, and Best Supporting Actress (Andrea Leeds).

Having Wonderful Time

An RKO-Radio Picture (1938)

Cast: Ginger Rogers (Teddy Shaw); Douglas Fairbanks, Jr. (Chick Kirkland); Peggy Conklin (Fay Coleman); Lucille Ball (Miriam); Lee Bowman (Buzzy Armbruster); Eve Arden (Henrietta); Dorothea Kent (Maxine); Richard "Red" Skelton (Itchy Faulkner); Donald Meek (P. U. Rogers); Jack Carson (Emil Beatty); Clarence H. Wilson (Mr. G.); Allan Lane (Mac); Grady Sutton (Gus); Shimen Ruskin (Shrimpo); Dorothy Tree (Frances); Leona Roberts (Mrs. Shaw); Harlan Briggs (Mr. Shaw); Inez Courtney (Emma); Juanita Quigley (Mabel)

Credits: Pandro S. Berman (producer); Alfred Santell (director); Arthur Kober (screenplay), from play by Arthur Kober, as produced by Marc Connelly; Robert de Grasse (photography); Roy Webb (musical director); Van Nest Polglase (art director), Perry Ferguson (associate); Darrell Silvera (set decoration); Edward Stevenson and Renié (gowns); John E. Tribby (recording); James Anderson (assistant director); William Hamilton (editor)

Songs: "My First Impression of You," "Nighty Night" (Sam Stept and Charles Tobias)

Release date: July 6, 1938 (Radio City Music Hall)

Run time: 70 minutes

Synopsis

Hardworking typist Teddy Shaw (Ginger Rogers) is anxious to escape to a "peaceful" vacation at Camp Kare-Free—it turns out to be crowded and noisy, but full of good-natured young people. A romance blossoms between Teddy and waiter Chick Kirkland (Douglas Fairbanks, Jr.). They have a lovely time joining in the activities over the next few days, but inevitably, her final night at camp arrives.

With no steady job, Chick feels he has no right to ask for Teddy's hand in marriage. In explaining his feelings, he ends up offending her with an improper proposition. Teddy runs off to the big final night festivities. To avoid Chick, she accepts an invitation to the cabin of the camp Don Juan, Buzzy Armbruster (Lee Bowman).

Once there, Teddy diverts him from romance to his backgammon board. Back at the party, Chick and Buzzy's main sweetheart, Miriam (Lucille Ball), are dying to know what is happening in Buzzy's bunk. Finally Chick bursts in and finds them still playing. Feeling foolish, he

Lucille becomes acquainted with her new bunkmate, Ginger Rogers. Peggy Conklin is at center. This was the last of very few films in which the stage actress appeared.

Emil takes it on the chin as Chick protects his lady's good name. Rogers struck Fairbanks as "an innocent high-spirited college kid, enthusiastic about ice cream sodas . . . "

goes back to wait for Teddy. Meanwhile, Buzzy gets fed up with backgammon and goes to bed. Teddy remains to make Chick jealous and falls asleep herself.

At breakfast the following day, Teddy's obnoxious ex, Emil (Jack Carson), shows up. He is oblivious, Chick is angry, Teddy is uneasy, and Miriam, fit to be tied, makes it known that she saw Teddy sneak out of Buzzy's cabin early in the morning. Emil believes the worst. Chick, on the other hand, has learned to trust her. He apologizes for the night before. Teddy and Chick reunite and plan to be married right away.

Notes and Comments

In the fall of 1937, a large cast and crew was rounded up at picturesque Big Bear Lake in California's San Bernardino Mountains for location filming on *Having Wonderful Time*. The youthful company enjoyed a festive time shooting the adaptation of Arthur Kober's play about Jewish vacationers at a Catskills resort. The play had been a hit for forty-seven weeks on Broadway and was awarded a prize as the best American comedy of 1937.

This commendation, however, did not mean it was a natural for the screen. The office of the Production Code Administration stated explicitly that the play

Reviews

" . . . refreshing movie fare, humorous, human and pleasant to take. It would take an old sorehead, hipped on the theatre, not to find it so. . . . Ginger Rogers takes the role of Teddy to her heart and makes her a charmingly naïve person . . . The honesty of Fairbanks' performance proves he is a versatile actor. . . . Lucille Ball turns in another grand performance as one of the girls."

—*New York Daily News*

" . . . generally, the show is smooth, well-tempered, gently satiric . . . Lee Bowman is faultless as the camp cad, and so—we might as well admit—are Richard Skelton as Itchy, the irrepressible master of ceremonies; Lucille Ball as Miriam, one of the harpies; Eve Arden as the radical; Jack Carson as Teddy's extinguished flame."

—*New York Times*

"Much of the charm, romantic tenderness and social problem features of Arthur Kober's stage play, 'Having Wonderful Time' are missing in the screen version. In their place the author [has] substituted some lively horseplay and occasional slapstick and has accentuated the comedy angles. . . . Public will accept it as a good time, and laugh heartily at its obvious humor."

—*Variety*

was unacceptable source material for a film on the basis of its "dialogue and sex situations." Approval was eventually granted with express assurance that certain plot points, including a scene in which the lead male character propositions the leading lady, would be handled with great delicacy.

When RKO secured the film rights, Kober himself was engaged to write the screenplay. In transposing his play, the Jewish flavoring of the camp and idiomatic phrases also had to be diluted for the censors. The characters' names were changed, starting with the leads, Teddy Stern and Chick Kessler, who became Teddy Shaw and Chick Kirkland. The basics of Kober's story remained intact, as did some of the campers' traits. "I had to pull out the 'gesundheits,'" Kober said, " . . . But the characteristic overemphasis of social amenities and cultural refinements was left in the movie script because we felt that such overemphasis is a trait of all socially ambitious young people of the lower middle class."

Working under the direction of Alfred Santell was a cast full of bright and promising young faces. Douglas Fairbanks, Jr. took the role of Chick, which had been originated on the stage by John Garfield. There was also Eve Arden, Jack Carson, Lee Bowman, and Richard—better known as Red—Skelton, who made his film debut as the camp clown. Ann Miller and Phyllis Fraser (the cousin of Ginger Rogers) had bit parts, and Lucille got *her* cousin, Cleo, in on the act too as one of the campers.

Having Wonderful Time was photographed (beautifully so by future *I Love Lucy* cameraman Robert De Grasse) between September 24 and November 29, 1937. Retakes were called for in March 1938. It was the second film Rogers made during a yearlong break from the series with Fred Astaire. They enjoyed their musicals but both were anxious to show what they could do independently. In this interim, Astaire made *A Damsel in Distress*

Douglas Fairbanks, Jr. helps Lucille stay warm on location at Big Bear Lake.

Lucille has a manicure while chatting with Lee Bowman.

with Joan Fontaine, and Rogers made *Stage Door*, *Having Wonderful Time*, and *Vivacious Lady* (a delightful comedy). Then, in September 1938, the team hit theaters again in *Carefree*.

As Miriam in *Having Wonderful Time*, Lucille made her fifth and final appearance in a film starring Rogers. On the set of these movies and around the lot, the two developed an enduring friendship, and called each other "cousin," because Rogers's grandmother was a Ball. They appeared together on the screen (television screen, that is) again when she guest starred on the "Ginger Rogers Comes to Tea" episode of *Here's Lucy*.

"To Lucille—Honey, you're the 'tops' All my love, Ginger"

Joy of Living

An RKO-Radio Picture (1938)

Cast: Irene Dunne (Maggie Garrett); Douglas Fairbanks, Jr. (Dan Brewster); Alice Brady (Minerva Garrett); Guy Kibbee (Dennis Garrett); Jean Dixon (Harrison); Eric Blore (Potter); Lucille Ball (Salina Garrett Pine); Warren Hymer (Mike); Billy Gilbert (Café Owner); Frank Milan (Bert Pine); Dorothy Steiner (Dotsy Pine); Estelle Steiner (Betsy Pine); Phyllis Kennedy (Marie); Franklin Pangborn (Orchestra Leader); James Burke (Mac); John Qualen (Oswego); Spencer Charters (Magistrate); George Chandler (Taxi Driver); Grady Sutton (Florist); Charles Lane (Reporter); Clarence Nash (Voice of Donald Duck)

Credits: Felix Young (producer); Tay Garnett (director); Gene Towne, Graham Baker, and Allan Scott (screenplay), from story by Dorothy and Herbert Fields; Joseph Walker (photography); Vernon L. Walker (special effects); Frank Tours (musical director); Russell Bennett (orchestral arrangements); Van Nest Polglase (art director), Carroll Clark (associate); Darrell Silvera (set decoration); Edward Stevenson and Kalloch (costumes); John E. Tribby (recording); Kenneth Holmes (assistant director); Jack Hively (editor)

Songs: "What's Good about Good Night?," "You Couldn't be Cuter," "Just Let Me Look at You," "A Heavenly Party" (Jerome Kern and Dorothy Fields)

Release date: April 15, 1938 (Radio City Music Hall)

Run time: 90 minutes

Synopsis

Overworked musical comedy star Maggie Garrett (Irene Dunne) never has a moment to enjoy her success or her $10,000 a week paycheck, which is drained by her parents and sister Salina's (Lucille Ball) family. The free-spirited Dan Brewster (Douglas Fairbanks, Jr.), who admires her from afar, makes it his duty to rescue Maggie and show her how to have a good time.

Dan's overzealous approach has him twice arrested for annoying the star. When his case is brought before a judge, an astonished Maggie is appointed his parole officer! Dan is to report to her twice a week, which allows him to continue his quest to make Maggie enjoy life. Eventually his persistence prevails and she agrees to spend one night on the town with Dan.

After a few drinks, Maggie lets loose and embarks on a night of revelry. The following morning her family is appalled, thinking only that

Salina runs through the scales.

Maggie, the much-abused family breadwinner, hands over her starring role to her dumfounded sister, Salina.

her friendship with Dan could prove damaging to her career. Maggie stands up to them at last but remains loyal to her family when Dan insults them. She sends him away. Later, upon learning that he plans to ship out, Maggie rushes to the pier and asks him to marry her.

After a quick ceremony, Dan learns that for the time being Maggie is unwilling to go away with him and break from her family or her demanding career. Fearing that she never will, he tells her their marriage can never work. Solemnly, Maggie goes back home. There, she realizes once and for all that her family is interested only in what her fortune can do for them, not in her happiness. Leaving them to stand on their own feet, Maggie returns to Dan and the promise of a fun-filled future.

Notes and Comments

Having begun her show business career in musical comedy on the stage, Irene Dunne entered the movies in 1930 and at once established herself as a leading actress in RKO's *Cimarron*. Thereafter, she primarily was known as a star of "weepies," until Columbia cast her in the screwball comedies *Theodora Goes Wild*

Reviews

"[It] is bereft of sufficient novelty or comedy plot to sustain itself through an hour and a half of gags . . . a cast of fine players try valiantly, but their joy of living is somewhat limited. . . . Short-coming of the production is the lack of development of plot after the simple premise is once established."

—*Variety*

"Miss Dunne gives all her charm, wist-fulness, womanliness to the role. . . . A delightful cast supports her. Doug Fairbanks, Jr., is an engaging hero. Alice Brady and Guy Kibbee are peerless stage parents. Eric Blore, Lucille Ball, Jean Dixon, Warren Hymer and Frank Milan are other polished players. . . . 'Joy of Living' is an exhilarating title and the picture measures up to it. It's a sparkling and exuberant comedy romance."

—*New York Daily Mirror*

"Irene Dunne and Douglas Fairbanks, Jr., employ their engaging sense of comedy in a pleasant manner in the brisk and amusing sophisticated farce called 'Joy of Living' . . . Under Tay Garnett's fresh and imaginative direction they frolic through the merry situations of this Towne-Baker script with considerable agility and sparkle."

—*New York World-Telegram*

and *The Awful Truth*. Her performances in both earned Oscar nominations and placed her in the top ranks as a comedienne with Carole Lombard, Myrna Loy, Ginger Rogers, and Jean Arthur. In 1937, RKO signed Dunne to a two-picture deal, returning her to her old home studio for the first time since *Roberta*.

With Alice Brady, Guy Kibbee, and Frank Milan

Tay Garnett (eight years before *The Postman Always Rings Twice*) directed *Joy of Living*, which he designed to showcase Dunne in a comedy once again. The film's original title, *Joy of Loving*, was ruled unacceptable by the censors. Garnett later commented, "Our title was mandatorily changed to *Joy of Living*, which is a gas if one accepts the Hays Office premise that one may experience the joy of living, *only* if one avoids the joy of loving."

Douglas Fairbanks, Jr., fresh from his success in *The Prisoner of Zenda*, co-starred with Dunne. Alice Brady, who specialized in playing manic society ladies (*The Gay Divorcee*, *My Man Godfrey*), was Dunne's mother and Lucille her freeloading sister Salina, who fancies herself an accomplished entertainer. The character had no redeeming qualities, and in a script satiated with gags and slapstick, provided Lucille with only one comic moment—at the piano, struggling to hit the high notes (or any note for that matter). During production of *Joy of Living*, between December 6, 1937 and February 8, 1938, Lucille was in awe of Dunne. While *Roberta* was being made three years earlier, she had observed the actress and was astounded by her talent in making take after take slightly different than the one that preceded it.

The film benefited from a score comprised of four new Jerome Kern-Dorothy Fields songs written specially for Dunne. Although the actress's comedic prowess was reaffirmed in *Joy of Living*, the cost of production had run up to over $1 million and RKO recorded a loss of $314,000. For the second half of her two-picture deal with the studio, Dunne was at her dramatic best again, in the original *Affair to Remember*, *Love Affair* (1939).

As Salina, Lucille had the most elegant wardrobe to date designed for her.

Go Chase Yourself

An RKO-Radio Picture (1938)

Cast: Joe Penner (Wilbur Meely); Lucille Ball (Carol Meely); Richard Lane (Nails); June Travis (Judith Daniels); Fritz Feld (Pierre Fontaine de Louis-Louis); Tom Kennedy (Ice Box); Granville Bates (Mr. Halliday); Bradley Page (Frank); George Irving (Mr. Daniels); Arthur Stone (Warden); Jack Carson (Warren Miles); Frank M. Thomas (Police Chief)

Credits: Lee Marcus (executive producer); Robert Sisk (producer); Edward F. Cline (director); Paul Yawitz and Bert Granet (screenplay), from story by Walter O'Keefe; Jack Mackenzie (photography); Vernon L. Walker (special effects); Roy Webb (musical director); Van Nest Polglase (art director), Feild M. Gray (associate); Renié (gowns); Richard Van Hessen (recording); Desmond Marquette (editor)

Song: "I'm from the City" (Hal Raynor)

Release date: April 22, 1938 (Palace Theater)

Run time: 75 minutes

With June Travis and Joe Penner

Synopsis

Dim-witted bank teller Wilbur Meely (Joe Penner) is elated because he has won a mobile home. The Meelys have no car to go with a trailer, but nevertheless he hauls it home to his wife Carol (Lucille Ball)—who orders him out to sleep in it alone. That night, bandits break into the bank, then hijack the trailer with Wilbur in it for their getaway. News reports tell Wilbur that he has become the main suspect in the robbery. Frank (Bradley Page), the brains of the gang, convinces him that his trailer hitched on to their car, and that they will help him evade the authorities. A frightened Wilbur contacts Carol.

Wilbur and the thieves continue on the road. During a rest stop, Wilbur helps Judy Daniels (June Travis), an heiress on the run to keep from marrying a title by way of a phony aristocrat named Pierre (Fritz Feld). The police find her, and she is taken home to her parents. Upon learning Judy's identity, Frank decides she would make an ideal hostage. They go after her, telling Wilbur that Judy *must* be saved from Pierre.

Elsewhere, Carol travels by train to rescue her husband. By chance, she meets Pierre onboard and latches on to him in order to shake police who are trailing her to lead them to Wilbur. Carol goes with Pierre to the Daniels estate. Wilbur also arrives there for Judy. Desperate to escape Pierre, Judy insists that Wilbur take her away, not knowing he is in the company of a trio of thugs. A ransom note is sent to her father—and Wilbur manages to send along with it a case containing the stolen bank funds.

Carol learns the location of the hunted trailer. The clumsy warden she brings with her bungles the rescue and makes them all the crooks' captives. More officers follow, and a high-speed chase ensues. Frank and his henchmen abandon the trailer. It perilously descends a mountain until finally smashing into a mass of hay. The cops catch the criminals. Thanks to Wilbur, the bank money is safe and he rejoices in the arms of his proud wife.

Notes and Comments

Joe Penner's inane brand of comedy made him one of radio's top performers during the '30s. The former vaudevillian—known for the catchphrase, "You Wanna Buy a Duck?"—forayed into films at Paramount in 1934 before moving to RKO three years later.

On Sunday evenings in 1938, Lucille could be heard on CBS Radio's top-rated variety program, *The Phil Baker Show*. She also performed on Jack Haley's *Wonder Show*. Listeners, one of whom was CBS's own Joe Penner, loved what Lucille brought to the shows. As she was also under contract to RKO, he requested that she be cast in his next picture, *Go Chase Yourself.*

Carol takes an urgent call from her hostage husband.

"The plot is an intricate one and the gags and lines are thoroughly amusing. Penner has been given substantial support. Lucille Ball, Richard Lane, Fritz Feld, June Travis, Tom Kennedy and Bradley Page all help to make the picture exciting and entertaining."

—*New York Daily News*

"The piece doesn't make much sense, nor was it supposed to, but it's funny if you're in the mood for simple-minded farce. There are plenty of gags, an exciting chase, and a plot of sorts that was made to order for the Penner personality. . . . The tall, blond and decorative Lucille Ball [as Wilbur's wife] checks in a thoroughly diverting performance."

—*New York Evening Journal*

"With the help of a bright script and a couple of experienced gagmen, vacuous Joe Penner has managed to turn out an amusing picture at last. . . . a lively bit of nonsense in much the style of the old feature comedies with Harold Lloyd, Buster Keaton and Harry Langdon."

—*New York Times*

Scheduled for production in February 1938, the picture was directed by Edward F. Cline, who was a Mack Sennett graduate and frequent collaborator with Buster Keaton in the early '20s. Penner was the star, but Lucille played her first female lead with assurance. She had to—that was part of domineering housewife Carol Meely's character. By making the most of a part that was hardly ideal, Lucille proved to studio executives that she warranted lead roles.

Go Chase Yourself was completed March 14, 1938. Of Penner's first three movies for RKO, this was his first hit. Screenwriters Paul Yawitz and Bert Granet (later a Desilu producer) succeeded in transferring Penner's appeal over the airwaves to the movie screen with a mix of slapstick and the comic's signature lamebrain humor. The picture briefly featured Hal Raynor's song "I'm from the City," from which Penner's next film took its title. In October 1938, Lucille was announced to star opposite him again in a picture called *Glamour Boy #2*, but *Go Chase Yourself* would be their only film together.

Lucille took her rise in status and joined the throng of actresses interviewed for *Gone with the Wind* after producer David O. Selznick asked the studios to send over their Scarlett O'Hara contenders. She did not take it seriously for a moment, but went around to Selznick's office about a month after finishing *Go Chase Yourself*.

The Affairs of Annabel

An RKO-Radio Picture (1938)

Cast: Jack Oakie (Lanny Morgan); Lucille Ball (Annabel Allison); Ruth Donnelly (Josephine); Bradley Page (Howard Webb); Fritz Feld (Vladimir); Thurston Hall (Major); Elisabeth Risdon (Mrs. Fletcher); Granville Bates (Mr. Fletcher); James Burke (Detective Muldoon); Lee Van Atta (Robert Fletcher); Anthony Warde (Bailey); Edward Marr (Martin); Leona Roberts (Mrs. Hurley)

Credits: Lou Lusty (producer); Ben Stoloff (director); Bert Granet and Paul Yawitz (screenplay), from story by Charles Hoffman; Russell Metty (photography); Douglas Travers (montage); Roy Webb (musical director); Van Nest Polglase (art director), Al Herman (associate); Darrell Silvera (set decoration); Renié (gowns); Earl A. Wolcott (recording); Jack Hively (editor)

Release date: September 9, 1938 (Palace Theater)

Run time: 68 minutes

Synopsis

Movie star Annabel Allison (Lucille Ball) needs publicity to revive her troubled career. Envisioning sensational headlines, her press agent, Lanny Morgan (Jack Oakie), puts her in prison to study life behind bars. The stunt backfires, and he nearly loses his job, but in no time, Lanny has another brainstorm inspired by Annabel's next picture, *The Maid and the Man*. He gets her a job as a domestic to gain experience for her role.

In the Fletcher residence lives an eccentric inventor (Thurston Hall), Mr. and Mrs. Fletcher, and their love-starved son, Robert (Lee Van Atta). The family does not recognize "Mary" and with substantial help from Lanny, she weathers her first day passably. The real trouble begins when guests of the Fletchers, Bailey (Anthony Warde) and Martin (Edward Marr), are exposed as criminals. They hold Annabel and the family hostage in the house while plotting out their next move.

At the studio, *The Maid and the Man* is shelved. Lanny tells Annabel that the stunt is called off, but when she says she "can't" leave, he smells

Cinema queen Annabel flanked by her press agent and her studio boss.

"Lucille Ball is practically a beginner, and a right good sport—besides which she has it on many movie mighties when it comes to looks. The gal should go places. . . . Not a big picture—'The Affairs of Annabel'—but we bet you'll want to see the sequel."

—*New York Post*

"First-rate comedy, speedily paced and acted with considerable spirit, brings back Jack Oakie in an amusing role and launches Lucille Ball to top billing that's justified by a good performance. . . . Much of the fun comes from Ben Stoloff's good direction. Production loses nothing in its modest settings which are adequate and the film bears the mark of good showmanship."

—*Variety*

"A promising first [of RKO's Annabel series] in a light farce vein, with some flip players in it. . . . with the help of a smartly written script, they have created an amusing trifle about a movie actress and a press agent with a svengali complex. . . . Miss Ball, who is rapidly becoming one of our brightest comediennes, plays it broadly and without a disruptive trace of whimsy."

—*New York Times*

trouble. After finding out dangerous men are holding her captive, Lanny and studio writers cook up a scheme to save her that involves a hundred extras dressed as police officers to scare the criminals.

Finally, the real cops arrive on the scene. Bailey and Martin make a run for it, using Annabel as a shield. Recalling her self-defense training, she turns the tables on the

Fortunately, the Fletchers do not connect the face of the new maid with the one on the cover of their latest issue of *Photoplay*.

crooks and they are arrested. Headlines around the globe declare Annabel a heroine. Her career is revitalized. Lanny has one more trick up his sleeve when the title of her new movie becomes *The Diamond Smuggler*. An unwitting and enraged Annabel bawls Lanny out as she is hauled off to prison as a suspected jewel thief!

Notes and Comments

The Affairs of Annabel marked a few significant firsts in Lucille's career. It provided her first starring role, her first title character, and was the first of a projected series in which she was to be showcased. Outside of Metro's *Andy Hardy*s, most film series of this period were mysteries and/or crime dramas; Fox had *Charlie Chan* and *Mr. Moto*, Warners had *Torchy Blane* and *Dead End Kids*, Paramount had *Bulldog Drummond*, MGM had the *Thin Man*. Not to be outdone, RKO followed the trend this year by initiating *The Saint* detective pictures, but they also made plans to launch a comedy series with their funniest female contract player, Lucille Ball.

Lucille and "moon-faced" comic actor Jack Oakie had supported Lily Pons in *That Girl from Paris* the previous year. They did not share many scenes in the film but showed potential as a comedy team. Lucille got the better of her co-star, a known scene-stealer, when they practiced the scene in which Annabel demonstrates her judo training on him. Lucille had taken a lesson to make it convincing but, in her diligence, ended up landing Oakie on his head in rehearsals. Angry perhaps, but undoubtedly embarrassed, the actor got to his feet and tottered off the set.

Go Chase Yourself co-writers Bert Granet and Paul Yawitz came up with a delightful screenplay based on Charles Hoffman's story "The Menial Star." Advance audience reception to the film was so positive that Lee Marcus, head of the B-picture unit, felt secure in producing follow-ups, and announced that the misadventures of Annabel and her agent would continue as a series.

The Affairs of Annabel was in production from May 23 until mid-June 1938. Lucille was endearingly dizzy as the victim of Oakie's hare-brained schemes in this Hollywood satire in the spirit of the Jean Harlow classic *Bombshell* (1933). It was also finely acted by cast members from Oakie to Lee Van Atta (Annabel's adolescent admirer), Elisabeth Risdon, Granville Bates, and Thurston Hall, who made up the nutty Fletcher household, to Ruth Donnelly, Bradley Page, and Fritz Feld as the studio personnel.

Lucille's hair and makeup as Annabel was the most flattering she yet had worn. The hair was darkened and parted in the middle. She modeled her look after Joan Bennett, who donned a brunette wig over her famously blonde hair this year for the movie *Trade Winds*. Bennett liked the color so much that she kept her own hair that way for the rest of her career. Lucille maintained it for about two years and also looked to Bennett for fashion tips. Lucille later said, "I sort of built my career as a Joan Bennett look-alike, hopefully. I admired her. I met her at RKO, and she was very nice to me." They both attracted producer-screenwriter Gene Markey, whom Bennett married in 1932 and Lucille dated in 1938, shortly after the couple separated. Incidentally, the next year Markey married Hedy Lamarr, the star who first made raven tresses with the mid-part the rage of Hollywood.

Annabel takes her judo lessons from Dr. Rubnick (Maurice Cass).

A judo demonstration performed a tad too earnestly caused headaches for Jack Oakie offscreen as well as on.

Room Service

An RKO-Radio Picture (1938)

Cast: Groucho Marx (Gordon Miller); Chico Marx (Harry Binelli); Harpo Marx (Faker); Lucille Ball (Christine); Ann Miller (Hilda); Frank Albertson (Leo Davis); Donald MacBride (Gregory Wagner); Cliff Dunstan (Joseph Gribble); Philip Loeb (Timothy Hogarth); Philip Wood (Simon Jenkins); Alexander Asro (Sasha); Charles Halton (Dr. Glass)

Credits: Pandro S. Berman (producer); William A. Seiter (director); Morrie Ryskind (screenplay), from play by John Murray and Allan Boretz, as produced by George Abbott; J. Roy Hunt (photography); Roy Webb (musical director); Van Nest Polglase (art director), Al Herman (associate); Philip Loeb (assistant to director); Darrell Silvera (set decoration); Renié (gowns); John L. Cass (recording); James Anderson (assistant director); George Crone (editor)

Release date: September 30, 1938 (Rivoli Theater)

Run time: 78 minutes

Synopsis

Gordon Miller (Groucho Marx) and the cast of his play, *Hail and Farewell*, have taken over the White Way Hotel. Supervising director Gregory Wagner (Donald MacBride) demands that their $1,200 bill be paid at once. Miller and his friends Binelli (Chico Marx) and Faker (Harpo Marx) prepare to skip out. Then Miller's girlfriend, Christine (Lucille Ball), arrives with news that she has found a backer for the show, so they can pay the hotel. Now the boys have to stay to keep an appointment with the backer in the morning, but they can't stay unless they pay, and they can't pay unless they stay and see the backer.

As Christine: office secretary, part-time actress, and Groucho Marx's sweetheart.

With Groucho (whose role was originated by Sam Levene), Harpo, and Chico—after polishing off a feast following enforced starvation in the hotel room, Christine arrives with papers regarding their backer.

Hail and Farewell author Leo Davis (Frank Albertson) turns up, and the boys hatch a scheme. Davis comes down with a homemade case of measles. As long as he is "sick," they cannot be put out of their room. The next morning, a Mr. Jenkins (Philip Wood) comes through with a check for Miller. But with Wagner kicking up a fuss, it seems like a bad investment, and the panicky Jenkins decides to stop payment. Wagner does not know this and allows Miller to draw against the check for the time being. This turns *Wagner* into Miller's backer.

On opening night, Wagner finds out about the check. The boys need to stall him from having them arrested until the show is over. Davis supposedly attempts suicide, and they spend an hour and a half trying to revive him. Following an extended farewell dirge, Faker is driven to the same dramatic end. Afterwards, Miller takes Wagner to catch the end of *Hail and Farewell*. He faints from shock when Faker appears as an actor on stage and he finds Davis enjoying the performance with his fiancée, Hilda (Ann Miller).

Notes and Comments

A record-setting $225,000 was spent by RKO on the screen rights to *Room Service*. The John Murray-Allen Boretz play had a run of five hundred

Reviews

" . . . the Marx Brothers superimpose characteristic Marxian madness upon a play already loaded with laughs. The mixture does not bring about the best possible results. . . . Groucho's mustache and rolling eyes are footnotes in phoniness. And at the same time the demands of the dramatic role prevent Groucho from reaching his own best levels of insanity."
—*New York Post*

"As comic pictures go, this ranks certainly above average; it has enough of the Marxian note for that. As Marx Brothers movies go, however, it is a minor effort. . . . There is a sick-bed scene followed by a wake which will tickle you, and there are spasms of good Marx byplay, but, as I say, no moments that blow the roof off."
—*New Yorker*

"While there may be some question about the play's being a perfect Marx vehicle, there can be none about its being a thoroughly daffy show. The White Way Hotel, where three producers are hanging around on a shoestring, remains a place where anything can happen, and usually does."
—*New York Times*

" . . . the change of pace is a good idea and, basically, the Marxes have a more staple [sic] story structure upon which to hang their buffoonery. . . . There are a number of highlight sequences punctuating the comedy [making] for a succession of strong laugh interludes."
—*Variety*

With Groucho, Chico, Ann Miller, and Harpo

performances on Broadway beginning in May 1937. Several members of the cast made it into Hollywood's version: Donald MacBride, Cliff Dunstan, Philip Wood, Alexander Asro, and Philip Loeb, each in their original roles with the exception of Loeb, who was replaced by Chico Marx. The play within the story was titled *Godspeed*—the movie changed it to *Hail and Farewell*, which was considered more permissible.

In 1938, the Marx Brothers' latest (and most financially successful) films, *A Night at the Opera* and *A Day at the Races*, had been made under the guidance of Irving Thalberg. After the producer's death in 1936, they lost their great champion at MGM. Zeppo Marx negotiated a lucrative deal for his brothers and they moved to RKO for their eighth picture. In *Room Service*, for the first time the Marx Brothers played stage characters they did not originate. The play was readjusted to suit their distinctive characteristics, but the outcome worked neither as a straight comedy nor entirely as a Marx vehicle, and *Room Service* failed at the box office. Groucho later said, "We've got to originate the characters and the situations ourselves. Then we can do them. Then they're us. But we can't do gags and play characters that aren't ours."

Though the Marx Brothers were considered to be "a wee bit soberer" (*New York Times*) than usual, the film was still brimming with lunacy, leaving very little for Lucille to do but run in and out of scenes looking beautiful but curiously less expressive. Ann Miller, coming off of *You Can't Take it with You*, was the other femme of the story. In her memoirs, Miller recalled that Lucille played a significant role in bringing her into movies: Ann was working in a club in San Francisco when Lucille arrived one night accompanied by Benny Rubin, an RKO talent scout. They both loved Miller's act. Lucille suggested that Rubin arrange a screen test for her and this led to a long-term contract with the studio.

A year later, Miller found herself making this film with Lucille and trying to cope with the off-screen pranks of the Marx Brothers. Asked in an interview years later about the making of *Room Service* with the Brothers, what instantly came to Lucille's mind was when the trio shocked some visiting priests and nuns by taking their clothes off on set!

In 1944, *Room Service* was remade and set to music, with Frank Sinatra and Gloria DeHaven, as *Step Lively*.

Christine, Faker, and Wagner think all their troubles are over after receiving a millionaire's check.

With her favorite Marx, Harpo

Annabel Takes a Tour

An RKO-Radio Picture (1938)

Cast: Jack Oakie (Lanny Morgan); Lucille Ball (Annabel Allison); Ruth Donnelly (Josephine); Bradley Page (Howard Webb); Ralph Forbes (Viscount Ronald River-Clyde); Frances Mercer (Natalie Preston); Donald MacBride (Thompson); Alice White (Marcella); Pepito (Poochy); Chester Clute (Pitcairn); Jean Rouverol (Laura Hampton); Clare Verdera (Viscountess River-Clyde); Edward Gargan (Longshoreman)

Credits: Lee Marcus (executive producer); Lou Lusty (producer); Lew Landers (director); Bert Granet and Olive Cooper (screenplay), from story by Joe Bigelow and Bert Granet, characters created by Charles Hoffman; Russell Metty (photography); Russell Bennett (musical director); Van Nest Polglase (art director), Albert D'Agostino (associate); Darrell Silvera (set decoration); Renié (gowns); Earl A. Wolcott (recording); Harry Marker (editor)

Release date: November 11, 1938 (Palace Theater)

Run time: 67 minutes

Lanny's hare-brained schemes are nothing but trouble for Annabel and the studio folk—no wonder he's always in hot water.

Synopsis

Fed up with scheming press agent Lanny Morgan (Jack Oakie), screen queen Annabel Allison (Lucille Ball) has him fired by the studio for the umpteenth time and then rehired just in time to accompany her on a publicity junket. As they reach Chicago, Lanny is back to his old antics. He has Annabel fall through a trap door on stage to gain public sympathy, a painful stunt carried out to no avail, as the story is sidelined in the papers by news of her rival Natalie Preston's (Frances Mercer) romance with a marquis.

At once, Annabel decides she wants her name linked with some nobleman. When she finds out she is staying in the same hotel as celebrated romance author Viscount Ronald River-Clyde (Ralph Forbes), she makes him her objective. Lanny helps bring them together, but before long, Annabel declares that their love is not to be tainted by publicity. What she does not know is that River-Clyde is already married and is being seen with her in hopes of boosting his book sales. Blissfully ignorant, Annabel thinks she has found true love and decides to quit show business.

Never at a loss for ideas, Lanny dreams up a plan to get Annabel back to Hollywood. That night, as she makes a farewell to films speech at her premiere with "Ronny" at her side, Lanny has Annabel's stage-struck manicurist storm the stage posing as the Viscount's wife. Just as Annabel recognizes her, his real wife shows up. When she finds out he was only using her for publicity, Annabel comes to the conclusion that Hollywood is where she belongs. The troupe heads back to Tinseltown for movies, mayhem, and certainly more misadventures.

Notes and Comments

In the second *Annabel* offering, originally called *Annabel Takes a Trip*, Lucille hit the road with Jack Oakie to find mischief in the Windy City. Lou Lusty again produced, but Lew Landers directed this time. Stalwarts Lucille and Landers were on what would be their sixth and eighth 1938 release, respectively. Within

Annabel asks Lanny to ride in the baggage car with her precious pup.

Reviews

"There is sparkle and zest to the comedy passages which are enlivened by snappy dialog. Picture rolls at a fast clip with no dull moments, and maintains quality set by first of the series. . . . Miss Ball handles assignment of the film star in capable fashion. . . . Direction of Lew Landers is at a steady gait, and his motivation and spacing of dialog is effective."
—*Variety*

"While it is unlikely that any publicity agent ever got himself as far out on a limb, or as often, as Annable's [sic] Lanny Morgan, the burlesque on some of the tricks of the trade provides audiences with a lot of fun. . . . Oakie and Miss Ball are well paired for comedy, besides which Miss Ball is extremely easy to look at and a capable little actress."
—*New York Daily News*

"In the field of catch-as-catch-can comedy the current exhibit is well above average, although the field is one in which, generally speaking, the average is well below average. Even in admittedly secondary pictures, however, Jack Oakie of the bacony cheeks, remains one of the screen's first comedians, and Lucille Ball still shows to advantage as one of the more attractive of colloquial comediennes."
—*New York Times*

With Ruth Donnelly, Jack Oakie, Donald MacBride, Bradley Page, and Pepito aboard a runaway train car.

twenty years, the director churned out well over one hundred low-budget movies.

Annabel Takes a Tour was Lucille's last picture with Jack Oakie, whose off-screen personality was known to resemble his brash onscreen persona. He was notorious for trying to upstage his co-stars. The two were friends off the set, however. They had fun making the *Annabel* films together, and a few years later Oakie helped newlyweds Lucille and Desi find a dream house near his own in the San Fernando Valley.

Cecil Kellaway, who went on to become a well-known character actor (and one of Lucille's *Easy to Wed* co-stars), played a small part as the Viscount's publisher in the film. The Viscount himself was portrayed by one of Lucille's old flames, British actor Ralph Forbes. They had been an item in 1934, but the romance had long since ended. Since their relationship, Forbes had married and divorced actress Heather Angel. Of Lucille's beaux of this period, she was the most serious about director Al Hall.

With her hair at its darkest yet and modeling the most glamorous wardrobe of her early period in B movies, Lucille was stunning in *Annabel Takes a Tour*. Despite its promising beginning, this entry saw the curtain come down on her first series. The follow-up to *The Affairs of Annabel* was put into production in August 1938 and completed on September 1. It was another funny, well-paced screwball spoof on Hollywood, but it did not match the financial success of its predecessor. *Annabel* never got a chance to recoup the loss after Jack Oakie raised his asking price to $50,000 per picture. Rather than increase the budget allotted to each installment, RKO pulled the plug on the series. Oakie left the studio, took a year off, and then moved to Fox.

Lucille on the other hand, was kept very busy. She advanced to starring roles during her seven 1938 films, each of them comedies. Though short-lived, the *Annabel* series advanced Lucille as a comedienne and firmly established her with the minor but affectionate title of Queen of the Bs. Other stock company actresses at RKO at this time that she reigned above were Anne Shirley, Frances Mercer, Ann Miller, Wendy Barrie, Lupe Velez, Sally Eilers, and Joan Fontaine.

Viscount "Ronny" goes "wading" in a Chicago hotel room as an ever-bemused Annabel contemplates quitting Hollywood for marriage to the publicity-minded romance novelist.

Annabel prepares to make a startling, albeit brief, personal appearance.

Next Time I Marry

An RKO-Radio Picture (1938)

Cast: Lucille Ball (Nancy Crocker-Fleming); James Ellison (Anthony J. Anthony); Lee Bowman (Georgi De Volknac); Granville Bates (H. E. Crocker); Mantan Moreland (Tilby); Elliot Sullivan (Red); Murray Alper (Joe)

Credits: Lee Marcus (executive producer); Cliff Reid (producer); Garson Kanin (director); John Twist and Helen Meinardi (screenplay), from story by Thames Williamson; Russell Metty (photography); Roy Webb (musical director); Van Nest Polglase (art director), Albert D'Agostino (associate); Renié (gowns); John L. Cass (recording); Jack Hively (editor)

Release date: December 1, 1938 (Palace Theater)

Run time: 65 minutes

Synopsis

In her father's will is the provision that Nancy Crocker-Fleming (Lucille Ball) must marry a "plain American" in order to inherit the family millions, and this is rigidly enforced by her guardian, Uncle Crocker (Granville Bates). In accordance with the will, Nancy weds the first free American she finds, Anthony J. Anthony (James Ellison), planning to obtain a quick divorce so she can then marry the gold-digging "Count" Georgi De Volknac (Lee Bowman).

When the press learns of the heiress's marriage, the story becomes front-page news, and Anthony is branded the Cinderella Man. In order to salvage his reputation, Anthony must go to Reno and file for divorce before Nancy does. To make certain she won't beat him to it, he locks her in his trailer. Pursued by newshounds, Nancy, Anthony, and his faithful Great Dane begin a raucous westward road trip.

After being "kidnapped" for a cross-country trek to Reno, Nancy's only change of clothes is Anthony's best suit. She later adds his hat to this ensemble and is mistaken for a teenaged boy. In the pictured scene, Nancy must put up a good fight for her dinner. Lucille said that this memorable "horse-sized" Great Dane "just couldn't get enough of me." In his enthusiasm, he would jump up and knock her down during the filming of their scenes together.

Just as their tempers cool and Nancy and Anthony warm to each other, Georgi catches up with them to reclaim his gold mine (i.e. Nancy). To Nancy's distress, newspapers turn up with stories that Anthony has another wife stashed away. Because of the rumors, she goes along with a plan of Georgi's to beat Anthony to Reno. Anthony is a step ahead of them.

"Running Away from Marriage . . . She Ran into Love!" ran the tagline.

He continues the journey alone, with Nancy and Georgi in hot pursuit, until they all arrive in Reno on the same day. There it is discovered that the story about Anthony's other woman was false. At Georgi's urging, Nancy files for divorce, but she no longer wishes to proceed with it.

When Nancy goes to court to withdraw her petition, Uncle Crocker arrives with news that he has had her marriage annulled so that she would be ineligible to collect her inheritance and thus be protected from Georgi. Nancy is outraged over losing Anthony. Frantic, she hatches a scheme for them to be remarried. Anthony knows what she is up to, but willingly plays along.

Notes and Comments

The formula of a beautiful heiress whose heedless ways are subdued by an average guy with above-average patience (and looks), became a favorite in screen comedies of the '30s after *It Happened One Night* swept the 1934 Oscars. When *Next Time I Marry* was released, it played at New York's Palace Theater on a double bill with another RKO comedy that utilized this theme, *The Mad Miss Manton*, starring Barbara Stanwyck and Henry Fonda.

Broadway director and former actor Garson Kanin came under contract to Samuel Goldwyn in 1937 wanting to direct a movie. With no such opportunities forthcoming after several months, he moved to RKO and triumphed in his

"John Twist, the author (with the aid of Miss Helen Meinardi) has given it plenty of twist; Mr. Kanin really gets his teeth into it. And of course there is Miss Ball—the former lanky and glass-eyed comedienne—who has prettied herself up, put her eyebrows in the wrong place and everything. . . . the members of its cast [acquit] themselves with class A charm and gusto. In search of an un-qualified superlative, we can confidently say that 'Next Time I Marry' is the best picture to open on a double bill this year."

—New York Times

"Mr. James Ellison, who plays the husband delightfully, and Mr. Lee Bowman, who is an amusing rival, cooperate with the sprightly Miss Ball in making 'Next Time I Marry' a jaunty little light comedy . . . Miss Ball has individuality and wears smart clothes exceptionally well. She's a very interesting addition to Hollywood's roster of madcap heiresses."

—New York Daily News

"All the slightly mad movies of the past season could be rolled into one bolt of celluloid—and the result wouldn't be quite so much daffy slapstick as is included in 'Next Time I Marry' . . . Lucille Ball is as screwy and spoiled as any of Hollywood's poor little rich gals."

—New York Post

With James Ellison, as newlyweds Mr. and Mrs. Anthony J. Anthony. Lucille lamented to an interviewer at the time her unpleasant memory of shooting a similar scene for this film, out of doors in scorching weather wearing a fur coat.

directorial debut with the sleeper *A Man to Remember*. Before that film was released and proven a success, Kanin was assigned another small production, *Next Time I Marry*, which he constructed into what was called one of the finest and most entertaining program comedies of 1938. He soon was the studio's hottest young director, having gone directly into *The Great Man Votes* with John Barrymore and then *Bachelor Mother* with Ginger Rogers—just a few among many directing and writing achievements Kanin's career would include.

Lucille, meanwhile, received top billing for the first time playing one of the dizzy heiresses that ran rampant in the '30s screwball genre. It was a part once intended for Miriam Hopkins. Her leading man this time was James Ellison, who had gained a following as a movie cowboy playing William Boyd's sidekick in several *Hopalong Cassidy* movies. Lee Bowman, who played the phony count, was the original George Cugat (later renamed Cooper) of Lucille's radio series, *My Favorite Husband*; they performed the pilot together, but thereafter he was replaced by Richard Denning.

Next Time I Marry was originally named *Trailer Romance*, but fortunately that was changed just prior to release. Thomas Williamson's story was adapted by John Twist and Helen Meinardi with some punching up by Dudley Nichols (who this year also wrote *Carefree* and *Bringing Up Baby*). Outdoor scenes were shot in the San Fernando Valley. The picture went into production on September 19, was completed on October 8, 1938, and became RKO's final offering of the year. Its wacky plot was admittedly familiar, but *Next Time I Marry* featured many hilarious moments and was enhanced by an enthusiastic cast and Kanin's lively direction.

This formal version of the lead characters' marriage was not played out onscreen, but was staged in publicity stills for *Next Time I Marry*.

The bridesmaid at far left is Lucille's own cousin Cleo.

Beauty for the Asking

An RKO-Radio Picture (1939)

Cast: Lucille Ball (Jean Russell); Patric Knowles (Denny Williams); Donald Woods (Jeffrey Martin); Frieda Inescort (Flora Barton-Williams); Inez Courtney (Gwen Morrison); Leona Maricle (Eve Harrington); Frances Mercer (Patricia Wharton); Whitney Bourne (Peggy Ponsby); George Andre Beranger (Cyril); Kay Sutton (Miss Whitman); Ann Evers (Lois Peabody)

Credits: Lee Marcus (executive producer); B. P. Fineman (producer); Glenn Tryon (director); Doris Anderson and Paul Jarrico (screenplay), from stories by Edmund L. Hartman and Grace Norton and Adele Buffington; Frank Redman (photography); Douglas Travers (montage); Frank Tours (musical director); Van Nest Polglase (art director), Carroll Clark (associate); Darrell Silvera (set decoration); Edward Stevenson (gowns); Stanley Cooley (recording); George Crone (editor)

Release date: February 9, 1939 (Palace Theater)

Run time: 68 minutes

Synopsis

Jean Russell's (Lucille Ball) three-year romance with Denny Williams (Patric Knowles) is brought to a heartbreaking end when he marries a ten-million-dollar pot of gold named Flora Barton (Frieda Inescort). Lifting Jean's spirits, however, is her faith in a cold cream she has developed, and she gives this work her complete attention.

To give the product a compelling buildup, Jean enlists the help of advertising executive Jeff Martin (Donald Woods). A benefactor he finds for her turns out to be Flora, of all people, who is unaware of Jean and Denny's romantic past. Flora seeks to establish her husband in business to quiet gossipy friends. Thus, Denny and Jean become partners in what becomes a hugely successful cosmetics line and beauty salon. The downside for Jean is Denny being a part of the business. Inevitably, he begins to pursue her, saying he does not love Flora. Meanwhile, Jeff is in love with Jean, and she confesses to him that she still loves Denny.

Lobby card for *Beauty for the Asking* with Patric Knowles and Donald Woods.

Jean and Jeff admire their respective favorite views while riding atop a double-decker bus.

To ease the situation, Jean sends Denny away on business. While he is gone, she endeavors to help Flora hold onto him by putting her through an intensive glamorizing routine. But the makeover is of no use. When Denny returns, he still wants Jean, and Jean can no longer fight her feelings.

Jean wants to relinquish the company's profits to Flora and make a fresh start with Denny. The thought of losing those millions sends the cad right back to Flora, but Flora leaves him out in the cold. The two women remain friends. Jean takes an extended vacation and returns ready to give her love to one who deserves it, Jeff.

Notes and Comments

As hinted by the onscreen writing credits, the story of *Beauty for the Asking* went through many incarnations. Grace Norton and Adele Buffington's original story was called *The Glorious Graft*, a tale about one Elizabeth Marden, whose rise to the top of the beauty profession is motivated by a custody battle for her child against the wealthy and wicked mother of her late husband. Besides the obvious nod to Elizabeth Arden, the story contained references to another remarkable

"Lucille Ball plays the young career woman with a good deal of zest and a competence in handling the dialogue that infuses the mediocre story with an atmosphere of reality usually lacking in films of its type. As a matter of fact, Miss Ball rises high enough above her material to remind us that she is of the stuff that stars are made of."

—*New York Daily News*

"Yarn moves slowly and uneventfully. Miss Ball does well with the meagre [sic] opportunities afforded her. She is one of the more promising young players on the RKO contract list but she will be a long time getting anywhere unless the stories improve."

—*Variety*

"Lucille Ball plays Jean very well, and first-rate performances are turned in by Donald Woods, Patric Knowles, Frieda Inescort and Inez Courtney. Briefly, 'Beauty for the Asking' is a well acted, amiable little offering . . . "

—*New York World-Telegram*

"Unpretentiously made, it settles down to the business of providing an hour's casual entertainment and succeeds in its purpose. Lucille Ball [is] one of Hollywood's most promising players . . . "

—*New York Evening Journal*

businesswoman, Helena Rubenstein, who like the main character in the story, began by developing a face cream and then, to market it, opened a beauty shop, which she built into an international cosmetics empire.

Edmund L. Hartmann's outline and story notes submitted in the spring of 1938 come much closer to the basic story told in the released film. His provoking title, *The Beauty Racket*, perhaps suggested an exposé about the business of manu-facturing glamour, but Hartman described a framework "within which can be developed all the glamour and interest of the Beauty Industry, and all the acidly humorous outlook of women in their relations with other women." At this stage, Lucille's character was Betty Ayres, described as a "Gail Patrick type," the role of Jeffrey Martin was

Jeff, in turn, orders her to strip and pushes her into an ad for bath salts.

expanded (then called Martin Grant; Herbert Marshall was proposed to play him), and the part of the mercenary Denny was designated for Allan Lane. More writers, including Paul Yawitz and Jeanne Bartlett, had a crack at the story before Doris Anderson and Paul Jarrico whipped the script into the shape producers Lee Marcus and B. P. Fineman approved—a love triangle set against the backdrop of the beauty profession.

B. P. Fineman had a long history with the studio. In the mid-'20s, he was the production chief of Film Booking Offices of America (FBO), which a few years later became Radio-Keith-Orpheum, better known as RKO. *Beauty for the Asking* director Glenn Tryon had been a leading man in comedies of the late '20s before turning his focus to screenwriting and directing. Lucille played the sympathetic lead in this comedy-drama dressed in her usual stylish attire and earning the usual favorable reviews. Her co-star, Patric Knowles, would also appear with her in *Five Came Back*, and go on to support a succession of monsters in Universal horror films including *The Wolf Man* (1941). Comedienne Inez Courtney (best among the supporting cast), Donald Woods, and Frieda Inescort played Lucille's trio of best pals/business partners.

The fact that much of the action of *Beauty for the Asking* took place in a salon must have pleased Lucille immensely, for she often expressed to friends that if she had not become an actress, she would have been a beautician. In fact, she adored giving permanent waves, cutting, dying, and styling hair so much that she set up a beauty salon of her own at home where friends and family became the targets of her passion for makeovers—whether or not makeovers were called for or desired.

Beauty for the Asking was completed on November 19, 1938. It had been announced the previous month that Lucille would next make another comedy with Joe Penner, *Glamour Boy #2*, but she instead went directly into *Twelve Crowded Hours*. When Penner finally went before the cameras the following summer for *The Day the Bookies Wept*, it was opposite Betty Grable.

Jean talks a worn-out Flora into continuing the exercise portion of her beauty regimen. The film's tagline read, "For love's sake, make me beautiful."

Twelve Crowded Hours

An RKO-Radio Picture (1939)

Cast: Richard Dix (Nick Green); Lucille Ball (Paula Sanders); Allan Lane (Dave Sanders); Donald MacBride (Inspector Joseph Keller); Cyrus W. Kendall (George Costain); John Arledge (Red); Granville Bates (McEwen); Bradley Page (Tom Miller); Dorothy Lee (Thelma); Addison Richards (Berquist); Murray Alper (Allen); John Gallaudet (Jimmy); Joseph de Stephani (Rovitch)

Credits: Lee Marcus (executive producer); Robert Sisk (producer); Lew Landers (director); John Twist (screenplay), from story by Garrett Fort and Peter Ruric; Nicholas Musuraca (photography); Vernon L. Walker (special effects); Roy Webb (musical director); Van Nest Polglase (art director), Albert D'Agostino (associate); Renié (gowns); Hugh McDowell, Jr. (recording); Harry Marker (editor)

Release date: February 22, 1939 (Rialto Theater)

Run time: 64 minutes

Paula, Nick, and Dave seek an escape from both the police and the bad guys.

Synopsis

Newspaper reports issued by Nick Green (Richard Dix) helped send Dave Sanders (Allan Lane) to prison for a crime he didn't commit and consequently ended Green's romance with Sanders's sister, Paula (Lucille Ball). To right the injustice, Nick arranged for Dave's parole and secures him a job driving trucks for Manhattan Aggregates. Soon, Dave is linked to another crime, thanks to the ruthless boss of a numbers gang, George Costain (Cyrus W. Kendall).

Costain has two men who tried to skip town with a satchel of his money run down by an Aggregates truck. Evidence points to Dave as sole suspect in the homicides. Nick learns the truth behind the collision and sets out to prove it. He steals and then hides Costain's loaded satchel. Next, he warns Dave and Paula that the police are after Dave. They escape Inspector Keller (Donald MacBride), but Costain traps Nick and Paula. To buy time, Nick tells Costain the money will be handed over in

Paul and Nick try to figure their way out of a tight spot with a murderous thug.

return for help in freeing Dave from suspicion. The crime boss agrees, but he has plans of his own—namely arranging to turn his truck-driving assassin on Nick and Paula.

Keeping up the pretense to stall Costain, they go to Nick's apartment to wait for someone to bring the satchel. Nick and Paula wonder what their next move will be since they know no one is coming. With Inspector Keller of no help, Paula gets hold of a gun and shoots Costain, who then stumbles out to his car and into his own trap. Following orders, the hit man pursues the car to carry out his deadly mission. Dave is cleared and by now Nick has won back Paula's heart.

Notes and Comments

Twelve Crowded Hours was the last of Lucille's eight features filmed during 1938. Asked on the set when she would be given a break she joked, "I guess I'm having it now. They're letting me sit down between scenes in this picture." One thing she liked was that her role required less maintenance than usual, as she wore the same dress in all but one scene. Production wrapped on December 14. She actually did get some time off from filming before the start of *Panama Lady* in the spring.

Reviews

"Since melodrama is seldom synonymous with probability, perhaps it should be sufficient to report that 'Twelve Crowded Hours' [is] effective thriller entertainment. But there is so much in the film that is good that one cannot but regret that more care and attention weren't given to the development of the narrative. . . . Lucille Ball is exactly what a heroine in distress should be like . . . others in the cast help to make this a fast and diverting crime film."

—*New York World-Telegram*

"[Richard Dix] skips nimbly from peril to peril, covering ground so fast we hardly had a chance to see the familiar landmarks whisk by. . . . Lucille Ball plays it with just the appropriate air of somnambulism and Mr. Kendall, as the heavy, is obviously to the manner born."

—*New York Times*

"John Twist, in designing his script, [has] concentrated on melodramatic situations and on building up nerve-wracking suspense. His system is an interesting one; it makes a stale dish palatable again. . . . Richard Dix, Cyrus Kendall, John Arledge, Allan Lane, Lucille Ball and Donald McBride [sic] add their worthy talents to those of Messrs. Twist and Landers to make 'Twelve Crowded Hours' a rousing and engrossing screen thriller."

—*Brooklyn Daily Eagle*

This fast-moving crime drama, mixed with comedy, was another Robert Sisk B, guided by Lucille's *Annabel*

director, Lew Landers. *Next Time I Marry*'s John Twist wrote a taut script from a story by Peter Ruric and

horror screenwriter Garrett Fort.

The hero of the proceedings, Richard Dix, was one of RKO's first stars. He headed the cast of the only

"Best Picture" the studio ever produced, *Cimarron* (1931), in which he also played a daring newspaper

reporter (that time he earned an Oscar nomination for his efforts). In the silent era, Dix gained notoriety in

comedies until *Cimarron* made him a brawny adventure star of the early '30s.

Cyrus W. Kendall made an imposing villain in *Twelve Crowded Hours*, one of the most prominent roles he

was ever given during a long career of playing heavies (often without billing). Dorothy Lee, seen in a minor role,

was known as the love interest in over a dozen of RKO's Wheeler and Woolsey comedies. In 1936 she withdrew

from films as the comic duo's popularity waned. She returned in a small role in *Twelve Crowded Hours* but

retired again two years later.

Lucille is both decorative and efficient as Paula Sanders. She tags along with Richard Dix through his

various schemes to combat the bad guys and ultimately comes through for them at the finish of twelve hours

crowded with action and suspense.

Panama Lady

An RKO-Radio Picture (1939)

Cast: Lucille Ball (Lucy); Allan Lane (Dennis McTeague); Steffi Duna (Cheema); Evelyn Brent (Lenore); Donald Briggs (Roy Harmon); Bernadene Hayes (Pearl); Abner Biberman (Elisha); William Pawley (Panama Bartender); Earle Hodgins (Foreman); Joe Devlin (New York Bartender)

Credits: Lee Marcus (executive producer); Cliff Reid (producer); Jack Hively (director); Michael Kanin (screenplay), from story by Garrett Fort; J. Roy Hunt (photography); Vernon L. Walker (special effects); Roy Webb (musical director); Van Nest Polglase (art director), Albert D'Agostino (associate); Edward Stevenson (costumes); Hugh McDowell, Jr. (recording); Theron Warth (editor)

Release date: June 1, 1939 (Palace Theater)

Run time: 65 minutes

With Allan Lane and Joe Devlin. McTeague comes back into Lucy's life, conjuring a world of painful memories.

Synopsis

Fired from her job in the chorus at a Panama dive called Lenore's, Lucy (Lucille Ball) seeks consolation from her aviator boyfriend, Roy (Donald Briggs). Besides finding him unsympathetic, Lucy also discovers that he is an arms smuggler, but she is trusted to keep her mouth shut and sent on her way.

The penniless Lucy returns to Lenore's, where oil prospector Dennis McTeague (Allan Lane) enters her life. She gets caught trying to steal money from him, but he allows her to repay the debt by going to work as his housekeeper instead of to jail. At his home in an isolated area of South America, Lucy must fend off the advances of her host, as well as protect herself from a jealous native girl, Cheema (Steffi Duna). As promised, she keeps house for McTeague. Pacified by her woman's touch, he begins to mind his manners.

Reviews

"Save for the presence in its cast of the lovely Lucille Ball, there is little to recommend in the tropical melodrama . . . "
—*New York World-Telegram*

"'Panama Lady is a dull, poor story that has few redeeming features. . . . [Donald Briggs] does well enough, along with Miss Brent, who's in for a bit, and Lane . . . [Miss Ball's] dramatic emoting is too far a cry from her more sprightly, recent comedy roles."
—*Variety*

"'Panama Lady,' although a bit of a tawdry drama, is another minor triumph for Lucille Ball. But it is high time RKO recognized her potentialities and put her in something more deserving of her ability than the last things she has appeared in. I don't contend that she is a Duse, but she is one of the most up-and-coming young players around. Miss Ball's interpretation [is] an honest and restrained piece of work. Even when the story runs amok in melodrama, she makes you believe in the unfortunate Lucy. . . . The picture has glimpses of good drama, snatches of very natural dialogue and spurts of suspense, but, for all that, it doesn't measure up to standard."
—*New York Daily News*

McTeague tries to persuade Lucy to remain with him. In *Twelve Crowded Hours*, Allan Lane had portrayed Lucille's brother and in *Having Wonderful Time* he was the boyfriend of one of her roommates.

Back in Panama, Roy and his fellow gunrunners get into trouble. He believes Lucy tipped off the authorities and intends to punish her. When he arrives, Lucy is ready go away with him until he attempts to jump a claim to an oil gusher recently struck by McTeague's team. He becomes violent. There is a struggle. Lucy fires a gun and Roy falls dead. McTeague arranges for the overwhelmed girl to return to America.

Unable to forget her, the now wealthy McTeague moves to New York to search for Lucy. He finds her desolate, haunted by thoughts of killing a man. He informs her that Cheema later confessed that she framed Lucy. It was her shot, not Lucy's, that killed Roy. Finally able to begin putting the memories behind her, Lucy has hope for the future with the handsome McTeague by her side.

Notes and Comments

The first Lucy character Lucille played was the dramatic lead in *Panama Lady*. It was a change of pace, since up to then she had primarily played major roles in comedies. The film was a remake of a 1932 RKO-Pathé production, *Panama Flo*, which starred Helen Twelvetrees and Charles Bickford. Michael Kanin (writer of *Woman of the Year* and brother of Garson Kanin) adapted his script from Garrett Fort's story, "The Second Shot." The director was Jack Hively, an editor on several of Lucille's films who had begun directing earlier in the year.

Panama Lady's leading man, Allan Lane, went on to make a slew of westerns for Republic Pictures (many as "Rocky" Lane). If his face is forgotten today, at least his voice is not. In the '60s, Lane provided the off-screen vocals for TV's talking horse, Mister Ed. Lucille's female co-stars in the film were Evelyn Brent and Hungarian actress and dancer Steffi Duna. The former had made her mark during the silent era. In the mid-'20s, she was an important actress at FBO—the company that became RKO—but her career peaked at Paramount later in the decade in melodramas with George Bancroft including *Underworld* (1927).

Set in Central America and the Amazon jungle, *Panama Lady* was made right at RKO studios during the spring of 1939. A four-foot-deep pool doubling for the Guayas River was the scene of an alarming incident for Lucille toward the end of filming. While she was sitting in the seaplane used in several scenes, faulty overhead wiring rained sparks onto the craft's flammable cover. Lucille instantly leapt into the water.

More sparks flew from the direction of the Production Code Administration. The Breen Office requested delicate handling of many specific ascpects of the film. A few of their main concerns revolved around the questionable nature of Lenore's, the establishment in which Lucy is employed; that the character of Cheema, the

Cheema serves up an interesting plate for the new housekeeper. Steffi Duna played a very similar role in the prestigious *Anthony Adverse*, from 1936.

native girl, must not come across as anything more than a servant in McTeague's home; and that the gentleman who approaches Lucy at the end of the film should give no suggestion that she was ever a prostitute.

Panama Lady met with terrible reviews, but on the whole, the cast was spared the critics' scorn. Lucille's film career was not moving forward in the year widely regarded as the best in American movie history, 1939. The previous fall, RKO had acquired a new corporate president, George

The scene of the most tormenting nightmare from Lucy's past.

Schaefer. Between the management shuffles that took place this year (and that would prove on-going), no one seemed overly concerned with developing Lucille into a major star. She was, however, seen as a valuable asset for the studio's low-budget films, known as a hard-working, dependable actress, and thus kept continually busy while earning a sizeable salary of $1,000 a week. Meanwhile, she made a habit of rising above middling material, and critics took up the fight for her in their reviews by consistently expressing that she was a fine actress deserving of better roles.

The housekeeper and her oil prospector boss

Five Came Back

An RKO-Radio Picture (1939)

Cast: Chester Morris (Bill Brooks); Lucille Ball (Peggy Nolan); Wendy Barrie (Anne Melhourne); John Carradine (Mr. Crimp); Allen Jenkins (Pete); Joseph Calleia (Vasquez); C. Aubrey Smith (Professor Henry Spengler); Kent Taylor (Joe); Patric Knowles (Judson Ellis); Elisabeth Risdon (Martha Spengler); Casey Johnson (Tommy Mulvaney); Dick Hogan (Larry); Pat O'Malley (Mike Mulvaney)

Credits: Lee Marcus (executive producer); Robert Sisk (producer); John Farrow (director); Jerry Cady, Dalton Trumbo, and Nathanael West (screenplay), from story by Richard Carroll; Nicholas Musuraca (photography); Vernon L. Walker (special effects); Douglas Travers (montage); Roy Webb (musical score); Van Nest Polglase (art director), Albert D'Agostino (associate); Edward Stevenson (gowns); John E. Tribby (recording); Harry Marker (editor)

Release date: July 4, 1939 (Rialto Theater)

Run time: 75 minutes

Synopsis

The Silver Queen, an airplane bound for Panama, departs with nine passengers, two pilots, and a steward on board. The motley group of passengers consists of an engaged couple, Alice Melhourne (Wendy Barrie) and Judson Ellis (Patric Knowles); professor of botany Henry Spengler (C. Aubrey Smith) and his wife Martha (Elisabeth Risdon); Vasquez (Joseph Calleia), an anarchist held under guard of Detective Crimp (John Carradine); and Tommy (Casey Johnson), a child traveling with Pete (Allen Jenkins), a warm-hearted hood. Lastly, there is Peggy Nolan (Lucille Ball), a striking young woman trying to put a troubled past behind her. She is snubbed by most of her traveling companions, who do not know what to make of her.

As the plane makes its way toward Panama they run into a tropical storm, which precipitates the accidental death of the steward (Dick Hogan). The craft is sent far off its course, but the pilots manage to bring

When Pete is killed, the group becomes aware of the fact that they are keeping company with headhunters in the jungle.

Reviews

First regarding her as a tramp, after getting to know the real Peggy, Bill comes to love and respect her.

it down safely. Professor Spengler deduces that they have landed somewhere east of the Andes. Co-pilots Bill (Chester Morris) and Joe (Kent Taylor) set about repairing the damaged plane, but this will take a few weeks. The individuals work together to try and survive until then. Their hardships bring out the best in many of them. Peggy develops a maternal instinct and looks after Tommy, and a kind spirit within Vasquez surfaces. Ellis, however, becomes a drunkard, bringing an end to his romance with the virtuous Alice.

After nearly three weeks, hostile natives make their presence known. Two of the men are killed. Upon hearing the rumble of drums rise from the jungle, Spengler warns the troop that it is a signal of headhunters who will attack when the drums cease. Bill and Joe have patched up the plane just in time. But there are high mountains to pass and the now-crippled aircraft cannot make

it with the weight of the remaining nine. Only four can go back, and the little boy, but who will it be, and how are they to decide?

One among them has nothing to lose if he does not return—Vasquez, a criminal who is to be executed. He would have been happy to remain in their "ideal community" forever. He will choose who goes—and who stays behind. As the beating of the drums comes to a standstill, it is time for his decision. Peggy, who has become a mother to little Tommy, will go, along with Bill, the once-jaded pilot who wants to begin a life with her. The other two to be saved are Alice and Joe, who have also formed a bond. One remaining twist is how the four left behind face the next few moments. Overhead, *The Silver Queen* returns to civilization with the five young survivors.

Struggling to survive the wilds of the jungle . . .

The same five clean up very nicely. Lucille is pictured with Kent Taylor, Wendy Barrie, Casey Johnson, and Chester Morris.

Chester Morris, Lucille, Allen Jenkins, John Carradine, Joseph Calleia, Patric Knowles, Elisabeth Risdon, C. Aubrey Smith, Wendy Barrie, and Kent Taylor

Jungle mud is applied to Lucille's leg before a take.

Notes and Comments

Five Came Back, an ensemble adventure drama crafted in the *Grand Hotel* mode, was not only Lucille's best film of 1939 but also one of RKO's best. She replaced her friend Ann Sothern in a sympathetic bad-girl-with-a-heart-of-gold role that placed her in the South American jungle for the second picture in a row (on the screen at least).

There were no "star" personalities among the large cast, but there were several reliable character actors, and the acting was commendable down the line. The second, and less interesting, young female character of the story was portrayed by Wendy Barrie. While considered lower on the studio's status scale than Lucille, she was another of RKO's B-picture stalwarts. As seen in *Five Came Back*, Barrie's British society heritage made her a different type than Lucille.

Five Came Back completed filming April 26, 1939, having cost approximately $225,000 to make. It opened on the Fourth of July to stellar reviews and became a surprise hit, a "sleeper" that brought attention to all involved—John Farrow as director, the writers, and the cast. As for its box-office success, the *New York Herald-Tribune* reported that the Rialto Theater was "operating on a twenty-four hour schedule to accommodate the crowds." Fondly remembered by cinephiles, the film is widely viewed as having paved the way for disaster epics of the '70s, like *Airport* and *The Poseidon Adventure*. There were several more high-profile movies of the disaster genre in the late '30s (though they dealt with natural calamities), such as *San Francisco*, *The Good Earth*, and *The Rains Came*.

Jerry Cady, Nathanael West (author of *The Day of the Locust*), and Dalton Trumbo turned out a fine script from Richard Carroll's story. Having come to RKO the previous year, Trumbo had already distinguished his writing with another acclaimed B picture, *A Man to Remember*. He soon moved on to larger-scale hits for the studio like *Kitty Foyle* and had continued success into the '40s. Later, when Trumbo was blacklisted for his communist ties and writing under pseudonyms and behind "fronts," his screenplay for *The Brave One* (1956) won the Oscar, as did his story for *Roman Holiday* (1953).

Director John Farrow would also have further triumphs in movies both as a director and writer. Seventeen years after *Five Came Back*, he attempted to repeat its success with a remake, *Back from Eternity*, but it did not generate the excitement of the original. One review called it "about as average a picture as it is possible to conceive." Swedish import Anita Ekberg stepped into Lucille's role, and Robert Ryan was the pilot she loves.

Lucille signs child actor Casey Johnson's autograph book on the set of *Five Came Back*.

Chester Morris remained memorable to Lucille for the struggle she had keeping her romantic co-star's hands in check.

That's Right—You're Wrong

An RKO-Radio Picture (1939)

Cast: Kay Kyser (as himself); Adolphe Menjou (Stacey Delmore); May Robson (Grandma); Lucille Ball (Sandra Sand); Dennis O'Keefe (Chuck Deems); Edward Everett Horton (Tom Village); Roscoe Karns (Mal Stamp); Moroni Olsen (Jonathan D. Forbes); Hobart Cavanaugh (Dwight Cook); Dorothy Lovett (Miss Cosgrave); Lillian West (Miss Brighton); Denis Tankard (Thomas); Kay Kyser's Band, featuring Ginny Simms, Harry Babbit, Sully Mason, Ish Kabibble, and "The College of Musical Knowledge"

Credits: David Butler (producer and director); William Conselman and James V. Kern (screenplay), from story by David Butler and William Conselman; Russell Metty (photography); Vernon L. Walker (special effects); George Duning (musical arrangements); Eddie Prinz (dance director); Van Nest Polglase (art director), Carroll Clark (associate); Darrell Silvera (set decoration); Edward Stevenson (gowns); Earl A. Wolcott (recording); Fred A. Fleck (assistant director); Irene Morra (editor)

Songs: "The Answer is Love" (Sam Stept and Charles Newman); "The Little Red Fox (N'ya, N'ya You Can't Catch Me)" (James V. Kern, Lew Porter, Johnny Lange, and Hy Heath); "Fit to Be Tied" (Walter Donaldson); "Happy Birthday to Love" (Dave Franklin); "Chatterbox" (Jerome Brainin and Allan Roberts)

Release date: November 29, 1939 (Loew's Criterion Theater)

Run time: 94 minutes

Synopsis

Hoping to boost a slump in ticket sales, the producers at Four Star Studios decide to turn out a surefire hit by starring radio's Kay Kyser in a film. An offer is dispatched to the bandleader. Kay reluctantly accepts only to please the jubilant boys in his band and their female singer, Ginny Simms. Once in California, Kay's worst fears are realized as, one by one, his musicians "go Hollywood."

Producer Stacey Delmore (Adolphe Menjou) is in trouble when his best writers, Village (Edward Everett Horton) and Cook (Hobart Cavanaugh), hand in a script calling for a matinee idol rather than a Kay Kyser. Unable to invent an original story suited to Kay, Delmore schemes to make him quit, telling him that Ginny will be replaced onscreen by glamour girl Sandra Sand (Lucille Ball). Kay is ready to start packing—until he begins to sense Delmore has something up his sleeve.

To teach the producer a lesson, Kay tells him that he will play the lover in the original Village and Cook script. The press have a field day with the antics of "Casanova Kyser," and Delmore is in a worse spot than ever. After viewing a disastrous screen test Kay makes with Sandra, Delmore calls off the picture, putting him in hot water with studio head Jonathan Forbes (Moroni Olsen) and clearing the way for Kay and his musicians to happily go back to "their own backyard," on the radio.

Notes and Comments

That's Right—You're Wrong introduced the "Ol' Professor" of the airwaves, Kay Kyser, and his "Kollege of Musical Knowledge" to the movies. The film was an amusing satire on Hollywood producers' efforts to recruit radio performers, and their lack of invention in constructing projects for them. Kyser portrayed himself, the famous orchestra leader host of a lively quiz program that merged offerings from his swing band, comedy, and music-related questions, complete

With Adolphe Menjou

Reviews

" . . . one of the smartest script jobs seen hereabouts in some time . . . A thoroughly amusing piece, the film romps gaily through one comedy scene after another, with several musical interludes deftly woven into the action. Mr. Kyser plays Mr. Kyser with an engaging humor . . . "
—*New York Journal-American*

" . . . a welcome variation from the usual band-leader pictures. . . . After a slow start, the picture progresses rapidly and the second half produces some really funny scenes, particularly the results of Kay's screen test. . . . May Robson, Lucille Ball, Edward Everett Horton [are] among the regular Hollywoodites who assisted Kyser in making this a topnotch comedy."
—*New York Daily Mirror*

"Story is a most glib one on which to launch Kyser's try in films . . . the maestro displays comedy ability far above the ordinary for screen newcomers in two good laugh sequences. [The screen test and the garden party] . . . The songs are all above par, put over in showmanship style by Kyser and his gang."
—*Variety*

With Kay Kyser, the bandleader and radio personality who starred in seven films. The title of this one came from the catchphrase of his radio show.

with "diplomas" (this was all illustrated in the film's final sequence). Kyser's own musicians were shown, including Harry Babbitt, Ish Kabibble, Sully Mason, and his female vocalist, Ginny Simms.

To support them, writer-producer-director David Butler cast the movies' own Adolphe Menjou (as a producer, a role in which he was completely at home), Lucille, Dennis O'Keefe, and character actors May Robson, Edward Everett Horton, and Roscoe Karns for additional comedy. Hollywood columnists Hedda Hopper and Sheilah Graham, among others, dropped by to add a touch of authenticity to the Tinseltown spoof.

1939 had been filled with melodramas for Lucille, but she was back to comedy for her final release of the year, as the glamorous movie star of *That's Right—You're Wrong*. She had a choice comedy sequence—in fact the highlight of the picture—a screen test scene in which she endeavors to make Kyser convincing as a great lover. She later worked more closely with the co-writer of the script, James V. Kern, after he became an *I Love Lucy* director (in 1955–57). Kern, who would also direct episodes of *My Three Sons* and *My Favorite Martian*, earned his first screenwriting credit with this film.

Principal photography on *That's Right—You're Wrong* took place from September until October 23, 1939. It garnered a hearty profit, which signaled that more Kay Kyser pictures were to come. He and his band would make one RKO feature a year until 1943.

The Marines Fly High

An RKO-Radio Picture (1940)

Cast: Richard Dix (Lieutenant Danny Darrick); Chester Morris (Lieutenant Jimmy Malone); Lucille Ball (Joan Grant); Steffi Duna (Teresa); John Eldredge (John Henderson); Paul Harvey (Colonel Hill); Horace MacMahon (Monk O'Hara); Dick Hogan (Corporal Haines); Robert Stanton (Lieutenant Hobbs); Ann Shoemaker (Mrs. Hill); Nestor Paiva (Fernandez); Ethan Laidlaw (Barnes); Abner Biberman (Gomez); John Sheehan (Airplane Seller)

Credits: Lee Marcus (executive producer); Robert Sisk (producer); George Nicholls, Jr. and Ben Stoloff (directors); Jerry Cady and Lt. Commander A. J. Bolton (screenplay), from story by A. C. Edington; Frank Redman (photography); Roy Webb (musical director); Louis Betancourt (native music); Van Nest Polglase (art director), Albert D'Agostino (associate); Renié (gowns); Earl A. Wolcott (recording); Frederic Knudtson (editor)

Release date: March 4, 1940 (Rialto Theater)

Run time: 68 minutes

Synopsis

A rebel leader known as "El Vengador" drives Joan Grant (Lucille Ball) off of her Central American cocoa plantation to the protection of a nearby Marine post. This places her in close proximity to her boyfriend, Lt. Danny Darrick (Richard Dix), but their relationship is jeopardized by the arrival of the romatic Lt. Jimmy Malone (Chester Morris). On top of that, Teresa (Steffi Duna), an old flame of Danny's, turns up, sending Joan into Jimmy's waiting arms.

By day the men unite in the hunt for El Vengador. By night they contend for Joan. The two escort her back to her plantation and find it overrun with comrades of El Vengador, who is found to be Henderson (John Eldredge), the foreman of Joan's ranch. Danny is knocked out, and Joan is taken captive.

The base learns who El Vengador is and that he has fled to the town of La Rita. Jimmy is sent after him, while the injured Danny must stay behind. Not wanting Jimmy to reach Joan first, Danny sets out for the town himself by plane.

Reviews

"This is a modest adventure picture without pretensions of anything but that, and so if you are adventurously inclined and admire pretty faces like that of Lucille Ball, well, why not?"

—*New York Daily Mirror*

"Long experience and good veteran records fail to keep Lieutenants Richard Dix and Chester Morris from being ambushed by an army of trite scenes and situations. . . . The principals will have to solace themselves with a 'doing as well as can be expected' because of inferior story material and poor direction."

—*New York Daily News*

" . . . this is mighty thin fare [though] Lucille Ball again demonstrates that she's an up-and-coming young actress. . . . Dialog is nearly as trite as the yarn. Frank Redman's photography is first-rate. The production is impressive, the background music always telegraphs impending developments, as if the audience didn't know."

—*Variety*

" . . . this is not a bad little adventure picture. What with shooting, flying and Marine Corps badinage, it is a fair enough vehicle for the continuance of the Richard Dix-Chester Morris friendly feud."

—*New York Post*

In La Rita, Henderson releases Joan, using her as an unwitting instrument to lead the Marines into an ambush upon entering town. Jimmy is shot. As he lies wounded, he asks Joan to marry him. To calm him, she agrees.

Overhead flies Danny and he witnesses the conflict. He picks up Joan and Jimmy and they go for reinforcements. A panicky Henderson flees La Rita. Danny spots him from the plane, shots are fired, and Henderson is killed.

Peace is restored and at the post Jimmy is on the mend. Joan has given her word to marry him, but her face shows him that Danny has her heart. With Jimmy's blessing, she runs back to Danny.

Notes and Comments

The Marines Fly High entered production in late October 1939 with George Nicholls, Jr. directing. Midway through filming, Nicholls was killed in an auto accident. Lucille had worked with the director of the folksy hit *Anne of Green Gables* once before—on *Chatterbox*. Ben Stoloff picked up where Nicholls left off.

With Richard Dix and Chester Morris

The film cast Lucille in a love triangle with Richard Dix and Chester Morris, who had already competed for the affections of a woman, first Dolores Del Rio and then Joan Fontaine, in two earlier pictures. *Panama Lady*'s native girl, Steffi Duna, resurfaced as an amorous Spanish dancer. The Hungarian-born Duna began in British cinema and then came to Hollywood, where she worked for various studios throughout the '30s before retiring from the screen in 1940. That year, she married actor Dennis O'Keefe, who appeared in her final picture, *The Girl from Havana*. *The Marines Fly High* was Lucille's second and last film with each of these three actors.

France and England declared war on Germany less than two months before the start of filming on this action yarn in which the Marine Corps comes to the rescue. It was an unpretentious diversion for audiences to enjoy on a double bill.

The Marines Fly High was Lucille's last of a string of assignments for producer Robert Sisk. He departed from RKO after George Schaefer took complete charge and continued producing at MGM. Lucille's first release of the new decade was another drama, but she would soon return to lighter fare. The new year would bring enhancement in her career and far greater still in her personal life.

From his sickbed, Jimmy presents Joan with an engagement ring. Will she or won't she accept?

As cocoa plantation owner Joan Grant

You Can't Fool Your Wife

An RKO-Radio Picture (1940)

Cast: Lucille Ball (Clara Hinklin/Mercedes Vasquez); James Ellison (Andrew Hinklin); Robert Coote (Battincourt); Virginia Vale (Sally); Emma Dunn (Mom Fields); Elaine Shepard (Peggy); William Halligan (J. R. Gillespie); Oscar O'Shea (Chaplain); Norman Mayes (Porter)

Credits: Lee Marcus (executive producer); Cliff Reid (producer); Ray McCarey (director); Jerry Cady (screenplay), from story by Richard Carroll and Ray McCarey; J. Roy Hunt (photography); Roy Webb (musical score); Van Nest Polglase (art director), Carroll Clark (associate); Edward Stevenson (gowns); Hugh McDowell, Jr. (recording); Theron Warth (editor)

Release date: May 23, 1940 (Palace Theater)

Run time: 68 minutes

Synopsis

Married five years, Andrew (James Ellison) and Clara (Lucille Ball) Hinklin are settled into a humdrum existence until Andrew's boss at the accounting firm designates him to entertain the head of the office's London branch, the happy-go-lucky Mr. Battincourt (Robert Coote). As Andrew is thrust into a world of soirees and debutantes, the Hinklin marriage suffers. Brokenhearted by evidence that Andrew has been unfaithful, Clara throws him out of the house.

Andrew moves in with Battincourt. He tries to reconcile with Clara, but all of his efforts are thwarted by his meddlesome mother-in-law (Emma Dunn). Before long, Andrew begins living it up with Battincourt. Sensing that his friend's new attitude is only a front, Battincourt intervenes to reunite the Hinklins. One look at Clara gives him a plan of action—he will turn her into the glamour girl that is hidden behind her unflattering clothes. He arranges a costume party, which Clara is to attend made up to look like the town's leading playgirl, Mercedes Vasquez (also played by Lucille).

With Robert Coote and James Ellison

Andrew tries to convince Clara that he has been faithful to her.

The night of the masquerade, Clara gets cold feet, Andrew gets wind of the scheme, and worst of all, the real Mercedes Vasquez shows up. Mistaking the masked Mercedes for his wife, Andrew plays along by flirting with her. Soon Clara arrives, also masked. After Mercedes leaves, Clara continues the deception and tests Andrew's fidelity by pretending to be Mercedes. Things go too far. They wind up at Andrew's apartment, bedtime arrives, and Andrew leans in for a kiss, signaling the time to end to the charade. Clara unmasks herself and runs home. Andrew follows to make a revelation of his own. He knew when the real Clara stepped into Mercedes's place because she neglected to remove her wedding ring! The Hinklins are quickly back in each other's arms, their romance reignited.

Notes and Comments

The second (and final) teaming of Lucille Ball and James Ellison was a farce of suspicious wives and wandering husbands that was a variation on the well-known Ferenc Molnár tale of *The Guardsman*, which had been enacted on both stage and screen by Alfred Lunt and Lynn Fontanne. In that earlier work, the roles of masquerading wife and unsuspecting husband are reversed. But actually, *You Can't Fool Your Wife* was based on a story by Richard Carroll and Ray McCarey

Reviews

"Skirting the farcical, a number of ticklish situations are met in what amounts to an entirely wholesome manner . . . The direction of Ray McCarey brings out the best in comedy values and the story [maintains] a pretty good crispness. . . . The cast is consistently good."

—*Variety*

"[Ball and Ellison] are good at comedy and it's bad that the picture lets them, as well as us, down with a climax that I thought had been put away in moth balls . . . Yet up to this commonplace ending the picture furnishes quite a few hearty laughs at the expense of an average married couple with mother-in-law trouble."

—*New York Daily News*

"The plot is fairly complicated for such a small picture. Lucille Ball [has] to don a Spanish mantilla and go in for a dual role. She manages it quite well. The cast, in fact, is the best part of the picture. Miss Ball and Mr. Ellison keep natural, even in the face of the usual high-pitched farce situations."

—*New York Sun*

Lonely Clara wonders where her husband spends his evenings.

called "The Romantic Mr. Hinklin," with a script by Jerry Cady.

This was Lucille's last picture for RKO's B-unit executive Lee Marcus and for producer Cliff Reid. Through reorganization, both exited the studio over the next several months. Storywriter Ray McCarey also directed the film. Brother of the celebrated director Leo McCarey, he had worked with Lucille previously on the Three Stooges short *Three Little Pigskins* during her tenure at Columbia in 1934. In the top supporting roles were Robert Coote (who would play a small part in her 1947 film *Lured*) and Emma Dunn (a regular in the *Dr. Kildare* movies).

You Can't Fool Your Wife gave Lucille two characters to portray—a dowdy housewife and an Argentine glamour girl. She studied for the film with a linguistics coach who taught her a few words of Spanish and helped her affect the requisite accent for the Mercedes Vasquez scenes. She finished principal photography on February 20, 1940.

Near the time *You Can't Fool Your Wife* was made, early in 1940, Lucille captured the imagination of the young "genius" on the studio lot, Orson Welles, who had been signed by the new corporate president, George Schaefer, in the summer of 1939.

With James Ellison

One of the productions Welles wanted to make early on, but that never took form, was *The Smiler with a Knife*. He later described it as "a farce about a very likeable, handsome, extremely attractive young man who's planning to be the dictator of America . . . he comes to a bad end, but not until [the girl's] been a department store Santa Claus and a lot of other things." Welles wanted Lucille to star, playing a girl who is on to the would-be tyrant's game and trying to figure out the best way to bring him down. Welles could not come to terms with RKO about casting, but at any rate he had already begun developing *Citizen Kane*. While Lucille seemed locked in the "up and coming" stage

Lucille makes a visitor welcome to the set.

in modest films, she was nevertheless attracting a great deal of attention from talents who saw her capable of a far greater future than her RKO bosses did. Scripts for the studio's more prominent comedies were earmarked for Ginger Rogers, whom they also kept busy making several films per year.

As Clara, in the beguiling disguise of Mercedes

Dance, Girl, Dance

An RKO-Radio Picture (1940)

Cast: Maureen O'Hara (Judy O'Brien); Louis Hayward (Jimmy Harris); Lucille Ball (Bubbles); Virginia Field (Elinor Harris); Ralph Bellamy (Steve Adams); Maria Ouspenskaya (Madame Basilova); Mary Carlisle (Sally); Katherine Alexander (Miss Olmstead); Edward Brophy (Dwarfie); Walter Abel (Judge); Harold Huber (Hoboken Gent); Ernest Truex (Bailey #1); Chester Clute (Bailey #2); Lorraine Krueger (Dolly); Lola Jensen (Daisy); Emma Dunn (Mrs. Simpson); Sidney Blackmer (Puss in Boots); Vivian Fay (The Ballerina); Ludwig Stossel (Caesar); Erno Verebes (Fitch)

Credits: Harry E. Edington (executive producer); Erich Pommer (producer); Dorothy Arzner (director); Tess Slesinger and Frank Davis (screenplay), from story by Vicki Baum; Russell Metty (photography); Vernon L. Walker (special effects); Edward Ward (musical director); Ernst Matray (dance director); Van Nest Polglase (art director), Al Herman (associate); Darrell Silvera (set decoration); Edward Stevenson (gowns); Hugh McDowell, Jr. (recording); James H. Anderson (assistant director); Robert Wise (editor)

Songs: "Morning Star," "Jitterbug Bite" (Edward Ward, Chester Forrest, and Robert Wright); "Mother, What Do I Do Now?" (Forrest and Wright)

Release date: August 30, 1940 (Palace Theater)

Run time: 90 minutes

Synopsis

Judy (Maureen O'Hara) and Bubbles (Lucille Ball) are members of a struggling dance troupe, both ambitious, but with very different goals in mind. Judy has a gift for ballet, while Bubbles has a more seductive style that puts her in greater demand. At a club where they are appearing, they meet young millionaire Jimmy Harris (Louis Hayward) as he drowns his sorrows over his failed marriage. He and Judy hit it off until he notices her eyes, which remind him all too much of his estranged wife. He suddenly turns his attention to Bubbles, leaving Judy bewildered. But of greater concern to her is for the troupe to find its next booking.

Bubbles lands a job hula dancing in a Hoboken nightspot where she gets discovered and turned into "Tiger" Lily White, burlesque queen. The act that is dreamed up for her calls for a ballerina to perform in between her numbers, provoking the striptease fans to demand for more of Tiger Lily. Bubbles offers the job to Judy, who ecstatically accepts, not

Bubbles, Judy, and the police officer who is leading a raid on their nightclub.

Bubbles dances the hula to get the troupe booked into a nightclub, but she alone is hired.

realizing she is to be a stooge. The night of her debut, the crowd's jeers and

catcalls break Judy's heart but not her spirit. All that matters to her is that she gets

to dance, so she stays on. As Bubbles becomes a sensation on Broadway, Judy

ascends to fame along with her.

One night their old pal Jimmy attends the show, still trying to get over his

divorce. He and Judy agree to pick up where they left off before Bubbles came between them. Romance blooms briefly until a scene explodes in a nightclub where they run into his ex-wife, Elinor (Virginia Field), on the arm of her divorce attorney. Judy instantly recognizes that Jimmy is still in love with the former Mrs. Harris, and she walks out on him. He tries to win Judy back the next day, but she refuses to see him. The fortune-hunting Bubbles takes advantage of the vulnerable (drunken) state Jimmy is in to trap him into wedlock.

Sporting a black eye after a tussle with Judy, Bubbles grants Jimmy the freedom to reunite with his ex-wife—but with a catch (a $50,000 settlement!).

At the theater that night, Bubbles tells Judy of the elopement, finally pushing the reserved Judy over the edge. Fed up with the audience of hecklers, she tells them off. Afterwards she receives a rousing ovation—and a slap across the face from Bubbles. A full-scale fight ensues onstage, ending up in a night court. As Bubbles gripes about her

black eye, the unharmed Judy calmly relates her story to the judge and admits her mistakes. She and Bubbles make amends, and Judy is given a short prison term.

Bubbles agrees to let Jimmy go, allowing him to reunite with Elinor at last. Steve Adams (Ralph Bellamy), a ballet producer, had been interested in Judy for some time (both professionally and romantically), but his attempts to meet her had been repeatedly misconstrued. He bails her out and offers her the opportunity of her dreams—dancing for the American Ballet Company.

Notes and Comments

Lauded by the studio as a "feminine hit," *Dance, Girl, Dance* was conceived by *Grand Hotel* author Vicki Baum and adapted for the screen by Tess Slesinger and Frank Davis. Working titles for it had been *Have it Your Own Way* and *Dance, Girls, Dance*. After production commenced on April 15, 1940, creative differences mounted between producer Erich Pommer and director Roy Del Ruth. Before long, Dorothy Arzner, the most prominent of the few female directors of her time, assumed Del Ruth's post. Having risen from typist at Famous Players-Lasky, her credits included Clara Bow's first talkie, *The Wild Party*, and *Nana*, in which Lucille appeared in a bit part.

Arzner turned the main focus of *Dance, Girl,*

Dance to the women and less on the various love angles. She scrapped Del Ruth's footage and made revisions that brought Maria Ouspenskaya into the cast as the girls' manager—originally the character had been a male role for Maurice Moscovitch, who fell ill while the film was in production and then died a short time later. The men of the picture were handsome Louis Hayward and Ralph Bellamy, the supporting actor who didn't get the girl in many great films (this time he did!). The editor, Robert Wise, moved on to directing classics such as *The Sound of Music*.

Lucille had one of her showiest movie roles in Bubbles. She played it to the hilt, turning in an exciting performance that was recognized by critics as the film's highlight. In her musical moments, she danced a torrid hula and simulated a striptease that received ample attention in fan magazines (and slipped by the censors). She worked on the routines with choreographer Ernst Matray for weeks prior to filming. Erich Pommer was very impressed by Lucille and wanted to work with her again in 1941 on a drama called *Passage to Bordeaux*, which would have co-starred Joseph Cotten, with Ruth Warrick in support, had the project come to fruition. In the opening sequence, the girls wore costumes reminiscent of Marlene Dietrich's in *The Blue Angel*, another of the renowned German filmmaker's productions.

As Bubbles

Bubbles is greeted backstage by Judy and her benefactor, Dwarfie (Edward Brophy), following her sensational debut. In her memoirs, O'Hara said while making this film, she and Lucille became "inseparable chums."

Jimmy takes up a collection for the out-of-work showgirls after watching them perform "Roll Out the Barrel."

Having just come from a brawl with Maureen O'Hara for *Dance, Girl, Dance*, Lucille looked like this the first time she met Desi— and behind the eye bandage fell in love with him at first sight.

Pommer fled Hitler's Germany and made films in England in the late '30s. There, in 1938, he and his partner, Charles Laughton, discovered stage actress Maureen O'Hara. They gave her a contract with Mayflower Pictures and then took her to America in 1939 to play Esmeralda in *The Hunchback of Notre Dame* at RKO. While Lucille covered the "oomph" department, Pommer placed O'Hara at the opposite end of the dancing spectrum as the ballerina. The Irish actress was at the threshold of a career that would continue for well over half a century.

Dance, Girl, Dance took longer to make than usual for Lucille, finishing up in July at a budget of around $700,000. Though the reviews were mixed in 1940, the movie has held up well over the years, and it is highly regarded for its various depictions of relationships among strong-willed, ambitious women. Lucille is not simply the bad girl to O'Hara's good girl. She does not become a villain. An underlying spirit of kinship permeates the production through the contrasting women's quarrels and catfights.

Lucille's career gained momentum with *Dance, Girl, Dance*, but there was greater excitement coming into her personal life. After shooting the film's well-publicized fight scene, Lucille and Maureen walked over to the studio commissary for lunch. There she came face to face for the first time with one of the co-stars of her next film, the handsome Cuban, Desi Arnaz.

Now dubbed "Tiger" Lily, Bubbles offers Judy a spot in her act. Fellow dancer Sally (Mary Carlisle) offers encouragement.

On the set with Dorothy Arzner

Too Many Girls

An RKO-Radio Picture (1940)

Cast: Lucille Ball (Connie Casey); Richard Carlson (Clint Kelly); Ann Miller (Pepe); Eddie Bracken (Jojo Jordan); Frances Langford (Eileen Eilers); Desi Arnaz (Manuelito Lynch); Hal LeRoy (Al Terwilliger); Libby Bennett (Tallulah Lou); Harry Shannon (Harvey Casey); Douglas Walton (Beverly Waverly); Chester Clute (Harold L. Lister); Tiny Person (Midge Martin); Ivy Scott (Mrs. Tewksbury); Byron Shores (Sheriff Andaluz); Grady Sutton (Football Coach); Averill Harris (Detective); Van Johnson (Chorus Boy)

Credits: Harry E. Edington (executive producer); George Abbott (producer and director); John Twist (screenplay), from play by George Marion, Jr., Richard Rodgers, and Lorenz Hart, as produced by George Abbott; Frank Redman (photography); Vernon L. Walker (special effects); George Bassman (musical director); LeRoy Prinz (dance director); Hugh Martin (vocal director); George Bassman and Gene Ross (orchestral arrangements); Frank Tours (orchestra conductor); Van Nest Polglase (art director), Carroll Clark (associate); Edward Stevenson (wardrobe); Dewey Starkey (assistant director); Earl A. Wolcott (recording); William Hamilton (editor)

Songs: "Heroes in the Fall," "You're Nearer," "Pottawatomie," "'Cause We Got Cake," "Spic and Spanish," "Love Never Went to College," "Look Out," "I Didn't Know What Time it Was" (Richard Rodgers and Lorenz Hart)

Release date: November 20, 1940 (Loew's Criterion Theater)

Run time: 85 minutes

All of Pottawatomie celebrates the football team's first victory since 1918 with a rousing production number, "Look Out."

Synopsis

To keep his unruly daughter Connie (Lucille Ball) out of trouble, millionaire Harvey Casey (Henry Shannon) enlists four handsome football heroes to work as her undercover bodyguards. Connie has just returned from Europe in unusually bright spirits and decides to attend a college on the Mexican border called Pottawatomie, which unbeknownst to Casey is near the ranch of her new beau, Beverly Waverly (Douglas Walton).

As the new semester approaches, Connie is off to college, with a quartet of bodyguards tailing her: Clint (Richard Carlson), Jojo (Eddie Bracken), Al (Hal LeRoy), and Manuelito (Desi Arnaz). To the boys' delight, Pottawatomie has ten girls to every male, and a peculiar tradition—a girl wears a beanie on her head to show that she does not "neck"! As Manuelito, Jojo, and Al get to know the co-eds, Clint becomes better acquainted with Connie, who is unaware that he is her bodyguard. He soon makes her forget Beverly Waverly, but a "hands-off policy" in his contract with her father stands in the way of romance.

Meanwhile, with the help of four of the best athletes in college football, Pottawatomie becomes the leading team in the league. Amidst this excitement, Clint resolves to come clean to Connie, but before he can do so, she discovers his identity on her own. Hiding hurt feelings behind a mask of glacial indifference, she insists they leave school immediately, in spite of the fact that they are being counted on to play in the big game the next day. As her guardians, the boys are obligated to return her home safely.

When the student body hears their stars are running out on them, they form a mob to stop them. Manuelito is caught and the others narrowly escape. This scene makes Connie see it was her own antics that caused her to require constant supervision. She spends the night searching for Clint. Her ex, Beverly, finds Clint, Jojo, and Al and returns them to Pottawatomie in time for the game the next day. The crowd's enthusiasm fills the stadium. A contrite Connie makes the first apology of her life to Clint. After they win the game, a celebration is held with Manuelito leading the conga line. Clint and Connie are reunited, and Al, Manuelito, and Jojo become friendly with co-eds Eileen (Frances Langford), Pepe (Ann Miller), and Tallulah Lou (Libby Bennett).

With Frances Langford, Ann Miller, Eddie Bracken, Hal LeRoy, and Richard Carlson

"'Too Many Girls' is lively, fast-moving, gay and nonsensical, with these attributes paraded against a colorful collegiate background. It is studded with several good tunes . . . Lucille Ball is a beaut for the lead . . . LeRoy Prinz incorporates some new twists to the dances . . . "

—*Variety*

" . . . pleasant, light-hearted and wholly ingenuous campus film . . . it is mainly the young people—conceivable collegiates for a change—who give to 'Too Many Girls' the snap and bounce that is has. Lucille Ball, Frances Langford and Ann Miller are a trio of dangerous co-eds, and Richard Carlson and Eddie Bracken are a couple of smooth lads with the quips. At various moments, they all sing or dance with pleasing exuberance . . . "

—*New York Times*

"Desi beats the bongo with Latin-American fervor, Hal does some spectacular tapping and Eddie [is] an all around good comedian . . . the producers couldn't have selected a better Connie than Lucille Ball, who plays the willful heiress of the story with zest . . . the picture [is] thoroughly entertaining."

—*New York Daily News*

Richard Carlson, Lucille, Desi Arnaz, Ann Miller, Hal LeRoy, Frances Langford, Eddie Bracken, and Libby Bennett. The camaraderie among the stars made the filming of *Too Many Girls* a joyous experience.

Notes and Comments

In Lucille's entrance in *Too Many Girls*, she approaches a restaurant, gives a fleeting nod to a waiter standing nearby, and steps inside. So awed is the waiter by her beauty that he faints. These are Lucille Ball and Desi Arnaz's first moments together on film, but essentially the only interaction between them in the movie.

In late 1939, RKO purchased the film rights to the hit musical *Too Many Girls* for $100,000. Lucille was primed to replace stage star Marcy Wescott in the lead. While in New York doing publicity, Lucille made her way to the Imperial Theater to see what all the buzz was about concerning one of the show's stars, Desi Arnaz. She noted his "electrifying charm" but soon returned to Hollywood, where she was slated for another project while *Too Many Girls* completed its run on Broadway.

The show played to rave notices with its Rodgers and Hart score and spirited cast.

While Richard Carlson was Lucille's love interest on the screen, off screen everyone at RKO witnessed the start of a great love affair between her and Desi.

Twenty-two-year-old Desi was already a local celebrity with his show at the La Conga nightclub, where he had New Yorkers dancing *la conga*, but he had never acted. Director George Abbott took a chance on him. What Desi lacked in experience he made up for in charisma, and when RKO bought the rights, he was among the original cast members chosen to recreate his role.

The day Desi arrived in Hollywood, Lucille filmed a fight for *Dance, Girl, Dance*, and it was in the disheveled makeup and costume for this scene that she first encountered him. Later the same day, Lucille was neatly groomed again for a gathering of the *Too Many Girls* company. Thereafter she and Desi were inseparable.

Romance blossomed on the set, which made for a happy atmosphere during the six-week shoot (It also became an exciting, unexpected publicity angle). Desi remembered, "I don't think that we ever made another picture in which everyone had so much fun as we did on that one." They formed lifelong friendships with several of their co-stars, as well as with George Abbott. Abbott had directed a number of Paramount pictures in the early sound era. He came to RKO from New York to direct his first film in nine years, bringing with him seven members of his original cast: Libby Bennett, Ivy Scott, Byron Shores, Hal LeRoy, and three future stars who made their screen debuts in

With Ann Miller (above) and Richard Carlson, who played a timid football hero who shyly woos Lucille.

Playing up Desi's heartthrob status with Ann Miller, who remarked, "God, he was attractive!" Then seventeen-year-old Miller had just returned to Hollywood after a successful run in *George White's Scandals*. Playing a Mexican spitfire named Pepe, she replaced Desi's partner from both the stage production and his nightclub act, Diosa Costello. This was Miller's fourth and final film with Lucille.

Too Many Girls—Desi, Eddie Bracken, and Van Johnson. Bracken became a popular comedian. All-American, freckle-faced Johnson, who understudied each of the male leads in the stage version (even Desi) signed with MGM two years later and was soon the nation's favorite Boy Next Door.

Filming wrapped on July 31, 1940, nine days ahead of schedule and under budget. The cast received bright reviews, though most agreed that Abbott's stage version had been better. It was a light-weight film made enjoyable by a dynamic young cast. This was Lucille's fourth and last 1940 release, a year in which her characters ranged from drab housewife to burlesque queen to pampered heiress. Of the role of Connie Casey, she later said, "I had never played an ingénue before, nor did I want to. But I did it." In spite of her qualms, she performed with vivacity and brought warmth to the headstrong character. No doubt finding love on the set helped her bring the necessary enthusiasm into the part.

A Girl, a Guy and a Gob

An RKO-Radio Picture (1941)

Cast: George Murphy (Coffee Cup); Lucille Ball (Dot Duncan); Edmond O'Brien (Steven Herrick); Henry Travers (Abel Martin); Franklin Pangborn (Pet Shop Owner); George Cleveland (Pokey); Kathleen Howard (Jawme); Marguerite Chapman (Cecilia Grange); Lloyd Corrigan (Pigeon); Mady Correll (Cora); Frank McGlynn (Parkington); Doodles Weaver (Eddie); Frank Sully (Salty); Nella Walker (Mrs. Grange); Richard Lane (Recruiting Officer); Irving Bacon (Mr. Merney); Rube Demarest (Ivory)

Credits: Harold Lloyd (producer); Richard Wallace (director); Frank Ryan and Bert Granet (screenplay), from story by Grover Jones; Russell Metty (photography); Vernon L. Walker (special effects); Roy Webb (musical score); Van Nest Polglase (art director), Albert D'Agostino (associate); Darrell Silvera (set decoration); Edward Stevenson (wardrobe); Hugh McDowell, Jr. (recording); James H. Anderson (assistant director); George Crone (editor)

Release date: April 23, 1941 (Loew's Criterion Theater)

Run time: 90 minutes

The guy, the girl, and the gob

Synopsis

From her balcony seat at the concert hall, Dot Duncan (Lucille Ball) accidentally drops her purse on the head of the affluent businessman Steven Herrick (Edmond O'Brien), then makes a quick getaway, leaving him furious. Dot reports to her new secretarial job the next morning and finds that the same man is to be her boss. He forgives her clumsiness, she his superior attitude, and they begin working together.

Dot's boyfriend, a flighty sailor and part-time wrestler, Coffee Cup (George Murphy), comes ashore for good—Dot hopes. The happy-go-lucky couple and Dot's wacky family begin softening Steven's stuffy demeanor. Dot and Coffee Cup take him out for a round of gaiety and before long, Steven falls in love with Dot. Even after his engagement to a haughty debutante ends, Steve hides his feelings, knowing Dot and Coffee Cup intend to marry.

Keeping the pair from becoming engaged is a matter of $200 for a ring. Steven provides the cash and Coffee Cup pops the question.

Reviews

"Harold Lloyd has sent along a rib-ticklish little comedy . . . If this doesn't make sense, it makes perfect nonsense. The important thing is not who gets the girl but how much fun they have along the way. The cast is giddy as can be. Lucille Ball may not be made of India rubber, but she has as much bounce . . . "

—*New York Times*

" . . . a dizzy riot of wacky fun. Directed with freshness and skill by Richard Wallace and played to perfection by a cast that includes George Murphy, Lucille Ball and Edmund O'Brien. It will roll you out of your seats with laughs. . . . A great deal of invention and imagination have gone into the gags . . . "

—*New York World-Telegram*

"Into 'A Girl, a Guy and a Gob' [Harold Lloyd] has injected the same rollicking, high-speed, effervescent gaiety which always has marked the best of his own comedies. . . . Lucille Ball is delightful as the girl, handling her role with charming ease and skill . . . "

—*Hollywood Reporter*

"It is full of life and bouncing energy . . . and in the acting of its three principals, Lucille Ball, George Murphy and Edmund O'Brien, it has a curiously ingratiating quality that seems to get under your skin and make you like everybody."

—*New York Morning Telegraph*

As the wedding approaches, Dot has misgivings, and notices that her fiancé appears to as well. Still confused, they soon stand side by side at a chapel. Steven is selected as best man, and the look between he and Dot tells Coffee Cup that Steven is the best man for her, too. He sends them into each other's arms and returns to his true love—the Navy.

Notes and Comments

A Girl, a Guy and a Gob was produced by Harold Lloyd, legendary bespectacled, straw-hatted comedian of the movie's silent era, known for his daredevil stunts (like the famous image of him dangling from the clock of a twelve-story building, from *Safety Last*). At his peak during the '20s, Lloyd began producing his own films. He withdrew from movie acting after 1938, then went to RKO in 1940 for *A Girl, a Guy and a Gob*, his first production in which he did not also star.

As originally conceived, the picture was to be called *Three Girls and a Gob*, with Maureen O'Hara and Jack Carson in the leads. The story was altered and

The nutty Duncans look forward to Coffee Cup becoming an official member of the family after he proposes to Dot in this scene.

Sea-faring Coffee Cup sails back to favorite girl, Dot ("Spindle" to him).

given a new title to suit it, along with a different cast. Official writing credit went to Frank Ryan and Bert Granet for their script from a story by Grover Jones. Additional dialogue was contributed by husband-and-wife writing partners Victor Heerman and Sarah Y. Mason (Oscar winners for *Little Women*, 1933), and in his memoirs, co-star George Murphy recalled nightly scriptwriting sessions after the day's filming with director Richard Wallace.

Lucille went to work on *A Girl, a Guy and a Gob* in late September 1940. It was filmed during the time Desi was fiercely courting her, which probably accounts for the particular radiance and bounce she seems to have as the carefree Girl of the title. She later recalled, "It was a rosy, wonderful time for me. I adored the movie; I had a great time making it." The film is sprightly, fast-paced, and funny, featuring a giddy, carefree family that resembles the Vanderhofs of *You Can't Take it with You*, and it was a success at the box office.

Onscreen Lucille's "Guy" was Edmond O'Brien, who was to become a good friend of the Arnazes. This, his second major role following *The Hunchback of Notre Dame*, showed O'Brien slimmer and more handsome than in his

Lucille and Edmond O'Brien play a then popular board game, Citadel, between scenes.

acclaimed character parts of the '50s. George Murphy played the titular Gob. Lucille had bit parts in his first three pictures, but this was her only time starring opposite the future California senator. Murphy also worked as an executive of public relations at Desilu in the '50s.

Production ended on *A Girl, a Guy and a Gob* on November 18, 1940. Once her work was through, Lucille left immediately on a promotional tour with Maureen O'Hara for *Dance, Girl, Dance*. She spent a short time with Desi in New York before continuing with the tour in the Midwest, but after a few days apart, she was lured back east. On November 30, 1940 came the news that they had eloped to Connecticut.

Lucille's confidence in producer Harold Lloyd and director Richard Wallace (pictured here) was badly shaken by the extensive script revisions handed out daily throughout production. She became convinced of failure until the first screening before an audience, after which she told Hedda Hopper, "You could have knocked me over with a feather at the preview. The audience just howled. It was a smash hit."

Look Who's Laughing

An RKO-Radio Picture (1941)

Cast: Edgar Bergen (as himself); Charlie McCarthy (as himself); Jim Jordan (Fibber McGee); Marian Jordan (Molly McGee); Lucille Ball (Julie Patterson); Lee Bonnell (Jerry Wood); Dorothy Lovett (Marge); Harold Peary (Throckmorton P. Gildersleeve); Isabel Randolph (Mrs. Uppington); Walter Baldwin (Bill); Neil Hamilton (Hilary Horton); Charles Halton (Sam Cudahy); Harlow Wilcox (Mr. Collins); Spencer Charters (Hotel Manager); Jed Prouty (Mayor Duncan); George Cleveland (Kelsey)

Credits: Allan Dwan (producer and director); James V. Kern (story and screenplay); Zeno Klinker and Dorothy Kingsley (material for Edgar Bergen); Don Quinn and Leonard L. Levinson (material for Fibber McGee and Molly); Frank Redman (photography); Vernon L. Walker (special effects); Roy Webb (music); C. Bakaleinikoff (musical director); Van Nest Polglase (art director), Al Herman (associate); Edward Stevenson (gowns); John L. Cass (recording); Edward Donahue (assistant director); Sherman Todd (editor)

Release date: December 24, 1941 (RKO Palace and Albee Theaters)

Run time: 79 minutes

Synopsis

After the last show of the season for radio's Edgar Bergen and Charlie McCarthy, a party is held to celebrate the engagement of Bergen's assistant, Julie Patterson (Lucille Ball), to his business manager, Jerry Wood (Lee Bonnell). It's Edgar Julie really loves, but he takes her for granted.

Bergen and Charlie head by plane for a vacation, but a faulty sense of direction lands them in sleepy Wistful Vista instead. There they stay with the scatterbrained Fibber McGee (Jim Jordan) and his wife, Molly (Marian Jordan). McGee believes his town will prosper if Hilary Horton (Neil Hamilton) builds his aircraft factory on the Wistful Vista flying field. Throwing a wrench into the plan is Fibber's neighbor, Throckmorton P. Gildersleeve (Harold Peary). He is in cahoots with Cudahy (Charles Halton) of Ironton Realty, who wants Horton's business for Ironton. Bergen, a friend of Horton's, volunteers to bring him to Wistful Vista.

Charlie McCarthy, playing a patient in a show within the film, is awestruck by his nurse.

Reviews

"It's no wow effort, but will please as a better-than-average B. . . . as the harried worrier for Bergen's well-being, Lucille Ball is fetching . . . Jim and Marian Jordan are capital in their tried and proved Fibber and Molly roles. . . . Allan Dwan produced-directed with expert hand and canny pacing."

—*Variety*

"The McCarthy and the McGee gags are cleverly woven into the script. Charlie, for instance, falls for Molly's telephone impersonation of Sis, the 'I betcha' child on Fibber's program. Lucille Ball plays Bergen's glamorous secretary and her presence in the film lends it an aura of romance, as Lucille tries to interest the indifferent Bergen . . . whether or not you'll like the comedy depends on your enthusiasm for the Bergen and McGee type of gags, which have settled into a pattern by this time."

—*New York Daily News*

"As might be expected with an assortment of funny people [in a cast], the plot is not precisely the straightest line between two points. . . . It is a homely comedy, and fortunately it doesn't try to be anything more. . . . Lucille Ball shows a pretty and animated face. Nothing astonishing, mind you, but amusing in spots."

—*New York Times*

Bergen and the McGees listen in as Julie places a call to her jilted fiancé.

Bergen does not head directly to Horton. He goes to New York for Julie first. Instead of getting married on her wedding day, she is dragged away to help the McGees. In Wistful Vista, Julie pieces things together—Gildersleeve tricked Charlie into having Bergen detour to New York before picking up Horton to give Cudahy a chance to negotiate with Horton first. Julie uses her feminine charms on Cudahy and fools him into thinking that a worthless tract of land owned by Fibber is the site Horton is interested in purchasing.

Thanks to Julie, Cudahy and Gildersleeve wind up with Fibber's swampland, and Horton's business comes to Wistful Vista. Meanwhile, Bergen realizes he can't live without Julie, and they plan to marry.

Notes and Comments

Past success with delivering radio stars to the screen (e.g. Kay Kyser in *That's Right—You're Wrong*) convinced RKO executives to produce more of the same. *Look Who's Laughing* featured some of radio's brightest: Edgar Bergen and his wooden pal, Charlie McCarthy; Jim and Marian Jordan, better known as Fibber McGee and Molly; along with the Great Gildersleeve, Harold Peary, with his signature laughter. Allan Dwan, a prolific crafts-man in the business since 1911, produced and directed the comedy. (Some of his better known products of the sound era include *Heidi*, 1937, and *Suez*, 1938.)

Lucille was something of a radio star herself, or at least would be soon. During 1938 she had been a regular on the programs of Phil Baker and Jack Haley and often performed on radio thereafter. Seven years after this picture, she would truly make it big over the airwaves with her own series, *My Favorite Husband*.

In March 1941, the studio announced that Desi was to play a "romantic lead" in *Look Who's Laughing*. This was just one of many projects

With Fibber McGee and Molly

With Dorothy Lovett and Bergen

With Edgar Bergen

Lucille and Desi could not come together on during the early years of their marriage. This initial casting decision did not stick, but the couple did do a brief vaudeville tour together around the forth-coming New Year, when this film was in theaters.

With the working title of *Look Who's Talking*, the movie was shot between May 13 and June 23, 1941. *Look Who's Laughing* is a pleasant artifact of its time, showcasing performers the public tuned in to regularly. Viewed today, it is curious to see the flesh-and-blood actors speak and interact with Charlie, who in the movie is a live character. In 1941, it was a major blockbuster for RKO. The bombing of Pearl Harbor had taken place earlier in the month of the film's opening, and this giddy entertainment provided a welcome diversion. *Look Who's Laughing* was followed up in 1942 by *Here We Go Again*, another hit featuring the same five radio personalities (including Charlie).

Valley of the Sun

An RKO-Radio Picture (1942)

Cast: Lucille Ball (Christine Larson); James Craig (Jonathan Ware); Sir Cedric Hardwicke (Warrick); Dean Jagger (Jim Sawyer); Peter Whitney (Willie); Billy Gilbert (Justice of the Peace); Tom Tyler (Geronimo); Antonio Moreno (Chief Cochise); George Cleveland (Bill Yard); Hank Bell (Shotgun); Richard Fiske, Don Terry (Lieutenants)

Credits: Graham Baker (producer); George Marshall (director); Horace McCoy (screenplay), from story by Clarence Budington Kelland; Harry Wild (photography); Vernon L. Walker (special effects); Paul Sawtell (music); C. Bakaleinikoff (musical director); Albert D'Agostino and Walter E. Keller (art directors); Edward Stevenson (costumes); Bailey Fesler and John C. Grubb (recording); Edward Donahoe (assistant director); Desmond Marquette (editor)

Release date: February 6, 1942 (Rialto Theater)

Run time: 78 minutes

A close call for Sawyer, Jonathan, and Christine after Sawyer triggers a battle with the Indians.

Synopsis

In the 1860s Arizona territory, Army scout Jonathan Ware (James Craig) is one of the few who are interested in giving Native Americans a fair deal. Helping a trio of falsely accused Apache Indians escape the authorities gets Jonathon into trouble and he is nearly jailed. Certain he can remedy the situation by pleading his case in Washington, he escapes the guards and heads east.

Jonathan pauses for a rest at the home of Christine Larson (Lucille Ball), fiancée of the crooked agent in charge of Indian affairs, Jim Sawyer (Dean Jagger). After Jonathan sabotages their first ceremony, Sawyer and Christine head to Tucson to be wed, but a tribe of Indians seizes the coach and takes them to their camp—Sawyer has been cheating the Indians out of their dues from the government. Jonathan intervenes. The Indians trust him and spare Sawyer's life on condition that he return horses and cattle that are rightfully theirs.

They are safe again, thanks to Jonathan. Christine sees Sawyer for the scoundrel he is and calls off their engagement—Jonathan is the man for her. The jilted Sawyer turns Jonathan in to the military police who are after him and wages war with the Indians by taking hostage their leader, Cochise (Antonio Moreno).

Lucille and James Craig as Jonathan and Christine

Christine and her friends help Jonathan escape, and he then retrieves what belongs to the Indians from Sawyer's ranch, but it may be too late. The Indians have made their way down the hills to do battle and rescue Cochise. At last, Sawyer cooperates and Jonathan sets the Indian chief free to call an end to the destruction. Afterwards, newlyweds Jonathan and Christine continue the journey to Washington together.

Notes and Comments

If Lucille Ball seems an unlikely choice for a western, bear in mind that it was *Valley of the Sun* director George Marshall who turned Marlene Dietrich into the wild west's favorite chanteuse in *Destry Rides Again* (1939), eliciting one of the German siren's best performances. Alas, *Valley of the Sun* was no *Destry*, and neither were the lead female characters of equal caliber.

Christine shares a laugh with the Justice of the Peace (Billy Gilbert) and Sawyer before Jonathan steals her heart.

" . . . out of material which might easily have been turned into a whooping Wild West show, Director George Marshall and his writers have made an ambling and cross-purposed film which wobbles [sic] between blood-and-thunder and nondescript Western farce. Apparently the boys were not quite certain whether they were shooting Mr. Kelland's novel or Joe Miller's joke book."

—*New York Times*

"Good histrionic performances are very much in evidence. Lucille Ball, who is more a product of the twentieth century, nevertheless makes a spirited and attractive western heroine, and James Craig and Dean Jagger are good in their respective roles."

—*Motion Picture Herald*

" . . . a studio typewriter has removed all traces of [Clarence Budington Kelland's] sophisticated touch. And in its place there's a rip-roaring, hard-riding, two-fisted film that is half Indian story in the 1860s and half Hollywood of the 1930s. . . . peopled with some fine actors and paced as swiftly as it is, you will find a few bright spots on the Rialto screen this week."

—*New York World-Telegram*

In a career that spanned over fifty years, Marshall proved himself capable of handling any genre, from film noir (*The Blue Dahlia*) to comedies with Will Rogers, Bob Hope, and Jerry Lewis, among others. He later directed Lucille again for a spell on *Here's Lucy*. Marshall was known for his blending of drama and broad comedy, but critics complained that he missed the mark attempting this in *Valley of the Sun*.

The story by Clarence Budington Kelland (*Mr. Deeds Goes to Town*) ran as a serial in the *Saturday Evening Post*. Lucille's role was earmarked for Dorothy Comingore (of *Citizen Kane*) in early stages. Though she may have seemed out of place in Arizona pioneer days, it was not the setting but the part itself that let her down, for it did not adequately exploit her versatile abilities. Lucille's other film set in the Old West, *Fancy Pants*, was one of her best (also directed by Marshall). Her character in that film was more colorful, and her discomfort in period costumes was played for laughs from start to finish. In *Valley of the Sun*, most of the comedy was handled by Billy Gilbert.

Lucille, Desi (in back), and members of the cast and crew enjoy the Native American dances.

The stars are entertained by Native-American extras featured in *Valley of the Sun.*

James Craig, who had recently emerged from bit parts after appearing with Ginger Rogers in *Kitty Foyle*, co-starred, along with the venerable Sir Cedric Hardwicke. Silent screen Latin lover Antonio Moreno was seen in a minor role as Cochise. In the '20s, he was leading man to the greats—Greta Garbo, Gloria Swanson, Clara Bow (in the 1927 classic *It*). Producer Graham Baker infused some authenticity into *Valley of the Sun* by rounding out the cast with the less-familiar faces of Native Americans employed from the areas in and around Taos, New Mexico, where exteriors were shot. Principal photography took place from late September until November 15, 1941. The production budget of $646,000 was not recouped at the box office.

A Native American child shares a cone with Lucille on the set.

The Big Street

An RKO-Radio Picture (1942)

Cast: Henry Fonda (Little Pinks); Lucille Ball (Gloria Lyons); Barton MacLane (Case Ables); Eugene Pallette (Nicely Nicely Johnson); Agnes Moorehead (Violette Shumberger); Sam Levene (Horsethief); Ray Collins (Professor B); Marion Martin (Mrs. Venus); William Orr (Decatur Reed); George Cleveland (Colonel Venus); Vera Gordon (Mrs. Lefkowitz); Louise Beavers (Ruby); Millard Mitchell (Gentleman George); Juan Varro (Lou Adolia); Hans Conried (Louie); Harry Shannon (Doctor); William Halligan (Detective); John Miljan (McWhirter); Don Barclay (Emcee); Julius Tannen (Judge Bamberger); Eddie Dunn (Mulvaney); Bert Hanlon (Philly the Weeper); Anthony Blair (O'Rourke); Art Hamburger (Joel Duffle); Addison Richards (Dr. Mitchell); Ozzie Nelson and His Orchestra

Credits: Damon Runyon (producer); Irving Reis (director); Leonard Spigelgass (screenplay), from story by Damon Runyon; Russell Metty (photography); Vernon L. Walker (special effects); Roy Webb (musical score); C. Bakaleinikoff (musical director); Albert D'Agostino and Al Herman (art directors); Darrell Silvera and Claude Carpenter (set decoration); Mel Berns (makeup supervisor), Westmore (Miss Ball's makeup); Chester Hale (dance director); Renié (gowns); Freddy Wittop (Miss Ball's dance costume); Richard Van Hessen (recording); Clem Beauchamp (assistant director); William Hamilton (editor)

Song: "Who Knows?" (Mort Greene and Harry Revel)

Release date: August 13, 1942 (Palace Theater)

Run time: 88 minutes

Synopsis

Little Pinks (Henry Fonda) is the ultimate fan of Gloria Lyons (Lucille Ball), a singer with a heart of stone. One night, Pinks meets Gloria and rescues her dog. To repay him, she gets him a job bussing tables at her nightclub. Pinks is so grateful and awed by Gloria that he begins calling her "Your Highness."

Though she is the girlfriend of the dangerous Case Ables (Barton MacLane), Gloria makes a date with handsome millionaire Decatur Reed (William Orr). When she tells Ables they are through, he pushes her down a flight of stairs and she is paralyzed from the waist down. Pinks takes on the task of helping her through this difficult time. He scrimps and saves to pay Gloria's medical bills, then takes her to his home to recuperate. He keeps her spirits up by telling her she will be well in no time, though doctors have informed him she will never

Gloria, with Little Pinks and her beloved Baby, on her first day out of the hospital.

With Henry Fonda and Barton MacLane as Case Ables. Runyon is said to have modeled the Ables character on gangster "Bugsy" Siegel.

walk again. Gloria shows no gratitude and treats Pinks cruelly. She begins to believe she cannot survive the New York winter. Unable to afford any other means of transportation, Gloria asks Pinks to wheel her to Florida.

The two hitch a few rides and finally make it to sunny Miami, where they stay with Pinks's friends, Violette (Agnes Moorehead) and Nicely Nicely (Eugene Pallette). While relaxing on the beach, Gloria encounters Decatur Reed, who does not realize she is paralyzed. They plan to see more of each other, but when he discovers her condition, he dismisses her as "damaged goods."

Gloria sinks into a deep depression, realizing that she will never be her old self again. Her health deteriorates. The doctor tells Pinks she will die unless her illusions are restored. Pinks knows what to do. Gloria had told him that she envisioned herself looking beautiful at a grand party, men fawning over her—the envy of every woman. Pinks will do anything to make this dream come true. He steals a gown and jewelry for her, then obtains a ballroom, as well as food, champagne, and decorations by blackmailing the man that caused Gloria's accident, Case Ables.

With help from Pinks's friends, many threats to the success of the party that arise are thwarted. Now Gloria has become humbled and appreciative of the

Reviews

"Damon Runyon has finally got a screen production that does credit to one of his stories. . . . Lucille Ball does the best acting job of her career as a gold-digger, and the usually virile Henry Fonda is perfectly grand as the dopey Lindy character."
—*New York Daily Mirror*

"'The Big Street,' typical Damon Runyon story, shapes up as the sturdiest b.o. bet from this studio in months . . . It shows Lucille Ball as a first-rate actress . . . [She] comes through with high laurels. Fonda [is] at his best. Eugene Pallette is well teamed with Agnes Moorehead . . . Ray Collins achieves top supporting honors . . . "
—*Variety*

"Chalk up a winner for Damon Runyon. . . . Lucille is harsh, unyielding, self-centered to the very end. . . . This motion-picture has all the comedy, pathos, peculiar Broadway jargon, descriptive names and unexpected plot twists associated with a Runyon tale . . . has gone far afield in acting, direction, theme and story treatment . . . "
—*Screen Guide*

"Pretty Lucille Ball, who was born for the parts Ginger Rogers sweats over, tackles her 'emotional' role as if it were sirloin and she didn't care who was looking. . . . Good shot: Miss Ball, crippled and propped up in bed, trying to do a conga from the hips up. She does it very nicely."
—*Time*

trouble Pinks went through for her. Toward the end of the evening he joins the party, dressed in white tie and tails. Holding her up, he glides Gloria across the dance floor and she tells him, "I'm happy for the first time in my life, Pinks." With his help and encouragement, Gloria stands on her own two feet one last time, then collapses and dies in his arms.

A tender moment when Pinks and Gloria stop for the night on their way to Florida in a wooded clearing where they rest, build a fire, and meet up with hold-up men. Filmed on June 8, 1942, an exterior set was built for this lengthy sequence that was cut from the final print of *The Big Street*.

Notes and Comments

The Big Street began as "Little Pinks," a short story by Damon Runyon featured in *Collier's* magazine. Many Runyon tales had been filmed previously (*Lady for a Day*, *Little Miss Marker*, et al.), but this was the writer's first time assuming authority over the screen adaptation as a producer. Soon after his arrival at RKO in 1941, Runyon was introduced to Lucille by Walter Winchell* and quickly made up his mind that in her he had found his Gloria Lyons, the venomous showgirl of the story. Studio heads insisted that a bigger name was needed for the part and tried at different times to get Barbara Stanwyck and Jean Arthur, but Runyon was adamant, and Lucille was cast in what would be her favorite film.

Working titles were *It Comes up Love* and *Little Pinks*. Fledgling director Irving Reis was assigned to the project and Leonard Spigelgass, who had adapted Runyon stories in the past, prepared the script. The start of production was delayed for several months, until April 22, 1942. Part of the wait was for Henry Fonda, whom RKO borrowed from Fox for $60,000 to play the devoted Little Pinks. The actor was occupied at his home studio playing another "magnificent dope" in a movie of that name.

To Lucille, Gloria Lyons was the most stimulating part she had yet been given. She squelched her initial concerns about the character's ruthless nature and followed the advice of Charles Laughton (who at one time RKO announced as her co-star)—"play the bitchiest bitch that ever was." In 1946, she told the *Saturday Evening Post*, "it was exciting because it was so meaty—so rich in humor, pathos and tragedy . . . The challenging

*Many sources indicate Carole Lombard, but in her autobiography, Lucille names Winchell as the person who introduced her to Runyon.

difficulty of portraying Gloria adequately was what made the task so much fun." She was outstanding, moving in her portrayal while exhibiting the showgirl's contemptible qualities, her moments of frailty, and the traumatic discovery that she will never walk again. This performance brought her to the attention of MGM's Arthur Freed, who was preparing to make the musical *Du Barry Was a Lady*.

The climactic final scene of *The Big Street* has a humbled Gloria finding happiness with Pinks before collapsing into his arms. He then carries her up a flight of stairs toward a balcony. Nearly forty years later, at the American Film Institute's tribute to Henry Fonda, Lucille remembered that Irving Reis called for six takes of this scene as the increasingly exasperated Fonda murmured, "If he has me do this one more time I'm going to throw you off the balcony." In recounting the story, she joked that if they ever made another picture she would carry *him* up a flight of stairs.

Along with Lucille and Fonda in the leads, *The Big Street* was aided by a prominent supporting cast: Ray Collins and Agnes Moorehead had both made impressive debuts in *Citizen Kane* a year earlier. Sam Levene, Eugene Pallette, Louise Beavers, Barton MacLane, and Hans Conreid all

Before fade out, Pinks is as much Gloria's idol as she is his.

fleshed out interesting Runyon characters. Playboy Decatur Reed was played by William Orr, a handsome young actor who later became the head of Warner Bros. television, and a bit part was essayed by monologist Julius Tannen, one of teenaged Lucille's great inspirations for going into show business. Tannen is best remembered as the man who demonstrates talking pictures in *Singin' in the Rain*.

The film cost $544,844 to make and was completed on June 13, 1942. Three men central to its creation were no longer on hand during the post-production period—Runyon was no longer at RKO, Reis went to war, and the film editor died, all of which left *The Big Street* in the hands of others who could not turn out the film as conceived by its creators. Furthermore, Fonda was back at Fox and Lucille had signed on with MGM by the time it was released. Consequently, the picture did not receive the promotional campaign it merited. In spite of these circumstances, which made her feel the production was "jinxed," Lucille always looked back on *The Big Street* with great pride, and Runyon was so touched by it that it was known to move him to tears after endless screenings.

Choreographer Chester Hale was engaged to create a dance for Lucille. Publicity shots of her rehearsing and performing her rumba solo remain, but it did not make it into the film's final cut, except for the glimpse we see Gloria perform from the waist up in her hospital bed. Hale said, "Lucille is tall, lithe, willowy and has much talent as a dancer. She has a beautiful back; holds herself well, and is extremely graceful."

Seven Days' Leave

An RKO-Radio Picture (1942)

Cast: Victor Mature (Johnny Grey); Lucille Ball (Terry Havelock-Allen); Harold Peary (Throckmorton P. Gildersleeve); Mapy Cortés (Mapy); Ginny Simms (Ginny); Marcy McGuire (Mickey Havelock-Allen); Arnold Stang (Bitsy); Peter Lind Hayes (Jackson); Walter Reed (Ralph Bell); Wallace Ford (Sergeant Mead); Buddy Clark (Clarky); Charles Victor (Charles); King Kennedy (Gifford); Charles Andre (Andre); Harry Holman (Justice of the Peace); Addison Richards (Captain Collins); Lynn, Royce, and Vanya (Specialty Dancers); Ralph Edwards & Co.; Freddy Martin and His Orchestra; Les Brown and His Orchestra

Credits: Tim Whelan (producer and director); George Arthur (associate producer); William Bowers and Ralph Spence, Curtis Kenyon and Kenneth Earl (screenplay); Robert de Grasse (photography); Vernon L. Walker (special effects); C. Bakaleinikoff (musical Director); Ken Darby (vocal and musical advisor); Charles Walters (dance director); Albert D'Agostino and Carroll Clark (art directors); Darrell Silvera and Michael Ohrenbach (set decoration); Renié (gowns); Robert Guhl (recording); Sam Ruman (assistant director); Robert Wise (editor)

Songs: "Please Won't You Leave My Girl Alone," "You Speak My Language," "A Touch of Texas," "I Get the Neck of the Chicken," "Can't Get Out of this Mood" (Frank Loesser and James McHugh)

Release date: October 15, 1942 (Capitol Theater)

Run time: 87 minutes

A soldier and his girl—with Victor Mature

Synopsis

When Private Johnny Grey (Victor Mature) and the men of his company are given seven days' leave, they head for the USO canteen, where Johnny is reunited with his sweetheart, Mapy (Mapy Cortés). The same night, he learns that the descendants of General John Jacob Grey stand to receive a substantial legacy. But the next day, Mr. Gildersleeve (Harold Peary), executor of the general's estate, informs Johnny of a provision—General Grey's will states that the only Grey who may inherit his fortune is the one who marries a Havelock-Allen, thereby ending a feud between the two families dating back to the Civil War.

Gildersleeve takes Johnny to the girl he is supposed to ensnare, Terry Havelock-Allen (Lucille Ball). She is already engaged to Ralph Bell (Walter Reed). Thinking it would be dirty trick, Johnny wants to forget the matter, but he decides he will later make it up to Terry later by giving her

With Victor Mature, Harold Peary, Arnold Stang, Peter Lind Hayes, and Walter Reed

a share of the inheritance. He gets right to work and with the help of his friends, who get Terry's fiancé out of the way, his brash brand of charm works its magic. She falls for him—and Johnny falls in love with her, too.

At a garden party held at Terry's home, Johnny plans to tell her about the inheritance. But she finds out before he gets a chance, which sends her back to Ralph. A skirmish ensues between the two men, and Johnny and his friends land in the guardhouse. His ex-fiancée, Mapy, harboring no hard feelings, knows Johnny loves Terry. Along with Terry's sister, Mickey (Marcy McGuire), she convinces her of this. Terry and Johnny have a speedy marriage ceremony before he goes overseas.

Notes and Comments

In early 1942, Charles Koerner, head of the RKO theater chain, became production chief of the studio, bringing with him the motto "Showmanship in Place of Genius."* To pull his studio out of a financial crisis, he wanted surefire crowd-pleasers. Aiming to satisfy each customer, performers of all varieties were paraded through *Seven Days' Leave.* Among the acts were two radio programs (*The Court of Missing Heirs* and Ralph Edwards's *Truth or Consequences*),

*This slogan pointed an accusing finger at Orson Welles, whose groundbreaking productions at RKO were generating a great deal more headaches than profits.

"Producer-director Tim Whelan seems to have been embarrassed by talent riches wherein the cast is concerned, but the conglomerate of film, radio and variety names in the army-theme comedy has resulted in a loose-ends pic that superlative editing couldn't clarify."

—*Variety*

"Loaded with music, hot, sweet and solid, primed with comedy of the strictly now brand and peppered with snatches from a couple of the best air shows, 'Seven Days' Leave' [made] a whole lot of local audiences very happy. . . . Lucille Ball gives a charming performance."

—*Brooklyn Daily Eagle*

"Into a strictly prefabricated story about the soldier and the girl the producers have chucked as many gags, songs, dances and snappy sayings as they could well cull from the joke books or snatch out of thin air. . . . 'Seven Days' Leave' is an unsteady mélange. But on a thin tire the producers are still getting a little mileage. The audience seemed to enjoy the ride."

—*New York Times*

two name bands (Freddy Martin and Les Brown), comic dancers (Lynn, Royce, and Vanya), and Peter Lind Hayes doing impersonations, along with many singers and comedians. Four screenwriters joined forces to string together all of these specialty acts.

Lucille and Marcy McGuire as sisters Terry and Mickey

Production began on June 17, 1942, under the working title of *Sweet or Hot*. It cast Lucille as a wartime debutante who, by the finish, trades in her feminine frills for a uniform and waves her soldier, Victor Mature, goodbye. At this time, the

beefy actor was nicknamed "The Hunk," known as Betty Grable's leading man onscreen, and Rita Hayworth's off. He had just made *Footlight Serenade*, in which Lucille would have supported her old friend Betty, but Lucille refused to be loaned to Fox for the musical comedy. She did not relish the idea of being parceled out to another studio and its schedule was likely to clash with that of *The Big Street*.

The dynamic performer of Spanish and Mexican cinema, Mapy Cortés, made her only American film appearance as Mature's jilted fiancée in *Seven Days' Leave*. Arnold Stang, who played a pipsqueak private, was for years the voice of various animated characters including TV's *Top Cat*. Producer-director Tim Whelan's sixteen-year-old discovery, Marcy McGuire, made her screen debut as Lucille's boy-crazy kid sister. This was the first movie task for Broadway dance director Charles Walters, too. Afterwards, he continued his career at MGM, first as a choreographer and later directing such musicals as *Easter Parade* (1948) and *High Society* (1956).

Mature joined the Coast Guard following completion of *Seven Days' Leave*, making it his last film until after the war. The picture was also Lucille's last under contract to RKO. The previous spring she had signed a new seven-year agreement for an increased salary, yet she remained a star of B pictures. Koerner was a friend and knew RKO had nothing great in store for her, so when MGM expressed interest in Lucille, he agreed to let her go. It pained her to leave behind the hairdressers, seamstresses, grips, etc., whom she had come to regard as family. But at MGM, producer Arthur Freed awaited to star her in his next musical extravaganza.

Though *Seven Days' Leave* was another example of RKO's inability to provide Lucille with ideal vehicles, in a way, the film let her leave on a high note. It was one of the studio's top moneymakers of 1942.

Sharing a laugh with Victor Mature

Lucille watches the future *Samson* have his hair cut on the set.

MGM and Beyond

(1943 to 1974)

By 1942, Lucille knew it was unlikely she would ever break out of Queen of the Bs status at RKO. She had enjoyed working there, but it was time to move to a new studio. She chose the biggest of them all, MGM, where she received the "star treatment" and was made over to fit in with their extravagant style. MGM was distinguished for its big-budget musicals. In the early '40s, the output was designed to build the morale of audiences living in a world at war. Lucille became a dynamic addition to such films.

In the second half of the '40s, she worked for other studios such as United Artists, Paramount, and Columbia in a variety of films, from whodunits to screwball comedies, portraying characters including Ellen Grant (*Miss Grant Takes Richmond*) and Sally Elliot (*The Fuller Brush Girl*) that capitalized on her mastery of physical comedy and handling of props.

Riding high on the success of *I Love Lucy*, she made two more films at MGM in the mid-'50s with Desi. Then, during the '60s and '70s, Lucille made sporadic returns to the big screen that served as delightful reminders of the past film career of a star who had become the First Lady of Television.

At MGM. *Easy to Wed.* Costume by Irene, hairstyle by Sydney Guilaroff, photographed by Clarence Sinclair Bull.

Du Barry Was a Lady

A Metro-Goldwyn-Mayer Picture (1943)

Cast: Red Skelton (Louis Blore/King Louis XV); Lucille Ball (May Daly/Madame Du Barry); Gene Kelly (Alec Howe/Black Arrow); Virginia O'Brien (Ginny); Rags Ragland (Charlie/Dauphin); Zero Mostel (Rami the Swami/Taliostra); Donald Meek (Mr. Jones/Duc de Choiseul); Douglass Dumbrille (Willie/Duc de Rigor); George Givot (Cheezy/Count de Roquefort); Louise Beavers (Niagara); Tommy Dorsey and His Orchestra

Credits: Arthur Freed (producer); Roy Del Ruth (director); Irving Brecher, Nancy Hamilton, and Wilkie Mahoney (screenplay), from play by Herbert Fields and B. G. DeSylva, as produced by B. G. DeSylva; photographed in Technicolor by Karl Freund; Natalie Kalmus (Technicolor color director), Henri Jaffa (associate); Warren Newcombe (special effects); Georgie Stoll (musical director); Roger Edens (musical adaptation); George Bassman, Leo Arnaud, Alec Stordahl, and Sy Oliver (orchestration); Merrill Pye (musical presentation); Charles Walters (dance director); Cedric Gibbons (art director); Edwin B. Willis (set decoration), Henry Grace (associate); Irene (costumes), Shoup (associate); Gile Steele (men's costumes); Jack Dawn (makeup); Douglas Shearer (recording); Blanche Sewell (editor)

Songs: "Du Barry Was a Lady," "Madame, I Love Your Crepes Suzettes" (Burton Lane and Ralph Freed); "Salome" (E. Y. Harburg and Roger Edens); "I Love an Esquire Girl" (Lew Brown, Freed, and Edens); "Ladies of the Bath," "Song of the Rebellion" (Edens); "Do I Love You," "Katie Went to Haiti," "Friendship" (Cole Porter)

Release date: August 13, 1943 (Capitol Theater)

Run time: 101 minutes

Synopsis

Hat-check boy Louie Blore (Red Skelton) and dancer Alec Howe (Gene Kelly) are both head over heels for May Daly (Lucille Ball), the nightclub star. Louie is May's pal, but her heart belongs to Alec. There's just one problem. Alec is broke and May "can't afford to marry for love." She explains this to him and they argue, leaving her with a heavy heart, but still seeing dollar signs.

As luck would have it, Louie wins the Sweepstakes the following day and abruptly announces that he and May will be wed. May lets him know that her only interest is his money, but Louie intends to marry his dream girl under any circumstances. To keep Alec from posing a threat, Louie attempts to slip him a Mickey Finn, but their glasses are switched, and Louie downs the knockout drink himself. Within seconds, his subconscious sends him to a far-off time and place.

Lucille and Red Skelton as May and Louie

Gene Kelly, Lucille, Red Skelton, Virginia O'Brien, and Tommy Dorsey perform the Cole Porter classic, "Friendship."

Louie awakens as King Louis XV, whose mistress is the notorious Madame Du Barry. Trying to put an end to the affair is the Black Arrow, whose followers protest the king's lavish spending of the people's tax dollars on luxuries for Madame. When he and Du Barry finally come face to face, she falls in love. The Black Arrow assembles a mob to bring down the king, but he is arrested and sentenced to the guillotine. Du Barry begs Louis to spare his life. Seeing how deeply she loves him, the king agrees.

Shortly after, Louie regains consciousness. He is in present-day New York again, and his dream has made him see that May belongs to another. May realizes she would rather be poor and happy with Alec than marry for money. Louie, meanwhile, finds romance with the singing cigarette girl, Ginny (Virginia O'Brien).

Notes and Comments

Lucille's contract with MGM went into effect August 1, 1942 and shortly thereafter, cameras rolled on *Du Barry Was a Lady*. It was her first picture away from RKO in seven years. At a cost of $1.2 million, never before had so much money been expended on one of her films. But then, she had never worked for Arthur Freed, the top musical producer at Hollywood's top studio. "At first, I was plain scared," she later wrote, " . . . Pliable as a rag doll, I submitted to

Reviews

"The underlying motif is girls, girls, girls, with photogenic Lucille Ball at the head of this department. The proceedings are further blended to the popular taste by music old and new, a top-flight orchestra, a comedy cast and a silk-and-satin production in Technicolor. . . . To her red-headed and later bewigged beauty Miss Ball adds vivaciousness and excellent comedy timing, proving once again that she is a musical-comedy star of the first magnitude."
                —*New York Herald-Tribune*

"Metro has made a film version of 'Du Barry Was a Lady' [for] the delight of the multitudes. And take it from us, that's the purpose which it is certain to fulfill. . . . they have tossed the juicy dame role to Lucille Ball, who carries it well . . . they have given the whole show a Technicolor sheen, an eye-filling opulence and splendor, which is fabulous in these rationed times."
                —*New York Times*

"The film is full of fun. . . . Red Skelton clowns absurdly and Lucille Ball is tops as the tough singer who becomes Du Barry. The songs are great . . . "
                —*New York Journal-American*

The riotous Du Barry

being re-styled, or revamped from the clothes on my back to the hair on my head to many of the ideas inside of it."

This film gave the public its first sight of Lucille Ball in color, a vision so astounding that *Life* magazine proclaimed her "Technicolor Tessie," the "best subject for color films." Her naturally brown hair had already been platinum blonde, dark brown, and finally strawberry blonde, but for *Du Barry*, hairstylist Sydney Guilaroff opted for a more startling effect, a shade known as "Tango Red." She initially hated it, but it worked well in the lush Technicolor photography of Karl Freund (later a key member of the *I Love Lucy* crew).

On the stage, *Du Barry Was a Lady* was a sensation of the 1939–40 Broadway season (Lucille had enjoyed it during a trip to New York when she first saw Desi in *Too Many Girls*). In spite of the play's success, MGM was required to make a great deal of changes in their translation. They even toyed with the idea of changing the title to *Gentlemen's Choice*. The story's off-color humor called for extensive rewrites at the outset, and then the script was submitted many times to the Production Code Administration for approval. Various lines and scenes, such as the one set in Du Barry's bedroom with her palace guards, were considered too suggestive and had to be modified repeatedly. A few other lines the censors objected to, like, "I couldn't tell you how, but she got along" (from the title song), remained in the final print.

MGM also handpicked an entirely new cast. Lucille's dual role had been originated by her longtime friend Ethel Merman. The stage edition also featured Betty Grable (now a Twentieth

Gene Kelly, as Alec, expresses his love with a song, "Do I Love You."

Century-Fox star, unavailable to MGM) and Charles Walters, who was brought in as the film's choreographer. Other replacements were Red Skelton (for Bert Lahr) and Gene Kelly, who had just scored a hit in his debut film, *For Me and My Gal*.

Only three numbers from the original Cole Porter score made it into the movie, and new tunes were added by MGM talent. Lucille later said, "Though I've been called on to do plenty of singing and dancing in my career, I've never been expert at it." This was a source of apprehension to her when in the company of seasoned musical performers. Martha Mears dubbed her singing voice, but she worked diligently with Walters to master the dance routines. The "Madame, I Love Your Crepes Suzettes" number with Red Skelton called for exhaustive rehearsals bouncing on a trampoline bed, which made her intensely nauseated.

In the character of May Daly, Lucille played it straight for the most part, while the bulk of the clowning came from Red Skelton, but she was best in her comedy scenes as Du Barry and in the musical sequences. The film did admirably at the box office, earning back more than twice its production cost. Ingredients of Cole Porter music, comedy, color, girls galore, and a likeable cast guaranteed success. In the depths of World War II, it was just the kind of escapism the public wanted to help them endure the day's headlines.

As Madame Du Barry, Lucille tries to ward off the advances of ardent lover King Louis XV.

Best Foot Forward

A Metro-Goldwyn-Mayer Picture (1943)

Cast: Lucille Ball (as herself); William Gaxton (Jack O'Riley); Virginia Weidler (Helen Schlessenger); Tommy Dix (Elwood C. Hooper, "Bud"); Nancy Walker (Nancy the Blind Date); June Allyson (Minerva); Kenny Bowers (Dutch); Gloria DeHaven (Ethel); Jack Jordan (Hunk); Beverly Tyler (Miss Delaware Water Gap); Chill Wills (Chester Short); Henry O'Neill (Major Reeber); Sara Haden (Miss Talbert); Donald MacBride (Captain Bradd); Bobby Stebbins (Greenie); Darwood Kaye (Killer); Morris Ankrum (Colonel Harkrider); Nana Bryant (Mrs. Dalyrimple); Harry James and His Music Makers

Credits: Arthur Freed (producer); Edward Buzzell (director); Irving Brecher and Fred Finklehoffe (screenplay), from play by John Cecil Holm, Hugh Martin, and Ralph Blane, as produced by George Abbott; photographed in Technicolor by Leonard Smith; Natalie Kalmus; (Technicolor color director), Henri Jaffa (associate); Lennie Hayton (musical director); Jack Matthias, Leroy Holmes, Conrad Salinger, George Bassman, and Leo Arnaud (orchestration); Charles Walters (dance director); Cedric Gibbons (art director), Edward Carfagno (associate); Edwin B. Willis (set decoration), Mildred Griffiths (associate); Irene (costumes); Gile Steele (men's costumes); Jack Dawn (makeup); Douglas Shearer (recording); Blanche Sewell (editor)

Songs: "Buckle Down, Winsocki," "Wish I May, Wish I Might," "Three Men on a Date," "Ev'ry Time," "The Three Bs," "I Know You by Heart," "My First Promise (The Ring Waltz)," "Alive and Kickin'," "You're Lucky" (Hugh Martin and Ralph Blane)

Release date: June 29, 1943 (Astor Theater)

Run time: 94 minutes

With William Gaxton, trumpet man Harry James, and youngsters Tommy Dix and Virginia Weidler.

Synopsis

As the Senior Prom approaches, the cadets at Winsocki Academy are full of joy—all except Bud Hooper (Tommy Dix), that is. He wrote to his favorite star, Lucille Ball, asking her to be his date and to his amazement, she accepted. The problem is Helen Schlessenger (Virginia Weidler)—his girlfriend, whom he was already set to take to the prom.

Lucille arrives in town the day of the dance, talked into the stunt by her press agent, Jack O'Riley (William Gaxton). Bud informs her she will have to attend as "Helen Schlessenger," the name he submitted to the faculty. No one at school is to know Lucille Ball is at the prom (so no publicity). She is ready to call the scheme off, but Jack assures her he will make it pay off. Meanwhile, the real Helen is furious with Bud for breaking their date.

Bud gets a kiss from his favorite movie star.

At the prom, Lucille is hit on by Bud's friends Dutch (Kenny Bowers) and Hunk (Jack Jordan) and before long, her identity is revealed. Bedlam breaks loose. Lucille has had enough, but Bud talks her into one last dance. Helen chooses this time to get even with Lucille for stealing her man. She tears her dress, leading the crowd in a "souvenir collecting" frenzy as Lucille is stripped down to her slip.

The administration searches for those responsible for bringing a movie star to the dance. Lucille's unsavory incident makes the newspapers, Helen and Bud have yet to reconcile, and Bud receives a severe punishment—he won't graduate. Lucille assumes the blame for everything. She patches up Bud's quarrel with Helen, squares him with Winsocki, then proudly watches her greatest fan accept his diploma at the commencement exercises.

Notes and Comments

Inspired as he often was by the magic of Broadway, Arthur Freed decided to transfer *Best Foot Forward* to the movie screen. MGM paid $150,000 for the rights and announced plans to star Lana Turner and possibly Gene Kelly under the

O'Riley (outfitted to match his star client) tries to sell Lucille on the idea that attending a prom with a teenaged boy will regenerate her fading career.

With Kenny Bowers, Tommy Dix, and Jack Jordan. Bowers and Jordan swapped the characters they portrayed in the stage version. Meanwhile, Dix, who had played "Greenie" on the stage, took the lead male role previously essayed by Gil Stratton.

direction of Vincente Minnelli. The John Cecil Holm story had been presented at the Barrymore Theater by George Abbott during 1941–42, and with a Hugh Martin-Ralph Blane score containing the hit "Buckle Down, Winsocki," *Best Foot Forward* was a rousing success.

In their adaptation, the screenwriters turned an ordinary boarding school into a military academy peopled by a talented and lively bunch, five of whom were members of the New York cast: Tommy Dix, Nancy Walker, Kenny Bowers, Jack Jordan, and June Allyson. Within the Hollywood contingent were MGM starlets Virginia Weidler and Gloria DeHaven. This was seventeen-year-old Weidler's final film. In previous years, she had portrayed memorable youngsters in *The Women* and *The Philadelphia Story*. The members of the large cast were each provided their moment to shine.

When Lana Turner, pregnant with daughter Cheryl, had to pass up *Best Foot Forward*, Lucille was called in to play the movie star—whom they named Lucille Ball. Her wit and dry humor hit the mark as the actress who suffers in Annabel Allison style at the hands of an overly imaginative press agent, played by Broadway musical comedy star William Gaxton.

This was Lucille's first time working with Eddie Buzzell, whom she later named as the first

Though beautiful, the Irene creation Lucille wears to the senior prom is no match for Winsocki's ravenous "souvenir collectors."

director to understand and bring forth her particular style of comedy. In a 1976 interview, Buzzell called *Best Foot Forward* his "favorite" of the thirty-four movies he made (among them the Marx Brothers' *At the Circus* and *Go West*). In addition to starring his "dear friend" Lucille, he said the film, "holds special memories for me because I had a chance to work with talented people who were just getting started in movies—June Allyson. Gloria DeHaven. Nancy Walker. Not to mention a young fellow in the chorus named Stanley Donen. Because of such talents, *Best Foot Forward* was the most fun I ever had directing a picture."

Production ended on March 23, 1943. The feature earned $2,700,000 in domestic film rentals—another hit musical for Lucille at MGM.

Primping on the set

Thousands Cheer

A Metro-Goldwyn-Mayer Picture (1943)

Cast: Kathryn Grayson (Kathryn Jones); Gene Kelly (Eddy Marsh); Mary Astor (Hyllary Jones); Jose Iturbi (as himself); John Boles (Colonel William Jones); Ben Blue (Chuck Polansky); Frances Rafferty (Marie Corbino); Mary Elliott (Helen); Frank Jenks (Sergeant Koslack); Frank Sully (Alan); Dick Simmons (Captain Fred Avery); Ben Lessy (Silent Monk); Guests: June Allyson, Lucille Ball, Maxine Barrat, John Conte, Gloria DeHaven, Judy Garland, Sara Haden, Lena Horne, Marsha Hunt, Don Loper, Marilyn Maxwell, Frank Morgan, Margaret O'Brien, Virginia O'Brien, Eleanor Powell, Donna Reed, Mickey Rooney, Red Skelton, Ann Sothern; the MGM Dancing Girls; Benny Carter and His Band; Bob Crosby and His Orchestra; Kay Kyser and His Orchestra

Credits: Joe Pasternak (producer); George Sidney (director); Paul Jarrico and Richard Collins (screenplay), from story by Jarrico and Collins; photographed in Technicolor by George Folsey; Natalie Kalmus (Technicolor color director), Henri Jaffa (associate); Herbert Stothart (musical director); Cedric Gibbons (art director), Daniel B. Cathcart (associate); Edwin B. Willis (set decoration), Jacques Mersereau (associate); Irene (costumes); Jack Dawn (makeup); Douglas Shearer (recording); George Boemler (editor)

Songs: "Sempre libera" from opera *La traviata* (Giuseppe Verdi); "Daybreak" (Ferde Grofe and Harold Adamson); "I Dug a Ditch" (Lew Brown, Ralph Freed, and Burton Lane); "Three Letters in the Mail Box" (Walter Jurmann and Paul Francis Webster); "Let There Be Music" (Earl Brent and E. Y. Harburg); "United Nations on the March" (Dmitri Shostakovitch, Harold Rome, and Harburg); "Honeysuckle Rose" (Fats Waller and Andy Razaf); "In a Little Spanish Town" (Mabel Wayne, Sam M. Lewis, and Joe Young); "Should I" (Nacio Herb Brown and Arthur Freed); "The Joint is Really Jumpin' in Carnegie Hall" (Roger Edens, Ralph Blane, and Hugh Martin)

Release date: September 13, 1943 (Astor Theater)

Run time: 126 minutes

Synopsis

Singing sensation Kathryn Jones (Kathryn Grayson) travels with the Army to entertain the troops. She meets Private Eddy Marsh (Gene Kelly), whose only wish is to be transferred to the air corps. Her father, Colonel Jones (John Boles), arranges it for him, but Eddy changes his mind about leaving after falling in love with Kathryn.

Kathryn's mother, Hyllary (Mary Astor), is against the romance. She loved a soldier once herself—Colonel Jones. It caused her much heartache to come second to his duties. She does not want the same for her daughter. Eddy voices his own thoughts to Hyllary and lands in the guardhouse until Colonel Jones comes to his rescue.

Before the troops are sent away to the fields of battle, Kathryn puts on a final show, featuring a parade of superstars. Afterwards, she has just enough time to tell Eddy she loves him and that she will be waiting for him at the war's end.

Notes and Comments

Lucille, June Allyson, and Gloria DeHaven, each in *Best Foot Forward* wardrobe, stepped over from the set of their film to make cameo appearances in *Thousands Cheer*. With few exceptions, virtually every

Reviews

Frank Morgan, as a phony physician, takes Lucille's pulse.

star on the Metro roster turned up, converting producer Joe Pasternak's intimate musical into an all-star extravaganza. Allyson and DeHaven were paired for the "In a Little Spanish Town" number, and Lucille performed a comedy sketch. She played a potential Wave who submits to a physical examination administered by an amorous barber (Frank Morgan) posing as a doctor.

Director George Sidney had Gene Kelly and Kathryn Grayson, both relatively new MGM musical stars, in the principal roles, supported by screen veterans Mary Astor and John Boles. Classical musician Jose Iturbi made his film debut. Beside Iturbi, Kay Kyser, Benny Carter, and Bob Crosby were in on the act with their big bands, to give some idea of the range of music heard in *Thousands Cheer*.

The flag-waving tribute to the soldiers had its patriotic premiere at the Astor Theater in New York, where some $534,000 was raised in the sale of war bonds for the Third War Loan Drive.

Meet the People

A Metro-Goldwyn-Mayer Picture (1944)

Cast: Lucille Ball (Julie Hampton); Dick Powell (William "Swanee" Swanson); Virginia O'Brien ("Woodpecker" Peg); Bert Lahr (The Commander); Rags Ragland (Mr. Smith); June Allyson (Annie); Steve Geray (Uncle Felix); Paul Regan (Buck); Howard Freeman (Mr. Peetwick); Betty Jaynes (Steffi); John Craven (John Swanson); Morris Ankrum (Monte Rowland); Miriam LaVelle (Miriam); Ziggie Talent (Ziggie); Kay Medford (Mrs. Smith); Joey Ray (Dance Director); Mata and Hari (Oriental Dancers); Vaughn Monroe and His Orchestra; Spike Jones and His City Slickers

Credits: E. Y. Harburg (producer); Charles Riesner (director); S. M. Herzig and Fred Saidy (screenplay), from story by Sol Barzman, Ben Barzman, and Louis Lantz; Robert Surtees (photography); Lennie Hayton (musical director); Wally Heglin, Conrad Salinger, Hugo Winterhalter, and John Watson (orchestration); Kay Thompson (vocal arrangement); Merrill Pye (musical presentation); Sammy Lee, Charles Walters, and Jack Donahue (dance directors); Cedric Gibbons (art director), Hubert Hobson (associate); Edwin B. Willis (set decoration), Mac Alper (associate); Irene (costumes), Sharaff (associate); Gile Steele (men's costumes); Douglas Shearer (recording); Alexander Troffey (editor)

Songs: "In Times Like These," "Shicklegruber" (Sammy Fain and E. Y. Harburg); "Meet the People" (Henry Myers and Jay Gorney); "Heave Ho" (Harold Arlen and Harburg); "I'd Like to Recognize the Tune" (Richard Rodgers and Lorenz Hart); "Say That We're Sweethearts Again" (Earl Brent); "Smart to be People" (Burton Lane and Harburg)

Release date: April 21, 1944 (Loew's State Theater)

Run time: 100 minutes

Synopsis

For raising over $10,000 for the war effort, "Swanee" Swanson (Dick Powell) wins a date with Broadway star Julie Hampton (Lucille Ball). He uses their date as and opportunity to pitch his play, *Meet the People*. Julie likes the music, and soon the play goes into production. Swanee is appalled to see it remade into a glamorous affair, clashing with his aim of celebrating the average American. He raises a ruckus, rehearsals stop, and Swanee returns home to Morganville, leaving a message for Julie—to do *Meet the People*, she must *meet the people*.

Following his advice, Julie takes a job as a welder in the Morgan Shipyards. At first, she only wants to get the show back,

With Dick Powell

Reviews

"Except [for] a few isolated bright spots in the production, the picture lags lamentably and its efforts to be gay and airy are obliterated by the heavy left hands of the authors . . . Lucille Ball is amusing in spots, as a musical comedy star who takes a job in the shipyards [and,] when she is allowed to dress up in her capacity of stage star, she looks something gorgeous."

—*New York Daily News*

" . . . one of those pictures which simply switch the backstage boy-girl yarn, and it has actors threatening to 'put on the greatest show you ever saw,' which they don't. 'Rags' Ragland and little June Allyson, who is a honey, are lost in the pile. They may build iron ships in that shipyard but they certainly have got a wooden plot."

—*New York Times*

"Story is both innocuous and unimportant, dragging in many spots, and only serves to mount a number of production numbers and specialties. . . . There's a flock of talent on display. Some is spotlighted to fine advantage, while other personalities are lost in the shuffle."

—*Variety*

As Broadway star Julie Hampton, Lucille goes from glamour queen to welder shortly after getting mixed up with a character named Swanee.

but after a few days, she begins to enjoy herself and share Swanee's views on the war workers. Romantic sparks fly, and he agrees to give Broadway another chance with his play. But then he becomes convinced that Julie has been using the shipyard for publicity, and cancels the show again!

Newspapers announce that the war workers are frozen to their jobs for the duration, so Julie remains in Morganville. She plans a celebration for the launching of the shipyard's 300th ship. Swanee's cousin John (John Craven), composer of *Meet the People*, returns from overseas expecting to see their play performed on the stage. Julie cannot bear to disappoint him. She cancels her own show and prepares to put on *Meet the People*, rounding up talent from within the shipyard for the cast. The night of the launching, the crowd is enthusiastic, but backstage Julie yearns for Swanee, who has left town. He returns in time to see the show done exactly as he had envisioned, and dries Julie's tears.

Notes and Comments

Producer E. Y. "Yip" Harburg described *Meet the People* as "a musical with a viewpoint—that is, revue plus story." It was the only producing effort from this prolific lyricist from the Arthur Freed unit whose hits included "Over the Rainbow." Charles Riesner, a veteran director of comedians such as Buster Keaton and W. C. Fields, was called upon to bring the story to life. With Lucille and Dick Powell the only actors centrally involved in the plot, supporting cast members were confined to an assortment of musical routines and comedy sketches.

Meet the People originated as a musical stage revue, showcasing mostly newcomers, that played successfully in Los Angeles, but fizzled out when it reached New York in 1941. Virginia O'Brien benefited most from the show by virtue of her unique rendition of "Say That We're Sweethearts Again." It is said the deadpan expression that became her trademark came from an acute case of stage fright on opening night. She reprised the song for the film.

The world's most glamorous welder and her man.

Bert Lahr and Rags Ragland also contributed brief, amusing sequences.

Dick Powell had been a top star throughout the '30s in Warner Bros. musicals, but this was his first for MGM. He played against type later this year, in *Murder, My Sweet*, which revived his career and led to more tough-guy roles, before focusing his energy behind the camera as a producer-director. He impressed Lucille as a "Great natural performer. So natural that lots of people do not give him credit for many fine performances, because they take him for granted too readily. He

does not make a noise with his acting. He does, however, make a large noise in the business world."

Lucille again played a famous actress—this time of the Broadway stage. Though she did not care for the movie, she at least enjoyed herself while making it with Dick Powell and June Allyson, whose talents she greatly respected and with whom she became fast friends. The future Mrs. Dick Powell, June Allyson, sang Rodgers and Hart's "I'd Like to Recognize the Tune" in *Meet the People*. Powell and Allyson had met briefly backstage of *Best Foot Forward* on Broadway before Allyson came to California. It was this film that brought the pair together again, though there was no romance yet, as he was still married to Joan Blondell.

Championing war workers and the average soldier, *Meet the People* had good intentions and a bright score, but even so, it was a letdown at the ticket window. The picture was in production from June 7, 1943 through the end of the summer. Lucille did not do anymore filming for the rest of the year. This was a trying time for her because Desi had been drafted in May. During the rest of 1943 and the early part of 1944, she performed frequently on radio and in wartime activities. Over the holidays, she participated in the "Hollywood Bond Cavalcade," a bond tour that featured a glorious array of stars and raised millions of dollars for the war effort.

The stars relax with some of the music talent at MGM during a break from filming.

With Virginia O'Brien and Dick Powell

Lucille poses in her dressing room doing needlework between scenes in July 1943.

Ziegfeld Follies

A Metro-Goldwyn-Mayer Picture (1946)

Cast: William Powell (The Great Ziegfeld); Edward Arnold, Fred Astaire, Lucille Ball, Marion Bell, Bunin's Puppets, Lucille Bremer, Fannie Brice, Cyd Charisse, Hume Cronyn, William Frawley, Judy Garland, Kathryn Grayson, Lena Horne, Gene Kelly, Robert Lewis, James Melton, Victor Moore, Virginia O'Brien, Red Skelton, Esther Williams, Keenan Wynn

Credits: Arthur Freed (producer); Vincente Minnelli (director); Lennie Hayton (musical director); photographed in Technicolor by George Folsey and Charles Rosher; Natalie Kalmus (Technicolor color director), Henri Jaffa (associate); Roger Edens (musical adaptation); Conrad Salinger and Wally Heglin (orchestration); Kay Thompson (vocal arrangements); Robert Alton (dance director); Cedric Gibbons, Merrill Pye, and Jack Martin Smith (art directors); Edwin B. Willis (set decoration), Mac Alper (associate); Irene and Helen Rose (costumes); Sidney Guilaroff (hairstylist); Jack Dawn (makeup); Douglas Shearer (recording); Albert Akst (editor); William Ferrari (puppet sequence)

Songs: "Bring on the Beautiful Girls" (Roger Edens and Arthur Freed); "Bring on the Wonderful Men" (Edens and Earl Brent); "Libiamo" from opera *La traviata* (Giuseppe Verdi); "This Heart of Mine," "Beauty" (Harry Warren and Freed); "Love" (Hugh Martin and Ralph Blane); "Limehouse Blues" (Philip Braham); "An Interview (Madame Crematon)" (Edens and Kay Thompson); "The Babbitt and the Bromide" (George and Ira Gershwin)

Release date: April 8, 1946 (Capitol Theater)

Run time: 118 minutes

Synopsis

Up in the heavens, "The Great Ziegfeld" (William Powell) looks back on his illustrious career and wonders what his *Follies of 1946* might have been. For the opening he envisions a pink number—a tribute "to the beautiful girls" starring a ravishing Lucille Ball. A fitting commencement to a show featuring such musical and comedy talents as Judy Garland, Lena Horne, Fannie Brice—and William Frawley.

Notes and Comments

Arthur Freed's fabulously expensive, Technicolored musical revue, like Ziegfeld's own *Follies*, had no storyline, but it had MGM's arsenal of first-rate musical and comedy talents in front of and behind the cameras. In a brief prologue, William Powell reprised his turn as the master showman from the Oscar-winning *The Great Ziegfeld* (1936).

When *Ziegfeld Follies*' original director, George Sidney, withdrew from the picture, Freed asked Vincente Minnelli to take over. Ultimately, however, several directors worked on various segments. Filming took place primarily between April and August 1944, but the film underwent many changes before finally being released two years later. At the first preview in November 1944, *Ziegfeld Follies* had an epic three-hour running time. Poor audience response led to more cutting and reshooting the following month and in early 1945. In spite of its staggering $3,240,000 price tag, the production made money for MGM by grossing over $5,000,000.

Lucille went to work on her portion of the show in April and May 1944 (between *Meet the People* and *Without Love*), under the direction of George Sidney. Freed had planned comedy segments for her, but the continual revising of his material left her with only the opening musical number. She makes a stunning impression in pink with flaming red curls and a feathered headdress and cape as she enters atop the Lone Ranger's horse, "Silver," and then cracks her whip in front of dancers in black sequined panther costumes; all to the tune of "Bring on the Beautiful Girls," which is sung by Fred Astaire before her entrance. Though she was disappointed by the exclusion of her comedy skits, Lucille's opening is probably the most famous image of the all-star spectacular.

Lucille the chorus girl tamer in May 1944

Reviews

"In show business parlance, Ziggy had flops as well as boffs. And so this $3,000,000 kaleidoscopic film glorification of Florenz and his lush extravaganzas also has its flops and boffs . . . The show as a whole is dazzling, colorful, imaginatively conceived, splendidly produced by Arthur Freed and tastefully directed by Vincente Minnelli. It is an interesting innovation in movie entertainment . . . "
—*Cue*

"Metro, through producer Arthur Freed and Director Vincente Minnelli . . . have routined a show with right proportions of glittering spectacle, comedy skits, experienced dancing and fair, if not distinguished, tunes. As in usual revues (not Ziegfeld's!), some are good, some are not—and a few have theatrical distinction, lacking only the character of cinema. . . . Strictly episodic, with inevitable ups and downs, this 'Ziegfeld Follies' is entertaining—and that's what it's meant to be."
—*New York Times*

Without Love

A Metro-Goldwyn-Mayer Picture (1945)

Cast: Spencer Tracy (Pat Jamieson); Katharine Hepburn (Jamie Rowan); Lucille Ball (Kitty Trimble); Keenan Wynn (Quentin Ladd); Carl Esmond (Paul Carrell); Patricia Morison (Edwina Collins); Felix Bressart (Professor Grinza); Emily Massey (Anna); Gloria Grahame (Flower Girl); George Davis (Caretaker); George Chandler (Elevator Boy); Clancy Cooper (Sergeant)

Credits: Lawrence A. Weingarten (producer); Harold S. Bucquet (director); Donald Ogden Stewart (screenplay), from play by Philip Barry, as produced by the Theatre Guild, Inc.; Karl Freund (photography); A. Arnold Gillespie and Danny Hall (special effects); Peter Ballbusch (montage); Bronislau Kaper (musical score); Cedric Gibbons and Harry McAfee (art directors); Edwin B. Willis (set decoration), McLean Nisbet (associate); Irene (costumes), Marion Herwood Keyes (associate); Douglas Shearer (recording); Frank Sullivan (editor)

Release date: March 22, 1945 (Radio City Music Hall)

Run time: 110 minutes

Her entrance as Kitty Trimble. The part had been portrayed on stage by Audrey Christie.

Synopsis

Scientist Pat Jamieson (Spencer Tracy) arrives in Washington at the height of the wartime housing shortage. He is out on the streets until he bumps into the inebriated but hospitable Quentin Ladd (Keenan Wynn), who leads him to the home of his cousin, Jamie (Katharine Hepburn). Pat is developing an oxygen mask for the military, and Jamie's cellar is an ideal workplace. He and Jamie get off to a rocky start, but she opens her home to him to aid the war effort.

Concerning love, Pat and Jamie have one thing in common—they are both through with it. Pat because he has been hurt, Jamie because her beloved died. Jamie wants to stay with Pat in the house and help him with his project, but to make it proper, she proposes marriage—without love. Pat accepts. Their union appears peculiar to outsiders, but they are content to work side by side for months until the oxygen mask is completed.

Inevitably, Jamie feels the lack of love in her life, seeing the romance between Quentin and her friend Kitty Trimble (Lucille Ball). When Pat is called to Chicago to test the invention, Jamie follows. Chicago is the home of the woman who broke his heart, and Jamie fears losing Pat to her. When Jamie's jealous streak begins to show, they argue and Jamie goes home. When the oxygen mask is a success, Pat finds himself wishing Jamie were still there to share the moment.

Back home, Pat hears from Kitty that Jamie has been seeing playboy Paul Carrell (Carl Esmond). The thought arouses *his* jealousy. Pat and Jamie start anew with a relationship built on love, and Quentin pops the question to Kitty.

Notes and Comments

After Lucille completed her sequence in *Ziegfeld Follies*, there was a five-month lapse in her filming schedule in 1944. At the studio, she spent a good deal of time learning comedy from two masters, Buster Keaton and director Ed Sedgwick (the latter she had first met at RKO during the making of *That Girl from Paris*).

With Spencer Tracy, who ranked fifth this year on the list of top box-office draws.

Reviews

"Without Love is a satiny translation of a Philip Barry play . . . a good deal of the dialogue is happy to hear and happier in its skill; Katharine Hepburn and Spencer Tracy are exactly right for their jobs; it is good to see Lucille Ball doing so well with a kind of role new to her . . . "
—*The Nation*

"There is a nice love-story hidden somewhere in the picture, and though there is practically no attempt really to explore or explain its possibilities, it somehow gets itself satisfactorily told. To a great extent Philip Barry, and Donald Ogden Stewart, who wrote the skillful screenplay, are to be thanked for this. . . . Lucille Ball handles her lowly wisecracks so well as to set up a new career for herself."
—*Time*

" . . . despite its gab and weaknesses in spots, 'Without Love' is really most amusing. And that goes for its bright particular stars. Miss Hepburn gives a mischievous performance . . . Mr. Tracy is charmingly acerbic . . . Keenan Wynn is delightfully diverting . . . and Lucille Ball throws the wise-cracks like baseballs as a good old wise-guy friend."
—*New York Times*

With Spencer Tracy, Keenan Wynn, Katharine Hepburn, and Carl Esmond

Kitty and Quentin play hard to get until . . .

Quentin decides to stop their frustrating games and proposes to her.

When Lucille returned to filming, it was alongside two other performers she admired tremendously—Spencer Tracy, one of her favorite actors, and Katharine Hepburn, whom she had idolized since Hepburn's days as RKO's most revered star.

Having superbly revitalized Hepburn's career with *The Philadelphia Story* a few years earlier, playwright Philip Barry set out write another story especially for her; *Without Love* was the result. She starred in the stage edition, which opened in New York in November 1942. In Hollywood the play was adapted by Donald Ogden Stewart as the third co-starring vehicle for Tracy and Hepburn. *Keeper of the Flame*, a suspenseful drama of political intrigue (also with a script by Stewart) had been the follow-up to *Woman of the Year*, the sparkling comedy that began the pair's alliance (both onscreen and off).

Without Love was a return to lighter fare for Tracy and Hepburn, with strong comedy players in support. Catch Gloria Grahame in an amusing bit as a flower seller with hayfever. Lucille and Keenan Wynn contributed expert performances and won praise as a promising new comedy combination. Wynn had been signed by MGM in 1942 and played mostly wisecracking secondary characters throughout the decade, but his career continued both in films and television up into the mid-'80s.

This was the final film from Harold S. Bucquet before his death a year later. The director of most of the *Dr. Kildaire* series for Metro ended his career on a high note. *Without Love* was a polished comedy strikingly photographed by Karl Freund and charmingly played by its stars.

Lucille began work on the film on October 16, 1944, the same day she appeared in court seeking a divorce from Desi for the first time. She told columnist Louella Parsons the split was caused by "A clash of temperaments. . . . I'm just as much to blame as Desi. We both have tempers and we're both difficult when we're battling." This measure served as a wake-up call rather than an ending. They immediately reconciled, and she later said it was "the shortest-lived interlocutory in the history of the California courts."

The casting of Lucille and Wynn as a tempestuous twosome led to their pairing in an even better comedy, *Easy to Wed*.

Bud Abbott and Lou Costello in Hollywood

A Metro-Goldwyn-Mayer Picture (1945)

Cast: Bud Abbott (Buzz Kurtis); Lou Costello (Abercrombie); Frances Rafferty (Claire Warren); Robert Stanton (Jeff Parker); Jean Porter (Ruthie); Warner Anderson (Norman Royce); Mike Mazurki (Klondike Pete); Carleton G. Young (Gregory LeMaise); Donald MacBride (Dennis Kavanaugh); Edgar Dearing, Robert Emmett O'Connor (Studio Guards); Katharine Booth (Louise); Lyttle Sisters (Singers); Marion Martin (Miss Milbane); Arthur Space (Director); Wm. "Bill" Phillips (Kavanaugh's Assistant); Chester Clute (Mr. Burvis); Marie Blake (Secretary); Wheaton Chambers (Pedestrian); In guest appearances as themselves: Rags Ragland, Lucille Ball, Preston Foster, and Robert Z. Leonard

Credits: Martin A. Gosch (producer); S. Simon Sylvan (director); Nat Perrin and Lou Breslow (screenplay), from story by Nat Perrin and Martin A. Gosch; Charles Schoenbaum (photography); George Bassman (musical director); Ted Duncan (orchestration); Charles Walters (dance director); Cedric Gibbons and Wade B. Rubottom (art directors); Edwin B. Willis (set decoration); Irene (costumes), Kay Carter (associate); Valles (men's costumes); Jack Dawn (makeup); Douglas Shearer (recording); Ben Lewis (editor)

Songs: "Fun on the Midway," "As I Remember You," "I Hope the Band Keeps Playing," "The Cocabola Tree" (Ralph Blane and Hugh Martin)

Release date: October 5, 1945

Run time: 83 minutes

Synopsis

Ambitious barbers Buzz (Bud Abbott) and Abercrombie (Lou Costello) decide to become talent scouts, making crooner Jeff Parker (Robert Stanton) their first client. Temperamental star Gregory LeMaise (Carleton G. Young) drops out of a film he is to make with their actress friend Claire (Frances Rafferty). Buzz and Abercrombie go to see the director on Jeff's behalf. They wind up dodging cops all over the studio lot instead, but with Claire's help, Jeff is chosen to be her new leading man.

When LeMaise finds out he has been replaced, he steps back into the role. To keep him out, Buzz and Abercrombie make him believe he has killed Abercrombie. LeMaise goes into hiding, and Jeff is put back in the picture.

Before long, LeMaise sees Abercrombie is alive, and once again, Abercrombie finds himself hunted throughout the lot. He eludes the enraged actor until the most expensive scene of Jeff's picture is shot.

On the set with Bud Abbott

This secures him the role for good. Now agents to a star, Buzz and Abercrombie purchase the old barbershop.

Notes and Comments

Lucille played herself yet again in a cameo role in this comedy. At "Mammoth Studios," Lou Costello intrudes as she tries to work out a scene for a fictional film with Preston Foster and Robert Z. Leonard. Actor Preston Foster was an old friend whom Lucille had dated occasionally in the mid-'30s; Leonard was the acclaimed director of *The Divorcee* (1930) and *The Great Ziegfeld* (1936). Though she never got to make a picture with Leonard, she did work several times with this film's director, S. Sylvan Simon, in coming years. Simon's comedies with Lucille best projected the qualities that were later ingrained in her television persona.

The famed comedy team was borrowed from Universal for *Bud Abbott and Lou Costello in Hollywood*. The stage veterans had been among the top ten box-office draws since 1941, only a year after their screen debut, but they did not make the list in 1945. This picture did nothing to bolster their standing, but their popularity swelled again later in the decade.

At this point, three of Lucille's last five assignments had been guest appearances. The hectic pace of her first year at MGM had slowed considerably. Unlike RKO, Metro had an immense roster of top stars. Consequently, Lucille was not kept as busy as she was accustomed to being, occasionally losing roles to other actresses, including Angela Lansbury. Luckily though, her best comedy role at MGM was just around the corner.

Guest stars Preston Foster, Lucille, and Robert Z. Leonard chat with the film's director, S. Sylvan Simon (right).

Easy to Wed

A Metro-Goldwyn-Mayer Picture (1946)

Cast: Van Johnson (Bill Chandler); Esther Williams (Connie Allenbury); Lucille Ball (Gladys Benton); Keenan Wynn (Warren Haggerty); Cecil Kellaway (J. B. Allenbury); Carlos Ramirez (as himself); Ben Blue (Spike Dolan); Ethel Smith (as herself); June Lockhart (Babs Norvell); Grant Mitchell (Homer Henshaw); Josephine Whittell (Mrs. Burns Norvell); Paul Harvey (Curtis Farwood); Jonathan Hale (Hector Boswell); James Flavin (Joe); Celia Travers (Farwood's Secretary); Sybil Merritt (Receptionist); Sondra Rodgers (Attendant)

Credits: Jack Cummings (producer); Edward Buzzell (director); Maurine Watkins, Howard Emmett Rogers, and George Oppenheimer (screenplay, *Libeled Lady*), Dorothy Kingsley (adaptation); photographed in Technicolor by Harry Stradling; Natalie Kalmus (Technicolor color director), Henri Jaffa (associate); Johnny Green (musical director and score supervisor); Ted Duncan (orchestration); Jack Donohue (dance director); Cedric Gibbons and Hans Peters (art directors); Edwin B. Willis (set decoration), Jack Bonar (associate); Irene (costumes), Marion Herwood Keyes (associate); Valles (men's costumes); Jack Dawn (makeup); Douglas Shearer (recording); Blanche Sewell (editor)

Songs: "The Continental Polka" (Ralph Blane and Johnny Green); "Acercate Mas" (Osvaldo Farres); "Viva Mexico" (Pedro Galindo); "Boneca de Pixe" (Ary Barroso); "Toca Tu Samba" (Raul Soler)

Release date: July 11, 1946 (Capitol Theater)

Run time: 111 minutes

Synopsis

When the *Morning Star* falsely accuses spoiled heiress Connie Allenbury (Esther Williams) of husband stealing, her father, J. B. (Cecil Kellaway), sues the newspaper for $2 million. It's Warren Haggerty's (Keenan Wynn) job to save the paper. His plan of action is to is turn the slanderous headline into the truth.

Casanova Bill Chandler (Van Johnson) is just the man to assist him in this endeavor. Bill is to marry any willing young woman, make Connie fall in love with him, then have his wife create a scandal by blaming Connie for the breakup of her happy home. Gladys Benton

Connie and Gladys make one too many brides for Bill in *Easy to Wed*.

With Keenan Wynn and Van Johnson

(Lucille Ball) is Warren's short-tempered and long-suffering fiancée. She is persuaded to pretend to marry Bill—but Warren has them legally wed!

Bill goes to work. Connie is suspicious at first but before long, he wins the confidence of both father and daughter. Connie lets down her guard and falls in love with Bill. The change in her makes him feel like a heel. He stalls the proceedings of the scheme and tries to get Connie to drop the lawsuit of her own accord. Bill also works his charm on Gladys to put her on his side, because Warren intends to continue with his smear campaign. While romancing Gladys, Bill has her believing that there is nothing between he and Connie except negotiations for her to drop the charges.

As he gets more deeply involved, Bill tells Connie about Gladys, Warren, and the planned frame-up. Learning of their romance, the affection-starved Gladys refuses to give Bill his freedom, but after a woman-to-woman chat with Connie, she sees that it is Warren she really loves. Almost losing Gladys to another man makes Warren appreciate the terrific girl he has. The *Morning Star* is saved, Gladys has her man's full attention, and our libeled lady, Connie, can now legally marry Bill.

A few drinks bring out the romantic—and the Shakespeare—in Gladys, and make her nearly too hard to handle for Bill.

Notes and Comments

Easy to Wed was a remake of MGM's 1936 screen triumph *Libeled Lady*, which starred William Powell, Myrna Loy, Jean Harlow, and Spencer Tracy. The original story (updated by Dorothy Kingsley) remained much the same, with music, dancing, Technicolor, and a south of the border setting all thrown in for good measure. Lucille and Keenan Wynn, who had proved a winning pair in *Without Love*, assumed the Harlow and Tracy parts, while Van Johnson and Esther Williams stepped into Powell and Loy's roles. It all spelled surefire success. Johnson and Wynn had recently made *Weekend at the Waldorf*, another glossy remake of a 1930s MGM blockbuster (*Grand Hotel*).

The Jack Cummings production was initially called *Early to Wed*. Frank Morgan had been designated to support the four stars as J. B. Allenbury, but ultimately the role went to Cecil Kellaway, who had previously been named for the part of Farwood, the newspaper publisher. His *Postman Always Rings Twice* co-star, Lana Turner, was at one point announced to star in this film as well.

Lucille gave one of her finest performances in *Easy to Wed* and stole the best notices from her then more famous co-stars. She played an inspired drunk scene with Van Johnson, impersonated a female duck ("a red-haired pintailed widgeon") and made each scene she was in hers. Lucille credited director Eddie Buzzell with helping her to discover her uniqueness. He encouraged her to use her own instincts and rather than trying to force a performance, he allowed her to be herself.

The musical sequences were another matter. The day following her first rigorous rehearsals of "The Continental Polka," Lucille played a joke on choreographer Jack Donahue by coming onto the set in a wheelchair, elaborately made up to look battered and bruised, carrying a sign that read, "I am not working for Donahue . . . Period." Of course, she did then and years later as well, when Lucille called on him to direct some of her television series' episodes and specials.

Easy to Wed came on the heels of Johnson and Williams's successful pairing in *Thrill of a Romance*. Water-spectacle star Williams was required to sing for the first time, and in Spanish, no less. She and Johnson also had a duet in Portuguese. They were coached by a musician from Carmen Miranda's band, and then Miranda herself demonstrated the correct pronunciation. Williams told an interviewer, "I do enjoy coming up for air once in a while. That is why Connie Allenbury in *Easy to Wed* is my favorite role so far . . . I learned a great deal about acting from the always-helpful veterans in the cast, Van Johnson, Lucille Ball and Keenan Wynn."

Lucille and Van had been friends since his debut in *Too Many Girls*. Certain he would succeed, she insisted Johnson remain in Hollywood when he was ready to give up. She introduced him to Bill Grady, an MGM talent scout, and this led to a contract with the studio. Within three years he was second only to Bing Crosby in Quigley's nationwide popularity poll. Johnson memorably twirled Lucille around the dance floor as a guest on "The Dancing Star" episode of *I Love Lucy*.

Easy to Wed was completed June 26, 1945, and opened in New York in July 1946 to critical praise and great business. It brought in $4.5 million at the box office. In October of that year, Stanton J. Tolamn, president of the Associated Drama Guilds of America, announced that Danny Kaye and Lucille had been voted the "King and Queen of Comedy."

Gladys takes part in the mating call portion of Bill's duck-hunting lesson.

With Esther Williams and Van Johnson

Two Smart People

A Metro-Goldwyn-Mayer Picture (1946)

Cast: Lucille Ball (Ricki Woodner); John Hodiak (Ace Connors); Lloyd Nolan (Detective Bob Simms); Hugo Haas (Señor Rodriguez); Lenore Ulric (Señora Maria Ynez); Elisha Cook, Jr. (Fly Feletti); Lloyd Corrigan (Dwight Chandwick); Vladimir Sokoloff (Jacques Dufour); David Cota (Jose); Clarence Muse (Porter)

Credits: Ralph Wheelwright (producer); Jules Dassin (director); Ethel Hill and Leslie Charteris (screenplay), from story by Ralph Wheelwright and Allan Kenward; Karl Freund (photography); George Bassman (musical score); Cedric Gibbons and Wade Rubottom (art directors); Edwin B. Willis and Keogh Gleason (set decoration); Irene (costumes); Valles (men's costumes); Sydney Guilaroff (hairstylist); Jack Dawn (makeup); Douglas Shearer (recording); Chester W. Schaeffer (editor)

Song: "Dangerous (Peligrosa)" (Ralph Blane and George Bassman)

Release date: June 4, 1946 (Rialto Theater)

Run time: 93 minutes

As larcenous lovers Ricki and Ace

Synopsis

Ace Connors (John Hodiak) has stolen a large sum in government bonds. Detective Simms (Lloyd Nolan) catches up with him in Beverly Hills, where Ace has met fellow con artist Ricki Woodner (Lucille Ball). Ace agrees to go to prison willingly, provided Simms allows him to make the ride east a pleasure trip. Ace has hidden the bonds to make a handsome reward at the end of his five-year sentence. Fly Feletti (Elisha Cook, Jr.), a hood who believes he is entitled to the bonds, also catches up with Ace. Fly tries to persuade Ricki to help him get them, but she prefers to work alone. She boards the train with Ace and Simms. Within a short time, the charming crooks are in love. They agree to make the most of their limited time together as they arrive in New Orleans in time to celebrate Mardi Gras.

Amid the revelers, Ricki and Ace lose Simms. Ricki proposes they catch a ship to South America that night. Ace agrees and tells her where the bonds are hidden. They lose each other in

A burgeoning romance under the watchful gaze of Detective Simms.

the crowd. Fly, who had been trailing them, grabs Ricki and demands a share of the fortune. She outwits him and escapes. When Ace finds that both Ricki and the bonds are missing, he thinks she has played him for a fool. Both Simms and Fly find Ace. In the confrontation, Fly is shot. Hearing a ship pull away, Ace is certain Ricki is gone. He gives himself up.

To Ace's surprise, Ricki is waiting at the eastbound train to say goodbye when he arrives with Simms. Simms reveals that he found Ace's hidden treasure days ago. Ace is on his way to jail for five years, and Ricki has matters of her own to settle in order to clear out of life as a con artist.

Notes and Comments

Lucille's high hopes for good comedy assignments following her success in *Easy to Wed* were dashed when MGM next starred her in a melodrama. Originally called *Time for Two*, Ralph Wheelwright's first writing and producing endeavor was retitled *Two Smart People*. The script was by Ethel Hill and Leslie Charteris; the latter was the author of the oft-interpreted *Saint* detective stories.

The director, Jules Dassin, worked at MGM and other Hollywood studios during the '40s. After being blacklisted in the early '50s he went to Europe, where

Reviews

"'Two Smart People' is flippantly-treated melodrama. It's never as bright as it tries to be and as a consequence overall results fail to stack up to expectations. . . . Script of the basically okay plot has been packed with awkward dialogue. Over-direction and under-editing are other handicaps. . . . Miss Ball and Hodiak have some good moments in bouncing the plot around, but never quite overcome dialog handicap."

—*Variety*

"Except for a lively and colorful series of Mardi Gras sequences in New Orleans, which are introduced quite late in the picture, 'Two Smart People' is an otherwise dreadfully boring hodgepodge . . . John Hodiak and Lucille Ball are the principals and they are painfully defeated by the script at almost every turn. Lloyd Nolan as the patient sleuth fares a little better, however."

—*New York Times*

"It is a neat idea—assembled, of course, from dozens of other previously-exploited neat ideas—matching John Hodiak and the always enjoyable Lucille Ball . . . Any cat-and-mouse film, to hold interest, has to be helped a lot by characterization and smart photography and direction. Two Smart People has both."

—*PM*

Princess Lucille
and Pirate John
Hodiak on the
set of the Mardi
Gras scenes.

he directed as well as acted in a number of acclaimed films. John Hodiak was cast opposite Lucille. He had

recently been Judy Garland's leading man in *The Harvey Girls*. Lucille thought him "A beautiful man. Huge

inferiority complex. Consistently in love with the unattainable or what he didn't understand. His only love

Anne Baxter." (A few months after completion of this picture Hodiak married Baxter.) Alongside the stars

were compelling supporting actors Lloyd Nolan and Elisha Cook, Jr. Cook's sinister, blackmailing character of

Two Smart People was his specialty. He played such a menace more memorably in *The Maltese Falcon* (1941).

Also, Lucille's cousin Cleo participated, playing a bit part in a Mardi Gras scene, costumed as Cleopatra.

Two Smart People was in production from September to November 15, 1945. The cast did as best they could, but the proceedings never quite came to life, outside of a few fleeting moments. Unfortunately, this year MGM seemed to be too preoccupied with pictures about children and pets (*The Yearling*, *Courage of Lassie*, *My Brother Talks to Horses*) to come up with a second vehicle worthy of this first-class comedienne.

Also in November 1945, Sergeant Desi Arnaz was released from the service and Lucille had concerns closer to her heart than her career. In December she told the *Los Angeles Times*, "Desi is out of the Army and I want to be with him and I want to have a baby. In fact, twins." Children were years away yet. In the meantime, she left Metro a few weeks after *Two Smart People* and decided to continue as a freelance artist.

Stars Lucille, John Hodiak, and Lloyd Nolan on the costume shop set.

A cigarette break with co-star Lenore Ulric and close friend Ed Sedgwick.

With John Hodiak

Sketching on the set. Lucille enjoyed making *Two Smart People*.

A Twentieth Century-Fox Picture (1946)

Cast: Lucille Ball (Kathleen Stuart); Clifton Webb (Hardy Cathcart); William Bendix (Stauffer, a.k.a. White Suit); Mark Stevens (Bradford Galt); Kurt Kreuger (Tony Jardine); Cathy Downs (Mari Cathcart); Reed Hadley (Lieutenant Frank Reeves); Constance Collier (Mrs. Kingsley); Molly Lamont (Lucy Wilding); Forbes Murray (Mr. Bryson); Regina Wallace (Mrs. Bryson); John Goldsworthy (Butler); Charles Wagenheim (Fred Foss); Minerva Urecal (Mother); Raisa (Daughter); Matt McHugh (Milkman); Hope Landin (Scrubwoman); Gisela Werbisek (Mrs. Schwartz); Vincent Graeff (Newsboy); Frieda Stoll (Frau Keller); Thomas Martin (Majordomo); Mary Field (Cashier); Ellen Corby (Maid); Eloise Hardt (Saleswoman); Steve Olsen (Barker); Eddie Heywood and His Orchestra

Credits: Fred Kohlmar (producer); Henry Hathaway (director); Jay Dratler and Bernard Schoenfeld (screenplay), from story by Leo Rosten; Joseph MacDonald (photography); Fred Sersen (special effects); Cyril Mockridge (music); Emil Newman (musical director); Maurice De Packh (orchestration); James Basevi and Leland Fuller (art directors); Thomas Little (set decoration), Paul S. Fox (associate); Kay Nelson (costumes); Ben Nye (makeup); W. D. Flick and Harry M. Leonard (sound); J. Watson Webb (editor)

Release date: May 8, 1946 (Roxy Theater)

Run time: 99 minutes

Synopsis

Private eye Bradford Galt (Mark Stevens) has started fresh in New York with a new office and a budding romance with his secretary, Kathleen (Lucille Ball). But now his painful past is coming back to haunt him in the form of a man in a white suit (William

Bendix) who has been tailing him. Brad forces the man to confess he was hired by Tony Jardine (Kurt Kreuger), Brad's former business partner.

After Brad is nearly run down in the street, Kathleen makes him open up to her about his past to try and comprehend what is happening. Jardine once set Brad up on a charge of manslaughter that sent him to prison. It now looks as if Jardine is not through with him. Brad roughs Jardine up as a warning to lay off, but his ex-partner is innocent this time.

The atmospheric cinematography by Joseph MacDonald in *The Dark Corner* exemplifies the film noir genre.

Brad and Kathleen's growing intimacy illuminates Brad's dark corner.

Jardine has another nemesis in well-known art dealer Hardy Cathcart (Clifton Webb) because he is having an affair with Mrs. Cathcart (Cathy Downs). Knowing the history between Jardine and Brad, Cathcart hired White Suit to make Brad think Jardine was out to get it him. Then, Cathcart hoped, Brad would be provoked to murder Jardine. Since that plot failed, Cathcart turns to plan B—he has White Suit murder Jardine in Galt's apartment.

Searching for clues as to who is framing him, Brad hunts for White Suit, but by the time he tracks him down, the man has been killed by Cathcart. Just when he and Kathleen think they are back at square one, they make the connection between Jardine and Cathcart. Brad goes to his art gallery. While Brad is at last face to face with the man that pushed him into a "dark corner," Mrs. Cathcart puts an end to the nightmare by shooting her husband for the murder of her lover. Brad has his life back, and he and Kathleen have an appointment with the justice of the peace first thing in the morning.

Notes and Comments

Toward the close of 1945, Lucille reported to work at Fox studios for the first time since her Goldwyn days for *The Dark Corner*. At the time, she was caught in

"It's tough, rugged, grim in spades—and won't be topped in this category for some time. . . . In the acting department, Lucille Ball is entitled to heavy honors. When this young lady is given half a chance she demonstrates a quality of work that is all too rare in pictures. She has been given ample opportunity in this to display her superior ability."
— *Los Angeles Examiner*

"As whodunits go, 'The Dark Corner' is a rough, tough-talking melodrama that lacks the Sunday punch for a genuine knockout but scores deftly on points. . . . Fortunately, [Mark] Stevens's dilemma includes Lucille Ball as his ever-loving secretary, which is all to the good for the film's brighter moments. . . . 'The Dark Corner' is a good cut above the run of Hollywood homicide."
— *Newsweek*

"When a talented director and a resourceful company of players meet up with a solid story, say one such as 'The Dark Corner,' then movie-going becomes a particular pleasure. . . . [a] sizzling piece of melodrama."
— *New York Times*

the midst of legal wrangles with MGM while trying to break away from her agent. Ultimately she won independence from her agent and, in the process, from the studio. With Desi away from home so often, it was a terribly distressing time for Lucille personally as well as professionally.

The prospect of acting in a psychological murder mystery increased the strain on her already frayed nerves. Playing a secretary, Lucille spent the first morning of filming behind a typewriter. When lunch was called, a crew member discovered what

With Mark Stevens. The secretary falls in love with the boss. Stevens later directed himself in a crime drama similar to *The Dark Corner*, *Cry Vengeance* (1954).

she had been typing and showed it to director Henry Hathaway: "Dear Mr. Hathaway," she wrote, "If you knew how—nervous I was today you wouldn't dare shoot the picture and you would call the whole thing off and then you wou" She halted abruptly and followed with "LUCY IS A SISSY," repeated three times. When Lucille sat down at her typewriter again after the break she found a response from Mr. Hathaway: "Dear Lucy: Would it help you to know that I'm nervous as hell

myself? Love, H.H." It was a kind gesture on the part of Hathaway, who had a reputation for being difficult with his actors. Unfortunately, further into filming he did not continue to show the compassion Lucille needed in her director at this time and the movie was to remain an unpleasant memory for her.

Based on a novel by Leo Rosten, *The Dark Corner* was Fred Kohlmar's first production for Fox under a new contract with the studio. Lucille had known Kohlmar since her arrival in Hollywood when he was a production assistant to Samuel Goldwyn. He went on to produce such hits as *Picnic* and *Pal Joey* in the '50s. The film had a seasoned and respected director in Hathaway, whose credits include *Lives of a Bengal Lancer* (1935), *Kiss of Death* (1947), and *True Grit* (1969).

Jay Dratler and Bernard Schoenfeld co-wrote the screenplay. Dratler had also collaborated on the script of *Laura*, and *The Dark Corner* emerged with traces of the earlier film noir classic. Clifton Webb was still the unstable egotist who worships the girl in a portrait—Cathy Downs this time, instead of Gene Tierney. *Laura*'s Waldo Lydecker had been the musical comedy veteran's first role in a sound film and in it he earned a supporting actor Oscar nomination. In Webb's next film, *The Dark Corner*, Fox cast him as another urbane character with a sinister esteem for feminine and artistic beauty. Leading man Mark Stevens was another relative newcomer to movies. He was signed by Fox in 1945 and given his first lead the same year.

Kathleen was a more serious role than Lucille was accustomed to, but even her dramatic characters had an abundant supply of wisecracks under the most tense of circumstances. She handled it impeccably, though she could never bring herself to view the film because of the difficulties during production. The suspense-filled *Dark Corner* introduced Lucille to a downbeat genre that had begun to emerge in recent years and truly took hold immediately following World War II—film noir (though it was not so named at the time). 1946 alone also saw the release of noir archetypes *The Killers*, *The Big Sleep*, *Gilda*, *Notorious*, *The Blue Dahlia*, and *The Postman Always Rings Twice*.

An uncommonly virtuous noir heroine, Kathleen Stuart

Lover Come Back

A Fessier-Pagano Production (1946)

Released by Universal Pictures

Cast: George Brent (Bill Williams); Lucille Ball (Kay Williams); Vera Zorina (Madeline Laslo); Charles Winninger (William Williams, Sr., "Pa"); Carl Esmond (Paul Millard); Raymond Walburn (J. P. Winthrop); Wallace Ford (Joe Tubbs); Elisabeth Risdon ("Ma" Williams); William Wright (James Hennessy); Louise Beavers (Martha); Franklin Pangborn (Hotel Clerk); George Chandler (Walter); Joan Fulton (Janie); J. Henry Peeples (Wm. B. Davidson); Pat Alphin (Receptionist); Ellen Corby (Rita)

Credits: Howard Benedict (executive producer); Michael Fessier and Ernest Pagano (producers and screenplay); William A. Seiter (director); Joseph Valentine (photography); Hans J. Salter (music); Jack Otterson and Martin Obzina (art directors); Russell A. Gausman and Ted Offenbecker (set decoration); Travis Banton (costumes); Al Teitelbaum (furs); Carmen Dirigo (hairstylist); Jack P. Pierce (makeup); Bernard B. Brown (sound), Rupert Pritchard (technician); Fred Frank (assistant director); Ray Snyder (editor)

Release date: June 19, 1946 (Loew's Criterion Theater)

Run time: 90 minutes

With George Brent

Synopsis

While her correspondent husband, Bill (George Brent), has been covering the war overseas, Kay Williams (Lucille Ball) has remained on the home front designing gowns for Styles, Inc. and blocking the advances of her male co-workers. When Bill returns, they have a briefly happy reunion before it comes out that while away he professed devotion to many women, including his photographer associate, Madeline (Vera Zorina). He deems his philandering to be his right. Kay plots to get even.

She arouses his jealousy by inviting the amorous Paul Millard (Carl Esmond) over for cocktails. Bill demands she explain herself. Kay says she will be happy to—if he comes clean about his misdeeds. He maintains that a man does not have to explain. Incensed, Kay departs for Las Vegas to seek a divorce.

Millard follows, hoping to benefit from her vulnerable state of mind. Bill and Madeline turn up in Las Vegas too, on an assignment. All at the same hotel, the two mismated couples encounter each other. Kay accepts Millard's marriage proposal. Bill reacts by asking Madeline for her hand. But unable to deny they still love their spouses, Kay and Bill promptly call off their respective engagements. Bill and his similarly unfaithful father (Charles Winninger) have a man-to-man talk that reforms them both and leads Bill and Kay to mend their broken marriage.

Notes and Comments

Since her departure from MGM and her former agent, Lucille had signed with a new representative, Kurt Frings, and on his advice began freelancing. Many stars would soon be taking this route, but when Lucille struck out on her own, she was among a small minority. Lucille herself had doubts about it and was still at an emotional low point following *The Dark Corner*. It took coaxing from Frings and director William Seiter to get her to make *Lover Come Back* at Universal in the spring of 1946. She went into the production unsure of herself and nervous to the point of stuttering, but bolstered by the kindness and understanding shown to her by Seiter and the company, Lucille's mood brightened within days. For this reason, in spite of the film's shortcomings, she felt that making *Lover Come Back* at this time "was the best thing I could have done."

Paul (left) piques the jealousy of Kay's Casanova husband, Bill.

At various stages known as *Lesson in Love*, *Lucy Goes Wild*, and *When Lovers Meet* (the last two reissue titles), *Lover Come Back* was the official title of the film. The producing/writing team behind it, Michael Fessier and Ernest Pagano, turned out numerous comedies for Universal in the mid-'40s. They signed up for *Lover Come Back* veteran director William Seiter, whom Lucille had known for years, having worked with him on *Roberta* and *Room Service* at RKO.

Her errant husband was played by George Brent who, though never a first-string star himself, supplied onscreen romantic interest for the movies' foremost actresses, most frequently Bette Davis. This was ballet dancer Vera Zorina's cinematic exit (she does not dance in the film). Formerly of the Ballet Russe, Zorina made her Hollywood debut in *The Goldwyn Follies* (1938). Supporting roles in *Lover Come Back* were filled by Carl Esmond (who had played another passionate "Paul" in *Without Love*), Charles Winninger, Wallace Ford, and Elisabeth Risdon.

Playing a couturier, Lucille was seen in the height of fashion in every scene. She and designer Travis Banton garnered the picture's highest accolades. Best known for his costumes in the Josef von Sternberg-Marlene Dietrich films, Banton dressed fashion plate Carole Lombard even more often than Dietrich in his days as head designer at Paramount, and costumed many Twentieth Century-Fox musicals during the '40s.

While Lucille made *Lover Come Back*, Desi was appearing at Ciro's in Hollywood, but he would soon be leaving for New York's Copacabana nightclub. *Lover Come Back* was completed April 6, 1946. After that, Lucille was finally able to take a leave of absence from Hollywood without a studio's permission. She took advantage of her freedom and prevented another prolonged separation from her husband by joining him for several months in New York. She could certainly afford a vacation. During the summer of 1946, there were five Lucille Ball films either in theaters or about to be released. She made a round of personal

appearances and was so well received by audiences that the New York papers began calling her the "Female Frank Sinatra."

Lucille's *Lover Come Back* has no relation to the 1961 Doris Day-Rock Hudson comedy of the same name.

Wallace Ford, playing a friend of the Williamses, observes with anxiety the birth of a scheme.

With Vera Zorina

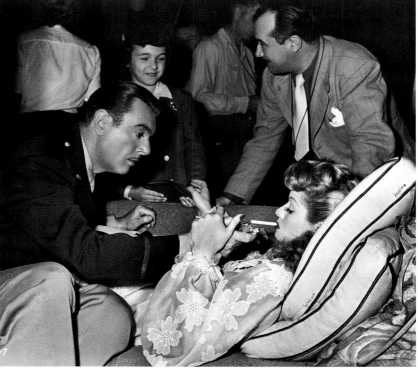

Between scenes with George Brent, a script girl, and cinematographer Joseph Valentine.

Lured

A Hunt Stromberg Production (1947)

Released by United Artists

Cast: George Sanders (Robert Fleming); Lucille Ball (Sandra Carpenter); Charles Coburn (Inspector Temple); Boris Karloff (Charles van Druten); Sir Cedric Hardwicke (Julian Wilde); Joseph Calleia (Dr. Nicholas Moryani); Alan Mowbray (Lyle Maxwell); George Zucco (Officer Barrett); Robert Coote (Officer); Alan Napier (Inspector Gordon); Tanis Chandler (Lucy Barnard)

Credits: Hunt Stromberg (executive producer); James Nasser (producer); Henry Kesler (associate producer); Douglas Sirk (director); Leo Rosten (screenplay), from story by Jacques Companeez, Ernest Neuville, and Simon Gantillon; William Daniels (photography); David Chudnow (musical director); Nicolai Remisoff (production designer and art director), Victor Greene (assistant); Elois Jenssen (gowns); Josephine Sweeney (hairstylist); Don Cash (makeup); John Carter and Joe Kane (sound); Clarence Eurist (assistant director); James E. Newcom (supervising editor); John M. Foley (editor)

Song: "All for Love" (Michel Michelet)

Release date: August 28, 1947 (Victoria Theater)

Run time: 102 minutes

Synopsis

A serial murderer is on the loose in London, and Scotland Yard has received a signal that he is about to strike again. Known as the "Poet-Killer," he sends poems to the police with cryptic clues as to who will be next. Sandra Carpenter (Lucille Ball), a friend of the last victim, is asked to help in the investigation by Inspector Temple (Charles Coburn). The madman preys upon beautiful women, and Sandra is a perfect lure.

The Poet-Killer meets his victims through ads in the personal columns. Sandra answers those calling for young women. After a few wrong turns, including a run-in with an insane dress designer (Boris Karloff), she lands in a home from which three maids have disappeared. It turns out the servants are involved in other offenses. They are brought

With a menacing Boris Karloff

Sandra is safe from harm with Robert.

to justice, but the Poet-Killer remains at large. Scotland Yard receives another poem—this time it appears Sandra will be next.

While working undercover, Sandra has captured the heart of playboy theatrical impresario Robert Fleming (George Sanders), and they are to be married. Sandra's happiness is shattered when her fiancé becomes the prime suspect. Evidence against him mounts to such a degree that Inspector Temple believes Robert is being framed. He puts together a profile of the killer, one which Robert does not fit. However, it describes his business partner, Julian Wilde (Sir Cedric Hardwicke), exactly.

Because he is in love with Sandra, Wilde incriminated Robert, who in Wilde's deluded mind, was taking Sandra away from him. Sandra steps back into her role of decoy to trap Wilde. The killer is apprehended. Sandra and Robert put the nightmare behind them and look ahead to life as Mr. and Mrs.

Notes and Comments

Following her holiday in New York to be with Desi, Lucille returned to moviemaking in an intriguing murder mystery. *Lured* went before the cameras in November 1946. *Personal Column* was the working title of this remake of the 1939 French film *Pieges* (meaning "Traps," or *Snares*, as the French film was also known). The suspense of director Robert Siodmak's earlier version,

Reviews

"It is mystery and melodrama served up with intelligence, mighty fine production, interesting backgrounds and performances many cuts above the ordinary. . . . General suspenseful buildup to climax is smartly handled in direction of Douglas Sirk."

—*Film Daily*

"The slick production dress assisted by some neat camera handling, highly effective score and motionful direction by Douglas Sirk almost, but not quite, succeed in obscuring flaws in the underlying plot structure. . . . Performances are good down the line despite many obvious situations. Miss Ball registers best in comic bits as a wisecracking showgirl . . ."

—*Variety*

" . . . a competently plotted melodrama, only mildly on the sensational side, with the requisite amount of suspense. . . . Miss Ball gives chipper account of herself as the intrepid lady dick, and the others are proportionately helpful. Douglas Sirk invests his direction with a piquant European flavor . . ."

—*Los Angeles Times*

"Lucille Ball is quite a girl and an engaging comedienne. Coburn, Sanders, Hardwicke and Alan Mowbray are natural foils for her comedy."

—*New York Herald-Tribune*

Sandra and Robert drink a toast to their engagement with Robert's partner Julian, played by Sir Cedric Hardwicke (right). When the distinguished Sir Cedric had knighthood bestowed upon him at age forty-one, in 1934, he was the youngest actor to be so honored (until Laurence Olivier in 1947).

With Joseph Calleia, who played a suspicious visitor to the home where Sandra's investigation leads her to be employed as a maid.

starring Maurice Chevalier, Marie Déa, and Erich von Stroheim, was interpolated with music and comedy. *Lured* retained the comic touches and featured the song "All for Love," by Michel Michelet, to lessen the tension.

Released by United Artists, *Lured* was produced by Oakmont Pictures, the then newly formed company of distributor James Nasser and producer Henry Kesler. The film's executive producer, Hunt Stromberg, was one of MGM's most outstanding producers from the silent era through to the early '40s, now working independently. In his past, he had brought about the perfect fusion of comedy, mystery, suspense, and romance (all of which *Lured* combined) in the first four installments of the *Thin Man* series. The screenplay of *Lured* was penned by *Dark Corner* author Leo Rosten. German director Douglas Sirk, in one of his first American films, guided the production a few years before hitting his stride with sumptuous melodramas like *Magnificent Obsession* (1954) and *Imitation of Life* (1959). He brought the picture to completion on January 10, 1947.

Lucille was engaging as the heroine of *Lured*. It was a different kind of role for her but still brought her comedic talent into play, and she looked stunning before the lens of Greta Garbo's favorite cinematographer, William Daniels. Co-star George Sanders, Hollywood's favorite cad, starts out the

With her faithful bodyguard, played by George Zucco

film as another of his rogues, but turns out a sterling character. Charles Coburn, always a memorable personality, as a Scotland Yard inspector, set the tone for the rest of the supporting cast with an absorbing portrayal. The mad couturier, Boris Karloff, had by this time been one of the most bone-chilling of horror film stars for many years. He had only about a five-minute sequence in *Lured* but instilled it with his usual ominous presence. Other important roles went to Alan Mowbray, Sir Cedric Hardwicke, and Joseph Calleia.

Lucille formed a lasting alliance with the woman who created her wardrobe in *Lured*, Elois Jenssen. The designer went on to dress her for years on television, beginning in 1953, when the *I Love Lucy* budget could first afford to have Lucy Ricardo stop dressing "off-the-rack."

Lucille's Sandra was exquisitely groomed, gowned, and made-up throughout *Lured*.

Resting against a board to prevent her gown from wrinkling between takes, Lucille is pictured with co-star George Sanders and dialogue director Stuart Hall.

Her Husband's Affairs

A Columbia Picture (1947)

Cast: Lucille Ball (Margaret Weldon); Franchot Tone (William Weldon); Edward Everett Horton (J. R. Cruikshank); Mikhail Rasumny (Professor Glinka); Gene Lockhart (Peter Winterbottom); Nana Bryant (Mrs. Winterbottom); Jonathan Hale (Governor Fox); Paul Stanton (Dr. Frazee); Mabel Paige (Mrs. Josper); Frank Mayo (Vice President Starret); Pierre Watkin (Vice President Beitler); Carl Leviness (Vice President Brady); Dick Gordon (Vice President Nicholson); Douglas Wood (Tappel); Jack Rice (Slocum); Clancy Cooper (Window Washer); Charles C. Wilson (Police Captain); Charles Trowbridge (Brewster); Selmer Jackson (Judge); Arthur Space (District Attorney); Virginia Hunter (Cruikshank's Secretary)

Credits: Raphael Hakim (producer); S. Sylvan Simon (director); Ben Hecht and Charles Lederer (screenplay); Charles Lawton, Jr. (photography); George Duning (musical score); M. W. Stoloff (musical director); Stephen Goosson and Carl Anderson (art directors); Wilbur Menefee and Louis Diage (set decoration); Jean Louis (gowns); Helen Hunt (hairstylist); Clay Campbell (makeup); Frank Goodwin (recording); Earl McEvoy (assistant director); Al Clark (editor)

Release date: November 12, 1947 (Capitol Theater)

Run time: 83 minutes

A trick cream causes Margaret and Bill to awake to a shock.

Synopsis

Advertising man Bill Weldon (Franchot Tone) and his wife Margaret (Lucille Ball) love each other, but the fact that Margaret comes to his rescue both in business and personal matters is a steady source of friction between them. Eccentric inventor Professor Glinka (Mikhail Rasumny), whom Bill finances, develops a hair-removal system with which Bill and his boss, Cruikshank (Edward Everett Horton), think they have struck gold. The product is tested on many men. The following morning, they all awake with full-grown beards!

Margaret convinces Cruikshank and the board of directors to market the cream as a hair-restoring treatment. Bill, who had plans of his own for it, decides she has butted in one too many times. Meanwhile, Glinka tries to tell them that the cream is completely unpredictable. Margaret finds out what he means when the most peculiar growth of all forms on the head of the governor, who orders the arrest of Bill and Glinka.

Bill is caught, then the police find a cadaver from Glinka's experiments and think Bill has killed the professor. Bill sees a way to make his murder trial the ultimate publicity stunt for yet another of Glinka's crackpot inventions.

He tells Margaret to let him handle the situation his own way, but she cannot help herself. After trying to prove Bill is insane, she finds out Glinka is actually alive. She brings him to court, and the case against Bill is dismissed. All is forgiven between Margaret and Bill as she promises to let him handle his own affairs from now on.

Notes and Comments

Lucille went directly from *Lured* into *Her Husband's Affairs*, the first Columbia picture she appeared in since 1934, when she was a $75-a-week contract player for the studio. Franchot Tone played opposite her. He was at his peak as a leading man in MGM pictures of the '30s, frequently appearing with his then wife, Joan Crawford, but he was still very active throughout the '40s. The dependable Edward Everett Horton led the supporting cast of character actors, with Gene Lockhart and Mikhail Rasumny, in contributing to the reckless proceedings of the Raphael Hakim production. This was Lucille's third and final film with Horton. He would later be the first movie personality to make a guest appearance on *I Love Lucy* (in episode fifteen, "Lucy Plays Cupid").

Margaret inquires about Professor Glinka to save her husband.

" . . . a welcome relief to a box-office overrun with psychosis melodrama. It's zaney [sic], well-premised fun that has a laugh a minute. There's production polish, sure direction and extremely deft performances that add up to pleasurable entertainment."

—*Variety*

"Lucille Ball, an able an comedienne, works hard and adroitly as the wife, and Franchot Tone springs about as the husband, but they labor to little avail. . . . in nonsense as well as serious drama, there must be a pattern, a plan, to sustain the humor. This film has none."

—*New York Times*

" . . . there are some hilariously funny situations that director Sylvan Simon carried off with a high, wide and handsome sweep, disregarding anything that stands in the way of high-tension laughs. . . . Franchot Tone and Lucille Ball carry the ball for Simon all the way here. Tone was never better—nor funnier, while the ever-entrancing Lucille is right in there with him pitching as only she can. Both parts were made to order for this team and they really make a romp of it."

—*Hollywood Reporter*

In a year that theaters were filled with hard-hitting dramas like *Crossfire*, *Out of the Past*, and *Gentleman's Agreement*, *Her Husband's Affairs* hearkened back to the golden age of the screwball comedy. The script came from Ben Hecht and

Bill tries in vain to convince his wife to butt out.

Charles Lederer, an ace writing team who between them generated screenplays for a great many outstanding films. Hecht had contributed to two of the films that defined the screwball era, *Twentieth Century* (1934) and *Nothing Sacred* (1937), both of which starred Carole Lombard. *Life* magazine paid Lucille a great compliment by

comparing her to her favorite star in their review: "Lucille Ball, as [Tone's] Miss Fix-it wife, could give any actress lessons in how to play comedy, will remind many of Carole Lombard at her best."

Her Husband's Affairs encountered opposition when the British film censors saw that the *married* couple's twin beds had been pushed together. Scenes were reportedly reshot at a cost of $30,000 to conform to their standards, but no separation between the beds is seen in prints available today. Hollywood's own censorship board was mainly concerned about the wife of the title's perjured testimony during a trial sequence going unpunished, but Lucille's comedic playing allowed the scene to pass unchanged.

Lucille had known the film's director, S. Sylvan Simon, at MGM, where he directed comedies with Abbott and Costello and Red Skelton. They established a fine working relationship that led to the deal Lucille made with Columbia in early 1949 to star in three films in which Simon was intended to function as producer.

Production wrapped on *Her Husband's Affairs* on March 24, 1947, and it went into release that November. No new Lucille Ball films arrived at theaters in 1948. Two months after this picture was completed, Lucille took to the stage with a road company of the Elmer Rice play *Dream Girl*, which toured the country for six months of success.

In a series of publicity photos, Lucille and Franchot Tone poked fun at the morality standards imposed by film censors in 1947.

Hair and makeup test

Edward Everett Horton, Lucille, and S. Sylvan Simon celebrate Franchot Tone's forty-second birthday.

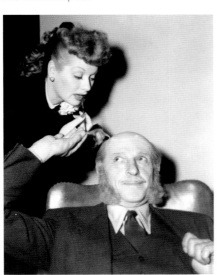

Professor Glinka's invention turns the governor's (Jonathan Hale) head into glass! Lucille applies her lipstick on the set by the reflection.

Taking a break with Mikhail Rasumny and director S. Sylvan Simon.

Sorrowful Jones

A Paramount Picture (1949)

Cast: Bob Hope (Sorrowful Jones); Lucille Ball (Gladys O'Neill); Mary Jane Saunders (Martha Jane Smith); William Demarest (Regret); Bruce Cabot (Big Steve Holloway); Thomas Gomez (Officer Reardon); Tom Pedi (Once Over Sam); Paul Lees (Orville Smith); Houseley Stevenson (Doc Chesley); Ben Weldon (Big Steve's Bodyguard); Emmett Vogan (Psychiatrist); Narration by Walter Winchell

Credits: Robert L. Welch (producer); Sidney Lanfield (director); Melville Shavelson, Edmund Hartmann, and Jack Rose (screenplay), from story by Damon Runyon and screenplay by William R. Lipman, Sam Hellman, and Gladys Lehman; Daniel L. Fapp (photography); Gordon Jennings (special effects); Farciot Edouart (process photography); Robert Emmett Dolan (musical score); Hans Dreier and Albert Nozaki (art directors); Sam Comer and Bertram Granger (set decoration); Mary Kay Dodson (costumes); Wally Westmore (makeup); Harold Lewis and John Cope (sound); Oscar Rudolph (assistant director); Arthur Schmidt (editor)

Songs: "Havin' a Wonderful Wish (Time You Were Here)," "Rock-a-Bye Bangtail" (Jay Livingston and Ray Evans)

Release date: July 5, 1949 (Paramount Theater)

Run time: 89 minutes

Synopsis

Broadway's favorite penny-pinching bookie, Sorrowful Jones (Bob Hope), loses a bundle when a horse named Dreamy Joe comes in first. Its owner, Big Steve (Bruce Cabot), rigs the next race in favor of the local bookies, so Sorrowful is accepting all bets on Dreamy Joe. One gambler leaves his daughter, Martha Jane (Mary Jane Saunders), with Sorrowful as collateral. The man is killed after learning of Big Steve's racetrack scam. Sorrowful's old flame, Gladys O'Neill (Lucille Ball), convinces Sorrowful to take in the four-year-old orphan.

Big Steve offers to guarantee Dreamy Joe will win his next race, with the help of a final, deadly "speedball." In return, Sorrowful must loan him $5,000 and allow Steve to pass the horse off as belonging to Martha Jane while the racing commission is suspicious of him. The girl falls in love with the nag, while Sorrowful and Gladys fall in love with Martha Jane. They decide to stall turning her over to the welfare services until after the

With Bob Hope, William Demarest, and Mary Jane Saunders

race so Martha Jane can collect the purse money. Officer Reardon (Thomas Gomez) is aware the girl is the murdered man's daughter. The horse makes him connect her to Big Steve—Reardon knows who the killer is.

Martha Jane is severely injured after a fall. In her daze she calls for Dreamy Joe. The horse is her only hope for survival. Sorrowful and his pal Regret (William Demarest) sneak the horse away from Big Steve before the big race, and take it to Martha Jane. With Dreamy Joe's help, her recovery begins immediately. Reardon arrests Big Steve for the murder of the girl's father. Sorrowful and Gladys decide they love Martha Jane, and each other, enough to form a family.

Notes and Comments

After the January 1948 conclusion of her *Dream Girl* tour, Lucille went back before the camera for *Sorrowful Jones* in late April. It was the first production to

As nightclub singer Gladys O'Neill, gowned by Mary Kay Dodson

Reviews

"The comedy is warm, played with a lot of heart, and is slated for a broad audience appeal. . . . Lucille Ball was a slick choice for the femme lead, interpreting Runyon's idea of a Broadway doll with considerable skill to make it entirely believable. . . . Sidney Lanfield's affectionate direction gets all to be had from the story and the players, making it very satisfactory entertainment."
                    —*Variety*

"Bob Hope is at his clowning best in 'Sorrowful Jones.' . . . [Lucille Ball] is a fine foil for the star, building up bits of business to a point where they are comically consequential, even though they have next to nothing to do with the plot. . . . 'Sorrowful Jones' is familiar material, made fresh and funny by Hope's superb jesting."
                    —*New York Herald-Tribune*

"Three energetic gag writers have provided [Hope] with a script that is loaded with farce situations and explosively funny gag lines. . . . Mary Jane Saunders is a cipher of juvenile cuteness in the 'marker' role, and Lucille Ball is a girl who knows her small place and keeps it as the night-club singing queen."
                    —*New York Times*

Gladys naturally takes to mothering the little girl.

pair her with Bob Hope on the screen. They had performed together on radio and in shows for the troops during the war, but Lucille did not realize she had ever made any particular impression on Hope until word came from Paramount that he had requested her to star opposite him in his next film. The screenplay was based on Damon Runyon's *Little Miss Marker* and was a remake of the 1934 film starring Shirley Temple, Adolphe Menjou, and Dorothy Dell. *Sorrowful*

Jones placed the accent on humor more than did the earlier version, but it still had sentimental, heartwarming moments that highlighted a new aspect of Bob Hope's persona.

In 1934, Menjou had been the nominal star of *Little Miss Marker*, but Shirley Temple stole the show. Paramount conducted a six-month-long search for an "unknown" to fill her shoes. Five-year-old Mary Jane Saunders of Pasadena, California was selected among the estimated 5,000 applicants interviewed. Lucille, meanwhile, replaced Dell as Sorrowful's girl. Bob Hope was the number one box-office draw in America that year. He took center stage, but in her supporting role, Lucille

Lucille and Hope created a special magic onscreen that she found with a select few other male co-stars. The two repeated their characterizations of Gladys and Sorrowful for the popular *Lux Radio Theatre* in November 1949.

showed that they were perfectly matched. They were close friends who would be teamed in three more films and often work together on television.

The crew behind the cameras had worked with Hope often and scored another hit with *Sorrowful Jones*. Robert Welch, who made his producing debut with Hope's latest blockbuster, *The Paleface*, oversaw production and Sidney Lanfield directed. Along with his previous Hope pictures, Lanfield, a former vaudevillian, was noted for his Fox musicals of the late '30s.

Lucille thoroughly enjoyed the experience of working on a film with Bob Hope. She told a reporter, "His humor always keeps the whole company rolling which is a pretty wonderful thing because [there] is always a certain amount of tension and temperament in most companies." Hope kept his fellow studio employees smiling by riding around the lot on a bicycle bearing a sign that read, "Bob Hope—Available for Parties, Banquets, Weddings, etc." Lucille posted a sign of her own on her dressing room door: "Lucille Ball. Wife of Desi Arnaz. Stooge for Bob Hope. Sympathetic Friend of Dolores Hope. New Fan of Bing Crosby's."

Production came to a close on June 9, 1948. The reviews were excellent, and it earned greater profits than any of Hope's previous pictures. The two factors that made *Sorrowful Jones* vary from his other films were that it offered a slightly

different character to portray and gave him a new and equally funny leading lady.

Little Miss Marker was remade again under that name in 1980 with Walter Matthau. Tony Curtis starred in still another version from 1962 called *Forty Pounds of Trouble*.

A month after *Sorrowful Jones* was completed, Lucille embarked on an entirely new project. Her very own radio series, *My Favorite Husband*, premiered on CBS-Radio. She was soon to become one of the country's best-loved radio personalities.

With director Sidney Lanfield

Little Mary Jane Saunders had modeling experience, but no film credits when she was cast in *Sorrowful Jones*.

Easy Living

An RKO-Radio Picture (1949)

Cast: Victor Mature (Pete Wilson); Lucille Ball (Anne); Lizabeth Scott (Liza Wilson); Sonny Tufts (Tim McCarr); Lloyd Nolan (Lenahan); Paul Stewart (Argus); Jack Paar (Scoop Spooner); Jeff Donnell (Penny McCarr); Art Baker (Howard Vollmer); Gordon Jones (Bill Holloran); Don Beddoe (Jaegar); Dick Erdman (Buddy Morgan); William "Bill" Phillips (Ozzie); Charles Lang (Whitey); Kenny Washington (Benny); Julia Dean (Mrs. Belle Ryan); Everett Glass (Virgil Ryan); James Backus (Dr. Franklin); Robert Ellis (Urchin); Steven Flagg (Gilbert Vollmer); Alex Sharp (Don); Russ Thorson (Hunk Edwards); June Bright (Billy Duane); Edward Kotal (Curly); Audrey Young (Singer); Dick Ryan (Danny the Bartender); the Los Angeles Rams

Credits: Robert Sparks (producer); Jacques Tourneur (director); Charles Schnee (screenplay), from story "Education of the Heart" by Irwin Shaw; Harry J. Wild (photography); Russell Cully (special effects); Roy Webb (music); C. Bakaleinikoff (musical director); Albert D'Agostino and Alfred Herman (art directors); Darrell Silvera and Harley Miller (set decoration); Edward Stevenson (gowns); Gordon Bau (makeup); Earl Wolcott and Clem Portman (sound); James Lane (assistant director); Fredric Knudtson (editor)

Song: "Easy Living" (Leo Robin and Ralph Rainger)

Release date: October 8, 1949 (Loew's Criterion Theater)

Run time: 77 minutes

Synopsis

Pete Wilson (Victor Mature) is "King Football," star of the New York Chiefs. The team secretary, Anne (Lucille Ball), has a habit of falling for the wrong men. She loves Pete, but he is utterly enraptured by his beautiful, social-climbing wife, Liza (Lizabeth Scott). Liza is opening a design firm. The wealthy Howard Vollmer (Art Baker)—more interested in her than in the business—finances Liza Inc., in spite of her lack of talent.

Knowing his wife is intolerant of weakness, Pete keeps quiet about a heart condition he has developed and continues playing football against doctor's warnings. He has the alternative of becoming an assistant coach of a college team, but fears it would mean losing Liza. He cannot perform like he used to, and his best friend, Tim McCarr (Sonny Tufts), replaces him as team star. As Pete's game founders, so does his marriage. After he and Liza separate, Pete pours his heart out to Anne, letting the truth slip

With Victor Mature and Paul Stewart

Anne's popularity with the team players proves to be no cure for loneliness.

about the state of his health. Anne cannot keep the secret when Pete vows to put his all into the next playoff game to impress Liza. Anne and Tim make Pete come to his senses, and he finally retires from playing.

Liza takes a turn for the worse after their split. She sees what a mistake it was to put Liza Inc. before Pete, and to have taken up with Vollmer. Happy to be in Pete's arms again, Liza is ready to stand by her man as assistant coach or anything else he may become.

Notes and Comments

Lucille returned to her alma mater, RKO, in this tale of a football hero's fall from glory by Irwin Shaw. The studio had become a very different place from the one she had left six years earlier. In May 1948, it was purchased by Howard Hughes. In July, seventy-five percent of the personnel was laid off and production was cut to a bare minimum. *Easy Living*, then titled *Interference*, began filming in the midst of these upheavals, in mid-July 1948.

Jacques Tourneur (*Cat People*, *Out of the Past*), directed for producer Robert

Reviews

"Its story is more complicated than the usual pigskin drama, but from the general audience viewpoint its over-drawn situations hold up fairly well. If action seems lacking there is strong personal motivation to compensate. The Robert Sparks production shoots the works in casting with five important players spotted in the leading roles. They perform the intriguing characterizations with expected finesse."

—*Hollywood Reporter*

" . . . the cast names are good, but, on the whole, it's disappointing film fare that lacks the common touch to put it over. . . . Lucille Ball's starring role, while expertly done, doesn't realize on the possibilities of her name and talent."

—*Variety*

" . . . a slick, quick, nervous melodrama, in which pseudo-sophistication, obvious-ness, and artificial dialogue give cause for cringes. . . . Lucille Ball plays that wise-cracking secretary role that she can do with one arm tied behind her."

—*Hollywood Citizen News*

"Charles Schnee has written a bright, well-knit adaptation of an Irwin Shaw short story . . . The entire cast—particu-larly Mature, Tufts, Miss Ball and Lloyd Nolan—give attractive performances, and even Lizabeth Scott, as the wife, turns her lip-chewing to advantage."

—*New York Times*

Stars Victor Mature, Lizabeth Scott, Sonny Tufts, and Lucille

Sparks. During the late '30s and early '40s, Sparks turned out many installments of Columbia's *Blondie* series, which starred his wife, Penny Singleton. *Easy Living* starred Victor Mature, Lucille's *Seven Days' Leave* co-star, this time much more subdued and poignant in his performance. His career was back on track after serving in the war, and he was re-establishing himself as a regular in crime dramas, and soon in biblical epics. Lizabeth Scott was his selfish wife in the film (a part originally intended for Jane Greer). A discovery of producer Hal Wallis, Scott had attracted attention in 1947 opposite Humphrey Bogart in *Dead Reckoning*. The picture also featured Sonny Tufts, Lloyd Nolan (from *Two Smart People*), and a young Jack Paar who, like Lucille, found his greatest success in television, hosting his own show.

Anne temporarily takes Pete's mind off of the conspicuous absence of his wife at a party for the football club.

Lucille played the second female lead—a clever secretary who hides a heart of gold behind her keen wit. The character engenders more sympathy than Lizabeth Scott's, and makes the audience root for her to get the guy instead. The film had many commendable points, but Lucille was inexcusably wasted in *Easy Living*—further proof that while it grieved her to leave the place that felt like home, walking out of RKO in 1942 had been a wise move indeed.

Filming of her thirty-sixth and final RKO feature was completed on August 20, 1948. Within a decade, the studio's soundstages would be part of the Desilu television empire. Already the signs were showing. In 1948, the movie industry saw an alarming drop in business, while the sale of television sets quadrupled.

Anne receives counsel from her boss and former father-in-law, played by Lloyd Nolan.

Lucille poses at the football stadium.

Miss Grant Takes Richmond

A Columbia Picture (1949)

Cast: Lucille Ball (Ellen Grant); William Holden (Dick Richmond); Janis Carter (Peggy Donato); James Gleason (Mr. Gleason); Gloria Henry (Helen White); Frank McHugh (Mr. Kilcoyne); George Cleveland (Judge Ben Grant); Stephen Dunne (Ralph Winton); Arthur Space (Willacombe); Will Wright (Roscoe Johnson); Jimmy Lloyd (Homer White); Loren Tindall (Charles Meyers); Ola Lorraine (Jeanie Meyers); Claire Meade (Aunt Mae); Roy Roberts (Foreman); Charles Lane (Mr. Woodruff); Harry Harvey (Councilman Reed); Harry Cheshire (Leo Hopkins); Nita Mathews (Ruth)

Credits: S. Sylvan Simon (producer), Earl McEvoy (assistant); Lloyd Bacon (director); Nat Perrin, Devery Freeman, and Frank Tashlin (screenplay), from story by Everett Freeman; Charles Lawton, Jr. (photography); Heinz Roemheld (musical score); Morris Stoloff (musical director); Walter Holscher (art director); James Crowe (set decoration); Jean Louis (gowns); Helen Hunt (hairstylist); Clay Campbell (makeup); Lambert Day (sound); Carl Hiecke (assistant director); Jerome Thoms (editor)

Release date: October 2, 1949

Run time: 87 minutes

With William Holden . . . six years before the infamous *I Love Lucy* pie in the face.

Synopsis

For Ellen Grant (Lucille Ball), the worst pupil at the Woodruff Secretarial School, it comes as a great surprise when Dick Richmond (William Holden) selects her to work at his realty company. Actually, it is her apparent empty-headedness that wins her the position. The real estate firm, and now Ellen, are merely fronts for a bookmaking operation run from the back room of the office, where Dick and his cohorts take bets on the races.

Determined to become a good secretary, Ellen puts an ambitious venture into motion to help the business and the people of the town by creating affordable housing. Little does she know her plans are ruining Dick's organization. He cannot fire her for being efficient and cannot get her to quit. Ellen will stand anything (even passes from the boss!) to see the housing project through. Dick's troubles really begin when Ellen unwittingly accepts a bet placed by the malicious Mrs. Donato (Janis

Paige), putting him in debt to her for $50,000. Mrs. Donato, who would rather have Dick than the winnings, tells him that if he does not go away with her or pay up, her gang will deal with him.

Dick now allows Ellen to continue with her housing project so he can pay off the debt by stealing from the down payments on the new homes. So that no one will get wise to his scam, he puts the trusted Ellen in charge of the development. It becomes a nightmare for her when the funds run out before the houses are built and she cannot return the money to her friends. Ellen feels terrible, thinking that her own incompetence was to blame. Seeing the girl he's come to love suffer, Dick decides to go away with Mrs. Donato and pay the people back.

Dick must keep a close eye on what his secretary is doing as she unwittingly causes a string of calamities.

Reviews

" . . . a wacky comedy whose crazy story has about everything in the way of a gag, including the kitchen sink. . . . Lloyd Bacon's direction, filled with sock comedy hits and climaxed by an hilarious satire on gangster films, has the pace of a two-reeler. Bacon glosses over the holes in the script by keeping things fast, furious and funny . . . Lucille Ball gives her usual first-class performance as the girl, and William Holden is at his best in the part of the bookie."

—*Hollywood Reporter*

"It's a frothy item spun out of a light-weight yarn and skillfully sewn together under Lloyd Bacon's deft direction. . . . Miss Ball and Holden make a neat comedy-romantic team while McHugh, as a human adding machine, and Gleason, as a worried bookie, deliver plenty of laughs."

—*Variety*

" . . . it rollicks right along on the momentum created by three gagsmen-writers and sustained by Director Lloyd Bacon. The more improbable it gets the more you have been caught up in the swing of it and are willing to accept it at its face, or rib-tickling, value. . . . Miss Ball, who substitutes her own 'do-fers' whenever the dictation gets tough, brings all her skill, pantomimic as well as verbal, into play."

—*New York Times*

Ellen discovers the truth behind the missing money and the betting racket, but forgives Dick and cooks up an elaborate scheme involving her own "gang" to keep him from sacrificing himself to Mrs. Donato. With the stolen money returned,

The hilarious scene in which Ellen and her hold-up "gang" attempt to rescue Dick from Mrs. Donato (left) with a pencil sharpener.

the new homes can finally be constructed. Dick's partners come up with $50,000 to pay Mrs. Donato the same way they lost it—with a bet on a horse. Best of all, the love of a good woman makes Dick an honest man.

Notes and Comments

In early 1949, Lucille signed a contract with Columbia Pictures to make three films in three years at a salary of $85,000 each. S. Sylvan Simon, her director in *Her Husband's Affairs*, was now producing and anxious to make more films with her. In the first two under contract to Columbia,

she was to have Simon as her producer and Lloyd Bacon as director. As shown later in her career, when Lucille found colleagues she clicked with, she wanted to repeat the pleasure again and again.

Lloyd Bacon was a first-rate comedy director. He elevated from Mack Sennett two-reelers in the '20s and later at Warners directed hit musical comedies like *42nd Street* and *Footlight Parade*. The film's writers had experience with top comedians as well. The screenplay was the work of Nat Perrin, Devery Freeman, and Frank Tashlin. Tashlin had been a director of cartoon shorts. In the '40s he began writing comedy for feature films and later turned to directing them with continued success. This team behind *Miss Grant Takes Richmond* got Lucille's Columbia deal off to a solid start.

The talent in front of the cameras included the handsome William Holden, who made a fine foil for Lucille and demonstrated his own capacity for light comedy. James Gleason, Frank McHugh, and Janis Carter lent clever support to the stars. Two years later, Gleason would be among those asked to play the role of Fred Mertz in *I Love Lucy* before William Frawley came along.

Lucille reveled in her role as Ellen Grant in *Miss Grant Takes Richmond* and turned in one of her most entertaining film performances. The picture was fast-paced and full of sight gags that allowed her to display her proficiency with props—

Ellen requires much more than a helping hand to recover from her first day on the job as project manager.

making inanimate objects her partners in the fun-making. The character was a precursor to Lucy Ricardo. For all her loveable qualities and good intentions, she can't help attracting trouble. Just as Lucy puts all her gusto into becoming a champion candy dipper, Ellen struggles with her secretarial lessons, eliciting scowls from the instructor as she fumbles with the typewriter ribbon and makes a general ink-smearing mess of herself and her workstation. The picture went into production in February 1949 and continued filming until April 7. It was well received by critics and the public alike.

Now working at Columbia, Lucille got to continue her comedy training with Buster Keaton and Ed Sedgwick, who had relocated from MGM. They taught her more about the importance and handling of props, slapstick, timing, and even re-constructed classic comedy moments, all of which came into play in the movies she did at Columbia.

Ellen's typing mystifies her just as much as it does the teacher.

A Woman of Distinction

A Columbia Picture (1950)

Cast: Ray Milland (Alec Stevenson); Rosalind Russell (Susan Middlecott); Edmund Gwenn (Mark Middlecott); Janis Carter (Teddy Evans); Mary Jane Saunders (Louisa); Francis Lederer (Paul Simone); Jerome Courtland (Jerome); Alex Gerry (Herman Pomeroy); Charles Evans (Dr. McFall); Charlotte Wynters (Miss Withers); Clifton Young (Chet); Gale Gordon (Station Clerk); Jean Willes (Pearl); Wanda McKay (Merle); Elizabeth Flourney (Laura); Harry Tyler (Charlie); Lucille Ball (as herself)

Credits: Buddy Adler (producer); Edward Buzzell (director); Charles Hoffman and Frank Tashlin (screenplay), from story by Ian McLellan Hunter and Hugo Butler; Joseph Walker (photography); Morris Stoloff (musical director); Werner R. Heyman (musical score); Robert Peterson (art director); Louis Diage (set decoration); Jean Louis (gowns); Helen Hunt (hairstylist); Lambert Day (sound); Earl Bellamy (assistant director); Charles Nelson (editor)

Release date: March 16, 1950 (Radio City Music Hall)

Run time: 85 minutes

Synopsis

Nationally renowned scholar Susan Middlecott (Rosalind Russell) has "no room for romance" in her life. Professor Alec Stevenson (Ray Milland) is an equally diligent astronomer, embarking on a lecture tour when a publicist decides to invent a romance between the two intellectuals.

Susan is aghast by the reports. Her father (Edmund Gwenn), however, thinks it is about time she found a man and tries to throw them together—unsuccessfully. The predicament is made still worse when Susan's adopted daughter (Mary Jane Saunders), who desperately wants a daddy, tells Alec's publicist that the professor is her father!

Because of the ensuing gossip, Susan will lose her job as dean of Benton College unless the matter is cleared up. Alec attempts to help by

Movie star Lucille Ball has Alec hold just a few of her things while photographers snap her picture.

saying they are married. Armed with proper adoption papers, Susan has no need to play along, but just as she is about to show the college board her paperwork, Alec's charm and gallantry sinks in. No longer caring what her colleagues believe, she goes after Alec, and they end in a clinch at the Benton train station.

Notes and Comments

Rosalind Russell and Ray Milland were seen in their only onscreen pairing in *A Woman of Distinction*, a slapstick comedy—not among their best work, although both were already proven proficient actors in comedy as well as drama. Little Mary Jane Saunders from *Sorrowful Jones* portrayed Russell's daughter in what was her third film. The role was her last of significance in films, although she did make several television appearances well into the 1960s. *A Woman of Distinction* was directed by Eddie Buzzell, whom Lucille had so enjoyed working with at MGM.

Lucille made a cameo appearance as herself. She and Ray Milland are seated next to each other on an airplane. Upon landing, she obliges the waiting cameramen with pin-up poses, stealing the spotlight from Milland, playing a notable British astronomer.

One of Lucille's most beloved co-stars, Gale Gordon, also appears in a small but funny role as an exasperated train-station clerk. At the time, Gordon had just become a regular on Lucille's radio series, *My Favorite Husband*, in which he played her husband's boss, bank president Rudolph Atterbury. Gordon became her choice for the role of Fred Mertz on *I Love Lucy*, but he was already committed to another program. However, he did appear twice on *I Love Lucy* at the end of the first season, once on *The Lucy-Desi Comedy Hour*, co-starred on all three of Lucille's subsequent series thereafter, and appeared with her in several television specials, making him by far her most frequent co-star.

Reviews

" . . . this mélange of misadventures, in which Miss Russell is involved with Ray Milland as her hapless associate, is no more than a custard-pie farce, with all of the humor evolving from physically violent episodes."

—*New York Times*

"Sans much logic, the Rosalind Russell-Ray Milland teamwork is good for more laughs than not and the gags overcome a yarn that lacks sound motivation. . . . Director Edward Buzzell gets his picture off the ground with a fast start and is generally successful in keeping its developments sprightly."

—*Variety*

Fancy Pants

A Paramount Picture (1950)

Cast: Bob Hope (Humphrey); Lucille Ball (Agatha Floud, "Aggie"); Bruce Cabot (Cart Belknap); Jack Kirkwood (Mike Floud); Lea Penman (Effie Floud); Hugh French (George Van Basingwell); Eric Blore (Sir Wimbley); Joseph Vitale (Wampum); John Alexander (President Theodore Roosevelt); Norma Varden (Lady Maude); Virginia Keiley (Rosalind); Colin Keith-Johnston (Twombley); Joe Wong (Wong)

Credits: Robert L. Welch (producer); George Marshall (director); Edmund Hartmann and Robert O'Brien (screenplay), from story by Harry Leon Wilson; photographed in Technicolor by Charles B. Lang, Jr.; Francis Cugat (Technicolor color consultant); Gordon Jennings (special effects); Farciot Edouart (process photography); Van Cleave (musical score); Billy Daniels (dance director); Hans Dreier and Earl Hedrick (art directors); Sam Comer and Emile Kuri (set decoration); Mary Kay Dodson (women's costumes); Gile Steele (men's costumes); Wally Westmore (makeup); Gene Merritt and Don Johnson (sound); Oscar Rudolph (assistant director); Archie Marshek (editor)

Songs: "(Hey) Fancy Pants!," "Humphrey," "Home Cookin'" (Jay Livingston and Ray Evans)

Release date: July 19, 1950 (Paramount Theater)

Run time: 92 minutes

With Bob Hope as the ultimate gentleman's gentleman, and Hugh French as George van Basingwell, her gentlemanly admirer.

Synopsis

Effie Floud (Lea Penman) takes her daughter Aggie (Lucille Ball) to England in the hope that she will pick up some refinement. A suitor (Hugh French) tries to impress Aggie by hiring a group of actors with impeccable manners to pose as his family. When Effie sees the "butler," Humphrey (Bob Hope), she decides she must take him home to Big Squaw, and offers him a salary he can't refuse.

At the Floud homestead, Pa (Jack Kirkwood) and Aggie quickly have all they can stand of "Fancy Pants" trying to improve them. Aggie sicks her jealous admirer, Cart Belknap (Bruce Cabot), on him. But just then, the Flouds sorely need Humphrey. Pa had been confused and told the town Effie was bringing home from England the "Earl of Brinstead." The message spread to Theodore Roosevelt (John Alexander) himself and now the president plans to make a stop in Big Squaw to call on the visitor from

England. Humphrey confesses to Aggie that he is an actor and agrees to play the Earl during the president's visit. His willingness to help the family out of a jam wins him Aggie's respect—and her heart.

Everything runs smoothly during Roosevelt's stay until a foxhunt is proposed. Humphrey slips away, faking an injury. As the others begin the hunt, Cart stays behind to sabotage the "Earl." He finds Humphrey's press clippings and learns that he is an actor, not an aristocrat. Cart threatens to expose him. Following a comic high-speed chase for the actor's scrapbook, Cart makes his revelation to President Roosevelt and the townspeople. Humphrey and Aggie hightail it out of Big Squaw—unpopular, but in love!

Notes and Comments

After the exceptional box-office returns of *Sorrowful Jones*, Lucille was invited back to Paramount to make a second film with Bob Hope. Her contract, dated April 22, 1949, offered $8,750 per week ($1,250 more per week than *Sorrowful Jones*). Lucille readily accepted the opportunity to work with her pal again, and in the summer of 1949 she began making *Fancy Pants*. Originally called *Where Men are Men*, the film was to be a remake of 1935's *Ruggles of Red Gap*, starring Charles Laughton. It was quite altered from its predecessor, however, and added music and Technicolor. The well-known Harry Leon Wilson story had also been adapted for the screen in 1918,

Aggie heckles Humphrey with a song, "Hey! Fancy Pants!".

Joseph Vitale, Bob Hope, Lucille, Joe Wong, and Jack Kirkwood have a sing-a-long while preparing some "Home Cookin'." Annette Warren provided the vocals for Lucille.

starring Taylor Holmes, and again in 1925, with Edward Everett Horton in the lead. Studio records show that Paramount began planning *Fancy Pants* in 1947 as a vehicle for Betty Hutton, calling it *Lady from Lariot Loop* at the time. When Hutton passed on the part, the project was cancelled, only to be reinvented in 1949 as a Bob Hope film.

Director George Marshall had worked with both stars prior to *Fancy Pants*; Bob Hope in *The Ghost Breakers* and *Monsieur Beaucaire* and Lucille in *Valley of the Sun*. Lucille had superior material in *Fancy Pants* than in her earlier Marshall film. Between she and Bob, the laughs were continuous, and she glowed in Charles Lang's Technicolor photography. Lucille had a particularly contemporary look that kept her away from costume pictures. Here, she rebuffs the bustles and bows in favor of buckskins, and hairstyling reaches new heights of absurdity when Bob discovers a new use for birdcages.

Humphrey makes a much better butler than he does a hairdresser.

Between takes with Bob Hope (top) and director George Marshall (bottom).

Home movies from the set of *Fancy Pants* show Lucille taking her pratfalls bravely, but it was an accident involving Hope that garnered nationwide publicity for the film. It occurred while shooting a scene in which Lucille teaches him to ride a horse using a mechanical barrel. Hope took a nasty tumble and was knocked unconscious. Production halted while he recuperated at Hollywood Presbyterian Hospital.

Robert Welch as producer and Bruce Cabot as the villain of *Sorrowful Jones* repeated these roles for *Fancy Pants*. Songwriters Jay Livingston and Ray Evans and supporting cast members Jack Kirkwood, Lea Penman, and Eric Blore contributed merry moments to the production. *Fancy Pants* was a hit with audiences, grossing $2.6 million. Bob and Lucille enacted the film again on *Lux Radio Theatre* in 1951.

As the new decade approached, Lucille's career was doing well, and she was performing more of the kind of comedy she wanted to with her comedies at Columbia, with Bob Hope at Paramount, and *My Favorite Husband*. The radio program went into its second season just as shooting was finishing up on *Fancy Pants*, in September 1949.

The Fuller Brush Girl

A Columbia Picture (1950)

Cast: Lucille Ball (Sally Elliot); Eddie Albert (Humphrey Briggs); Carl Benton Reid (Mr. Christie); Gale Robbins (Ruby Rawlings); Jeff Donnell (Jane Bixby); Jerome Cowan (Harvey Simpson); John Litel (Mr. Watkins); Fred Graham (Rocky Mitchell); Lee Patrick (Claire Simpson); Arthur Space (Inspector Rodgers); Sid Tomack (Bangs); Billy Vincent (Punchy); Lorin Raker (Mr. Deval); Lelah Tyler (Mrs. North); Sarah Edwards (Mrs. East); Lois Austin (Mrs. West); Isabel Randolph (Mrs. South); Isabel Withers (Mrs. Finley); Donna Boswell (Sue/Lou Finley); Gregory Marshall (Alvin/Albert Finley)

Credits: S. Sylvan Simon (producer); Lloyd Bacon (director); Frank Tashlin (screenplay); Charles Lawton, Jr. (photography); Heinz Roemheld (musical score); Morris Stoloff (musical director); Robert Peterson (art director); James Crowe (set decoration); Earl Bellamy (assistant director); Lambert Day (sound); Jean Louis (gowns); Clay Campbell (makeup) Helen Hunt (hairstylist); William Lyon (editor)

Song: "Put the Blame on Mame" (Allan Roberts and Doris Fisher)

Release date: October 5, 1950

Run time: 84 minutes

Synopsis

Sally Elliot (Lucille Ball) and her fiancé, Humphrey (Eddie Albert), are employed at the Maritime Steamship Company. Unaware that their boss, Mr. Simpson (Jerome Cowan), is involved in illegal activities, the couple is more mindful of planning their future. They have their eyes on a new home, but the price is beyond their means. Then Simpson gives Humphrey a promotion that suddenly puts their house within grasp—until Sally does battle with the office switchboard and gets fired.

Sally applies for a job as a Fuller Brush girl, but it requires a recommendation from her former employer. This seems impossible to get until Simpson finds himself in need of her help. When she was fired, Sally accidentally sneezed a powder on him that left behind a woman's fragrance. She is to explain the scent to his suspicious wife. Though not yet hired, the following day Sally tries her hand at selling Fuller Brush

At the encouragement of her girlfriend (Jeff Donnell, to the right of Lucille), Sally applies for a position with the Fuller Brush Cosmetics company.

Reviews

"[Lucille Ball] proves to be an expert slapstick comedienne in 'The Fuller Brush Girl,' super-escape entertainment. Indeed, the film escapes right out of this world. Miss Ball dominates the farce, appearing in almost every scene, and it's a good thing she does. . . . Miss Ball carries the ball for a comedy touchdown in this one."

—*Los Angeles Times*

"'The Fuller Brush Girl' is hardly more than a vehicle for Lucille Ball, and she makes capital of the situation. If ever there were any doubts as to Miss Ball's forte, 'Fuller Brush' dispels them. She's an excellent comedienne, and in this rowdy, incoherent yarn with its Keystone Kop overtones, she garners the major laurels. In fact, she is on so much of the time that the story's weaknesses can thus be overlooked."

—*Variety*

" . . . the hilarious and frequently strenuous gags follow each other at a breathless pace, without ever slowing down for a moment. Lloyd Bacon, always tops in comedy direction, never misses a bet to win guffaws of laughter . . . Lucille Ball, with her wide-eyed beauty and buoyant charm, puts over her comedy with perfect timing, and just the right amount of pathos and bewilderment to arouse the filmgoer's sympathy while she keeps them laughing."

—*Hollywood Reporter*

These four bridge-playing matrons have no idea what they're in for after opening the door to this Fuller Brush girl!

cosmetics—it has disastrous results and delays her arrival at the Simpson home. Impatient, Simpson sends another woman posing as Sally to speak to his wife.

By the time Sally arrives, Mrs. Simpson (Lee Patrick) has been murdered. The other woman clubs Sally and plants the gun in her hand. Humphrey arrives on the scene, Sally comes to, and they escape, but she is now a murder suspect hunted by the police. Sally recognizes the woman that struck her as burlesque queen Ruby Rawlings (Gale Robbins). When Mr. Simpson is found dead later the same day, Sally is suspected of killing him, too. She and Humphrey must get hold of Ruby Rawlings!

At the burlesque hall, Sally sneaks into the star's dressing room. When Ruby comes in, Sally ties her up and calls for the police. A pair of goons who were in on the Simpson murders overhear her conversation with the cops and chase after her and Humphrey as they escape the theater. Sally and Humphey wind up trapped by the gang, alone out to sea on a ship full of murderers. Back at the theater, Ruby comes clean to the cops about a diamond-smuggling racket and who masterminded both killings.

Meanwhile, through a series of entertaining ruses, Sally and Humphrey elude the band of criminals until the police reach the ship. While still on deck, a barrel full of dynamite explodes, putting an end to the craft's days of smuggling in diamonds, but the two lucky lovebirds are safe, and Sally's name is cleared.

Notes and Comments

Lucille's next Columbia assignment was filmed in the early months of 1950. Co-starring Eddie Albert (later of *Green Acres* fame), it was a spin-off of Red Skelton's *The Fuller Brush Man*. The comedian blessed his successor by popping up in a cameo playing (what else?) a Fuller Brush man who swindles Lucille into buying products from *him* during her discouraging first day on the job.

The Fuller Brush Girl was shaped by much of the *Miss Grant Takes Richmond* team. S. Sylvan Simon produced, Lloyd Bacon directed, and Frank Tashlin wrote the script. Simon made only one more film before his death a year later, a classic that earned him an Oscar nomination, *Born Yesterday*. Tashlin's script was tailor-made for Lucille's comedic talents. A graduate of Warner Bros. cartoons, he wrote scenes that seemed designed for Daffy Duck. Betty Hutton was a lovely, energetic musical comedienne, but really there was no female star like Lucille Ball on the scene—a beauty who specialized in such broad slapstick, taking her pratfalls and seltzer water without losing her feminine allure.

Escaping the cops with her beau, Humphrey

A pair of glasses drawn on a window give Sally her first lead in unraveling the mystery that threatens to put her behind bars.

Sally goes incognito to gain access to the backstage area of a burlesque hall.

Just hanging around

Lucille had a fearless, *try anything* attitude toward physical comedy that had painful repercussions when it came to filming the strenuous antics of *The Fuller Brush Girl*. "I sprained both wrists and displaced six vertebrae, then irritated my sciatic nerve . . . I also suffered a two-day paralysis of the eyeball when talcum powder was accidentally blown into my eye by a wind machine. A three-day dunking in a wine vat gave me a severe cold, and I also was bruised by several tons of coffee beans." In addition, gulping down a barrel of what was supposed to be wine made her sick to her stomach. The talcum powder incident required a four-day absence from work until her eye recovered, and at the end of filming she had to be hospitalized because that "cold" developed into pneumonia. As some consolation, the reviews applauded Lucille for her unique brand of comedy.

Whether hanging from a clothesline, fumbling with a crazed switchboard, or wearing an absurd get-up performing a striptease to "Every Baby Needs a Da Da Daddy," Lucille was in top form as the loveable bungler Sally Elliot and again, Lucy Ricardo is clearly in bloom. Indeed, outside of the Columbia gates at this time loomed television. Talks with CBS had recently begun about adapting Lucille's radio show, *My Favorite Husband*, to the small screen. Filming ended on *The Fuller Brush Girl* in March. Three months later, she and Desi embarked on a nationwide vaudeville tour to prove that audiences would accept them as the husband and wife stars of the proposed series.

With co-star Eddie Albert. Even before his signature television role came along, in the '40s and '50s, Albert enjoyed a busy career in small and big-screen comedies and dramas, including *Roman Holiday* (1953) and *The Sun Also Rises* (1957).

The Magic Carpet

A Columbia Picture (1951)

Cast: Lucille Ball (Princess Narah); John Agar (Ramoth); Patricia Medina (Lida); George Tobias (Razi); Raymond Burr (Grand Vizier Boreg al Buzzar); Gregory Gaye (Caliph Ali); Rick Vallin (Abdul); Jo Gilbert (Maras); William Fawcett (Ahkmid); Doretta Johnson (Tanya); Linda Williams (Estar); Perry Sheehan (Copah); Eilean Howe (Vernah); Minka Zorka (Nedda); Winona Smith (Ziela)

Credits: Sam Katzman (producer); Lew Landers (director); David Mathews (screenplay); photographed in Supercinecolor by Ellis W. Carter; Jack Erickson (special effects); Mischa Bakaleinikoff (musical director); Paul Palmentola (art director); Sidney Clifford (set decoration); Jean Louis (gowns); Herbert Leonard (unit manager); Josh Westmoreland (sound); Wilbur McGaugh (assistant director); Edwin Bryant (editor)

Release date: September 25, 1951

Run time: 84 minutes

As Princess Narah

Synopsis

Caliph Omar and Queen Yasmina are murdered, but before the assassins reach young Prince Abdullah, he is whisked away by a magic carpet to the home of Ahkmid (William Fawcett), the physician. Raised as the good doctor's son, the boy grows into a man called Ramoth (John Agar), knowing nothing of his noble lineage. Ramoth becomes a Robin Hood of sorts known as the Scarlet Falcon to oppose the tyrannical Caliph Ali (Gregory Gaye).

By curing the caliph's hiccups, Ramoth is appointed the royal physician and thus gains access to the palace. His Majesty's sister, Princess Narah (Lucille Ball), takes particular interest in him, as does Vizier Boreg (Raymond Burr), after he finds out that Ramoth is the true caliph. Boreg goes to Ahkmid looking for the magic carpet and stabs him for not relinquishing it. With his last breaths, Ahkmid tells Ramoth of his royal parentage and where to find the carpet that saved his life.

In order to overthrow the caliph, weapons are needed. Ramoth learns the path of a caravan carrying arms to the palace, but then new difficulties arise. Narah knows Ramoth is heir to the throne. After he refuses to make her queen, she tells the caliph that Ramoth is his enemy, the Scarlet Falcon. At the last moment, the magic carpet rescues him from execution. He and his men overtake the cargo of weapons and overthrow the despot. Ramoth takes his place as ruler, with his sweetheart, Lida (Patricia Medina), at his side.

Notes and Comments

More interesting than anything that happens onscreen in *The Magic Carpet* is the story of how Lucille became involved in this Arabian Nights potboiler. It actually began auspiciously in the fall of 1950, when Cecil B. DeMille offered her

Ramoth grills Narah to find out who killed the kind physician who raised him.

Reviews

"'The Magic Carpet' is a fair escapist picture that will level off in the more general situation as a modest attempt at entertainment, pretentiously dressed up beyond its worth. Lucille Ball is wasted in her role of a princess but does supply a fair amount of marquee value. John Agar, as the dashing hero, is stilted."
—*Variety*

"Exceptionally well-made for a program offering, it carries an abundance of action, has top-budget production values and is a treat to the eye because of its beautiful Supercinecolor photography."
—*Showmen's Trade Review*

an important role in his upcoming epic about life under the big top, *The Greatest Show on Earth*. Lucille was ecstatic, certain her Columbia contract would not stand in the way. She was due to make one more film for the studio but nothing was

With John Agar, who started in films in the late '40s, after his marriage to Shirley Temple.

scheduled for her yet, and she had been loaned to Paramount in the past. Although Columbia chief Harry Cohn was widely known as a "tyrant," Lucille did not count on his trying anything underhanded. Cohn, in turn, underestimated her intelligence.

Lucille was to be paid $85,000 for her last Columbia picture. Cohn would not release her from her obligation, nor would he postpone it so that she could make *The Greatest Show on Earth*. Instead, he presented her with a dreadful script

then waited for her to refuse it and go with DeMille. That would allow him to break her contract and save money. What was happening was not a new story in Hollywood—Lucille knew what he was up to. To her, making *The Magic Carpet* meant Cohn would pay her $85,000 for one week of work and she would fulfill her contract—as well as enjoy the pleasure of outfoxing Harry Cohn. Therefore Lucille accepted the assignment, without mentioning the fact that she had just discovered she was pregnant! This too would have released Cohn from his financial commitment. She kept her secret from him and the studio personnel until after the film was made.

Having Lucille Ball agree to make *The Magic Carpet* caused additional headaches for quickie producer Sam Katzman, because her salary alone took up a substantial portion of his budget. Meanwhile, Lucille's personal maid, Harriet McCain (the only one on the set in on the baby secret), let out her costumes to accommodate the extra weight she was putting on. Filmed in Supercinecolor, the picture was made in just over a week in December 1950. Lucille had worked with the director, Lew Landers, on four of her RKO Bs of the '30s. She played the unsympathetic character of Princess Narah, who spends her days lying around the palace thinking up new ailments to be examined by a young physician played by John Agar.

The Princess makes a startling discovery that clues her in on the true identity of Ramoth.

The production was completed December 16, 1950, in time for *The Greatest Show on Earth*, which was to begin filming at the end of January, but Lucille turned the DeMille project down because of her pregnancy. Gloria Grahame took the part of Angel for DeMille. This allowed the expectant mother to rest and concentrate on her television series that was taking form, because in January CBS finally consented to Desi's co-starring in a show with Lucille—the only way she would have it.

The Magic Carpet marked the end of Lucille's pre-television career in films. Unprecedented success was yet to be achieved on the small screen, but her rise from obscurity to stardom and the length of her tenure in the movies could hardly be called a failure. Many take it for granted that she

and Desi, still a successful musician, "resorted" to television. Their essential purpose for beginning the series was that it offered what they had longed for since 1940—a project that kept Desi off the road, allowing them to work together in one location and raise a family. In 1951, the Arnazes accomplished both of these cherished goals.

A scene with Gregory Gaye and Raymond Burr, in which the villains discuss the greatest threat to Caliph Ali's regime—the "Scarlet Falcon."

The Long, Long Trailer

A Metro-Goldwyn-Mayer Picture (1954)

Cast: Lucille Ball (Tacy Collini); Desi Arnaz (Nicholas Carlos Collini); Marjorie Main (Mrs. Hittaway); Keenan Wynn (Policeman); Gladys Hurlbut (Mrs. Bolton); Moroni Olsen (Mr. Tewitt); Bert Freed (Foreman); Madge Blake (Aunt Anastacia); Walter Baldwin (Uncle Edgar); Oliver Blake (Mr. Judlow); Perry Sheehan (Bridesmaid)

Credits: Pandro S. Berman (producer); Vincente Minnelli (director); Albert Hackett and Frances Goodrich (screenplay), from novel by Clinton Twiss; photographed in Ansco Color by Robert Surtees, print by Technicolor; Alvord Eiseman (color consultant); A. Arnold Gillespie and Warren Newcombe (special effects); Adolph Deutsch (music); Cedric Gibbons and Edward Carfagno (art directors); Edwin B. Willis and Keogh Keason (set decoration); Helen Rose (women's costumes); Sidney Guilaroff (hairstylist); William Tuttle (makeup); Douglas Shearer (recording); Jerry Thorpe (assistant director); Ferris Webster (editor)

Song: "Breezin' Along with the Breeze" (Haven Gillespie, Seymour Simons, and Richard A. Whiting)

Release date: February 18, 1954 (Radio City Music Hall)

Run time: 96 minutes

Synopsis

As Tacy (Lucille Ball) and Nicky's (Desi Arnaz) wedding approaches, Tacy finds a new love—a trailer. She talks him into buying the longest, yellowest, most expensive motor home on the lot. After the ceremony, they start for Colorado, where they plan to make their home following a cross-country honeymoon. The first stop is at a trailer park, where their romantic wedding night becomes a block party.

The next night they are completely alone in the woods—with the trailer stuck in the mud. More calamities occur at Aunt Anastacia's (Madge Blake), but once on the road again there is good mixed with the bad. They pass beautiful countryside, collecting stones by which to remember their favorite spots. Trying to cook while Nicky drives, Tacy ends up bruised from head to foot, but the most trying ordeal is yet to come.

Before the final stop, there is an 8,000-foot mountain to climb. All unnecessary weight must be disposed of, meaning Tacy's large rocks and

"And then we saw *IT*."—at first sight of the Trailer

Ready to play the blushing bride, Tacy

canned fruits. She cannot bear to part with them, so instead she hides everything. After passing frightening roads, and almost falling off a cliff, they make it over the mountain, but when Nicky finds out Tacy endangered their lives with her stones and cans, it is the last straw. They have a heated argument.

Nicky goes for a drive to cool off, but when he returns, Tacy is gone. About to sell the trailer, Tacy and Nicky finally swallow their pride and apologize. Happily reunited, they make a fresh start at home in their long, long trailer.

Notes and Comments

1953 was turning out to be a banner year for Lucille and Desi. It began with the birth of their second child. The next month, *I Love Lucy* won an Emmy as Best Situation Comedy and Lucille was named Best Comedienne of 1952. The same year, movie studios were battling television with the technical advancements of CinemaScope, stereophonic sound, and 3-D. Producer Pandro Berman took a new approach. He sought to lure TV fans from their sets by making a film with the stars they tuned in to the most. Desi himself had attempted to purchase the rights to the Clinton Twiss novel *The Long, Long Trailer*. He was outbid by MGM,

Reviews

"It's a lighthearted, genuinely funny comedy that lapses into slapstick at the drop of a hat and shows both stars to best advantage. . . . Not a trick has been missed in squeezing the laughs from every conceivable situation. . . . Both Miss Ball and Arnaz deliver sock performances. Their timing is perfect and the dialog provided by Albert Hacket and Frances Goodrich is clever."

—*Variety*

" . . . most of the laughs [come] through the genuine acting skill and engaging personalities of the co-stars . . . Vincente Minnelli does a good job of highlighting the slapstick, and keeps the farce moving at a raucous rate."

—*Hollywood Reporter*

"Both Lucy and Desi rollick their way through the slapstick nonsense with a fine sense of timing, and an obvious zest that communicates itself to the audience immediately and makes for one big happy family in the zany antics."

—*Los Angeles Examiner*

"There's nothing lacking in the sprightly, colorful, comical and continuous movement departments . . . Vincente Minnelli, and the astute production staff, guides the show along a route of frequently hilarious incident."

—*Film Daily*

The result of trying
to be a chef aboard
a trailer in motion

but Berman wanted them for the project. Lucille and Desi accepted his offer and returned to MGM, where they had both been under contract in the mid-'40s, as full-fledged superstars. They were greeted as such, receiving a combined salary of $250,000 and given the former dressing rooms of Lana Turner and Clark Gable.

Vincente Minnelli directed them. Among his recent successes were *An American in Paris* and *The Band Wagon*. *The Long, Long Trailer* contained references to some of his earlier works. For instance, the Victorian-style home of Aunt Anastacia was part of the *Meet Me in St. Louis* set, and the story Tacy tells on their climb up the mountain resembles a scene from *Undercurrent*. In his memoirs Minnelli said, "Lucy is one of the few comedic

talents who can be broad and uniquely human at the same time. She can get away with things that less talented people wouldn't even presume to handle." The director and his stars each fondly recalled the making of *The Long, Long Trailer*.

Albert Hackett and Frances Goodrich collaborated on the script. The husband-and-wife team wrote the screenplays of many beloved classic films including *It's a Wonderful Life*, and were behind the witty banter of *The Thin Man*'s Nick and Nora Charles. Keenan Wynn, who was paired twice onscreen with Lucille during her MGM days, did more or less a cameo in the film (as a traffic cop), as did Marjorie Main, who at the time was having success as Ma Kettle in a series of films.

The Long, Long Trailer was made during the summer hiatus after I Love Lucy's second season, between June and July 16, 1953. It took two-thirds of the scheduled filming time. From their television experience, Lucille and Desi had been conditioned to work quickly. The Lucy-style comedy of the film made it like a lengthened episode of the series, but it visually enhanced their misadventures on a larger screen with color and took them to expansive outdoor locations including Yosemite National Park. The formula added up to a smash success. The behind-the-scenes team of Berman, Minnelli, Hackett, and Goodrich had produced Father of the Bride in 1950. At the time, it was the highest-grossing comedy ever released by MGM. The Long, Long Trailer surpassed it, earning $4.3 million in domestic film rentals.

The newlyweds make the best of a night stuck in the mud—with the trailer on a slant.

Tacy hides a stone memento in the oven before their mountain trek.

MGM gave Lucille and Desi the forty by eight-foot New Moon trailer with a musical doorbell that was used in the film. The Arnazes stationed it past a grape arbor behind their home in Chatsworth, where it served as a guesthouse for visiting friends. It was home to June Havoc for several months between plays.

Forever, Darling

A Zanra Production (1956)

Released by Metro-Goldwyn-Mayer

Cast: Lucille Ball (Susan Vega); Desi Arnaz (Lorenzo Xavier Vega); James Mason (The Guardian Angel); Louis Calhern (Charles Y. Bewell); John Emery (Dr. Edward R. Winter); John Hoyt (Bill Finlay); Natalie Schafer (Millie Opdyke); Ralph Dumke (Henry Opdyke); Mabel Albertson (Society Reporter); Nancy Kulp (Amy); Willis B. Bouchey (Mr. Clinton); Ruth Brady (Laura); Marilyn Maxwell (Leading Lady in Jungle Film)

Credits: Desi Arnaz (producer); Jerry Thorpe (associate producer); Alexander Hall (director); Helen Deutsch (story and screenplay); photographed in Eastman Color by Harold Lipstein, print by Technicolor; Howard Anderson Company (special effects); Bronislau Kaper (music); Ralph Berger and Albert M. Pyke (art directors); Edward Boyle (set decoration); Elois Jenssen (Miss Ball's wardrobe); Irma Kusely (hairstylist); Jack Young and Don Roberson (makeup); Glen Glenn Inc. (sound); Jack Aldworth and Marvin Stuart (assistant directors); Dann Cahn and Bud Molin (editors)

Song: "Forever, Darling" (Sammy Cahn and Bronislau Kaper), performed over the titles by the Ames Brothers

Release date: February 9, 1956 (Loew's State Theater)

Run time: 91 minutes

Father and husband try to believe in Susan's vision. An angel—with wings?

Synopsis

Five years into Larry (Desi Arnaz) and Susan (Lucille Ball) Vega's marriage, the honeymoon is long over. They have drifted apart, with Susan more influenced by her snobbish cousin Millie (Natalie Schafer) and Larry, a chemist, wrapped up in his work developing an insecticide called 383. Larry sees the two-year field project to test the product across the globe as a way to bring him and Susan together. Off by themselves, they could make it a romantic journey.

Larry's big news comes during a visit from Millie and her husband. They disapprove. Larry lets them know what he thinks of them, leading to a blowout between him and Susan. Afterwards Susan sees *him* for the first time—her Guardian Angel (James Mason), who has come to save her marriage. Larry gets word that he is to do a short testing of 383 before the two-year project. Susan takes the Angel's advice and accompanies him.

At once, Susan begins gaining a better understanding of Larry and his work. But try as she might, Susan is no good at roughing it. After she pokes a hole in their inflatable boat, leaving them waist-high in a swamp, Larry loses his temper. Susan declares she is through. Soon after, Larry's partner, Bill Finlay (John Hoyt), arrives for a demonstration of the insecticide. To Larry's bewilderment, 383 fails.

Susan's Angel botched Larry's mixture. Seeing him so dejected, Susan's anger vanishes. Finlay gives the insecticide a second chance and it works. The extended two-year field job is on, and Susan wants to be wherever Larry's work takes him. With a little help from a handsome angel, the Vegas love and understand each other better than ever.

Notes and Comments

Throughout 1955, *I Love Lucy* audiences delighted as the characters cavorted through Hollywood and attempted to break into the movies. In real life, the success of *The Long, Long Trailer* had studios vying for the services of Lucille and Desi. They went with MGM, the studio that agreed to finance and distribute a

Pure bliss two months after the wedding

Just a quiet dinner party with the Vegas. Pictured in this scene are Ralph Dumke, Desi, Lucille, Natalie Schafer, and Nancy Kulp.

After the first visit from her Angel

picture to be produced by Desi, under his new Zanra banner, at Desilu's Motion Picture Center. The property they chose to produce was a script by Helen Deutsch that MGM had been holding onto for years. It was once outlined for William Powell and Myrna Loy and then for Spencer Tracy and Katharine Hepburn, previously called *The Woman Who Was Scared* and *Her Guardian Angel*. Lucille and Desi's version was given the more melodic title of *Forever, Darling*, which went with a beautiful song composed by Sammy Cahn and Bronislau Kaper for the film.

With Desi guiding the course of the ever-expanding Desilu Productions, the Arnazes were

Susan daydreams herself into a movie starring the actor to whom her Guardian Angel bears a strong resemblance, James Mason.

busier than ever at the time of these negotiations with Metro. Desi now wanted to take their crew into film production, applying television methods to filmmaking in order to cut costs as well as production time. They went directly from the fourth season of *I Love Lucy* into *Forever, Darling.* The production cost $1.4 million and completed filming on July 14, 1955.

Forever, Darling was the swan song of director Al Hall, an old flame of Lucille's from the late '30s. Two of his biggest hits also concerned earthbound heavenly spirits providing guidance to the living, *Here Comes Mr. Jordan* (1941) and its sequel, *Down to Earth* (1947). James Mason (*A Star is Born*)

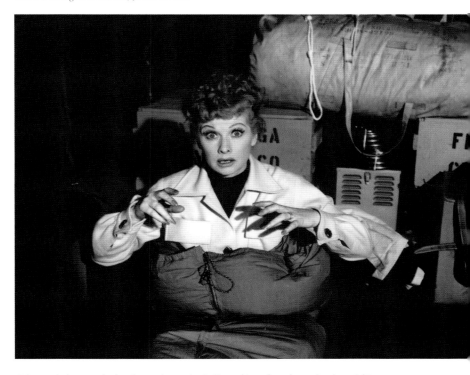

A jammed zipper and a hooting owl conspire in the making of one long, sleepless night.

co-starred with Lucille and Desi as the Angel, and the supporting cast featured two other actresses who made bigger names for themselves in television; Nancy Kulp is recognizable as Miss Jane Hathaway of *The Beverly Hillbillies*, and Natalie Schafer's roles as society women in films culminated in Lovey Howell of *Gilligan's Island*.

Louis Calhern, Schafer's former husband, played the prominent part of Lucille's father.

Lucille and Desi were accorded red-carpet treatment and she was reunited with old friends when they traveled to Jamestown for the world premiere of *Forever, Darling*. The film itself, however, received a cooler reception. It was panned by critics, and box-office receipts showed that the public too, was disappointed. In quality reviewers said it was not up to MGM standard, but more significantly, the script was not tailored to the stars in the way *Trailer* had been. Some of the warmth of the *Lucy* series was missing this time though it remains an enjoyable romantic fantasy. Other movie projects were considered for Lucille and Desi over the next few years but ultimately, *Forever, Darling* was their last film together.

A family visit on the set. Lucille's mother, DeDe, is seated with her back to the camera, while Desi's mother, Lolita, smiles up at her daughter-in-law.

The Facts of Life

A Panama and Frank Production (1960)

Released by United Artists

Cast: Bob Hope (Larry Gilbert); Lucille Ball (Kitty Weaver); Ruth Hussey (Mary Gilbert); Don DeFore (Jack Weaver); Louis Nye (Hamilton Busbee); Philip Ober (Doc Mason); Marianne Stewart (Connie Mason); Peter Leeds (Thompson); Hollis Irving (Myrtle Busbee); William Lanteau (Airline Clerk); Robert F. Simon (Motel Clerk); Louise Beavers (Gussie); Mike Mazurki (Husband in Motel Room)

Credits: Norman Panama (producer); Hal C. Kern (associate producer); Melvin Frank (director); Norman Panama and Melvin Frank (screenplay); Charles Lang, Jr. (photography); Howard Anderson Company (photographic effects); Joseph Lombardi (special effects); Paul Eagler (process photography); Leigh Harline (music composer and conductor); J. MacMillan Johnson and Kenneth A. Reid (art directors); Ross Dowd (set decoration); Edith Head and Edward Stevenson (Miss Ball's wardrobe); Irma Kusely (hairstylist); Layne Britton and Charles Blackman (makeup); Max Factor (fashion makeup); J. Walter Daniels (production manager); Glen Glenn Inc. (sound); Joseph Edmondson (sound mixer); Jack Aldworth (assistant director); Frank Bracht (editor); Saul Bass and Associates (titles)

Song: "The Facts of Life" (Johnny Mercer), performed over the titles by Eydie Gorme and Steve Lawrence

Release date: November 14, 1960

Run time: 103 minutes

Synopsis

Pasadena housewife Kitty Weaver (Lucille Ball) is fed up with her and her husband Jack's (Don DeFore) social routine. Coming along on their "intimate" Acapulco vacation are the Masons (Philip Ober, Marianne Stewart) and Kitty's best friend, Mary Gilbert (Ruth Hussey), with her husband, Larry (Bob Hope), whom Kitty can't stand. At the last minute, Mary and Jack have to stay behind, but both insist that Kitty and Larry go on to Acapulco with the Masons anyway.

When the Masons come down with stomach ailments after their first Mexican meal, Kitty and Larry are forced to become friends. At the end of an afternoon of fishing and the capture of a hundred and fifty-pound marlin, they find themselves in a romantic embrace. They spend an idyllic week together, but then it is time to return to their spouses. At home, Kitty and Larry are constantly thrown together in the old social group. They begin seeing each other secretly, but it just feels wrong in Pasadena, so a weekend rendezvous is arranged.

The myopic twosome fall for each other at a Mexican resort.

Reviews

" . . . the funniest U.S. film since The Apartment—a quick, slick, slyly satirical and sometimes wonderfully nutty comedy of middle-class manners and middle-aged morals. . . . Everybody knows that Hope and Ball are formidable clowns; this picture, in which they seldom make a funny face, should remind the public that they are skillful actors too."

—*Time*

"Lively, witty romp sparked by spirited work of Bob Hope and Lucille Ball . . . sharp, fast-moving screenplay [serves] as a sound, solid springboard for some of the year's best screen humor. . . . Hope exhibits refreshing restraint in his approach, admirably underplaying to his costar, but rattling off gags and handling reaction business as only he can. . . . Miss Ball thoroughly brightens up the comedy, be it farce, slapstick, sophisticated or satire, all of which are incorporated into the picture."

—*Variety*

" . . . refreshingly flip yet moral picture . . . they'll surely amuse married people who will wistfully recognize the clumsy and comical agitations of a cupid-plugged Lucy and Bob . . . It is humor about a ridiculous dilemma, and it should be enjoyable to teenagers, too. . . . It is a winning comedy, one of the liveliest from Hollywood."

—*New York Times*

Before leaving, Kitty leaves a note for Jack saying she has left him. In Monterrey, after being drenched in a rainstorm and arriving at their leaky cabin, Kitty and Larry quarrel, bicker, annoy each other, and quickly realize it is their own husband and wife each of them loves. They decide to catch the next flight home before Jack reads Kitty's message.

After a chance meeting with friends at the airport nearly ruins them, Kitty makes the plane and arrives at home—but Jack is there too. "Has he read the note?" she wonders. When she asks him to destroy it, Jack understands she has had a change of heart. Kitty is back with Jack, Larry is back with Mary, and they all have a renewed appreciation of each other.

Notes and Comments

Coming off of her divorce from Desi, Lucille sought to ease the pain by throwing herself into work. While plans developed for her Broadway debut, she agreed to make her return to the big screen opposite Bob Hope in *The Facts of Life*. The partners behind the picture, Norman Panama and Melvin Frank, collaborated on many treasured films, such as *Mr. Blandings Builds His Dream*

Here Lucille and Bob take direction from Melvin Frank before their characters proceed to a less than idyllic tryst in a leaky cabin. Frank, said, "They're perfect together . . . When they're in front of the camera, you can feel the magic."

Reunited with one of her favorite co-stars. Hope later called *The Facts of Life* his "favorite" of their four films together.

House, White Christmas, and several of Bob Hope's. They originally conceived *The Facts of Life* years earlier as a drama in the manner of David Lean's *Brief Encounter* for Olivia de Havilland and possibly James Stewart or William Holden. They knew a comic treatment of their daring (for its time) adultery-themed story would work with Bob Hope and Lucille Ball in the central roles. Both stars agreed to make it if the other would.

The Facts of Life went into production on June 2, 1960. It was Lucille's first post-*I Love Lucy* film, but it kept her on her home turf, as filming took place at Desilu on the former *Lucy* soundstage. The set was so beleaguered by accidents,

however, that Hope was on to something when he quipped, "This film should have been shot at Cedars of Lebanon Hospital."

There had been several mishaps during *Fancy Pants*. Hope got the worst of it then. This time it was Lucille's turn. Early on, in trying to hop aboard the boat used in some scenes, she fell, hit her head, and lost consciousness. At Cedars of Lebanon, she was treated for the lump that formed on her forehead, black eyes, various scrapes and bruises, and a laceration on her right leg. When Desi was informed, he wired Hope: "I played straight man to her for nine years and never pushed her. Why couldn't you control yourself?" Production shut

Bob Hope and Ruth Hussey admire Lucy as the Queen of the Gypsies. Lucille got along well with the Academy Award-nominated actress of *The Philadelphia Story*. Hussey hadn't made a movie since 1953, but returned for what would be her final film appearance as Hope's wife in *The Facts of Life*.

At the scene of her accident

"Was I 'Lucy?'" It was a change of pace for the two superstars that both critics and the public loved. *The Facts of Life* earned Oscar nominations for its clever screenplay and beautiful cinematography, art direction, and title song, while Edith Head and Edward Stevenson were awarded the prize for their costume designs.

In August, soon after production wrapped on *The Facts of Life*, Lucille went into rehearsals of her first and only Broadway show, *Wildcat*.

down for two weeks, until mid-June, while her face healed, after which she still required heavy makeup to conceal the wounds.

Lucille's misfortune was only the beginning. Before production ended, Hope injured a finger, co-star Don DeFore wound up in traction, troubled by a recurring back injury, the publicity man contracted the mumps, and Melvin Frank sprained an ankle during a golf game, necessitating crutches.

At a time when Doris Day-Rock Hudson "sex comedies" were doing great business and *The Apartment* was named the Best Picture of the year, *The Facts of Life* presented Lucille and Bob in a more adult comedy than fans were used to seeing them in. Trying to play it with more restraint, after shooting a scene Lucille would ask the director,

Sporting a bandage on her right leg as a result of the fall.

Critic's Choice

A Warner Bros. Picture (1963)

Cast: Bob Hope (Parker Ballantine); Lucille Ball (Angie Ballantine); Marilyn Maxwell (Ivy London); Rip Torn (Dion Kapakos); Jessie Royce Landis (Charlotte Orr); John Dehner (S. P. Champlain); Jim Backus (Dr. Von Hagedorn); Ricky Kelman (John Ballantine); Dorothy Green (Mrs. Champlain); Marie Windsor (Sally Orr); Evan McCord (Phil Yardley); Joan Shawlee (Marge Orr); Richard Deacon (Harvey Rittenhouse); Jerome Cowan (Joe Rosenfield); Donald Losby (Godfrey); Lurene Tuttle (Mother); Ernestine Wade (Thelma); Stanley Adams (Bartender)

Credits: Frank P. Rosenberg (producer); Don Weis (director); Jack Sher (screenplay), from play by Ira Levin, as produced by Otto Preminger; photographed in Technicolor and Panavision by Charles Lang; George Duning (musical score); Arthur Morton (orchestration); Edward Carrere (art director); William L. Kuehl (set decoration); Edith Head (costumes); Jean Burt Reilly (hairstylist); Irma Kusely (Miss Ball's hairstylist); Gordon Bau (makeup); Max Factor (Miss Ball's makeup); Stanley Jones (sound); Russell Llewellyn (assistant director); William Zeigler (editor)

Release date: April 13, 1963

Run time: 100 minutes

Lucille with Bob Hope and Ricky Kelman, who played her stepson.

Synopsis

Angie (Lucille Ball), the wife of a brutally honest drama critic, Parker Ballantine (Bob Hope), decides to write a comedic play. Parker waits for the idea to pass, but his heckling only makes her all the more determined. In a few weeks, the work is complete, and Angie hands it to Parker. Upon review, he says he honestly thinks it is terrible, but his behavior thus far has given her every reason to believe his opinion is biased.

In spite of Parker's critique, Angie is quickly able to put her play into rehearsals. When it opens on Broadway, Parker will either have to review it or pass the job to another critic. He decides he *must* do it himself to keep his integrity. This precludes him from offering the advice Angie asks for on the development of the production when problems arise. Further disrupting their union is Parker's ex-wife, Ivy (Marilyn Maxwell), who tries to convince him that there is more going on between Angie and director Dion Kapakos (Rip Torn) than rewriting.

On opening night, Angie again asks Parker not to cover her play. He relents, but while she is at the theater, he gets drunk, goes to see Ivy, and talks himself into writing his review anyway. For the night, Parker says, they are not husband and wife, but critic and playwright.

Dinner conversation at Sardi's includes talk about the play Angie intends to write. The story of *Critic's Choice* was suggested by a similar situation involving *New York Herald-Tribune* drama critic and author Walter Kerr and his playwright wife, Jean Kerr.

Reviews

"Jack Sher's adaptation hews to the main line of Levin's play, but neither film nor play contains much material for laughter. The action of the picture has been expanded to give Hope a couple of pure slapstick scenes which he performs with his usual zest for zany antics. . . . Most of the picture's running time is taken up with the couple's quarrels and these are not conducive to laughter."

—*New York Daily News*

"There are sporadic flashes of merriment in the film, the result primarily of the cheerful reassuring of Hope and Miss Ball and occasional chipper lines of dialog. . . . The vehicle provides Miss Ball with little opportunity to cut up in her accustomed manner, but her warm, sincere portrayal of the rather shallow-sighted unappealing wife is quite an achievement."

—*Variety*

"It is pleasing to look at in its expensive décor, color and scope, ably played by its experienced stars and ingratiating in its quieter insights into a sophisticated marital relationship. . . . unfortunately, the director, Don Weis, has tried to upholster the shaky plot with slapstick and broad burlesque . . . Both stars, old hands at this sort of thing, go through their paces with benign good humor, but their subtler comic talents remain untapped."

—*New York Times*

With Bob Hope

Parker pens a scathing analysis, which he tells Angie is his professional opinion. She is still furious. Parker finally finds the right words to reconcile with his wife when he realizes his mistakes; next time he will be supportive and ready to lend a hand instead of patronizing. Seeing that he is sincere, Angie goes back to Parker.

Notes and Comments

Critic's Choice had a fairly successful New York run, with Henry Fonda in the lead, before making it to the screen. Written by Ira Levin (author of

Rosemary's Baby and *The Stepford Wives*), the play was still on Broadway in early 1961, when Twentieth Century-Fox initiated plans to produce the film adaptation starring Bob Hope. Eventually the screen rights went to Warner Bros., and Lucille was signed as Hope's co-star in December.

Filming commenced in late March 1962. Don Weis, who had experience in television comedies, directed for producer Frank P. Rosenberg. The supporting cast featured Marilyn Maxwell, Rip Torn, Jessie Royce Landis, and a pre-*Gilligan's Island* Jim Backus. Throughout the '50s, Backus played supporting roles in films and provided the voice of the cartoon Mr. Magoo, before gaining eternal fame as shipwrecked millionaire Mr. Howell. In spite of the strong drawing power of its stars, *Critic's Choice* performed poorly at the box office. The frequent arguments between the main characters did not generate roars of laughter, but there were moments of affection and the expected great byplay between Lucille and Hope. The movie also featured an excellent score.

Another asset of the film was Edith Head's wardrobe for Lucille. Describing the preferred style of the former "Best-Dressed Girl in Town," the designer said, "She doesn't like extremes, or unusual or mad things . . . she doesn't let the clothes overpower her." Head garnered a remarkable thirty-five Oscar nominations (eight wins) throughout her legendary career. Lucille displayed her designs in two films.

Critic's Choice was Lucille's last picture with Bob Hope, but they would continue to be seen together occasionally on the small screen. Both often expressed that they "loved" working together. She made her final public appearance on the arm of Hope when they were presenters at the Academy Awards ceremony in March 1989. Hope paid posthumous tribute to her later the same year with a ninety-minute special in her honor called "Bob Hope's Love Affair with Lucy."

Shortly before *Critic's Choice* went into production, CBS announced that Lucille would return to television with a new series beginning in the fall. In the summer after the movie was made, filming began on the show, and in October 1962, Lucille made her debut as Lucy Carmichael on

The Lucy Show, alongside her old chum Vivian Vance. A month after that, she assumed Desi's position of president of Desilu Productions as he retired from the company. Full-time responsibilities as the head of a major studio, star of a hit series, mother of two, and wife to new husband Gary Morton kept Lucille from starring in a film for the next five years.

With Rip Torn

As Angie and Parker Ballantine, dressed by Edith Head

A Guide for the Married Man

A Twentieth Century-Fox Picture (1967)

Cast: Walter Matthau (Paul Manning); Robert Morse (Ed Stander); Inger Stevens (Ruth Manning); Sue Ane Langdon (Irma Johnson); Claire Kelly (Harriet Stander); Linda Harrison (Miss Stardust); Elaine Devry (Jocelyn Montgomery); Michael Romanoff (Maitre'd); Jason Wingreen (Harry Johnson); Fred Holliday, Pat Becker (Party Guests); Jackie Russell (Miss Harris); Aline Towne (Mousey Man's Wife); Eve Brent (Joe X's Blonde); Marvin Brody (Taxi Driver); In guest appearances as Technical Advisors: Lucille Ball (Mrs. Joe X), Jack Benny, Polly Bergen, Joey Bishop, Sid Caesar, Art Carney (Mr. Joe X), Wally Cox, Jayne Mansfield, Hal March, Louis Nye, Carl Reiner, Phil Silvers, Terry-Thomas; Also in cameos: Ben Blue, Ann Morgan Guilbert, Jeffrey Hunter, Marty Ingels, Sam Jaffe

Credits: Frank McCarthy (producer); Gene Kelly (director); Frank Tarloff (screenplay), from book by Frank Tarloff; photographed in DeLuxe color and Panavision by Joseph MacDonald; L. B. Abbott, Art Cruickshank and Emil Kosa, Jr. (special effects); Herbert Spencer (orchestration); Jack Martin Smith and William Glasgow (art directors); Walter M. Scott and Raphael Bretton (set decoration); Moss Mabry (costumes); Genesco, Inc. (apparel); Margaret Donovan (hairstylist); Ben Nye (makeup); Harry Caplan (unit production manager); Harry M. Lindgren and David Dockendorf (sound); Paul Helmick (assistant director); Dorothy Spencer (editor)

Song: "A Guide for the Married Man" (Johnny Williams and Leslie Bricusse), performed over the titles by the Turtles

Release date: May 26, 1967

Run time: 89 minutes

Synopsis

Paul Manning (Walter Matthau) has a perfect wife in Ruth (Inger Stevens), but still he decides to try his hand at infidelity. His pal Ed (Robert Morse) makes it his duty to first teach Paul the rudiments of how a "considerate" husband should commit adultery—meaning a man who loves his wife, would never hurt her by allowing her to find out he's been unfaithful.

Among the lessons are inventing an alibi, killing the smell of perfume, and how to pick a discreet location for a tryst. Following the training, an ideal "other woman" is selected for Paul and he is ready to take the plunge. But when the moment of truth arrives, all Paul can think of is his beautiful wife. He flees the motel room for the warmth of his own home. Having thoroughly studied the subject, Paul never wants to look at any woman but Ruth again.

Notes and Comments

A Guide for the Married Man abounded with guest stars, billed as technical advisors, enacting the various lessons in infidelity taught by Robert Morse to Walter Matthau. Lucille performed an entertaining sketch with Art Carney showing a husband whose system for getting out of the home for his rendezvous is to pick a fight with his wife, then apologize in the morning to restore domestic bliss until the next time.

The film was directed by Lucille's *Du Barry Was a Lady* leading man, Gene Kelly, who had made his directorial debut with

Between takes with Art Carney as her argumentative husband.

Reviews

"And they said it couldn't be done—a Hollywood comedy all about sex that isn't cause for leering and sneering. . . . Thanks primarily to the wonderful deadpan artistry of Matthau, backed by Kelly's consistently light touch, Morse's baby face baiting, and the comic wizardry of Art Carney, Carl Reiner, Sid Caesar and Jack Benny, who can make old gags young, for the most part, with a flourish, and without offense to anyone."

—*New York Daily News*

"[You will be] wildly entertained by the broadest and funniest farce that has come from Hollywood since the Russians came last year. . . . Of [the] always witty demonstrations, I find most amusing the one in which Art Carney teams with Lucille Ball . . . "

—*New York Times*

" . . . a picture of elaborately sly, sexy, stylish illustrations . . . The picture skates on fairly thin ice, but Kelly's taste, matched with Matthau's beautiful ability to project the ridiculous brimming into farce, keep the whole thing good, if not always clean, fun."

—*New York Post*

1949's *On the Town*. Kelly worked carefully with screenwriter Frank Tarloff to try and keep the story inoffensive by making Matthau the object of fun rather than the loyal wife. The movie opened to applause from critics and audiences, its success leading Kelly into his next feature film assignment for Fox—directing Barbra Streisand (and again Walter Matthau) in the over-the-top musical *Hello Dolly!*.

A Guide for the Married Man was released in May 1967, following the fifth season of *The Lucy Show*. During her tenure as president of Desilu, Lucille only found time to make a cameo appearance in one film. In early 1967, she sold the studio to Gulf and Western, and a few months later began work on a film that had been kept on the backburner for nearly a decade.

Yours, Mine and Ours

A Desilu-Walden Production (1968)

Released by United Artists

Cast: Lucille Ball (Helen North); Henry Fonda (Frank Beardsley); Van Johnson (Darrell Harrison); Louise Troy (Madeleine Love); Sidney Miller (Doctor Ashford); Tom Bosley (Family Doctor); Nancy Howard (Nancy Beardsley); Walter Brooke (Howard Beardsley); Mary Gregory (Sister Mary Alice); Marty Litis (Hospital Nurse); Harry Holcombe (Judge); Ben Murphy (Larry); Richard Angarola (French Actor on TV); Lilyan Chauvin (French Actress on TV); the Beardsley Children: Tim Matthieson (Mike); Gil Rogers (Rusty); Nancy Roth (Rosemary); Gary Goetzman (Greg); Suzanne Cupito (Louise); Holly O'Brien (Susan); Michele Tobin (Veronica); Maralee Foster (Mary); Tracy Nelson (Germaine); Stephanie Oliver (Joan); the North Children: Jennifer Leak (Colleen); Kevin Burchett (Nicky); Kimberly Beck (Janette); Mitch Vogel (Tommy); Margot Jane (Jean); Eric Shea (Phillip); Gregory Atkins (Gerald); Lynnell Atkins (Teresa)

Credits: Robert F. Blumofe (producer); Melville Shavelson (director); Melville Shavelson and Mort Lachman (screenplay), from story by Madelyn Davis and Bob Carroll, Jr.; photographed in DeLuxe color by Charles Wheeler; Howard Anderson Company (special effects); Fred Karlin (musical composition and arrangements); Ernie Sheldon (lyrics); Arthur Lonergan (art director); James Payne (set decoration); Renita Reachi and Frank Cardinale (costumes); Irma Kusely (hairstylist); Hal King and Bill Phillips (makeup); J. Paul Popkin (production supervisor); Kenneth Westcott (properties); Glenn Glen Inc. (sound); J. Richard Bremerkamp, Louis Nicoletti, and Jim Benjamin (assistant directors); Stuart Gilmore (editor)

Release date: April 24, 1968

Run time: 111 minutes

A fleeting moment of quiet during the two families' first night as one.

Synopsis

Widowed naval officer Frank Beardsley (Henry Fonda) comes ashore at San Francisco for good to finish raising his ten children. What he meets are eight sour faces who resent him for allowing his brother to care for the two youngest for a time. Also recently arrived in town is Helen North (Lucille Ball), a widow with eight kids. Frank and Helen are bringing up a combined eighteen children, but both are lonesome for companionship.

After two chance encounters, the pair officially meets when Helen, a nurse, cares for one of Frank's daughters. They begin dating, but have reservations because of the enormous brood between them. However, their friend Darrell (Van Johnson) sees to it that they realize they were made for each other. To the horror of their children, Frank and Helen soon decide to marry.

The twenty strong Beardsley-North clan moves into a large Victorian home and adjusts to an assembly line mode of living while Helen and Frank try to think of a way to generate unity between the two families. The solution Helen arrives at is to adopt Frank's kids and have Frank adopt hers. The children hate the idea.

Christmas day brings Helen news from her doctor—she is going to have a baby. Withholding this information from Frank temporarily, she soon after sends him off on a testing mission for the Navy that she knows he is anxious to take part in. This earns her the respect of Frank's boys. When he finally finds out about the pregnancy, Frank rushes home and a few weeks later, the first child is born to Frank and Helen Beardsley. It is the baby that finally makes them all feel like one family, and soon both groups of children agree to be adopted, making it official.

Notes and Comments

Yours, Mine and Ours' premise of a widowed mother of eight marrying a widowed father of ten, was actually based on a true-life story—that of the Beardsley family of Northern California. The real Helen Beardsley wrote a book about the family's experiences titled *Who Gets the Drumstick?*.

Helen and Frank work out a few kinks in their system for bed and bathroom assignments.

Their story was first envisioned as a possible film for Lucille to make with Desi in 1959. Beginning in the summer of 1962, plans for the project to go into production were continually postponed and rescheduled before everything finally came together for it to be made in the summer of 1967. Among the actors Lucille favored to co-star over the years were Fred MacMurray, Jackie Gleason, and Art Carney, while titles alternated from *The Beardsley Story*, to *His, Hers and Theirs*, *Full House*, *The Population Explosion*, and ultimately *Yours, Mine and Ours*.

A deal was struck with Robert F. Blumofe of United Artists to produce the film, and Melville Shavelson was signed to direct. The script of *The Beardsley Story* had changed hands several times through the years, but all versions up to then were considered by Blumofe and Shavelson to have too much *Lucy* in them. Shavelson and Mort Lachman, both of whom wrote frequently for Bob Hope, collaborated on a new screenplay.

Yours, Mine and Ours gave Lucille her first leading film role since 1963 and reunited her onscreen with her co-star from *The Big Street*, Henry Fonda, and with Van Johnson for the first time since *Easy to Wed*. *Happy Days'* Tom Bosley played a modest role as the family doctor, and among the eighteen Beardsley-North children were Tim Matheson, Tracy Nelson in her screen debut, and Suzanne Cupito, who later made a (new) name for herself in television as Morgan Brittany.

Preparing breakfast for eighteen children and two adults is no easy task.

With Lynnell and Gregory Atkins, real-life siblings who portrayed the youngest of the North children.

The movie was made during Lucille's summer break after making season five of *The Lucy Show*. On July 5, 1967, filming commenced aboard the *USS Enterprise* at the Alameda Naval Air Station. The crew then moved on to film the stars on location at some of San Francisco's most recognizable sights before returning to the Hollywood soundstages.

Made for $1.7 million, *Yours, Mine and Ours* exceeded expectations by becoming a box-office bonanza, one of the highest-grossing films of 1968. It was a genuine family picture, "—the only kind I'll do," Lucille told reporter Rex Reed on the set. "I hate all this violence and 007 stuff they're making. Turns me off." She was given a change from her television personality, but it was a true *Lucy* moment that was the film's highlight—a wonderful scene in which the Beardsley boys add an abundance of liquor to Helen's drink that makes her emotions run wild, from tears to hysterical laughter, and back again.

Dennis Quaid and Rene Russo played Frank and Helen Beardsley in a 2005 remake of *Yours, Mine and Ours*.

Playing her drunk scene, in which she alternates cries of sorrow between belly laughs. Shavelson commented, "It was tough but she did a great job. I don't know anybody else who could have carried off both of these emotions at the same time."

Mame

A Warner Bros. Picture (1974)

Cast: Lucille Ball (Mame Dennis); Beatrice Arthur (Vera Charles); Robert Preston (Beauregard Jackson Pickett-Burnside); Kirby Furlong (Young Patrick Dennis); Bruce Davidson (Older Patrick Dennis); Joyce Van Patten (Sally Cato); Don Porter (Mr. Upson); Audrey Christie (Mrs. Upson); Jane Connell (Agnes Gooch); John McGiver (Mr. Babcock); Doria Cook (Gloria Upson); Bobbi Jordan (Pegreen Ryan); George Chiang (Ito); Patrick Labyorteaux (Peter)

Credits: Robert Fryer and James Cresson (producers); Gene Saks (director); Paul Zindel (screenplay), from musical play by Jerome Lawrence, Robert E. Lee, and Jerry Herman, novel by Patrick Dennis, play by Lawrence and Lee, as produced by Fryer, Carr, and Harris; photographed in Technicolor and Panavision by Philip Lathrop; Albert Whitlock (special effects); Jerry Herman (musical adaptation); Ralph Burns and Billy Byers (orchestration); Fred Werner (music supervisor); Onna White (dance director), Martin Allen (associate); Robert F. Boyle (production designer); Harold Michelson (art director); Marvin March (set decoration); Theodora Van Runkle (costumes); Bruce Walkup and Robert Modes (men's wardrobe); Nancy McArdle and Renita Reachi (ladies' wardrobe); Jean Burt Reilly (hairstylist); Irma Kusely (Miss Ball's hairstylist); Fred Williams (makeup); Hal King (Miss Ball's makeup); Arthur Piantadosi (recording); Hal Klein (unit production manager); Al Overton, Jr. (sound); Jack Aldworth (assistant director); D. Michael Moore (second unit director); Maury Winetrobe (editor); Wayne Fitzgerald (titles)

Songs: "It's Today," "Open a New Window," "The Man in the Moon," "My Best Girl," "We Need a Little Christmas," "Mame," "Bosom Buddies," "Loving You," "Gooch's Song," "If He Walked into My Life Today," "What Do I Do Now?" (Jerry Herman)

Release date: March 27, 1974 (Radio City Music Hall)

Run time: 132 minutes

Synopsis

When his father dies, custody of nine-year-old Patrick Dennis (Kirby Furlong) is given to his only living relative—Auntie Mame (Lucille Ball). Mame, who holds court at lavish Beakman Place in Roaring Twenties New York, embraces her role as guardian and begins showing Patrick the world, everything from museums, to a speakeasy, to a police station when they get raided.

The toast of the '20s

Reviews

"In all fairness, it must be pointed out that with all her musical shortcomings, Lucille Ball provides Mame with what charm it does possess. . . . And in spite of the fact that Mame is a mess, Lucille Ball triumphs once again. She's a movie veteran, surviving yet another war. But it's an expensive victory, and everything that was an American classic has been left scattered around her like carnage on a Technicolor battlefield."

—*New York Daily News*

"Successful repeat of fun-loving Mame. . . . It is very much a woman's picture, a beguiling, funny and intermittently sentimental frolic. It may or may not be perennial Lucy's theatrical screen capstone. She is great in the role . . . 'Mame' is sometimes outrageously exaggerated, like, say, a fashion layout in Vogue. To vary the metaphor, it's a case of, if you don't like chocolate eclairs, stay out of the bakery. . . . 'Mame' is why movies were invented."

—*Variety*

"It's all relentlessly good-natured but unless you've been packed in storage somewhere it's so familiar it puts a tremendous burden on its star. . . . When the character of Lucy, an inspired slapstick performer, coincides with that of Auntie Mame, the Big-Town sophisticate, 'Mame' is marvelous. . . . Miss Ball has some great moments but she is not even a nonsinger who fakes singing very well."

—*New York Times*

The "Bosom Buddies" number. Lucille joked to Sidney Skolsky, "With Bea Arthur at my side, we sound like a couple of lady bullfrogs."

All is well until the fateful day of the Wall Street Crash of '29. Mame not only loses her fortune; Patrick is taken away by his trustee, Mr. Babcock (John McGiver).

Patrick adores Mame and finds a way to get back to her while her resilient nature kicks in. She takes a job as a clerk in a department store where she meets a wealthy Southern gentleman named Beauregard (Robert Preston). They fall in love and get married. While Patrick is away at school, the couple spends many beautiful years traveling the world until Beauregard's untimely death.

The grown Patrick (Bruce Davidson) becomes engaged to a pretty young snob, Gloria Upson (Doria Cook). When Mame meets her bigoted family, she finds out where Gloria gets her attitude. To her despair, some of their influence has rubbed off on Patrick too. She works out a plan to make him see the light.

Mame invites the Upsons to Beakman Place. While they are there, she has her dearest friend, Vera Charles (Beatrice Arthur) drop by, as well as many of her other colorful pals. Next comes an appearance by Patrick's former governess, Agnes Gooch (Jane Connell), who is in the delicate condition of being unmarried and pregnant. Then comes what the Upsons consider the ultimate insult. Mame announces that she has bought the property next to their estate with the intention of turning it into a home for unwed mothers. Outraged, they storm out of Beakman Place and Gloria calls off the engagement.

In time, Patrick sees that Auntie Mame was right. Years later, he is married to a former maid of Mame's, and they have a young son. As she departs on another world tour, Mame excitedly begins the task of teaching her great nephew all about life.

Notes and Comments

The first stage adaptation of Patrick Dennis's best-selling novel about the flamboyant Mame made it to Broadway in 1956, starring Rosalind Russell. Russell then brought the character to the screen for the first time in Warner Bros. 1958 film *Auntie Mame*. Eight years later, Mame hit Broadway again in an all-new musical edition starring Angela Lansbury. Each of

With Robert Preston, the actor most famous as *The Music Man*, a role for which he won a Tony on Broadway before recreating it on the cinema screen.

these interpretations had been supremely triumphant. When Warners purchased the rights to the musical (for $3 million), Lansbury was expected to repeat the role, but they instead turned to a more universally loved star, Lucille Ball. Lucille was anxious to become the next Mame, but always maintained that it was only because Lansbury herself had not been cast.

In January 1972, however, Lucille's participation in the musical was jeopardized when she broke her right leg in a skiing accident while on vacation in Snowmass, Colorado. Certain that making *Mame* was out of the question, she told producer Robert Fryer, "I'm not even sure I can walk, much less dance." His answer was, "We want you. You're our Mame. We'll wait until you're ready to play her."

With her injury written into her current series, *Here's Lucy*, Lucille filmed season five of the TV show before beginning work on *Mame* in January 1973. George Cukor, the original choice for director, was no longer available after the extended delay, so Gene Saks, the director of the stage version, was brought in. Tony award winner Bea Arthur, who was married to Saks, reprised her role of Mame's "bosom buddy," Vera Charles. Madelyn Kahn had been set to portray Agnes Gooch, but ultimately the part went to another Broadway cast member, Jane Connell.

During a trip to the South to meet her prospective in-laws, the Pickett-Burnsides.

Mame prepares to make her acting debut.

Mame was a physically demanding assignment and Lucille's first singing and dancing film role in nearly thirty years. Choreographer Onna White, yet another recruit from the stage company, had the task of coaching her for the dance numbers. Having always performed with unrestrained vigor, it was heartbreaking for Lucille to find that the accident put limits on what she could do. She still had an enormous capacity for work however, and appreciated the exhaustive but heartening rehearsals and exercise regimes White put her through for months prior to filming. Her own vocals were used for the first time in a full-scale musical. "Goodness knows I can't sing," she said at the

Mame wins the hearts of her disapproving
future in-laws after her triumph at a foxhunt.

A candid shot during filming

time, "but the words really mean something to me."

Mame was a grand, pretentious, $12 million production that took over five months to make. The critical reception was extremely mixed. Some reviews went overboard in their praise, but others were brutal and painful to Lucille, who was proud of *Mame*. She was very insecure about how her face would look on the big screen. The soft-focus lenses used to camouflage the signs of age became a prime complaint. Lucille embarked on a nation-wide promotional tour that boosted ticket sales, so the box-office returns were less disappointing. It set a record at Radio City Music Hall. *Mame* would be Lucille's final theatrical film release.

On the set with director Gene Saks

Stone Pillow

A Schaefer/Karpf Production (1985)

In association with Gaylord Production Company

Cast: Lucille Ball (Florabelle); Daphne Zuniga (Carrie Lang); William Converse Roberts (Max); Stephen Lang (Tim); Susan Batson (Ruby); Anna Maria Horsford (Collins); Stefan Schnabel (Mr. Berman); Rebecca Schull (Mrs. Nelson); Imogene Bliss (Violet); Michael Champagne (Supermarket Manager); Gloria Cromwell (Bus Terminal Matron); Patrick Kilpatrick (Young Thug); Matthew Locricchio (Tony); Pat MacNamara (Daggett); Josephine Nichols (Bag Lady in Lady's Room); Patricia O'Connell (Hargrove Shelter Guard); Peter Phillips (Bus Driver); Victor Raider-Wexler (Joe); John Ramsey (Older Thug); Alex Paez (Young Thug); Mary Lou Rosato (Bus Terminal Cop); Edward Seamon (Al); Raymond Serra (Stan); Gary Singer (Hargrove Shelter Guard)

Credits: Merrill H. Karpf (executive producer); Terry Donnelly (co-producer); George Schaefer (director); Rose Leiman Goldemberg (screenplay); Walter Lassally (photography); Georges Delerue (music); Warren Clymer (art director); Andy Blumenthal (editor)

Release date: November 5, 1985

Run time: 100 minutes

Synopsis

Carrie Lange (Daphne Zuniga) has just begun her career in social work. She wants to make a difference but must first learn what life is really like for the city's homeless. She meets an elderly woman named Florabelle (Lucille Ball), who makes it known she does not want company or help. Equipped with the precious cart that contains all of her belongings, Flora takes care of herself on the streets of Manhattan.

Carrie wins Flora's trust after saving her cart. Flora takes her for a runaway, and Carrie plays along as Flora finds her the best food and warmest places the streets have to offer. Flora even divulges painful memories about her past life. They go to Grand Central Station for the

Homeless in New York

With Daphne Zuniga

night, but are separated after the police throw everyone out. Flora looks for Carrie at a shelter and is stunned to find her working there. She feels she has been betrayed.

Against her will, Flora is shuttled off to a women's shelter in Brooklyn, where she is treated poorly, and then must find her own way back to Manhattan. Finding compassion difficult to come by even in those within her profession, Carrie decides she at least can make a difference, one person at a time. Finally realizing she cannot go on living the way does, Flora accepts Carrie's helping hand. Through Carrie's intervention, for the first time in years Flora has a place to call home.

Notes and Comments

Lucille knew that taking the role of a bag lady in the dramatic made-for-television feature *Stone Pillow* was a daring move. "I didn't think this was the greatest thing in the world to do," she said. "I knew I was taking a chance with my image." Admittedly having minimal concept of the plight of the homeless, the movie presented her with a challenge. She worked to understand the character by keeping detailed notes and developing ideas about the habits, traits, and eccentricities of Florabelle, whom she named after her grandmother, Flora Belle Hunt.

One of the reasons the project appealed to Lucille was the chance to work with George Schaefer, the producer-director behind many acclaimed Hallmark Hall of Fame television films including Emmy winners *Macbeth* (1960) and *Elizabeth the Queen* (1968). Her young co-star was Daphne Zuniga, just coming off of the hit teen comedy *The Sure Thing*, but seven years before the TV drama *Melrose Place*.

Filmed on the streets of Manhattan's Lower East Side, Lucille was unrecognizable to passers-

As Florabelle

by in her homeless guise. The production was originally scheduled to be shot during the winter beginning in late 1984, but it was postponed after the death of screenwriter Rose Leiman Goldemberg's daughter. When filming commenced in May 1985, a heat wave fell upon the city, causing the seventy-four-year-old star to suffer buried under heavy winter-weather garments. In addition to a shoulder injury, Lucille became dehydrated, lost twenty-three pounds, and had to be hospitalized at the end of the six-week shoot.

Stone Pillow premiered on CBS (the home of *Lucy*), garnering high ratings and some fine personal reviews for Lucille. But, as she anticipated, presenting herself in a manner so far removed from *Lucy* also brought forth strong criticism. Lucille too had difficulty beholding herself as Florabelle. "I saw the stills. Seeing myself made up to not look pretty, to have unkempt hair and no makeup—it upsets me."

She soon put on a more familiar face. In early 1986 came the announcement that Lucille would soon begin her fourth television series, *Life with Lucy*. The ill-advised program was cancelled within two months. The public still adored Lucy, but it was for the remarkable work she had done in the past. She had long since gained immortality, and nothing she did could diminish her star.

Short Subjects

$\mathcal{L}$ucille appeared in a handful of short subject features during the mid-'30s. With the exception of one, starring the Three Stooges, they are quite obscure, but what information could be compiled on the others has been documented.

Perfectly Mismated

A Columbia Short Subject Presentation (1934)

Cast: Leon Errol (Leon); Dorothy Granger (Hazel); Vivian Oakland (Rosita); Fred Malatesta (Mendoza); Phil Dunham (Landlord); Lucille Ball (Secretary)

Credits: Jules White (producer); James W. Horne (director); Andrew Bennison (story and screenplay); Al Siegler (photography); James Sweeney (editor)

Release date: November 1, 1934

Run time: 20 minutes

Synopsis

The union of bickering husband and wife Leon and Hazel Errol is pushed to the limit when Hazel finds out about Leon's former bride, Rosita, who ran away with a circus performer called the Great Mendoza. To make matters worse, the Mendozas move in down the hall from the Errols! Leon takes to drink and, inevitably, he wanders into the wrong apartment and gives rise to a night of bedlam that Hazel, Rosita, and her jealous husband will not soon forget.

Tidbit

During production, *Perfectly Mismated* was called *Scrambled Wives*.

With Leon Errol, publicity for *Perfectly Mismated*

Three Little Pigskins

A Columbia Short Subject Presentation (1934)

Cast: Moe Howard (Moe); Larry Fine (Larry); Curly Howard (Curley); Lucille Ball (Daisy Simms); Gertie Green (Lulu Banks); Phyllis Crane (Molly Gray); Walter Long (Joe Stacks)

Credits: Jules White (producer); Raymond McCarey (director); Felix Adler and Griffin Jay (story and screenplay); Henry Freulich (photography); James Sweeney (editor)

Release date: December 8, 1934

Run time: 20 minutes

Synopsis

Looking to earn a quick buck, the Stooges take part in a publicity stunt dressed as football players to advertise Boulder Dam College's upcoming game. Three gangsters' girlfriends (one of whom is Lucille) then mistake the boys for football heroes and ask them to play for the team of one of the hoods in order to assure a victory (and save the gangsters from losing $50,000). The next thing they know, the Stooges are holding the pigskin. The only problem is, they don't know a thing about the game! One hundred yards have never seen such chaos.

Tidbit

Asked what she remembered of this short fifty years later, Lucille replied, "Just a lot of seltzer squirting and trying to get dry."

His Old Flame

A Columbia Short Subject Presentation (1935)

Cast: Charles Murray; Geneva Mitchell; Billy Gilbert; Elaine Baker; Lucille Ball; Betty McMahon; Kay Hughes; Eve Reynolds; Doris Davenport, Doris McMahan, Alice Dahl, Carmen Andre

Directed by: James W. Horne

Release date: January 25, 1935

Run time: 18 minutes

Synopsis

The old flame of a mayoral candidate surfaces to stir up trouble at campaign time.

A Night at the Biltmore Bowl

An RKO-Radio Production (1935)

Cast: Jimmy Grier and His Orchestra; Betty Grable; Joy Hodges; Grady Sutton; Bert Wheeler; Edgar Kennedy; Lucille Ball; Anne Shirley; Preston Foster; Bud Flanagan

Credits: Lee Marcus (producer); Alf Goulding (director); Joseph A. Fields (screenplay); Roy Webb (musical director); Edward Mann (editor)

Release date: June 21, 1935

Run time: 17 minutes

Synopsis

A night of treasure hunting (initiated by Betty Grable) winds up at Hollywood's famous Biltmore Bowl.

Tidbit

Biltmore cast member Bud Flanagan later became Dennis O'Keefe, Lucille's co-star in *That's Right—You're Wrong*.

Lucille and *Biltmore* star Betty Grable

Dummy Ache

An RKO-Radio Short Subject (1936)

Cast: Edgar Kennedy (Edgar); Florence Lake (Florence); Dot Farley (Mother); Jack Rice (Brother); George Lewis (Al St. Claire); Lucille Ball (Lois); Harry Bowen (Cabbie)

Credits: Lee Marcus (producer); Bert Gilroy (associate producer); Leslie Goodwins (director); Leslie Goodwins and Charles Roberts (story); Jack McKenzie (photography); Denzil Cutler (recording); Edward Mann (editor)

Release date: July 10, 1936

Run time: 20 minutes

Synopsis:

Knowing that her husband, Edgar, would disapprove of her starring in a play, Florence acts very suspicious about where she is going when a rehearsal comes up. Edgar follows her to the home of co-star Al St. Claire and spies while they enact a scene in which Florence discovers that her lover is married (to Lucille). Florence becomes enraged and shoots Al. Edgar thinks the scene is for real. He comes in, finds a dummy of Al stuffed in a laundry basket, and before Florence can explain, carries it away to dispose of "the body." Limbs are spilling out of the hamper as he lugs it down the street and naturally the police soon catch up with Edgar, so before long, all confusion is cleared up.

Tidbit

Dummy Ache was nominated for an Academy Award as the Best Short Subject of 1936. It lost to *The Public Pays*, an installment of MGM's *Crime Does Not Pay* series.

In late 1935, *Follow the Fleet* period. She had appeared in two shorts earlier in the year.

So and Sew

An RKO-Radio Short Subject (1936)

Cast: Lucille Ball (Sally Curtis); Billy Gilbert (Rudolfo); Lorin Raker (Jimmy Drake); Constance Bergen (Elizabeth Campbell); Edward Keane (Jack Campbell); Bud Jameson (Whiters)

Credits: Lee Marcus (producer); Bert Gilroy (associate producer); Jean Yarbrough and Charles Roberts (story); Nick Musuraca (photography); James Stewart (recording); Edward Mann (editor)

Release date: July 1936

Run time: 15 minutes

Synopsis

Jimmy and Sally are soon to be wed. Jimmy, an interior decorator, has a job in the home of Mrs. Elizabeth Campbell, an old schoolmate of Sally's. While there, Rudolfo, an irate South American, arrives threatening to kill Elizabeth if she will not marry him—unless she can prove that she is happily married. With Mr. Campbell away, Elizabeth has Jimmy pose as her husband. All is well until Sally shows up. Jimmy is introduced to her as Elizabeth's husband, which nearly makes her go away with Rudolfo, who has transferred his affection from Elizabeth to Sally. When the real Mr. Campbell returns, Jimmy drops the pretense, knocks out Rudolfo, and wins Sally back.

Tidbit

So and Sew was second in a trio of shorts Lucille made in between *Bunker Bean* and her bit in *Winterset*, in June 1936, the same time she was appearing in newspapers because of her rumored engagement to Broderick Crawford.

Swing It

An RKO-Radio Short Subject (1936)

Starring: Louis Prima, Lucille Ball, Pee Wee Russell

Directed by: Leslie Goodwins

Release date: July 1936

Run time: 16 minutes

No Speeding! Fun on the RKO lot, 1936

Early 1936

One Live Ghost

An RKO-Radio Short Subject (1936)

Cast: Leon Errol (Henry Morton); Vivien Oakland (Ethel Morton); Robert Graves (Bert); Delmar Watson (Sonny); Lucille Ball (Maxine); Alan Curtis (Alan); Donald Kerr (Chauffeur); Jane Hamilton (Houseguest)

Credits: Lee Marcus (producer); Bert Gilroy (associate producer); Leslie Goodwins (director); Monte Collins and Leslie Goodwins (story); Jack MacKenzie (photography); W. C. Moore (recording); Edward Mann (editor)

Release date: November 7, 1936

Run time: 21 minutes

Synopsis

Henry Morton, an impulsive husband unhappy about his wife's nagging, fakes his death and then returns to his home posing as a British valet to see firsthand his family's reaction to his "death." Unaware that they are on to his scam, Henry is shocked that his wife appears to have forgotten him already. Hoping to scare her into shame, he goes out and returns home yet again—as his own ghost. Wearing the most unconvincing disguise imaginable, Henry is not fooling anyone (except Lucille as the maid!), and Mr. and Mrs. Morton are soon cheek to cheek again.

Tidbit

Lucille had a chance to expand her range in this short subject. Unlike her many stylish, smart-alecky characters of this period, here she played a jumpy, featherbrained maid with messy hair who flutters about the house giggling and hoping to get an earful of Leon Errol's British accent.

A Few That Never Were

*T*he following is a selection of film productions that never materialized for Lucille. During her fifty-six years in Hollywood she was assigned to, made tests for, or was desired by filmmakers to appear in many projects that for various reasons never came to pass.

There Goes My Girl

According to contemporary trade publications, Lucille was scheduled to participate in this romantic comedy as a supporting player in 1937, soon after returning from the east and her *Hey Diddle Diddle* stage experience. Ann Sothern and Gene Raymond starred as ace reporters employed by rival newspapers. The two happen to be in love with each other, but a murder case and a wily editor bent on keeping Ann single prevent the wedding from taking place. Modern sources state that Lucille's scenes ended up on the cutting-room floor; however, the film's daily production reports do not indicate that she worked a single day on this picture.

It Could Happen to You

This snappy 1939 comedy from *The Affairs of Annabel* storywriter Charles Hoffman might have been fun for Lucille. Fox's request for the loan of her services was declined by RKO. Her home studio was keeping her busy enough, assigning her to film after film (*Five Came Back* was slated for her at the moment). Fox wanted her to star as the wife of a reticent advertising man who lands in jail after innocently becoming involved in a murder. His spunky wife sets out to catch the real killer. Fox wanted Burgess Meredith for the male lead, but when he too was unavailable, Gloria Stuart and Stuart Erwin were cast.

Men Against the Sky

RKO assigned Lucille to this film in the spring of 1940. Shot in May and June of that year, at the time she was already working on two pictures at once, *Dance, Girl, Dance*, which was experiencing production delays, and *Too Many Girls*, which was going into rehearsals in mid-June. In this aviation drama, Lucille was to have played Kay Mercedes, the sister of a once first-rate but now alcoholic pilot named Phil. Kay's two-fold objective is to help her brother beat the habit and help the man she loves, Martin Ames, acquire a government contract for his aircraft factory, by selling Martin on a plane designed by Phil. Phil ends by sacrificing his life to test and perfect his plane. Martin gets his contract and consoles Kay. The part of Kay was reassigned to Wendy Barrie. Richard Dix and Kent Taylor played Phil and Martin, respectively.

Night of January 16th

Night of January 16th was based on the first play by Ayn Rand, who worked for a time in the wardrobe department at RKO. The studio purchased the rights to the work in 1939 and announced the possibility that either Lucille or Claudette Colbert would be cast in the lead role. The rights were sold to Paramount later the same year. Lucille would have portrayed Kit Lane, the private secretary of Bjorn Faulkner, a crooked business tycoon. Kit winds up on trial for her life when she is falsely accused of killing her boss. The odds are stacked against her, but with the help of Steve Van Ruyle, one of the victims of Faulkner's embezzling (who also is in love with Kit), clues to solving the mysterious murder are revealed. Robert Preston and Ellen Drew were co-starred as Steve and Kit in the 1941 Paramount production, with Nils Asther filling the role of Faulkner.

Parachute Battalion

RKO tried to put newlywed Lucille back before the cameras in March 1941 in this military drama. In it she was to have acted as the daughter of a Master Sergeant, an attractive feminine distraction for parachute jumpers stationed at a base in Georgia. Robert Preston starred as an ex-football hero with confidence to spare, Nancy Kelly supplied the love interest, and Edmond O'Brien was the shy recruit who earns the girl's love. All told, Lucille did not make any films for just over five months following her marriage to Desi in November 1940. When she did go before the movie cameras again it was May 1941, for *Look Who's Laughing*.

Ball of Fire

In early 1941, Lucille had her heart set on a part that had been rejected by a number of Hollywood's leading comedic actresses, first by Ginger Rogers, then Jean Arthur, then Carole Lombard, and then Barbara Stanwyck. Lucille, however, saw the jazzy "Sugarpuss" O'Shea in *Ball of Fire* as a terrific character. Knowing how she felt, Carole Lombard put in a good word for her with director Howard Hawks. A test convinced her old producer Samuel Goldwyn to offer her the part, and preproduction work got under way with Lucille slated to star. Barbara Stanwyck then changed her mind. Since she was a bigger name at the time, she won the role. Stanwyck gave a first-class performance, deserving of the Academy Award nomination she received, but watching the film, one cannot help feeling pangs of regret. *Ball of Fire* turned out to be outstanding, co-starring Gary Cooper and containing all the wit and dynamism one would expect of a Howard Hawks-directed comedy with a script by Billy Wilder and Charles Brakett. Lucille would most certainly have excelled as the flashy nightclub star who while hiding out from the police, turns the staid existence of a team of seven loveable scholars upside down and does the conga on it.

Yolanda and the Thief

Lucille, a so-called "non-dancer," came close to achieving the dream of millions of women—that of dancing with Fred Astaire—when MGM announced in March 1944 that she would star in *Yolanda and the Thief*. There were delays, and by the time the film was set to go into production, in the spring of 1945, the studio had found something even better for Lucille's talents, a juicy comedy role in *Easy to Wed*. Producer Arthur Freed cast another Lucille (Bremer) in his Technicolor musical fantasy. In spite of all its excess trimmings, including the magic presence of Fred Astaire and director Vincente Minnelli, *Yolanda and the Thief* failed at the box office. The story centers around a convent-bred heiress named Yolanda Aquaviva. She sends up a prayer and her guardian angel "materializes" in the form of Johnny Riggs. Johnny is, in reality, a crook scheming to get Yolanda's millions, that is, until he falls in love with the girl.

The Manchurian Candidate

Star Frank Sinatra, who was also influential behind the scenes of *The Manchurian Candidate*, wanted Lucille to play the deviously manipulative mother of Laurence Harvey in this classic political thriller from 1962. Director John Frankenheimer, who had just made *All Fall Down* with Angela Lansbury, wanted to cast Angela Lansbury in the role. After Frankenheimer screened *All Fall Down* for him, Sinatra agreed that Lansbury had the ability to make a great Mrs. Iselin (she proved it by earning an Academy Award nomination). Lansbury was given the part before Lucille even knew that she had been considered. Casting Lucille in such a role was an interesting idea from Sinatra that few others would have visualized. She was just regaining confidence after her divorce from Desi and subsequent remarriage to Gary Morton, so playing the mother of thirty-four-year-old Laurence Harvey may not have appealed to her at this time. She was also planning her return to television. All things considered, it seems likely Lucille would have passed on the part of Mrs. Iselin.

For information on more unrealized film projects, see Notes and Comments sections of the following entries:

Gone with the Wind (See *Go Chase Yourself*, page 156)

Glamour Boy #2 (See *Beauty for the Asking*, page 174)

Passage to Bordeaux (See *Dance, Girl, Dance*, page 200)

The Smiler with a Knife (See *You Can't Fool Your Wife*, page 196)

Footlight Serenade (See *Seven Days' Leave*, page 228)

Born Yesterday (See *Biography*, page 26)

The Greatest Show on Earth (See *The Magic Carpet*, page 306)

Endnotes

Page 8: "I just wanted": *Lucy and Desi: A Home Movie* (Arluck Entertainment, 1993).

Page 11: "I wasn't unloved": Lucille Ball, *Love, Lucy* (New York: G. P. Putnam's Sons, 1996), 26.

Page 11: "We didn't play": Fred Ball quoted from *Lucy and Desi: A Home Movie* (Arluck Entertainment, 1993).

Page 13: "the tragedy that": Cleo Smith quoted from *Lucy and Desi: A Home Movie* (Arluck Entertainment, 1993).

Page 13: "I'd run home": *TV Guide*, June 12, 1971.

Page 16: "I loved Hollywood": Lucille Ball interview, *Lucy and Desi: The Scrapbooks* (New York: Education Through Entertainment, 1996).

Page 17: "I've always been": Bart Andrews and Thomas J. Watson, *Loving Lucy* (New York: St. Martin's Press, 1980), 49.

Page 18: "Nothing was beneath": *Rolling Stone*, June 23, 1983.

Page 21: "We met and": *Rolling Stone*, June 23, 1983.

Page 21: "the first man": *McCall's*, September 1960.

Page 21: "I listed to": Gene Tierney with Mickey Herskowitz, *Self-Portrait* (Wyden Books, 1978), 47.

Page 23: "a cross between": Hedda Hopper column, circa 1943.

Page 24: "I had been trying": Lucille Ball, *Love, Lucy* (New York: G. P. Putnam's Sons, 1996), 176.

Page 25: "We'd been married": *Lucy and Desi: A Home Movie* (Arluck Entertainment, 1993).

Page 26: A year earlier: *New York Herald-Tribune*, June 2, 1949.

Page 27: "*was* Fred Mertz," "[the writers] took": *Finding Lucy* (American Masters, 2000).

Page 28: "I always felt": *McCall's*, September 1960.

Page 28: "All our good": Lucille Ball, *Love, Lucy* (New York: G. P. Putnam's Sons, 1996), 223.

Page 29: "In those days": *Los Angeles Times*, September 13, 1953.

Page 30: "I don't want": Desi Arnaz, *A Book* (New York: William Morrow, 1976), 284.

Page 31: "He has a": Lucille Ball, *Love, Lucy* (New York: G. P. Putnam's Sons, 1996), 207.

Page 31: "You can't go": Lucille Ball, *Love, Lucy* (New York: G. P. Putnam's Sons, 1996), 258.

Page 31: "I was about": Fan letter to Desi Arnaz, August 29, 1955. Lucille Ball file, Jack Hirshberg Collection, Margaret Herrick Library, Center for Motion Picture Study, Academy of Motion Picture Arts and Sciences (AMPAS).

Page 32: "a female 'Rainmaker'": *New York Times*, October 8, 1967.

Page 32: "'Wildcat' hasn't much": *New Yorker*, December 24, 1960.

Page 32: "the people came": *New York Times*, October 8, 1967.

Page 32: "Simple things like": Coyne Steven Sanders and Tom Gilbert, *Desilu: The Story of Lucille Ball and Desi Arnaz* (New York: William Morrow, 1993), 319.

Page 36: "It was a": Coyne Steven Sanders and Tom Gilbert, *Desilu: The Story of Lucille Ball and Desi Arnaz* (New York: William Morrow, 1993), 341.

Page 36: "I have to": *New York Times*, October 8, 1967.

Page 37: "went through some": *Woman's Day*, March 5, 1991.

Page 39: "I love you": Coyne Steven Sanders and Tom Gilbert, *Desilu: The Story of Lucille Ball and Desi Arnaz* (New York: William Morrow, 1993), 355.

Page 53: Stuart, who thought: *The Desilu Story* (Platinum/Bravo, 2003).

Page 55: The day that: Lewis Yablonsky, *George Raft* (New York: McGraw-Hill, 1974), 111.

Page 57: Less than a year: *The American Film Institute Catalog, 1931-1940*, 193.

Page 58: *Blood Money*, which: *New York Herald-Tribune*, August 15, 1933.

Page 60: It caused a stir: *Hollywood Reporter*, June 26, 1933.

Page 61: At least her director: *Modern Screen*, April 1939.

Page 64: On August 18, 1933: *Nana* production file, Special Collections, AMPAS.

Page 64: "complete deformation": *New York Sun*, May 11, 1934.

Page 64: *Lady of the Boulevards*: *Variety*, May 1, 1934.

Page 75: At the time: *Complicated Women* (Timeline Films/Turner Classic Movies, 2003).

Page 78: He came to: *The American Film Institute Catalog, 1931-1940*, 19.

Page 81: "toward a lighter": *New York Herald-Tribune*, August 1934.

Page 83: "Ice Cream Fantasy": A. Scott Berg, *Goldwyn, A Biography* (New York: Alfred A. Knopf, 1989), 254.

Page 84: "Lucille, you have": *Modern Screen*, April 1939.

Page 84: "Miss Ball—on": George Murphy, *Say, Didn't You Used to be George Murphy?* (Bartholomew House, Ltd., 1970), 170.

Page 85: *Fugitive Lady* synopsis: "Chic," *Variety* film review, November 1934; *Los Angeles Times* film review, 1934; *The American Film Institute Catalog, 1931-1940*, 717. Film not viewed by author.

Page 87: *Men of the Night* synopsis: "Chic," *Variety*, November 1934; *The American Film Institute Catalog, 1931-1940*, 1359. Film not viewed by author.

Page 93: For the star, Capra: Frank Capra, Jr. interview for *Broadway Bill* home video, Paramount, 1994.

Page 94: *Carnival* synopsis: Andre Sennwald, *New York Times*, February 1935; "Chic," *Variety*, February 20, 1935; *The American Film Institute Catalog, 1931-1940*, 294. Film not viewed by author.

Page 96: *Behind the Evidence* synopsis: *New York Times*, January 26, 1935; *New York Sun*, January 26 1935; "Bige," *Variety*, January 1935; *The American Film Institute Catalog, 1931-1940*, 134. Film not viewed by author.

Page 100: "I have tried": Edward G. Robinson, *All My Yesterdays* (New York: Hawthorn Books Inc, 1973), 52.

Page 101: *I'll Love You Always* synopsis: Andre Sennwald, *New York Times*, March 30, 1935; Thornton Delehanty, *New York Evening Post*, March 30, 1935; "Land," *Variety*, March 1935; *The American Film Institute Catalog, 1931-1940*, 1007. Film not viewed by author.

Page 102: "wasn't too easy": George Murphy, *Say, Didn't You Used to be George Murphy?* (Bartholomew House, Ltd., 1970), 184.

Page 111: "I cannot see": Ginger Rogers, *Ginger: My Story* (New York: HarperCollins, 1991), 139.

Page 112: "personal favorite": Undated *New York Times* clipping.

Page 112: The role started: Lucille Ball, *Love, Lucy* (New York: G. P. Putnam's Sons, 1996); Lucille Ball file, Special Collections, AMPAS.

Page 112: At her prompting: Lucille Ball interview, *Lucy and Desi: The Scrapbooks* (New York: Education Through Entertainment, 1996).

Page 112: For the dance: Ginger Rogers, *Ginger: My Story* (New York: HarperCollins, 1991), 141, 142, 143.

Page 115: had location filming: *Hollywood*, January 1943; Lucille Ball file, Special Collections, AMPAS.

Page 121: *Chatterbox* was budgeted: *Chatterbox* production file, RKO-Radio Pictures, Inc. Studio Collection, UCLA Arts Library Special Collections (UCLA).

Page 123: the film's final title: "Char," *Variety*, January 1936.

Page 127: Dance extras for: Paul Harrison, NEA Service Writer, November 22, 1935; *The American Film Institute Catalog, 1931-1940*, 676.

Page 129: His natural, homespun: "Chic," *Variety*, March 1936.

Page 129: San Fernando Valley: *New York Sun*, January 20, 1936.

Page 134: The New York Drama: *New York Daily News*, December 4, 1936.

Page 134: In the film's early: *New York Times*, June 22, 1936; July 23, 1936.

Page 138: In reality, however: American Film Institute, *Dialogue on Film*; Volume 3, Number 6, (Beverly Hills, CA: Center for Advanced Film Studies, 1974), 10.

Page 138: Pons herself wanted: James B. McPherson chapter of James A. Drake, *Lily Pons: A Centennial Portrait*; "Lily Pons in Hollywood," (Portland, OR: Amadeus Press, 1999), 131.

Page 141: "Lucille Ball, making": *Variety*, January 27, 1937.

Page 141: "She outlines a": *Variety*, January 27, 1937.

Page 146: With her box-office: Katharine Hepburn, *Me: Stories of My Life* (New York: Alfred A. Knopf, 1991), 238.

Page 147: "Being at RKO": Letter written by Lucille Ball to journalist Gladys Hall, July 20, 1962. Lucille Ball file, Gladys Hall Collection, AMPAS.

Page 147: Lucille would later: Lucille Ball interview, *Lucy and Desi: The Scrapbooks* CD-ROM (New York: Education Through Entertainment, 1996); Lucille Ball, *Love, Lucy* (New York: G. P. Putnam's Sons, 1996), 102.

Page 147: she was certain La Cava: *Modern Screen*, April, 1939.

Page 149: This commendation, however: *Having Wonderful Time* file, Production Code Administration papers, MPAA Collection, AMPAS.

Page 150: "I had to": Bosley Crowther interviews Arthur Kober, *New York Times*, 1938.

Page 154: "Our title was": Tay Garrett, *Light Your Torches and Pull Up Your Tights* (New Rochelle, York: Arlington House, 1973), 230.

Page 154: Lucille was in awe: American Film Institute. *Dialogue on Film*. Volume 3, Number 6 (Beverly Hills, CA: Center for Advanced Film Studies, 1974), 3.

Page 160: Lucille got the better: Oakie, Jack, *Jack Oakie's Double Takes* (San Francisco: Strawberry Hill Press, 1980), 135.

Page 161: "I sort of built": *Parade*, June 24, 1984.

Page 163: $225,000 was spent: *New York Times*, September 25, 1938.

Page 164: "We've got to originate": Acre, Hector. *Groucho: The Biography of Groucho Marx*. (New York: G. P. Putnam's Sons, 1978), 231.

Page 165: In her memoirs: Ann Miller, *Miller's High Life*. (Garden City, New York: Doubleday & Company, Inc., 1972), 55, 56, 57.

Page 165: Asked in an: Lucille Ball interview, *The Dick Cavett Show* (ABC; 1970).

Page 168: They had fun: Lucille Ball file, Special Collections, AMPAS.

Page 169: *Annabel* never got: *Variety*, 1938.

Page 170: Lucille said that: *Motion Picture*, October 1939.

Page 172: Lucille lamented to: *Motion Picture*, October 1939.

Page 172: It was a part: *The American Film Institute Catalog, 1931-1940*, 1500.

Page 175: As hinted by: *Beauty for the Asking* file, RKO Scripts Collection, UCLA.

Page 177: The fact that: Coyne Steven Sanders, Tom Gilbert, *Desilu: The Story of Lucille Ball and Desi Arnaz* (New York: William Morrow, 1993), 186; *Lucy and Desi: A Home Movie* (Arluck Entertainment, 1993).

Page 179: "I guess I'm": *Twelve Crowded Hours* pressbook (RKO-Radio Pictures, Inc., 1939).

Page 179: One thing she liked: *Motion Picture*, October 1939.

Page 183: More sparks flew: *Panama Lady* file, Production Code Administration papers, MPAA Collection, AMPAS.

Page 189: "about as average": *New York Times*, September 8, 1958.

Page 199: "a farce about": Peter Bogdanovich, *This is Orson Welles* (New York: HarperCollins, 1992), 34.

Page 205: After shooting the: Maureen O'Hara, *'Tis Herself* (New York: Simon & Schuster, 2004), 52.

Page 208: "electrifying charm," The day Desi arrived: Lucille Ball, *Love, Lucy* (New York: G. P. Putnam's Sons, 1996), 116, 117.

Page 209: "I don't think": Desi Arnaz, *A Book* (New York: William Morrow, 1976), 111.

Page 210: Filming wrapped on: *Too Many Girls* file, RKO Collection, UCLA.

Page 210: "I had never": *Parade*, June 24, 1984.

Page 212: As originally conceived: Kathleen Brady, *Lucille: The Life of Lucille Ball* (New York: Hyperion, 1994), 111.

Page 213: "It was a rosy": Lucille Ball, *Love, Lucy* (New York: G. P. Putnam's Sons, 1996), 127.

Page 214: "You could have": *Los Angeles Times*, May 25, 1947.

Page 224: Studio heads insisted: *Hollywood Reporter*, December 30, 1941; *Hollywood Reporter*, February 6, 1942.

Page 224: Part of the wait: *The Big Street* file, RKO Collection, UCLA.

Page 224: "it was exciting": *Saturday Evening Post*, March 23, 1946.

Page 225: "If he has": *AFI Lifetime Achievement Awards: Henry Fonda* (American Film Institute, 1978).

Page 226: "jinxed": *Saturday Evening Post*, March 23, 1946.

Page 226: Runyon was so: Jimmy Breslin, *Damon Runyon* (New York: Ticknor & Fields, 1991), 257.

Page 227: "Lucille is tall": *The Big Street* pressbook (RKO-Radio Pictures, Inc., 1942).

Page 235: "At first, I": Lucille Ball file, Gladys Hall Collection, AMPAS.

Page 236: The film gave: *Life*, Oct. 5, 1942, Lucille Ball, *Love, Lucy* (New York: G. P. Putnam's Sons, 1996), 156.

Page 236: The story's off-color: *Du Barry Was a Lady* file, Production Code Administration papers, MPAA Collection, AMPAS.

Page 237: "Though I've been": *New York Sunday News*, March 3, 1974.

Page 242: "holds special memories": *Action*, May/June 1976.

Page 247: "a musical with": MGM Production Facts sheet, 1943.

Page 248: "Great natural performer": Correspondence from Lucille Ball to journalist Gladys Hall, July 20, 1962. Lucille Ball file, Gladys Hall Collection, AMPAS.

Page 248: Though she did: Lucille Ball, *Love, Lucy* (New York: G. P. Putnam's Sons, 1996), 166.

Page 248: Powell and Allyson: June Allyson, *June Allyson* (New York: G. P. Putnam's Sons, 1982), 35.

Page 255: "A clash of temperaments": *Los Angeles Examiner*, September 8, 1944.

Page 261: "I do enjoy": *Saturday Evening Post*, April 12, 1947.

Page 261: Lucille and Van: Ronald L. Davis, *Van Johnson, America's Boy Next Door* (University Press of Mississippi, 2001), 46.

Page 261: In October of: Lucille Ball file, Hedda Hopper papers, AMPAS.

Page 264: "A beautiful man": Correspondence from Lucille Ball to journalist Gladys Hall, July 20, 1962. Lucille Ball file, Gladys Hall Collection, AMPAS.

Page 265: "Desi is out": *Los Angeles Times*, December 23, 1945.

Page 268: "Dear Mr. Hathaway": *Los Angeles Times*, December 23, 1945.

Page 268: further into filming: Lucille Ball, *Love, Lucy* (New York: G. P. Putnam's Sons, 1996), 175.

Page 269: she could never: Lucille Ball file, Special Collections, AMPAS.

Page 271: "was the best": Lucille Ball, *Love, Lucy* (New York: G. P. Putnam's Sons, 1996), 178.

Page 273: "Female Frank Sinatra": MGM publicist Tom Rogers report to studio by telegram, May 30, 1946.

Page 280: encountered opposition when: original caption attached to photos (Columbia Pictures, 1947).

Page 281: Hollywood's own censorship: *Her Husband's Affairs* file, Production Code Administration papers, MPAA Collection, AMPAS.

Page 284: They had performed: *Silver Screen*, April 1950.

Page 284: Paramount conducted a: *Paramount News*, April 19, 1948.

Page 285: "His humor always": *Silver Screen*, April 1950.

Page 288: Lizabeth Scott was: *The American Film Institute Catalog, 1941-1950*, 674.

Page 297: Her contract, dated: Lucille Ball file, Paramount Collection, AMPAS.

Page 298: Studio records show: *Fancy Pants* file, Paramount Collection, AMPAS; *The American Film Institute Catalog, 1941-1950*, 726.

Page 300: accident involving Hope: Bob Hope, Bob Thomas, *The Road to Hollywood: My 40-year Love Affair with the Movies* (Garden City, New York: Doubleday & Company, Inc., 1977), 73, 74.

Page 304: "I sprained both": Lucille Ball, *Love, Lucy* (New York: G. P. Putnam's Sons, 1996), 193.

Page 313: MGM gave Lucille: Lucie Arnaz to author, April 28, 2005.

Page 312: "Lucy is one": Vincente Minnelli, *I Remember it Well* (New York: Doubleday, 1974), 277.

Page 317: Desi now wanted: *New York Times*, July 10, 1955.

Page 320: "They're perfect together": *Newsweek*, August 22, 1960.

Page 322: They originally conceived: Bob Hope, Bob Thomas, *The Road to Hollywood: My 40-year Love Affair with the Movies* (Garden City, New York: Doubleday & Company, Inc., 1977), 87, 88, 89.

Page 322: "This film should": *New York Times*, July 31, 1960.

Page 322: "I played straight": *New York Times*, July 31, 1960.

Page 323: Lucille's misfortune was: *Newsweek*, August 22, 1960.

Page 323: "Was I Lucy?": Bob Hope, Bob Thomas, *The Road to Hollywood: My 40-year Love Affair with the Movies* (Garden City, New York: Doubleday & Company, Inc., 1977), 87, 88, 89.

Page 325: The story of *Critic's*: *New York Herald-Tribune*, May 2, 1963.

Page 326: Written by Ira: *Los Angeles Times*, March 31, 1961.

Page 326: "She doesn't like": Edith Head interview, *Lucy and Desi: The Scrapbooks* CD-ROM (New York: Education Through Entertainment, 1996).

Page 334: "the only kind": *New York Times*, October 8, 1967.

Page 336: "With Bea Arthur": Sidney Skolsky Collection, AMPAS.

Page 337: "I'm not even": *Ladies Home Journal*, April 1974.

Page 338: She still had: *New York Times*, February 18, 1973.

Page 338: "Goodness knows I": *New York Post*, February 28, 1974.

Page 341: "I didn't think": *New York Post*, November 4, 1985.

Page 342: One of the reasons: *New York Daily News*, October 21, 1985.

Page 345: "Just a lot of": *Rolling Stone*, June 23, 1983.

Page 351: Daily production reports: *There Goes My Girl* file, RKO Collection, UCLA.

Page 352: first by Ginger: A. Scott Berg, *Goldwyn: A Biography*. (New York: Alfred A. Knopf, 1989), 362.

Bibliography

A vast amount of information was compiled from original studio production files and contemporary newspaper clipping files preserved at the Academy of Motion Picture Arts and Sciences Center for Motion Picture Study, the UCLA Arts Library, the American Film Institute, the New York Public Library for the Performing Arts, the USC Cinema/Television Library, the Free Library of Philadelphia Theatre Collection, and the Museum of Modern Art.

Books:

Allyson, June, with Frances Spatz Leighton. *June Allyson*. New York: G.P. Putnam's Sons, 1982.

American Film Institute. *Dialogue on Film*. Volume 3, Number 6. Beverly Hills, CA, 1974.

The American Film Institute Catalog of Motion Pictures Produced in the United States, 1931-1940. Berkeley: University of California Press, 1993.

The American Film Institute Catalog of Motion Pictures Produced in the United States, 1941-1950. Berkeley: University of California Press, 1999.

Andrews, Bart, and Tom Watson. *Loving Lucy: An Illustrated Tribute to Lucille Ball*. New York: St. Martin's Press, 1980.

Arce, Hector. *Groucho: The Biography of Groucho Marx*. New York: G. P. Putnam's Sons, 1979.

Arden, Eve. *Three Phases of Eve*. New York: St. Martin's Press, 1985.

Arnaz, Desi. *A Book*. New York: William Morrow, 1976.

Astaire, Fred. *Steps in Time*. New York: Harper & Brothers, 1959.

Ball, Lucille, with Betty Hannah Hoffman. *Love, Lucy*. New York: G.P. Putnam's Sons, 1996.

Berg, A. Scott. *Goldwyn: A Biography*. New York: Alfred A. Knopf, 1989.

Berg, A. Scott. *Kate Remembered*. New York: G.P. Putnam's Sons, 2003.

Bergan, Ronald. *The United Artists Story*. New York: Crown Publishers, 1986.

Bogdanovich, Peter. *This is Orson Welles*. New York: HarperCollins, 1992.

Brady, Kathleen. *Lucille: The Life of Lucille Ball*. New York: Hyperion, 1994.

Breslin, Jimmy. *Damon Runyon*. New York: Ticknor & Fields, 1991.

Brochu, Jim. *Lucy in the Afternoon*. New York: William Morrow, 1990.

Capra, Frank. *The Name Above the Title*. New York: Macmillan, 1971.

Carlisle-Hart, Kitty. *Kitty*. New York: Doubleday, 1988.

Chierichetti, David. *Hollywood Costume Design*. New York: Harmony Books, 1976.

Croce, Arlene. *The Fred Astaire and Ginger Rogers Book*. New York: Outerbridge & Lazard, 1972.

Davis, Ronald L. *Van Johnson, MGM's Golden Boy*. University Press of Mississippi, 2001.

Deschner, Donald. *The Films of Spencer Tracy*. Secaucus, NJ: Citadel Press, 1968.

Drake, James A. *Lily Pons, A Centennial Portrait*. Portland, OR: Amadeus Press, 1999.

Eames, John Douglas. *The MGM Story, The Complete History of Fifty Roaring Years*. New York: Crown Publishers, 1975.

Eames, John Douglas. *The Paramount Story*. New York: Crown Publishers, 1985.

Fairbanks, Jr., Douglas. *The Salad Days*. New York: Doubleday, 1988.

Fonda, Henry. *Fonda, My Life. As Told to Howard Teichmann*. New York: New American Library, 1981.

Gallafent, Edward. *Astaire and Rogers*. New York: Columbia University Press, 2002.

Garnett, Tay, with Fredda Dudley Balling. *Light Your Torches and Pull up York Tights*. New Rochelle, NY: Arlington House, 1973.

Gregory, James. *The Lucille Ball Story*. New York: Signet, 1974.

Harris, Warren G. *Gable & Lombard*. New York: Simon and Schuster, 1974.

Harvey, Stephen. *Directed by Vincente Minnelli*. New York: HarperCollins, 1990.

Hay, Peter. *MGM: When the Lion Roars*. Atlanta: Turner Publishing, 1991.

Hepburn, Katharine. *Me: Stories of My Life*. New York: Alfred A. Knopf, 1992.

Hirschhorn, Clive. *The Columbia Story*. New York: Crown Publishers, 1989.

Hope, Bob, and Bob Thomas. *The Road to Hollywood, My 40-year Love Affair with the Movies*. Garden City, New York: Doubleday & Company, 1977.

Jewell, Richard B., with Vernon Harbin. *The RKO Story*. New Rochelle, NY: Arlington House, 1982.

Karney, Robyn (editor-in-chief). *Cinema Year by Year*. London: Dorling Kindersley Limited, 2001.

Kobal, John. *People Will Talk*. London: Aurum Press, Ltd., 1986.

Lasky, Betty. *RKO: The Biggest Little Major of Them All*. Englewood Cliffs, NJ: Prentice Hall, 1984.

Loy, Myrna, and James Kotsilibas-Davis. *Being and Becoming*. New York: Alfred A. Knopf, 1987.

Maltin, Leonard. *Leonard Maltin's Movie Encyclopedia*. New York: Plume, 1995.

Mayne, Judith. *Directed by Dorothy Arzner*. Indiana University Press, 1994.

McClay, Michael. *I Love Lucy*. New York: Warner, 1995.

Meredith, Burgess. *So Far, So Good*. Boston, MS: Little, Brown & Company, 1994.

Miller, Ann. *Miller's High Life*. Garden City, New York: Doubleday, 1972.

Minnelli, Vincente. *I Remember it Well*. New York: Doubleday, 1974.

Mitchell, Glenn. *The Marx Brothers Encyclopedia*. London: Batsford, 1996.

Mordden, Ethan. *The Hollywood Musical*. New York. St. Martin's Press, 1981.

Morella, Joe and Edward Z. Epstein. *Lucy: The Bittersweet Life of Lucille Ball*. Secaucus, NJ: Lyle Stuart Inc., 1973.

Murphy, George, with Victor Lasky. *Say, Didn't You Used to be George Murphy?*. Bartholomew House, Ltd., 1970.

Murray, Ken. *The Body Merchant: The Story of Earl Carroll*. Pasadena, CA: Ward Ritchie Press, 1976.

Oakie, Jack. *Jack Oakie's Double Takes*. San Francisco: Strawberry Hill Press, 1980.

O'Hara, Maureen, with John Nicoletti. *'Tis Herself, A Memoir*. New York: Simon and Schuster, 2004.

Oller, John. *Jean Arthur, The Actress Nobody Knew*. New York: Limelight Editions, 1997.

Parrish, James Robert. *The RKO Gals*. Carlstadt, NJ: Rainbow Books, 1974.

Robinson, Edward G. *All My Yesterdays*. New York: Hawthorn Books Inc., 1973.

Rogers, Ginger. *Ginger, My Story*. New York: HarperCollins, 1991.

Sanders, Coyne Stevens, and Tom Gilbert. *Desilu: The Story of Lucille Ball and Desi Arnaz*. New York: William Morrow, 1993.

Tannen, Lee. *I Loved Lucy: My Friendship with Lucille Ball*. New York: St. Martin's Press, 2001.

Thomas, Bob. *King Cohn*. New York: G.P. Putnam's Sons, 1967.

Tierney, Gene, with Mickey Herskowitz. *Self-Portrait*. New York: Wyden Books, 1978.

Vieria, Mark A. *Sin in Soft Focus: Pre-Code Hollywood*. New York: Harry N. Abrams, Inc., 1999.

Williams, Esther, with Digby Diehl. *The Million Dollar Mermaid*. New York: Simon Schuster, 1999.

Wray, Fay. *On the Other Hand*. New York: St. Martin's Press, 1989.

Yablonsky, Lewis. *George Raft*. New York: McGraw-Hill, 1974.

Yudkoff, Alvin. *Gene Kelly, A Life of Dance and Dreams*. New York: Watson-Guptill, 2000.

Documentaries:

AFI Lifetime Achievement Awards: Henry Fonda. American Film Institute, 1978.

Busby Berkeley: Going Through the Roof. Alternate Current/Turner Entertainment, 1997.

Complicated Women. Timeline Films/Turner Classic Movies, 2003.

Desilu Story, The. Platinum Productions/Bravo, 2003.

Finding Lucy. American Masters, 2000.

Goldwyn: The Man and His Movies. Columbia Tristar, 2001.

Harold Lloyd's World of Comedy. Continental, 1962.

Hollywood: The Golden Years: The RKO Story. BBC/RKO Pictures, 1987.

Lucy and Desi: A Home Movie. Arluck Entertainment, 1993.

Lucy and Desi: The Outtakes. Arluck Entertainment, 1993.

Musicals Great Musicals: The Arthur Freed Unit at MGM. Turner Entertainment, 1996.

MGM: When the Lion Roars. Turner Pictures, 1992.

CD-ROM:

Lucy and Desi: The Scrapbooks. Education Through Entertainment, 1996.

Index

Due to the detailed crew listings, and the general scope of this work, this is a selected index. It does include directors, writers, films, plays, family, co-stars, and other notables in the life of Lucille Ball and the entertainment world. Page numbers in italics refer to photographs.

Photo Credits

Courtesy of Desilu, too, LLC: 10, 11 12, 13, 14, 18, 19, 20, 22, 28, 29, 30, 31, 33, 34, 38, 39, 40 (first), 46 (bottom, right), 48 (second), 55, 57, 141, 350; 303 (top), 304 (bottom) Columbia; 15, 16, 47 (first), 48 (first, third), 51, 52, 53, 58, 84, Back Cover (top: first, second) Goldwyn; 36, 44 (top, right), 232 (second), 239, 247, 249 (top) MGM; 1, 8 (second), 9, 40 (second through eighth), 43 (top/bottom, right), 44, 45, 47 (left, third; right, first), 48 (fifth, sixth, eighth), 104, 138, 142 (first, third, fifth), 150, 152, 154, 156, 157, 158, 166, 173, 199 (top), 208 (bottom), 219 (top), 220 (bottom), 343, 350 RKO; 47 (right, fifth) United Artists; 65 (bottom, left) Twentieth Century; 71, 72 (bottom) Fox Films.

Courtesy of Tom Watson: 254 (top; bottom) MGM; 48 (seventh), 127 (bottom), 132, 142 (fourth), 175, 176 (bottom), 179, 180, 289 (left) RKO; 267 Twentieth Century-Fox.

Courtesy of Photofest: 24 MGM; 17, 121, 127 (top), 130, 151 (top), 214 (top), 224 RKO; 41 Fox Films; 274 United Artists.

Courtesy of the Academy of Motion Picture Arts and Sciences: 343 (left) RKO.

Collection of author: 47 (right, sixth), 48 (fourth), 86, 88, 89, 91, 92, 93, 95, 97, 99, 100, 101, 232 (fifth), 278, 279, 280, 281, 290, 291, 292, 293, 294, 301, 302, 303 (bottom), 304 (top), 305, 306, 307, 308, 309, 344, Back Cover (bottom: first, second) Columbia; 26, 340, 341, 342 Courtesy CBS; 49, 50, 62, 63, 64, 82, 83 Goldwyn; 2, 6, 7, 8 (seventh, eighth), 40 (right), 46 (top, left), 47 (left, eighth; right: second, third, fourth), 232 (first, third, fourth, sixth), 233, 234, 235, 236, 237, 238, 240, 241, 242, 244, 245, 246, 248, 249 (bottom), 251, 252, 253, 254 (center), 255, 256, 257, 258, 259, 260, 261, 262, 263, 264, 265, 310, 311, 312, 313, 314, 315, 316, 317, 318, 367, Back Cover (center; top, forth; bottom, third) MGM; 73, 74, 75, 282, 283, 284, 285, 296, 297, 298, 299, 300 Paramount; Front Cover, 5, 8 (first, third, fourth, fifth, sixth), 42, 43 (top, left; bottom, left), 47 (left: second, fourth, fifth, sixth, seventh), 103, 105, 106, 108, 109, 110, 111, 112, 113, 115, 116, 118, 119, 122, 124, 125, 126, 129, 133, 135, 136, 137, 139, 140, 142 (second, sixth, seventh, eighth), 143, 144, 145, 147, 148, 149, 151 (bottom), 153, 155, 159, 160, 161, 162, 163, 164, 165, 167, 168, 169, 170, 171, 172, 174, 176 (top), 177, 178, 181, 182, 183, 184, 185, 186, 187, 188, 189, 190, 191, 192, 193, 194, 195, 196, 197, 198, 199 (bottom), 200, 201, 202, 203, 204, 205 206, 207, 208 (top), 209, 210, 211, 212, 213, 214 (bottom), 215, 216, 217, 218, 219 (bottom), 220 (top), 221, 222, 223, 225, 226, 227, 228, 229, 230, 231, 286, 287, 288, 289 (right), 346, 349, 354, Back Cover (top, third) RKO; 54, 59, 61, 65 (top, right), 66, 67, 77, 78, 79, 80, 81 Twentieth Century; 69, 72 (top) Fox Films; 266, 268, 269, 329 Twentieth Century-Fox; 275, 276, 277, 319, 320, 321, 322, 323, 330, 331, 332, 333, 334 United Artists; 46 (top, right; bottom, left), 270, 271, 272, 273, 274 Universal; 35, 37, 47 (right: seventh, eighth), 232 (seventh, eighth), 324, 325, 326, 327, 335, 336, 337, 338, 339, Back Cover (bottom, forth) Warner Bros.

Photography, such as publicity stills, within the Hollywood studio system was released for free use for editorial purposes, frequently without proper credits provided. Any omissions or errors in crediting original owners are unintentional, and the publisher would be pleased to amend in future editions.

Acknowledgments

Lucy at the Movies was a work in progress for five years during which I was assisted by many willing and generous people who made it possible and to whom I am deeply grateful.

Thank you to a mother and father who were never any less than 100 percent supportive from day one. Trish, my all-purpose research helpmate, I couldn't imagine a better sister. Manny, Jess, Jenny, and all my encouraging family members and friends—thanks.

A very special thank you is extended to Lucie Arnaz, whose generosity, enthusiasm, and support of this project went beyond my dreams. Elisabeth Edwards, always helpful and a fount of knowledge, who became my favorite email buddy.

At Running Press: Greg Jones was the first to see this book and then became responsible for more good things that happened to me than he realizes, for which I am most grateful. Many thanks for the ongoing support of publisher Jon Anderson. Lisa Clancy was my expert editor. Corinda Cook, thanks for designing a beautiful book, and for your patience and dedication. My other friends in RP Editorial—Diana, Kelli, Teresa, all the Jens—and all other departments that worked toward the production of this book.

The expert staffs of the following research facilities were of invaluable aid to me at every turn and for every question that arose in pouring through their files and texts: the Academy of Motion Picture Arts and Sciences Center for Motion Picture Study, UCLA's Arts Library, the American Film Institute, the New York Public Library for the Performing Arts, the Free Library of Philadelphia, USC's Cinema/Television Library, and the Museum of Modern Art.

Locating the vast amount of photographs from Lucille Ball's early years necessary to illustrate this text was not an easy task, but it became an enjoyable (if frustrating) game of seek and find. For help in locating photographs, I would like to thank the staffs of the following firms: Photofest, the Academy of Motion Picture Arts and Sciences, Collector's Book Store, Baby Jane of Hollywood, and above all, Desilu too, LLC., for an enormous contribution of rare photographs.

The following individuals helped in many ways, from offering the voice of experience to a first-time author to providing photographs, research material, and various other invaluable aids: Much deserved thanks to Caren Roberts-Frenzel, Tom Watson, George Feltenstein, Milton T. Moore, Robert Osborne, Ric Wyman, Roy Windham, Ned Comstock, Michelle Vogel, Lauren Buisson, agent Peter Fleming for his help early on, and the erudite and methodical Elias Savada of Motion Picture Information Service.

And a nod to the studios of Hollywood's Golden Age, that created the images and stories represented in this text: RKO-Radio Pictures, Columbia Pictures, Metro-Goldwyn-Mayer, the Samuel Goldwyn Company, Paramount Pictures, United Artists, Warner Bros., Universal, and Twentieth Century-Fox.